Engaging with a Legacy: Nehemia Levtzion (1935-2003)

Engaging with a Legacy shows how Nehemia Levtzion shaped our understanding of Islam in Africa and influenced successive scholarly generations in their approach to Islamization, conversion and fundamentalism. The book illuminates his work, career and family life – including his own 'life vision' on the occasion of his 60th birthday. It speaks to his relationship with researchers at home and abroad as mentor, colleague and provocateur; in one section, several authors reflect on those dynamics in terms of personal and professional development. Levtzion's contemporaries also speak of interactions with him (and his life-long companion, wife Tirza) in the 1950s and 1960s; we see in these writings the birth of West African historical studies Levtzion's arrival as an Israeli graduate-student in Nkrumah's Egyptian-leaning Ghana, and the debate over what 'African Studies' should mean in an environment that included the personal intervention of W.E.B. Du Bois, are stories told for the first time. Most poignant is the account of Levtzion's commitment to building African Studies, complete with emphasis on Islam, in the heart of the Jewish state at The Hebrew University. His never-ending defence of the program reflected his determination to be both 'engaged historian' and 'engaged Israeli' – a legacy he chose for himself. Finally, an 'Epilogue' to the original publication shows how one aspect of this legacy, Levtzion's growing preoccupation with the 'public sphere in Muslim societies', has become even more relevant in 'post-Arab Spring' Africa and the Middle East.

This book was first published as a special issue of the *Canadian Journal of African Studies*.

E. Ann McDougall (Professor), Department of History and Classics, University of Alberta, Edmonton, Canada has researched social and economic history in southern Morocco and Mauritania for over thirty years. Her current project focuses on a comparative study of servile/marginal status in these regions, with attention to its importance in contemporary democratization.

Nehemia Levtzion 1935-2003

Engaging with a Legacy:
Nehemia Levtzion (1935-2003)

Edited by
E. Ann McDougall

LONDON AND NEW YORK

First published 2013
by Routledge
2 Park Square, Milton Park, Abingdon, Oxfordshire OX14 4RN

Simultaneously published in the USA and Canada
by Routledge
711 Third Avenue, New York, NY 10017

First issued in paperback 2015

Routledge is an imprint of the Taylor & Francis Group, an informa business

© 2013 Canadian Association of African Studies

This book is a reproduction of the *Canadian Journal of African Studies*, vol. 42, issue 2-3. The Publisher requests to those authors who may be citing this book to state, also, the bibliographical details of the special issue on which the book was based.

All rights reserved. No part of this book may be reprinted or reproduced or utilised in any form or by any electronic, mechanical, or other means, now known or hereafter invented, including photocopying and recording, or in any information storage or retrieval system, without permission in writing from the publishers.

Trademark notice: Product or corporate names may be trademarks or registered trademarks, and are used only for identification and explanation without intent to infringe.

British Library Cataloguing in Publication Data
A catalogue record for this book is available from the British Library

ISBN 13: 978-1-138-94663-7 (pbk)
ISBN 13: 978-0-415-63167-9 (hbk)

Typeset in Times New Roman
by Taylor & Francis Books

Publisher's Note
The publisher would like to make readers aware that the chapters in this book may be referred to as articles as they are identical to the articles published in the special issue. The publisher accepts responsibility for any inconsistencies that may have arisen in the course of preparing this volume for print.

Contents

Citation Information   vii
Notes on Contributors   xi

1. Engaging with the Legacy of Nehemia Levtzion: An Introduction
   E. Ann McDougall   1

Memoirs and Memories

2. The Legacy of Nehemia Levtzion 1935-2003
   Nehemia Levtzion   18

3. Nehemia Levtzion and Islam in Ghana: Reminiscences
   Ivor Wilks   38

4. Memories of Nehemia
   Martin Klein   53

5. Remembering Nehemia: Personal Tributes
   *Roland Oliver, William F.S. Miles, Naomi Chazan,
   and E. Ann McDougall*   69

6. In Memory of Tirtza Levtzion, 1935-2007   86

Engaging with a Legacy

7. Breaking New Ground in "Pagan" and "Muslim" West Africa
   David Robinson   88

8. Neo-Sufism: Reconsidered Again
   John O. Voll   102

9. Linking Translation Theory and African History: Domestication
   and Foreignization in *Corpus of Early Arabic Sources for West
   African History*
   Dalton S. Collins   119

CONTENTS

The Ancient Ghana and Mali Project

10. Reconceptualizing Early Ghana
    Susan Keech McIntosh 135

11. Captain of "We Band of Brothers": An Archaeologist's Homage to Nehemia Levtzion
    Roderick J. McIntosh 162

12. From the *Banan* Tree of Kouroussa: Mapping the Landscape in Mande Traditional History
    David C. Conrad 172

Developing "Themes": History of Islam in Africa

13. Christians and Muslims in Nineteenth Century Liberia: From Ideological Antagonism to Practical Toleration
    Yekutiel Gershoni 197

14. From the Colony to the Post-colony: Sufis and Wahhâbîsts in Senegal and Nigeria
    Irit Back 211

15. The Philosophy of the Revolution: Thoughts on Modernizing Islamic Schools in Ghana
    David Owusu-Ansah and Abdulai Iddrisu 234

16. A Question of Beginnings
    Kenneth W. Harrow 255

17. "Islamic Music in Africa" as a Tool for African Studies
    Michael Frishkopf 266

18. Hidden in the Household: Gender and Class in the Study of Islam in Africa
    E. Ann McDougall 296

The Last Word from Nehemiah

19. Resurgent Islamic Fundamentalism as an Integrative Factor in the Politics of Africa and the Middle East
    Nehemia Levtzion 334

20. Epilogue: Islam and the New Public Sphere
    John O. Voll 348

Works Cited 360
Index 398

Citation Information

The chapters in this book were originally published in the *Canadian Journal of African Studies,* volume 42, issue 2-3 (2008). When citing this material, please use the original page numbering for each article, as follows:

Chapter 1
Engaging with the Legacy of Nehemia Levtzion: An Introduction
E. Ann McDougall
Canadian Journal of African Studies, volume 42, issue 2-3 (2008)
pp. 213-229

Chapter 2
The Legacy of Nehemia Levtzion 1935-2003
Nehemia Levtzion
Canadian Journal of African Studies, volume 42, issue 2-3 (2008)
pp. 230-249

Chapter 3
Nehemia Levtzion and Islam in Ghana: Reminiscences
Ivor Wilks
Canadian Journal of African Studies, volume 42, issue 2-3 (2008)
pp. 250-264

Chapter 4
Memories of Nehemia
Martin Klein
Canadian Journal of African Studies, volume 42, issue 2-3 (2008)
pp. 265-280

Chapter 5
Remembering Nehemia: Personal Tributes
Roland Oliver, William F. S. Miles, Naomi Chazan, and E. Ann McDougall
Canadian Journal of African Studies, volume 42, issue 2-3 (2008)
pp. 281-297

Chapter 6
In Memory of Tirtza Levtzion, 1935-2007

Chapter 7
Breaking New Ground in "Pagan" and "Muslim" West Africa
David Robinson

Chapter 8
Neo-Sufism: Reconsidered Again
John O. Voll

Chapter 9
Linking Translation Theory and African History: Domestication and Foreignization in *Corpus of Early Arabic Sources for West African History*
Dalton S. Collins

Chapter 10
Reconceptualizing Early Ghana
Susan Keech McIntosh

Chapter 11
Captain of "We Band of Brothers": An Archaeologist's Homage to Nehemia Levtzion
Roderick J. McIntosh

Chapter 12
From the *Banan* Tree of Kouroussa: Mapping the Landscape in Mande Traditional History
David C. Conrad

Chapter 13
Christians and Muslims in Nineteenth Century Liberia: From Ideological Antagonism to Practical Toleration
Yekutiel Gershoni
Canadian Journal of African Studies, volume 42, issue 2-3 (2008)
pp. 409-422

Chapter 14
From the Colony to the Post-colony: Sufis and Wahhâbîsts in Senegal and Nigeria
Irit Back
Canadian Journal of African Studies, volume 42, issue 2-3 (2008)
pp. 423-445

Chapter 15
The Philosophy of the Revolution: Thoughts on Modernizing Islamic Schools in Ghana
David Owusu-Ansah and Abdulai Iddrisu
Canadian Journal of African Studies, volume 42, issue 2-3 (2008)
pp. 446-466

Chapter 16
A Question of Beginnings
Kenneth W. Harrow
Canadian Journal of African Studies, volume 42, issue 2-3 (2008)
pp. 467-477

Chapter 17
"Islamic Music in Africa" as a Tool for African Studies
Michael Frishkopf
Canadian Journal of African Studies, volume 42, issue 2-3 (2008)
pp. 478-507

Chapter 18
Hidden in the Household: Gender and Class in the Study of Islam in Africa
E. Ann McDougall
Canadian Journal of African Studies, volume 42, issue 2-3 (2008)
pp. 508-545

Chapter 19
Resurgent Islamic Fundamentalism as an Integrative Factor in the Politics of Africa and the Middle East
Nehemia Levtzion
Canadian Journal of African Studies, volume 42, issue 2-3 (2008)
pp. 546-559

Notes on Contributors

Irit Back is a lecturer in the Department of Middle East and African Studies, Tel Aviv University and The Open University. Her research interests relate to contemporary Islam in Africa (focusing on the relations between Sufis and Islamists) and conflict resolution. Her book, *Islam and Post-Colonial Identity in West Africa,* was published in Tel Aviv by Tel Aviv University in 2005.

Dalton S. Collins was a Masters' student in the Department of History and Classics at the University of Alberta. His thesis research re-considered studies of Ancient Ghana and Mali, in which the Hopkins-Levtzion *Corpus* was central. He currently lives and plays music in Vancouver, Canada.

David C. Conrad is Emeritus Professor of African History, SUNY-Oswego. He was a founder and, until very recently, President of the Mande Studies Association. His research in Guinea and Mali focuses on the oral traditions of the Mande world. His most recent book is *Empires of Medieval West Africa* (New York: Chelsea House, Revised Edition 2010).

Naomi Chazan is Professor Emerita of Political Science and African Studies at the Hebrew University of Jerusalem, where she chaired the African Studies Department and the Harry S. Truman Institute of Research for the Advancement of Peace. She served three terms as a member of the Knesset and is currently Dean of the School of Government and Society at the Academic College of Tel-Aviv-Yaffo.

Michael Frishkopf is Associate Professor of Music at the University of Alberta. He is also Associate Director of the Canadian Centre for Ethnomusicology and Research Fellow at folkwaysAlive! (UofA). His research focuses on the music and sounds of Islam, the Arab world and West Africa.

Yekutiel Gershoni, Professor of African History, is former Vice President and President of the Liberian Studies Association and former Chair of the

Department of Middle Eastern and African History, Tel Aviv University, Israel. His research focuses on West Africa, with a special emphasis on Liberia, and the relations between Africans and African-Americans. In recognition of his academic contributions, he received an honorary Doctorate from Ben Gurion University, Israel.

Kenneth Harrow is a Professor of English and African Literature at Michigan State University. He is the editor of *Faces of Islam in African Literature* (Heinemann, 1991), *The Marabout and the Muse* (Heinemann, 1996), *Postcolonial African Cinema* (Indiana University Press, 2007) and *Trash: African Cinema from Below* (Indiana University Press, 2012).

Abdulai Iddrisu, is Assistant Professor of African History at St. Olaf College, MN. He was previously Fellow of the Institute for the Study of Islamic Thought in Africa (ISITA), Program of African Studies, Northwestern University, Evanston, and Social Science Research Council-IDFR Fellow. He taught at Ghana's University for Development Studies and Illinois State University at Bloomington, IL. His work appears in many professional, peer-reviewed journals. Recent books: *Contesting Islam in Africa: Homegrown Wahhabism and Muslim Identity in northern Ghana* (Durham, NC: Carolina Academic Press, 2012); with David Owusu-Ansah and Mark Sey *Traditional Islamic Learning in Ghana* (Trenton, New Jersey: Africa World Press, Forthcoming).

Martin Klein is Professor Emeritus from the University of Toronto. Specializing in Islamic West Africa and in the study of slavery; his best known work is *Slavery and Colonial Rule in French West Africa* (Cambridge University Press, 1998).

E. Ann McDougall is Professor in the Department of History and Classics at the University of Alberta. Founder and former Director of its Middle Eastern and African Studies programme, her research focuses on the social and economic history of southern Morocco, Mauritania and Mali, especially in relation to desert salts and slavery.

Roderick J. McIntosh is Professor of Anthropology at Yale University and Curator of Anthropology at the Peabody Museum, both in New Haven, Connecticut, in addition to being Honorary Professor of Archaeology at the University of Pretoria. His major research interests include African and Old World comparative prehistory, intellectual history of prehistoric archaeology, geomorphology and palaeoclimate, and prehistoric symbols and ideology.

Susan Keech McIntosh is Professor of Anthropology at Rice University, Houston, Texas. Her archaeological research in Senegal and Mali during the past three decades has focused on the emergence of social and political complexity. She is past President of the Society of Africanist Archaeologists.

NOTES ON CONTRIBUTORS

William F.S. Miles is Professor of Political Science at Northeastern University, where he teaches religion, politics and third world development. His most recent book, *Zion in the Desert,* is an ethno-autobiography of American-Jewish baby boomers. He has also recently published, as originating editor and major contributor, *Political Islam in West Africa.*

Roland Oliver is Professor Emeritus from the University of London. A pioneer in the study of African History, he founded the African Studies Association (UK) in 1963 and was awarded its Distinguished Africanist Award in 1989. He was also elected a Fellow of the British Academy in 1993.

David Owusu-Ansah is Professor of African History at James Madison University at Harrisonburg, Virginia, where he is also Special Assistant to the President for Faculty Diversity. He was previously Director, Africana Studies Program (James Madison University) and Lester Martin Fellow at the Truman Institute (Hebrew University, Jerusalem). Research interests focus on the religion and politics of his native Ghana, on which he has authored many book chapters and articles. Book publications include *Islamic Talismanic Tradition in Nineteenth Century Asante* (1991); (with Daniel McFarl) *Historical Dictionary of Ghana* (2nd ed., 1995, sole author (3rd. ed, 2005), (4th ed., 2013, forthcoming); and (with Abdulai Iddrisu and Mark Sey), *Traditions of Islamic Learning in Ghana* (African World Press, forthcoming).

David Robinson is University Distinguished Professor Emeritus of History and African Studies at Michigan State University. He has focused his research and teaching on the history of Islam in Africa, especially francophone West Africa.

John O. Voll is Professor of Islamic History at Georgetown University and a past President of the Middle East Studies Association. His research and publications relate to Islamic movements of renewal in the modern era.

Ivor Wilks is Professor Emeritus of History, Northwestern University, Honorary Professor of History, University of Birmingham, and Honorary Professor of History, University of Wales, Lampeter. He has written extensively on Ghanaian history and on the spread of Islam in West Africa.

Engaging with the Legacy of Nehemia Levtzion: An Introduction

E. Ann McDougall

Résumé

Ce volume puise principalement dans les présentations faites au cours de deux réunions de l'Association des études africaines (2003, 2004) célébrant les contributions de Nehemia Levtzion au domaine de l'Islam en Afrique et évoquant nos interactions collectives et personnelles avec lui. Ce volume est d'autre part enrichi par les articles additionnels d'anciens étudiants, collègues et amis (les deux se confondent généralement), et par de jeunes érudits contemporains qui commencent tout juste à "connaître" Levtzion, grâce à la découverte de ses travaux. L'"Épilogue" donne le dernier mot, mot posthume, à Levtzion lui-même, dans un article qui examine le rôle contemporain du fondamentalisme vu par un historien dont la vie tout entière était engagée dans l'histoire de l'Islam au croisement entre le Moyen Orient et l'Afrique. Les pages qui suivent n'ont pas seulement pour but de rendre hommage à Nehemia Levtzion mais de réfléchir de manière critique, de reculer les limites et de présenter à d'autres érudits africanistes, engagés dans d'autres domaines d'études, et aux nouvelles générations d'érudits africanistes intéressés par ces questions, le rôle de Levtzion en ce qu'il a modelé notre compréhension de l'expérience de l'Islam en Afrique.

Abstract

This volume draws principally on presentations from two African Studies Association meetings (2003, 2004) that celebrated Nehemia Levtzion's contributions to the field of Islam in Africa and reminisced about our collective personal interactions with him. It is enriched by additional papers from former students, colleagues and friends (usually one and the same), as well as from contemporary young scholars just beginning to "know" Levtzion through his legacy. The "Epilogue" gives a final, posthumous word to Levtzion himself, in an article looking at the contemporary role of fundamentalism from the perspective of an historian who spent his life engaged in the history of Islam at its Middle Eastern and African crossroads. The following pages are meant not only to pay homage to Nehemia Levtzion but also to reflect critically, to push boundaries, and to introduce Africanist scholars, engaged in other areas of study and new generations of Africanist scholars in this field, to Levtzion's role in shaping how we have come to understand the experience of Islam in Africa.

Prologue

It seems regrettable that it so often takes the death of a colleague to generate this kind of collaboration. How much more fun it would have been to have had Nehemia Levtzion engage with us as we put forward these essays and respond in his inevitable challenging way to the resulting collection. Instead, this volume had its origins in an extremely sad set of panels. The first, referred to in the section below on "Ancient Ghana and Mali," was organized by Levtzion himself for the 2003 African Studies Association (ASA) meeting to re-launch work on a "new version" of his seminal work of the same name. The panel carried on, under David Conrad's chairmanship, and we are fortunate to have updated revisions of those presented in the following pages (David Conrad, Susan Keech McIntosh, and Roderick McIntosh).[1] The second was a consecutive set of two roundtables and a panel organized for the 2004 ASA in which several of our contributors participated (Ivor Wilks, Bill Miles, Martin Klein, David Robinson, John Voll, Yekutiel Gershoni, David Owusu-Ansah and Abdulai Iddrisu, and Kenneth Harrow). These were well attended by Levtzion's colleagues, several of whom added their own reminiscences and comments to the proceedings (and Roland Oliver kindly agreed to include them in this collection). Finally, over the past year or so, more essays and reminiscences were offered (Naomi Chazan, Irit Back, Michael Frishkopf, and Dalton Collins) — extending the "engagement" represented here from those who first experienced research in Ghana with Levtzion in the heady days of that country's early independence, through those for whom he was colleague, friend, mentor, or supervisor, to those who today carry on the next generation of research, influenced by his legacy, never having known the man. All are reflected in the following pages.

Thanks to Levtzion's generous family (and here I thank in particular Amos Nadan), we also have Levtzion himself in the words of a biography he delivered personally on the occasion of his sixtieth birthday ("The Legacy of Nehemia Levitzion 1935-2003"), and in one of the last essays he wrote but never published ("Resurgent Islamic Fundamentalism"). Sadly, we also have occasion here to say "good-bye" and "thank you" to his friend and partner of more than forty years, Tirtza ("In Memory of Tirtza"). "Good-bye" because Tirtza passed away only four years later. Thank you" because she was a part of everything Nehemia Levtzion did and integral to the relationships most of the people here developed with him over the years. The warmth of their home and their friendship is inseparable from our memories of, and respect for, Levtzion's contributions to the field of African Studies.

The following pages are meant to do more than "remember" Nehemia Levtzion. They are meant to pay homage, to reflect critically, to push boundaries and perhaps most importantly, to introduce to Africanist scholars engaged in other areas of study, and to new generations of Africanist scholars in this field, Levtzion's role in shaping how we have come to understand the experience of Islam in Africa.

Memoirs and Memories

In this section, Levtzion's own bare-boned version of "life" — marked by intersecting recollections of family marriages, births, and deaths with research trips, publications, and university positions — is fleshed out by the reminiscences of others. Ivor Wilks, already fully rooted in the collection of Arabic documents in newly-independent Ghana when Levtzion arrived, reveals the tensions involved in both Levtzion's choice of thesis research and the complications his arrival as an Israeli Fellow at the Institute of African Studies at the University of Ghana posed in the context of Nkrumah's pro-Egyptian politics. Wilks' reminiscences are themselves a piece of history, replete with actors like the late Thomas Hodgkin, Peter Shinnie, W.E.B. Du Bois, and President Kwame Nkrumah; one cannot read this piece without feeling a sense of the excitement, frustration, contestation, and negotiation that characterized the "early years" of shaping how Islam in Africa was to be studied.

Martin Klein's essay is an integration of reminiscences of Levtzion the man and the evolution of Levtzion the scholar — a very personalized appreciation of what Klein sees as Levtzion's major intellectual contributions to African studies. He approaches Levtzion's early work from the vantage point of a fellow traveller to newly independent Africa (he having arrived in Senegal at the same time as Levtzion came to Ghana), with full appreciation of the challenges research posed — not only physical but conceptual. As Klein says, "there were no models." He is also especially mindful of Levtzion's adventurous spirit in accepting that he must draw on oral information both to locate written documents relevant to Islam and to understand them, when this was not the methodology in which he had been trained. Moreover, it was not the "oral tradition" being proffered at the time as a viable research tool by another intrepid Africanist, Jan Vansina. Klein reminds us as well that seminal work is not without weakness, as he not only notes criticisms of Levtzion's *Muslim Chiefs* at the time but also points to areas in which the work has not fully stood the test of time. In engaging thusly, from personal and professional perspectives, with honesty and respect, Klein helps us to understand Levtzion's initial impact as a young Arabist in Africa — and why that impact remains profound and contentious.

Roland Oliver, who knew Levtzion when he first came to London for his PhD work, speaks of how Levtzion's knowledge of Arabic was the key that opened doors for him to the oral and written histories of northern Ghana's clerics. At a time when any scholars who would call themselves Arabists headed into Middle Eastern or religious textual work, Levtzion surprised people by turning his attention to sub-Saharan Africa, where he helped to sow the seeds that would reap a field called "Islam in Africa."

William Miles, Naomi Chazan, and I remember Levtzion in more personal terms, in a sense celebrating his humanity as much as his scholarship and professionalism. For Miles, it was Levtzion's Jewishness, as articulated in his scholarly work and personal life, that has left an indelible mark. He shares with us his moment of meeting Levtzion — he a brash, naïve young graduate student, Levtzion the "prickly," brusque master of the field who nevertheless gave generously of his time and advice and became a life-long mentor and friend. Similarly, my memories are rooted in Levtzion's critical responses to my early work, responses that were both flattering in their depth and detail, and challenging because Levtzion was not easily convinced to change his mind. These exchanges opened the door for a relationship that, while not "close," continued to influence my thinking — not to mention generating this project.

However, it is Chazan's piece that perhaps most brings Levtzion alive for us once again. As she says, he was "mentor, patron, colleague, counterpart, and friend for nearly forty years." And in this multi-faceted relationship that she enjoyed with him, most of us will recognize something familiar: his scrupulous devotion to solid research, his generosity of heart and spirit that nevertheless seldom led easily to "giving way" in an intellectual disagreement, his stubbornness — that could be frustrating in many situations on the one hand, admirable when it was directed to the right cause or project, on the other. In recounting her memories of Levtzion, Chazan also tells the history of African Studies in Israel. From training many who would become its first practitioners, to wooing friends and colleagues from all over to participate in this special community of scholars, to fighting the political battles that never seemed to end, Levtzion assured that African studies would flourish in a multi/inter disciplinary environment and that it would do so, ultimately, in conjunction with the older, more established Middle Eastern studies tradition. It is all the more sad, then, to read in Chazan's final paragraphs that so much of what he built in terms of infrastructure has not survived his death. It is notable that the "legacy" in Israel — as elsewhere — will now be measured in the inspiration that continues to drive his students and successors to work together and develop the field in an international context.

The section closes with the family "memory of Tirtza," a memory that completes Levtzion's story of the partnership and marriage that provided both context and support for his scholarship.

Engaging with a Legacy

In this section, which derives its focus from the larger goal of this volume, David Robinson, John Voll, and Dalton Collins respond directly to Levtzion's corpus of work. The first two are long-time colleagues and contemporaries of Levtzion whose own works on Islam in Africa (most especially West Africa) need no introduction to most readers. The last is a young graduate student only recently "introduced" to Levtzion's scholarship who reflects, perhaps, a new generation's approach to engagement.

Robinson chooses to focus on the early days of Levtzion's career, and therefore on *Muslim Chiefs*. While for Klein, the book's importance was largely in its foray into unchartered territory (almost literally) geographically speaking, for Robinson the impact lay principally in its challenge to the extant historiography of "Islamization." He points out that Levtzion's study was the first to stray from the traditional model that treated Islam prior to the great *jihads* of the nineteenth century as little more than a precursor to "real conversion," a "side-effect" of trade and commercial diaspora, and to suggest that the process of spreading Islam was also one of "acculturation"; moreover Muslim communities engaged in complex relationships with host political and state structures. This work, according to Robinson, "set in motion some very powerful vectors of research that have benefited the field and the understanding [of Islamization] of the last thirty years." He further highlights Levtzion's 1971 article, "A Seventeenth-Century Chronicle by Ibn al-Mukhtar: A Critical Study of Ta'rikh al-Fattash." Robinson describes it as revolutionary, challenging contemporary understanding both of a particular historical text and of the real meaning of nineteenth-century *jihad*. By proving that what was understood to be a sixteenth-century document in fact included a segment forged in the nineteenth century by an Islamic theocracy competing for legitimacy in an era of many "Islamic" states, he revealed that *jihad* was fought on a number of levels, using a range of "tools" that were not necessarily military in nature. Most importantly, again, Levtzion was challenging the extant view of that theocracy as a "pure and pristine" orthodoxy by revealing it to be much more troubled and complex than scholars to date had understood. Robinson himself gives a fascinating interpretation of how Levtzion's revelation of the forgery allows us to re-shape our understanding of the Middle Niger Delta region and of "Islamization" in the nineteenth century, expressing hope that these ideas will be pushed even further.

Voll worked with Levtzion in the mid-1980s on "Islamic renewal and revival in the eighteenth century," co-organizing a colloquium on the subject and giving context to a lively debate on the nature and significance of what was called "neo-sufism." This was a discussion not limited to Africa and as Voll makes clear, in spite of what might seem its particularisms, it remains relevant to understanding the dynamics of contemporary fundamentalist movements in Africa and elsewhere in Asia and the Middle East. His article gives an excellent overview of the historiography of this subject, situating Levtzion's views on what was "new" about "neo" Sufism in the eighteenth century within the ongoing debate. He notes what he sees as Levtzion's most important observation in the process of emerging neo-sufi movements — the growing use of local vernacular. And he traces, over several years, where Levtzion saw this as having impact: first in assisting the spread of Islam from the Arabic-speaking heartlands into Asia and Africa; second, in particular with the use of mystical verse, in facilitating the "move" from the urban to the rural populous; third, by allowing for the participation of more "common" people, in generating the expansion of the *tariqh* itself; and fourth, by extension, in assuring a growing impact of *tariqa*. Most significant, Voll quotes Levtzion as recently as 2002 tying use of the vernacular to activism: "A new Muslim leadership [in this context] emerged that articulated the grievances of the masses, criticized the rulers, and contributed to the radicalization of Islam." As Voll concludes, "The rise of vernacular religious literature and its role in the radicalization of some groups within the Muslim world as articulated by Levtzion ... suggests new lines for discussion of Islamic renewal movements." In particular, his placement of these movements within the conceptual framework of "the public sphere in Muslim societies" can be helpful for understanding twenty-first century movements as well as their eighteenth-century predecessors.

Finally, Collins "engages" from a very different vantage point — he looks back upon the recently reprinted *Corpus* (translated, annotated excerpted texts from Medieval authors writing about West Africa) as a graduate student just beginning his research and weighing the value of older "seminal" works in light of current theoretical and methodological paradigms. In particular, he revisits the *Corpus* as a student of translation theory who has been strongly shaped by the late 1970s discourse that Edward Said set in motion on "orientalism." As someone who will long continue to benefit from the Levtzion and Hopkins (1981) translations, there is a certain ambivalence reflected in his commentary about just how heavily historians should be resting on these accounts given that, even with the most studious attention having been given to literal and contextual meaning in their preparation, they still remain unsubjected to current "post modern" criticism. "Exoticising" is a practice inherent in Levtzion's attempt to give readers the "original flavour" of the language, but it is not considered as part of the ongoing debate about the role of the translator in shaping the relationship between the reader and the text, for example. "Othering" (now a verb for which Said might take dubious credit for inadvertently popularizing) was a process inherent in each of the layers integral to the *Corpus* (original Arabic texts, subsequent manuscript copies, colonial translations, not to mention the intervention of Levtzion and his colleague J.F.P. Hopkins) but is not discussed *per se* as part of what would today be an expected exploration of methodological challenges. Collins' ambivalence is understandable, given the rigour with which any student of history using translated documents today is interrogated, added to the rather disappointing decision made (by the publishers? by Levtzion?) not to address any of these questions in the 2000 re-issue of the *Corpus* in paperback. That said, he suggests that those who would engage with this work in the future should bring to it consciousness of what translators see as issues central to good translation, as well as critical applications of post-modernist concerns like "othering," in order to derive the richest meaning possible from a text that he readily realizes, will never be duplicated.[2]

The *Ancient Ghana and Mali* Project

While Levtzion's first book was the publication of his PhD thesis research, for his second — and many would argue equally important — monograph, he returned to the focus of his Masters thesis, the medieval "states" of Ghana and Mali. As Klein ably describes the work, it was largely influenced by pre-existing models of desert-sahel relations, including an emphasis on frontier conflict and trans-Saharan trade as transformative processes. How it made its impact was through Levtzion's ability to plumb the Arabic authors' texts, as well as West African chronicles written in Arabic to develop our understanding of these processes. He also drew upon the archaeological work and oral traditions available at the time to flesh out these accounts. As Klein says, he produced a work that was — once again — invaluable for teaching and research. Yet, it was sufficiently controversial to stimulate continued research in archaeology and oral history in particular, but also in other fields that bore upon its basic historical theses — numismatics, climate and environment, cultural studies (especially of desert nomads and desert-edge societies) and economic history. Levtzion's *Ancient Ghana and Mali* was soon in need of up-dating. And it was at this point that the "project" of which Susan Keech McIntosh, Roderick McIntosh, and David Conrad write in this section was born — this was the same project that languished during much of the time Levtzion undertook the major administrative duties that he describes in his life history and that he had hoped to "resurrect" or at least inject new life into, with the panel arranged for the 2003 ASA.

Susan Keech McIntosh and Roderick McIntosh evoke some of the discussions that took place over those many years in Texas, in Jerusalem, in Mali — and we "hear" the Levtzion of whom Chazan speaks — listening, provoking, challenging, arguing, grudgingly "negotiating" new positions, new terminology, gradually arriving at a new *Ancient Ghana and Mali* that remained essentially true to some of his original arguments while simultaneously moving in new directions. Susan Keech McIntosh and Roderick McIntosh speak in particular to the impact archaeological findings have had in evaluating the role of trans-Saharan (as distinct from regional) trade, for example, and in challenging notions of "the state" and "kingship." And the degree to which Levtzion had come to embrace these challenges and their implications. Susan Keech McIntosh simultaneously explores some of the most significant of these and brings us up-to-date on where current research would "push" the re-writing of *Ancient Ghana and Mali* today. She draws attention to the significance of decade-long climate changes in regional contexts, as well as regional and local environmental responses to such changes, to argue for a dynamic and complex Sahara that cannot usefully be seen only from the large-scale, long-dureé perspective. She situates an emergent "ancient Ghana" in a relatively wet frontier area where camel nomads would not have survived incursions and conquests, and where whatever "polity" emerged would have been based on a pastoral, not an agricultural, economy. Both findings challenge directly *Ancient Ghana and*

Mali's original theses. Following on this reconceptualization, we must begin to conceive of Ghana's society as one responding to seasonal changes — as a mobile entity rooted in transhumance and movement. This in turn raises questions about our assumptions of "power," government structures, social hierarchies, economic networks, rituals, and religion.

In many ways, Roderick McIntosh highlights some of the same issues as he approaches the project from the vantage point of discipline: the coming together of archaeology, oral history and textual history — a "band of brothers" captained by Levtzion in which archaeology no longer played a "hand-maiden's" role to the written word. And Levtzion's earlier skepticism of the value of oral tradition had given way to recognition of Conrad's role in their collective exploration of landscape — physical, cultural, metaphorical, and spiritual. He speaks of methodology and the degree to which the project was to have reflected this evolution, even as he takes issue with the doyen of African oral history, Jan Vansina with respect to his "limited" understanding of the role of archaeology in history. He also draws attention to the complex nexus in which archaeologists and anthropologists are conceptualizing and engaging with "landscape," a perspective which promises to give new shape to the "antecedents" section he proposes to write. Herein, he will return to the long-durée but not, as he puts it, as a "turgid narrative" (or as the deterministic climatic template of which Susan Keech McIntosh speaks) but rather as a "dialectical relation between culture and geography." "Mande" will be explained as a "deep-time physical and occult Landscape of Power"; archaeology will show its ability to move beyond a description of "mute artifacts." As Roderick McIntosh concludes, "what were the landscapes of ancient Ghana and Mali if not messages from deep-time, there to be read and acted upon by the successful Mande hero and heroine?" And with this, he sets the scene for Conrad's contribution — the "brother" bringing oral tradition to the "band."

Conrad, whose own earlier work (in partnership with Humphrey Fisher) in using the oral to challenge the written established a yet-to-be surpassed model for revisiting medieval African history (Conrad and Fisher 2002, 2003), shows rather than addresses, where the project is going and how the "successful Mande Hero and Heroine" did indeed write (orally) upon that landscape. He exemplifies the process by which Levtzion's *Ancient Ghana and Mali* has ultimately brought about its reincarnation as something the same but — "other." In his "Mapping the Landscape," Conrad takes us into a different way of conceptualizing space and by extension, into different expressions of memory and identity, some of which are still discernible today. "The spiritual elements of myth, legend and magic with iconic links to conspicuous landscape features are part of the soul of Manden, and no historical inquiry could be complete without acknowledging their importance," Conrad asserts. The concerns of kinship, power, and authority, the physical landscape, and spirituality that "are snugly interwoven in the oral discourse" of Mande history need not just inform or complement the concerns reflected in the "written discourse" of external Arab history (as early use of oral tradition tended to do and indeed, as Levtzion used it in the original *Ancient Ghana and Mali*), they must shape the way we conceptualize the experience and the reality of "ancient Ghana and Mali." In the world-view that it allows the reader to access, Conrad's work subtly argues for something much more revolutionary than an "update" of *Ancient Ghana and Mali*. In so doing, it simultaneously reinforces the aims McIntosh lays out in the account of his own proposed "antecedents" and underscores the radical reconceptualization that Susan Keech McIntosh is suggesting.

While it is not clear in any of these articles where the project is to go from here, it is notable that, following Levtzion's death, Paulo de Moraes Farias, professor emeritus Birmingham, UK, agreed to join the project. This is the same de Moraes Farias (1974) whose seminal article "Great States Revisited" (referred to by Klein) originally challenged aspects of Levtzion's conceptualization of frontier relations. In the intervening decades, his own work on "orality" and most recently his seminal book on medieval Gao tombstone inscriptions (de Moraes Farias 2003), has established his credentials as Levtzion's worthy successor in the project. Currently entitled "Emerging Polities in the Western Sudan: Ancient Ghana and Mali" (McIntosh), it promises to deliver a re-read of the past that will truly be testimony to Levtzion's commitment to multidisciplinarity in history and will genuinely launch a re-engagement with medieval West African history that will attract and engage a new generation of Africanist scholars.

Developing Themes: History of Islam in Africa

This section reflects something of Levtzion's multi-disciplinary interests and influences that were to some extent articulated in his last major edited collection, *A History of Islam in Africa* (Levtzion and Pouwels 2000a). Although history was the central discipline represented by contributors to the book and the main organizing perspective, a sizable section (approximately one-third) was deliberately "thematic" in approach — cross cutting chronology with discussions of particular aspects or facets of Islam. David Owusu-Ansah and Ken Harrow were contributors to that section. Harrow here addresses the same theme of "literature" but with a very different essay — one that explores through literature, rather than talking about it; Owusu-Ansah's (2000) original chapter had addressed the fascinating theme of "magic and amulets,"[3] while here he and his co-author, Abdulai Iddrisu, engage with one of Levtzion's personal passions — education. The book's chapter on sufi brotherhoods across Africa was by Knut Vikor (2000); here the topic is addressed in a more circumscribed fashion as a comparative study between Senegal and Nigeria by another of the "next generation," a former student of Levtzion's, Irit Back. Eric Charry (2000b) whose chapter on "Music and Islam" closed the section in the original volume was unable to participate; Michael Frishkopf, another of the generation to whom Levtzion will be but a well-known name, agreed to contribute an article on the subject. Coming from a very different background than Charry (Frishkopf's work spans sub-Saharan and north African terrain, drawing on research from both Ghana and Egypt), his article here reflects a "larger" Africa, one much more connected to Middle Eastern traditions than Charry's. Regrettably, Roberta Ann Dunbar (2000), author of the original thematic chapter on "Muslim Women" and participant in the memorial sessions devoted to Levtzion in 2004, had to withdraw from the project even as her fascinating essay looking at how such women shaped the public sphere in the past and the present, was taking shape. My somewhat differently oriented essay that looks at the intersection of women, slaves and the household is meant in some part to respect the attention the subject deserves. Finally, Yekutiel Gershoni who came from Israel to honour his friend and colleague in that same 2004 session by delivering a paper on education — homage to Levtzion's devotion to developing education in Israel — has developed a completely new essay here on a part of West Africa that has largely escaped the eyes of Islamic researchers, including Levtzion, namely Liberia.

These articles vary greatly in the extent to which they directly engage with Levtzion's scholarship — Harrow and Owusu-Ansah and Iddrisu in effect salute Levtzion in their opening paragraphs but then carry on to write independent articles that "engage" only to the extent that they reflect a continuing focus on the intersection of literature and education (respectively) with Islam. Harrow for example, acknowledges the centrality of the questions "How did Islam come to West Africa?" and "When did people convert?" to Levtzion's studies. But while he suggests that his alternative approach runs parallel to Levtzion's explorations of these questions, he actually begins with a very subversive proposition:

> What if we were to deny beginnings, deny there was a time we would label "before Islam" and "after Islam"? To be more precise, we might agree that people began to call themselves Muslim at well-defined moments and in specific places, but claim that their embrace of Islam was not simply a consequence of an originary conversion....

With this provocative suggestion, he proceeds to interrogate the experience of "being Muslim" through the lens of two African novels (or more specifically, their lead characters). While he does not return us, as readers, to Levtzion, were he to do so, we would find ourselves thinking quite differently about notions of "conversion" and "Islamization."

Owusu-Ansah and Iddrisu shift ground completely as they examine how Ghana is integrating the secular into the religious in order to retain "Muslim" education. In this probing of the intersection between the two, and the management of the potential tensions it suggests by Government policy, they are indeed speaking to a concern Levtzion occupied himself with during the many years he devoted to developing secular education in his own "religious" state, not to mention his sensitivity to the importance of non-Muslims studying Islam and non-Jews teaching and learning about Judaism (Miles). The success the Government's Education Service has had in simultaneously increasing the number of Muslim schools in a country loudly proclaiming a rise in Christian doctrines and then populating them with "secular" teachers and programmes (long suspect precisely because of their historical, as well as contemporary association with western Christianity), is nothing short of revolutionary, Owusu-Ansah and Iddrisu conclude.

Back and Frishkopf pay their respects purely in terms of the extent to which they share Levtzion's respect for the study of Sufism (to which Levtzion himself contributed so much — there is a certain "heritage" reflected in Back's choice of subject matter) and of music (which Levtzion himself appreciated but in no way ever attempted to address directly). While Back focuses in detailed fashion on the comparative interaction between sufists and Wahhabists in Senegal and Nigeria, attempting to explain similarities and differences between them in their "post colony" experiences, Frishkopf's chapter is very large in scope, beginning with the very contradictions inherent in talking about "Islam" and "Music," and moving on to outline in clearly accessible text how and why music has indeed become "Islamic" throughout Africa. That said, Back, like Levtzion, situates her Sufism in a much larger framework, both historical (the colonial experience is a key factor in her analysis) and thematic ("modernity, modernization and globalization," and their relation to specific Islamic brotherhoods in the post-colonial world). In contrasting Senegal's experience with sufi-Wahhabist tensions with that of Nigeria, she attempts to weigh the relative roles of "colonial" and "post colonial" realities, looking to explain future developments.

Frishkopf's "'Islamic Music in Africa' as a Tool for African Studies" while clearly generated from a different vantage point, is surprisingly conversant with Back's article, to the extent that it too brings what would seem to be a particularistic study to considerations of "modernity" and globalization. And like her exploration of how particular visions of Islam are mediated and take root, Frishkopf's approach to music is one of looking at it as facilitating the adoption of Islam in particular ways, at particular moments in time, in particular societies. His conclusion best signifies why "Islamic Music" is integral to the study and understanding of "Islamization":

> A deeper understanding of Islam in Africa depends upon research, both intensive and extensive, of the many local interpretations of Islam. For this purpose, an understanding of the

myriad expressive cultural practices carrying Islamic meanings, is essential, because of the ability of such practices to represent, and to reproduce or contest, core concepts and social relations characterizing Muslim societies. *Among these practices, music is central*, due to its collective and affectively charged nature. An enormous amount of feasible research on contemporary Islamic musical practices remains to be carried out. This research promises to illuminate the interactions of local and global forces — ideological, political, or economic — now shaping Muslim societies throughout the region [my emphasis].

The information in his article effectively supports this argument, from exploring the whole tension within Islam of speaking about "music," to showing (by isolating and describing the various components and purposes of that music) how it allows societies to mediate with the "new" and the "threatening," to giving examples of the above, to which anyone familiar with aspects of "world music" will relate. Like Back's, Frishkopf's "issues" resonate clearly with those which characterize Levtzion's work; that one worked with and was trained by Levtzion and the other knew him only vaguely by reputation is not evident in the insights both bring to building on his work.

Gershoni and I, on the other hand, are in fact responding to silences in Levtzion's work. That said, while Gershoni certainly draws on conventions well developed by Levtzion to draw Liberia into the larger discussion of "Islam in Africa," the piece stands entirely independent of the original book or its conceptualization. And whereas I use what I see as "missing" in terms of the role of women and slaves in shaping the process of Islamization as scaffolding for my article, I nevertheless draw extensively on material presented by several of the book's authors (with considerable attention to Dunbar's fine essay) to argue for "shifting the research paradigm" away from its current gender and class biases. The history of Muslims in Liberia, contrary to generally held understanding, is very much the history of Liberia itself prior to the twentieth century, Gershoni argues. As he recounts his narrative, his exploration of oral traditions echoes many of the "motifs" characterizing Islamization elsewhere and probes the debate in which Levtzion was active, over the relative role of traders and teachers in the process. In contrasting what he calls a "non-politicized" Islam with a "highly-politicized" Christianity in nineteenth century Liberia, he pulls a discussion which is usually bounded by considerations of *jihad* states into something broader, more relevant for looking not only at historical but contemporary situations. There are also resonances of Owusu-Ansah and Iddrisu's discussion of education here and its relation to secular state building, as Gershoni looks at Edward Blyden's plans to use education to integrate Liberia's successful Muslim communities into the "new," in this case "Christian" nation.

My essay, "Hidden in the Household: Gender and Class in the Study of Islam in Africa," would at first glance seem to have little support in *Islam in Africa*, and even less relevance for the issues that other essays in this section address. But in fact, just as Gershoni argues Levtzion's approach to Islamization could (and should) embrace the Liberian case, and Liberia in turn has something to "offer" us in understanding historical and contemporary Islam in Africa, I attempt to show that both "women" and "slaves" are there in the stories *Islam in Africa* tells, they simply have not been given sufficient voice. Moreover, where they are visible and voluble, they have something to say in terms of how we should understand the process of "becoming" and "being" Muslim. There is a methodological overlap here with Frishkopf's article in the sense of seeking catalysts, dynamics in "topics" too often treated as descriptive categories or as elements of Islam, subject to the power of males (traders, clerics, teachers) and class (middle and upper). Or in the case of music, as fixed "entities" that must be judged to be more or less "Islamic" according to some external measure of what it means to be Muslim. My article is preliminary, drawing on existing research — some of it very well known — to suggest that the vantage point of the household might lend new perspective to the roles women and slaves play in shaping, not merely responding to, Islam.

There is, then, certainly some level of "engagement with the legacy" to be seen in this section, but it is primarily directed at building upon it. Perhaps the ultimate "engagement" is reached when the next generations of scholars are only vaguely aware of the roots of so many of their resources, so "buried" have they become in the process of nurturing new growth. And perhaps this is why we share the desire, in this volume, not only to remember Levtzion as our personal friend and colleague but to introduce him anew to those who will continue to engage his legacy for many years to come.

Epilogue

Finally, we re-print one of the last pieces that Levtzion (2007) wrote and which was published posthumously. In "Resurgent Islamic Fundamentalism," he brings to bear his long-developed understanding of the dynamics of "reformism" and "renewal" to explain the emergence of the twenty-first century variations of the revitalization of Islam that he studied so long ago in the eighteenth- and nineteenth-century context. As always, he shows the relevance of these "historical" studies for understanding not only the present but the future. And as is appropriate in this volume dedicated to Nehemia Levtzion, his is the last voice that we shall hear.

Notes

[1] My thanks to Susan Keech McIntosh for providing me with audio copies of that remarkable session.

[2] He does, of course, acknowledge the earlier publication of Joseph Cuoq's French set of translated / annotated texts, *Recueil des sources arabes concernant l'Afrique occidentale du VIIIe au XVIe siècle* (Bilad al-Sudan) (Paris: Éditions de Centre national de la recherche scientifique, 1975). However, he points out that some "issues" translators would have with the work would derive specifically from the receptor language — that is, that there would be some aspects of Cuoq's work that would be specific to the Arabic-to-French, as distinct from the Arabic-to-English, translation involved. And from the "orientalism" perspective, the cultural "othering" predominant in France would not necessarily replicate that shaping some of the English manuscripts with which Levtzion and Hopkins worked.

[3] It was one of the most intriguing of the contributions, regrettably also one of the shortest. This perspective is not reflected in this volume, unfortunately. My paper on the memorial panel also treated the subject of "magic and Islam" in the context of the Sahara, but I have chosen not to publish it yet.

Memoirs and Memories

The Legacy of Nehemia Levtzion 1935-2003

Résumé

Le travail érudit de Nehemia Levtzion, publié dans un certain nombre de livres ou sous forme d'articles, a été partout acclaimé par les érudits et étudiants de l'Islam.... Nehemia Levtzion était un homme modeste qui répugnait à parler de lui-même. Pourtant, à l'occasion de son 60ème anniversaire en 1995, pour répondre à la demande de ses amis et de sa famille, il a parlé de sa vie en ces termes (traduits de l'Hébreu) pour en donner un résumé.

Abstract

The scholarly work of Nehemia Levtzion, published in a variety of books and articles, has been widely acclaimed by scholars and students of Islam.... Nehemia Levtzion was a modest man who was reluctant to talk about himself. At his 60th birthday celebration in 1995, however, when asked to speak to friends and family about his life, he gave the following account (translated from Hebrew), which sums up his life story.

I was born in Be'er-Tuvia on 24 November 1935, to Pnina (nee Perlow) and Aron Lubetski; this name was later changed to Levtzion. My sister Hanna was three years older than me.

At that time Be'er-Tuvia was the southernmost Jewish settlement in Palestine, and was surrounded by Arab villages. The *moshav* of Be'er-Tuvia was established in 1930, a few months after the destruction of the *moshavah*[1] of Be'er-Tuvia during the [Arab] Disturbances of 1929 and the expatriation of its inhabitants. We did not have a farm. My father worked as the secretary and accountant of the *moshav* and we lived in the workers' neighbourhood, but participated fully in village life.

Reproduced with minor editorial modifications from *Islam in Africa and the Middle East: Studies on Conversion and Renewal*, edited by Michael Abitbol and Amos Nadan, ix-xviii. Farnham, UK: Ashgate Variorum, 2007.

The events that we experienced were the activities of the British Army, first with much admiration during the Second World War, and later with much tension, when the British searched for weapons, or on the night when a ship with [illegal Jewish] immigrants landed on the coast at Nitzanim. During the War of Independence [1947/48] the village was bombed by the Egyptian Army and we, the children, were evacuated to the centre of the country.

In 1949, after the War of Independence, my family moved to Tel Aviv, and a new chapter began of five years of school (one year in the Ledogma primary school and four years in the 'Ironi Alef high school) and in the naval division *(Yamiya)* of the United Youth Movement *(Hatno'a Ha-meuhedet)*. Until 10th grade we were occupied in sea activities, including participating in (and winning) the Cities' Sailing Competition from Haifa to Tel Aviv. In the 11th and 12th grades my focus was the youth movement, in its guidance of pupils and its fostering of the *gar'in*.[2]

In December 1953 we [the members of the youth movement] enrolled in the Nahal, after three months of training in Kibbutz Tzora. At the end of this basic training, the gar'in moved to Kibbutz Ayelet Ha-shachar, and I was sent for hadracha [guidance] to Hatno'a Ha-meuhedet. I was posted to Haifa, and although the youngest leader, I was appointed coordinator of the movement in Haifa, and soon became a member of the national secretariat. In 1954 I cocrdinated the national summer camp in the Hulda forest.

In 1955, when the gar'in went to "advanced [military] manoeuvres" in the Nahal, my request to leave the *hadracha* and join the military practice in Camp Natan next to Beersheba was approved. In July the *gar'in* joined as "members" of Kibbutz Ma'ayan Baruch. It was a new chapter lasting two years, until July 1957. During this time I was a member of the Kibbutz's secretariat and in the second year I was also in charge of the sheep pen. In August and September 1956 I travelled to Holland and England with a delegation of leaders of the Habonim youth movement's summer camps.

In October 1957 I started my studies at the Hebrew University, at the Department of Arabic Language and Literature and the Department of Middle Eastern History. Three months after my arrival in Jerusalem I began to work at the Israeli Information Center as editor-in-chief of their publications, and continued there until 1961.

In all I have achieved, I am grateful to my teachers Baneth,

Plessner, Shamosh, Ashtor, Heyd and Baer, all of blessed memory, and to Ayalon and Shinar, may they live long. My interest in Islam was apparent in all my seminar papers during my BA studies: on the Khawâridj sects (for Baneth), Mohammad ʿAbdûh (for Baer) and on Ibn Taymiyya (for Ayalon). But beyond these individual studies, I was fascinated by the phenomenon of the spread of Islam — or Islamization.

In the first year of my MA course, around Hanukah 1961, I was invited to the home of the late Professor Uriel Heyd, head of the Institute for Humanities Studies. He spoke about the university's plan to enlarge the scope of the Center for African and Asian Studies. He said, "since you are interested in process of Islamization, go and study this process in Africa." The university, he promised, "would pay for your studies, and afterwards you would be able to establish a department for African Studies."

On 4 May 1961, the Gindel and Levtzion families celebrated our marriage [Nehemia Levtzion to Tirtza Gindel]. Tirtza had to finish teaching in a high school in Tiv'on, and a year later moved to teach at the regional school of Mate Yehuda in Kibbutz Kiriyat ʿAnavim. I was then an assistant in the department, and invested much effort into completing all my obligations for the MA, including a thesis and final exam, by July 1962.

At the beginning of November that year Tirtza and I travelled to London for my PhD studies in the history of Africa at the School of Oriental and African Studies (SOAS), University of London. During the first year I decided that my doctoral topic would be the expansion of Islam in Northern Ghana and neighbouring areas (the Volta River Basin). In July 1963 we spent a month in Paris, working in archives, and then travelled to Rome, via Switzerland and Italy, and at the beginning of September 1963 flew from Rome to Accra.

I dedicated about three months to studying the Arabic scripts collected at the University of Ghana, and in November we went north to Tamale. Tirtza decided to teach in a Ghanaian high school in Tamale, instead of at the Israeli school. Therefore we rented a house in Tamale. This was a base from which I travelled every Sunday to visit Muslim communities in Ghana, Togo and Upper Volta, returning to Tamale at the weekend. In all my travels in a Volkswagen "Beetle" I was joined by a translator, Hajj Ibrahim, with whom I spoke Arabic and who translated the local languages into Arabic.

In January 1964 Tirtza and I went on a long and adventurous journey via Upper Volta, south to Dahomey, north to Nigeria up to Niger on the Sahara border, and from there back to Ghana. We returned to London in August 1964, after visiting Austria, Prague and Copenhagen. In Copenhagen I worked on Arabic scripts from Kumasi, from the beginning of the 19th century, which had been seized by the Danes in Accra.

On 12 November 1965 our oldest son, Moshe, was born in London. He went to Israel with Tirtza in June 1965. I submitted my PhD in August 1965. and until it was read by the examiners, I participated in a conference on the history of Africa in Dar-es-Salaam, Tanzania, and also visited Kenya and Uganda. In November I defended my PhD thesis, and returned to Jerusalem as a lecturer in African and Islamic Studies at the Hebrew University.

On the eve of the Six Day War [1967] the faculty's board approved the proposal to establish a Department of African Studies for postgraduate students. Robert Shershevsky, who had partnered me in the preparatory work for it, died in that war, and I was appointed to coordinate the new department. Shmuel Eisenstadt, the dean of the Department of Social Science, was of great assistance at that time (the department came under the two faculties [Humanities and Social Sciences]).

The academic year 1967/68 was the department's first year, and we succeeded in getting an excellent group of students, among them Victor Azarya, Binyamin Neuberger and Michel Abitbol. We encouraged them to complete their PhD studies outside the country. Their first degrees were from different departments, so that the new department was as planned, interdisciplinary, with a historical approach as its integrative basis. After a year Naomi Chazan, who came with an MA in African Studies from Columbia, commenced her PhD thesis in the department.

On 22 February 1968 our daughter Osnat was born.

In 1968 my first book, based on my doctoral thesis, was published. Jan Vansina, a prominent historian of Africa, wrote in 1994, in a book that explored the development of African Studies in the field of Islam in Africa: "Less dismissive views became dominant after 1968, when Nehemia Levtzion published his Muslim and Chiefs in West Africa."

My MA thesis at the Hebrew University (supervised by Peesah

Shinar) was on the empire of Mali in the Middle Ages according to Arabic sources. Already, before coming to London, I had published an article in the very important *Journal of African History*, where I pointed out a mistake in the understanding of Ibn Khaldûn's text, which had caused confusion concerning the genealogy of Mali's rulers. Following the completion of [my] book on Northern Ghana, I then wrote a history of Ghana and Mali. In 1973 *Ancient Ghana and Mali* was published, and during the 1970s I wrote several chapters for the *Cambridge History of Africa* series on the history of Western Sudan up to 1800; I completed my contribution to a book on the History of West Africa in the Middle Ages. In 1981 the volume that I edited with John Hopkins *[Corpus of Early Arabic Sources for West African History]*, which includes the translation into English of Arabic texts up to the 16th century, was published. This volume, known to researchers of Africa by the abbreviation "Corpus," gave historians who do not read Arabic access to the sources. It is one of the most cited publications in the research literature.

In 1969 we went on our first sabbatical and got to know the United States.

On 2 June 1970 our daughter Noga was born.

In 1972/73 we went on sabbatical to Cambridge [UK]; I was a Fellow at St John's College. That year I had the opportunity to broaden my interest in the processes of Islamisation, and to return from the history of Islam in Africa to Islam in general. In the same year I ran a seminar at SOAS, with that institution's best researchers, on the process of Islamisation. The fruits of that seminar were published in a book that I edited, *Conversion to Islam* (1979).

On 5 July 1974 our son Avner was born.

In 1974 I was appointed head of the research committee of the Faculty of Humanities. In order to make better use of the limited resources for research, and after checking the needs of most researchers in the faculty, I set out new regulations that enabled every researcher to have access to printing and editing for his publications, and removed limitations on the number of photocopies. These arrangements exist today, with almost no changes, more than 20 years later.

In those years I dealt, for the first time, in the modern subject, as well as paying attention to the rising power of Islam in international relations. Thanks to a grant from the Leonard Davis Institute [for International Relations, Hebrew University] I completed some research, published in 1980 as *International Islamic Solidarity and its Limitations*.

In 1977 we again went on sabbatical to England, first to Oxford and then Manchester. While at Manchester I was chosen to be the Dean of the Faculty of Humanities at the Hebrew University and took up that position when I returned in September 1978. These were three fascinating years that I am not able to cover in this framework.

In Passover 1980 we lost our eldest son, Moshe, in a car accident.

After my term as dean, we went on sabbatical to Boston in 1981/82. I belonged simultaneously to the Center for Middle Eastern Studies at Harvard; the Center of African Studies in Boston; and the Department of Political Science at Brandeis. Between these, we managed to advance a joint endeavour of 20 years standing between myself and Ivor Wilks, which was published in 1986: *Chronicles from Gonja: A Tradition of West African Muslim Historiography*. Another [colleague] who greatly contributed to this work was Bruce Haight, a former student of Ivor's and mine.

After my return to Israel in August 1982 I was asked to become director of the Ben Zvi Institute, and hence to continue with the advancement of studies on the traditions of Judaism in the "East." It was also a first opportunity for me to dedicate effort to the field of Judaism.

In those five years, 1982-87, I was also the academic principal of a new programme, funded by the Rothschild Fund, to assist young diplomats from the Israeli Foreign Ministry, who did two years study at the Hebrew University.

Simultaneously, I became a member of the Planning and Budgeting Committee of the Israeli Council for Higher Education [PBC], after a previous term in 1980-81. As a member of the PBC I was the head of two committees, the committee for regional colleges and the committee for overseas students.

In 1983 we ran an international workshop at the Truman Institute for the Advancement of Peace [Hebrew University], on rural and urban Islam in Africa, which led to publication of the volume, *Rural and Urban Islam in West Africa* (1986).

In 1985 I coordinated a research group at the university's Institute for Advanced Studies, focusing on eighteenth-century renewal and reform movements in Islam. At the end of that year we held an international conference on the subject, leading to a book that I edited with John Voll, *Eighteenth Century Renewal and Reform in Islam* (1987).

In May 1987 I was chosen to be president of [Israel's] Open University, which opened a chapter of the five most fascinating years of my life. I received into my hands a well-established university, and I set a personal target to materialize its great potential. It seems to me that this was achieved in the doubling of the number of students to 20 000; in the establishment of colleges in which intensive studies could be conducted; in concentrating the studies in social sciences around occupations that were more in demand; and in presenting of the university as a valued alternative to other universities for youngsters finishing their military service. With this, the economic standing of the university was widened and stabilized.

In August 1992 we celebrated the marriage of Osnat and Amit, and in July 1993 the marriage of Noga and Amos.

Immediately after ending my term as president of the Open University, I agreed to replace Professor Moshe Davis as the academic chairperson of The International Center for the University Teaching of Jewish Civilization. This took me back to dealing with Jewish Studies.

From January 1994 I was the head of the Van Leer Institute in Jerusalem. I was asked to take this position after the institute had fallen into severe economic crisis and there were also personal difficulties. After a few months the institute was rehabilitated, and it gradually achieved a level of activity above what it had experienced in the past. The institute's emphasis is on continual intellectual dialogue.

In my research these days I focus on understanding the organisational and structural changes that took place in Sufi brotherhoods during the eighteenth century. These contribute to a more comprehensive understanding of the movements of reform and renewal. Simultaneously, I am cooperating with two archaeologists, Roderick and Susan McIntosh, and with an historian of oral traditions, David Conrad, in rewriting the book on Ghana and Mali, a book that has still not been superseded after 20 years. I am also engaged in another project, the Cambridge History of Islam in Africa, together with Randall Pouwels.

Since I live in an age where people gather things that they wrote, in 1994 a collection of essays of mine was published by Variorum under the title, *Islam in West Africa: Religion, Society and Politics to 1800*. On 23 June [1995] our first grandson, Yoav Moshe, was born to Osnat and Amit Korach.

[Editorial Epilogue]

Nehemia Levtzion passed away three months before his 68th birthday. If he had spoken to his friends and family on his 67th birthday, he would probably have added to the above that he chaired the Planning and Budgeting Committee of the Israeli Council for Higher Education (1997-2003) and was president of the Israel Oriental Society (1997-2003); he would have mentioned his new publications, especially the book he co-authored with J. Spaulding, *Medieval West Africa: Views from Arab Scholars and Merchants* and the book with M. Hoexter and S. N. Eisenstadt, *The Public Sphere in Muslim Societies*. Also, in September 1998 the family celebrated Avner and Tal's marriage; and by that time he had five grandchildren and another on their way.

Nehemia Levtzion in Ghana and with his translator Hajj Ibrahim

Nehemia Levtzion: Bibliography by Subject Area
[Editorial Note: This list, including the different categories, was prepared by Professor Levtzion.]

1. Conversion to Islam

Books

1.1 *Muslims and Chiefs in West Africa: A Study of Islam in the Middle Volta Basin in the Pre-Colonial Period.* Oxford: Clarendon Press, 1968, 256 pp.

1.2 (editor) *Conversion to Islam.* New York: Holmes & Meier, 1979, 270 pp.

Articles and Chapters

1.3 "Patterns of Islamization in West Africa." In *Aspects of West African Islam*, edited by D.F. McCall and N.R. Bennett. Boston: Boston University Press, 1971, 31-39. Reprinted in *Conversion to Islam*, edited by N. Levtzion, New York: Holmes & Meier, 1979, 207-216 (reprinted in 4.2).

1.4 "Conversion to Islam: Some notes towards a comparative study." *Actes de 29e Congrès International des Orientalistses: Etudes Arabes et Islamiques*, edited by C. Cahen. Paris: L'Asiatheque, 1975, 125-129.

1.5 "Towards a comparative study of Islamization." In *Conversion to Islam*, edited by N. Levtzion, 1981, 1-23 (see no. 1.2).

1.6 "Conversion under Muslim domination: a comparative study." In *Religious Change and Cultural Domination*, edited by David N. Lorenzen. Mexico City, 1981, 19-38.

1.7 "Shari'a and custom in the process of Islamization and sedentarization." *Cathedra* 20 (1981), 78-80 (Hebrew).

1.8 "Migration and settlement of Muslim nomads and conquerors: their contribution to Islamization. In *Emigration and Settlement in Jewish and General History*, edited by A. Shinan. Jerusalem: Zalman Shazar Center, 1982, 95-107 (Hebrew).

1.9 "Slavery and Islamization in Africa." In *Slaves and Slavery in Muslim Africa*, edited by J.R. Willis. London: Frank Cass, 1985, volume 1, 182-198 (reprinted in 4.2).

1.10 "Aspekte der Islmisierung: Eine kritische Wurdigungder Beobachtungen Max Webers." In *Max Weber Sicht des Islam: Interpretation und Kritik*, edited by W. Schluchter. Frankfurt: Suhrkamp, 1987, 142-155.

1.11 "Conversion to Islam in Syria and Palestine, and the survival of Christian communities." In *Conversion and Continuity: Indigenous Christian Communities in Medieval Islamic Lands*, edited by M. Gervers and R.J. Bikhazi. Toronto: Pontifical Institute of Medieval Studies, 1990, 289-312.

1.12 "Conversion and Islamization in the Middle Ages: how did Jews and Christians differ?" *Pe'amim* 42 (1990), 8-15 (Hebrew).

1.13 "Islamisierungmuster: Die Begegnung des Islam mit Achsenzeitreligionen." In *Kulturen der Achsenzeit II: Ihre institutionelle und kulturelle Dynamik*, edited by S.N. Eisnstadt. Frankfurt: Suhrkamp, 1992, volume 3, 226-241.

1.14 "Aspects of Islamization: Weber's observations on Islam reconsidered." In *Max Weber and Islam*, edited by T.B. Huff and W. Schluchter, New Brunswick, NJ: Transaction Publishers, 1999, 153-161 (an English translation of 1.10).

2. Renewal, Reform and Sufi Brotherhoods in the Eighteenth Century

Book

2.1 (co-editor with J.O. Voll) *Eighteenth Century Renewal and Reform in Islam*. Syracuse, NY: Syracuse University Press, 1987, 200 pp.

Articles and Chapters

2.2 "Notes on the Origins of Islamic Militancy in the Futa Jallon." *Notes Africaines* (Dakar), no. 132 (October 1971), 94-96 (reprinted in 4.2).

2.3 "Eighteenth-century renewal and reform movements in Islam." In *Renewal (tajdid) and Reform (islah) in Islam*, a special issue of *Hamizrah Hehadash* 31 (1986), 48-70 (Hebrew).

2.4 (with J. O. Voll) "Eighteenth-century renewal and reform movements in Islam: an Introductory Essay." In *Eighteenth Century Renewal and Reform in Islam*, edited by Levtzion and Voll, 1987 (see 2.1), 13-20.

2.5 "The Eighteenth Century: Background to the Islamic Revolutions in West Africa." In *Eighteenth Century Renewal and Reform in Islam*, edited by Levtzion and Voll, 1987 (2.1), 21-38 (reprinted in 4.2).

2.6 "Eighteenth-century renewal and reform in Islam: the role of Sufi turuq in West Africa." In *Islam in West Africa*, edited by Levtzion (no. 4.2), 1994 (from a collection of papers entitled *The Cloth of Many Colored Silks: Papers on History and Society Ghanaian and Islamic in Honor of Ivor Wilks*).

2.7 "al-Tijani, Ahmad." *Oxford Encyclopedia of the Modern Islamic World*, edited by John L. Esposito. New York: Oxford University Press, 1995.

2.8 (with G. Weigert) "Khalwatiyya." *Oxford Encyclopedia of the Modern Islamic World*. New York: Oxford University Press, 1995.

2.9 (with G. Weigert) "Religious Reform in Eighteenth-century Morocco." North African, Arabic and Islamic Studies in Honor of Pessah Shinar, published as *Jerusalem Studies in Arabic and Islam* 19 (1995), 173-197.

2.10 "Eighteenth-Century Sufi Brotherhoods: Structural, Organizational and Ritual Changes." In *Islam: Essays on Scripture, Thought and Society. A Festschrift in Honour of Anthony H. Johns*, edited by Peter G. Riddel and Tony Street. Leiden: Brill 1997, 147-60

2.11 (with G. Weigert) "The Muslim holy cities as foci of Islamic revivalism in the eighteenth century." In *Sacred Space: Shrine, City, Land*, edited by B.Z. Kedar and R.J. Zwi Werblowsky. The Israel Academy and Macmillan (UK), 1998, 259-77.

2.12 (with G. Weigert) "Renewal and reform of the Khalwatiyya in Egypt in the 18th century." Unpublished paper presented to the Middle East Studies Association annual meeting, San Antonio, TX, November 1990.

2.13 "The Dynamics of Sufi Brotherhoods." In *The Public Sphere in Muslim Societies*, edited by M. Hoexter, S.N. Eisenstadt and N. Levtzion. Albany: SUNY series in Near Eastern Studies, 2002, 109-118.

3. Studies on Islam

Books

3.1 *International Islamic Solidarity and its Limitations.* Jerusalem: Magnes Press for the Leonard Davis Institute for International Relations, 1980, 65 pp.

3.2 (with Daphna Ephrat and Daniela Talmon-Heller) *Islam: A History of the Religion.* The Open University of Israel, volumes 1 and 2, 1998; volume 3, 2000 (in Hebrew).

3.3 (co-editor with M. Hoexter and S.N. Eisenstadt) *The Public Sphere in Muslim Societies.* Albany, NY: SUNY Press 2002. 191 pp.

Articles and Chapters

3.4 "The Integration of the Muslim Northern Region into the Federation of Nigeria." *Hamizrah Hehadash* 12 (1962), 28-46 (Hebrew).

3.5 "Sects in Islam." In *Studies in the History of the Arabs and Islam*, edited by H. Lazarus-Yafeh. Tel-Aviv: Reshafim, 1967, 176-198 (Hebrew).

3.6 "Non-Arab Islam and the Middle East Conflict." In *Islamic Aspects of the Middle East Conflict.* Jerusalem: Truman Research Institute, 1974, 17-23 (Hebrew).

3.7 "Between `ulama' and rulers in the Muslim State." In *Priesthood and Monarchy: Studies in the Historical Relations of Religion and State*, edited by I. Gafni and G. Motzkin. Jerusalem: Zalman Shazar Center, 1985, 115-121 (Hebrew).

3.8 "The Spirit of the Mediterranean: Cultural Exchanges in Trade and War." *DOMUS: International Review of Architecture, Design, Art, Communication*, no. 813 (March 1999), 4-6.

3.9 "Islam and politics: lessons from the past." *Hamizrah Hehadash* 40 (1999), 5-8 (in Hebrew); *Prajna Vihara: Journal of Philosophy and Religion* (Assumption University, Bangkok) 1, no.2 (July-December 2000), 111-120.

3.10 "Tolerance in Islam." In *Education for Human Values, Tolerance and Peace,* edited by J. Iram. School of Education, Bar-Ilan University 2000, 15-19.

3.11 "Islam in African and Global Contexts: Adventures in Comparative Studies of Islam." Paper presented to the conference on Islam in Africa: A Global, Cultural and Historical Perspective, Binghamton University, NY, April 19-22, 2001.

4. Islam in Africa

Books

4.1 (co-editor with H.J. Fisher) *Rural and Urban Islam in West Africa.* Boulder, CO: Lynne Rienner, 1987, 176 pp.; first published as a special issue of *Asian and African Studies* 20, no.1 (1986).

4.2 *Islam in West Africa: Religion, Society and Politics to 1800.* London: Variorum, 1994, 300 pp.

4.3 (co-editor with R. L. Pouwels) *The History of Islam in Africa.* Athens, OH: Ohio University Press, 2000, 591 pp.

Articles and Chapters

4.4 "Islam in Africa: some central issues for research and teaching." *Hamizrah Hehadash* 17 (1967), 1-17 (Hebrew).

4.5 "The long march of Islam in the Western Sudan." In *The Middle Age of African History,* edited by R. Oliver. London: Oxford University Press, 1967, 13-18.

4.6 "Reflections on the Muslim historiography in Africa." In *Emerging Themes of African History,* edited by T.O. Ranger. Nairobi: East African Publishing House, 1968, 23-27.

4.7 "L'Islam et le commerce chez les Dagomba du Nord Ghana."

Annales: ESC 23 (1968), 723-743.

4.8 "Islam in Coastal West Africa." In *Islam in Tropical Africa*, edited by J. Kritzeck and W.H. Lewis. New York: Van Nostrand, 1969, 301-318.

4.9 "The `ulama' of the Western Sudan before the fifteenth century." In *The `Ulama' and Problems of Religion in the Muslim World: Studies in Memory of Uriel Heyd*, edited by G. Baer. Jerusalem: Magnes Press, 1971, 52-62 (Hebrew).

4.10 "Islam in West African politics: accommodation and tension between the `ulama' and the political authorities." *Cahiers d'Etudes Africaines* 18 (1979), 333-345.

4.11 "Sociopolitical roles of Muslim clerics and scholars in West Africa." In *Comparative Social Dynamics: Essays in Honor of S.N. Eisenstadt*, edited by E. Cohen, M. Lissak and U. Almagor. Boulder, CO: Westview Press, 1985, 95-107.

4.12 "Islam and religious pluralism in West African states." *Revue Francaise d'Histoire d'Outre Mer* 68 (1981), 154-155.

4.13 "Rural and urban Islam in West Africa." In *Rural and Urban Islam in West Africa*, edited by N. Levtzion and H.J. Fisher, Boulder, CO: Lynne Rienner, 1987 (4.1 above), 1-20 (reprinted in 4.2).

4.14 "Merchants vs. Scholars and clerics: differential and complementary roles." In *Rural and Urban Islam in West Africa*, edited by N. Levtzion and H.J. Fisher, Boulder, CO: Lynne Rienner, 1987 (1.8 above), 21-37 (reprinted in 1.10).

4.15 "Islam in Sub-Saharan Africa." *Encyclopaedia of Religion*, edited by Mircea Eliade *et al.* New York: Macmillan, 1987, volume 7, 344-357.

4.16 "Islam and state formation in West Africa." In *The Early State in Africa*, edited by S.N. Eisenstadt, M. Abitbol and N. Chazan. Leiden: E.J. Brill, 1987, 98-108.

4.17 "Muslim `ulama' and human rights in pre-colonial West Africa." In *Human Rights in Developing Countries: Problems and Prospects*, edited by C.E. Welch. Buffalo, NY, 1989, 122-138.

4.18 "Islam in Africa to 1800." In *The Oxford History of Islam*, edited by J. L. Esposito. New York: Oxford University Press, 1999, 475-507.

4.19 (with R. L. Pouwels) "Introduction: Patterns of Islamization and varieties of religious experience among Muslims of Africa." In *The History of Islam in Africa*. Athens: Ohio University Press 2000, edited by N. Levtzion and R.L. Pouwels (see above 4.3), 1-18.

4.20 "Islam in the Bilad al-Sudan to 1800." In *The History of Islam in Africa*, edited by N. Levtzion and R.L. Pouwels. Athens, OH: Ohio University Press, 2000 (see above 4.3), 63-91.

5. History of West Africa

Books

5.1 *Ancient Ghana and Mali*. London: Methuen, 1973, 283 pp. (hardcover and paperback); 2nd edition, New York: Holmes & Meier, 1980 (hardcover and paperback).

5.2 *An Introduction to African History*. Tel Aviv: The Open University of Israel, 1980, 147 pp. (Hebrew).

Articles and Chapters

5.3 "Salaga — a nineteenth century trading town in Ghana." *Asian and African Studies* 2 (1966), 207-244.

5.4 "Oral traditions and historical consciousness in Africa." In *Awareness of the Past in the Consciousness of the Nations and of the Jewish People*. Jerusalem: Zalman Shazar Center, 1969, 124-134 (Hebrew).

5.5 "The early states of the Western Sudan to 1500." In *History of West Africa*, edited by J.F.A. Ajayi and M. Crowder. London: Longman, 1971, volume 1, 120-157 (several later editions).

5.6 "Notes sur les états Dyula de Kong et de Bobo." *Bulletin de Liaison*. Centre Universitaire de Recherches de Development (Abidjan) 1 (1971), 61-62.

5.7 "Northwest Africa: from the Maghrib to the fringes of the forest in the seventeenth and eighteenth centuries." *Cambridge History of Africa*, volume 4, edited by J.R. Gray. Cambridge, 1975, 142-222.

5.8 "North Africa and the Western Sudan from 1050 to 1590." *Cambridge History of Africa*, volume 3, edited by R. Oliver. Cambridge, 1977, 331-462.

5.9 "The Sahara and the Sudan from the Arab conquest of the Maghrib to the rise of the Almoravids." *Cambridge History of Africa*, volume 2, edited by J.D. Fage. Cambridge, 1979, 628-674.

5.10 "Abdallah ibn Yasin and the Almoravids." In *Studies in West African Islamic History*, volume 1, edited by J.R. Willis. London: Frank Cass, 1979, 78-112 (reprinted in 4.2).

5.11 "Kotoko." *Encyclopaedia of Islam* 5 (1980), 278-279.

5.12 "Cad." *Encyclopaedia of Islam* (1981), 2nd edition, supplement, 163-167.

5.13 "The Jews of Sijilmasa and the Saharan trade." In *Communautés juives des marges sahariennes du Maghreb*, edited by M. Abitbol. Jerusalem: Ben-Zvi Institute, 1982, 253-263 (reprinted in 4.2).

5.14 "Mamluk Egypt and Takrur (West Africa)." In *Studies in Islamic History and Civilization in Honour of David Ayalon*, edited by M. Sharon. Leiden: E.J. Brill, 1986, 183-207 (reprinted in 4.2).

5.15 "Mali." *Encyclopaedia of Islam* 6 (1987), 257-261.

5.16 "Berber nomads and Sudanese states: the historiography of the desert-Sahel interface." In *Islam in West Africa*, edited by Levtzion, 1995 (no. 4.2).

5.17 "Kingdoms of the Western Sudan." *Encyclopedia of Africa*, edited by John Middleton. Simon & Schuster (forthcoming).

6. Textual Studies

ENGAGING WITH A LEGACY: NEHEMIA LEVTZION (1935-2003)

Books

6.1 (with J. F. P. Hopkins) *Corpus of Early Arabic Sources for West African History.* Cambridge, UK: Cambridge University Press, 1981 (Fontes Historiae Africanae: Series Arabica IV), 493 pp.

6.2 (with I.G. Wilks and B.M. Haight) *Chronicles from Gonja: A Tradition of West African Muslim Historiography.* Cambridge, UK: Cambridge University Press, 1986 (Fontes Historiae Africanae: Series Arabica IX), 258 pp.

6.3 (with Jay Spaulding) *Medieval West Africa: Views from Arab Scholars and Merchants.* Princeton, NJ: Markus Wiener, 2002, 126 pp.

Articles and Chapters

6.4 "The thirteenth and fourteenth century kings of Mali." *Journal of African History* 4 (1963), 341-353 (reprinted in 4.2).

6.5 "Early nineteenth-century manuscripts from Kumasi." *Transactions of the Historical Society of Ghana* 8 (1965), 99-119 (reprinted in 4.2).

6.6 "Ibn Hawqal, the cheque and Awdaghust." *Journal of African History* 9 (1968), 223-233 (reprinted in 4.2).

6.7 "Mahmud Ka`ti fut-il l'auteur de Ta'rikh al-Fattash?" *Bulletin de l'IFAN* (Dakar) 33 (1971), 665-674. Published also in English in *Research Bulletin: Centre of Arabic Documentation* (Ibadan) 6, nos.1-2 (1970), 1-12.

6.8 "A Seventeenth-Century Chronicle by Ibn al-Mukhtar: a critical study of Ta'rikh al-Fattash." *Bulletin of the School of Oriental and African Studies* 34 (1971), 571-593 (reprinted in 4.2).

6.9 "Was royal succession in ancient Ghana matrilineal?" *International Journal of African Historical Studies* 5 (1972), 91-93.

6.10 "Oral traditions and Arabic documents in the Muslim historiography of Africa." *Congrès International des Africanistes.* Paris, 1972, 47-59.

6.11 "Ancient Ghana: a reassessment of some Arabic sources." *Revue Française d'Histoire d'Outre-Mer* 66 (1979), 139-147 (reprinted in 4.2).

6.12 "The twelfth-century anonymous Kitab al-Istibsar: a history of a text." *Journal of Semitic Studies* 24 (1979), 201-217 (reprinted in 4.2).

6.13 "Muslim Travellers and Trade." *Trade, Travel and Exploration in the Middle Ages: An Encyclopaedia*, edited by John B. Friedman Kristen M. Figg. New York and London: Garland Publishing, 2000, 418-25.

6.14 "Arab geographers, the Nile, and the history of Bilad al-Sudan." In *The Nile: Histories, Cultures, Myths*, edited by H. Erlich and I. Gershoni. Boulder, CO: Lynne Rienner, 2000, 71-76.

6.15 "The Almoravids in the Sahara and Bilad al-Sudan: A Study in Arab Historiography." *Jerusalem Studies in Arabic and Islam (JSAI)* 25 (2001), 133-152.

7. Not mentioned by Professor Levtzion

7.1 "Facing the Future. In *Teaching Jewish Civilization: A Global Approach to Higher Education*, edited by Moshe Davis. New York: New York UP, (1995), 241-50.

Nehemia Levtzion: Curriculum Vitae
[Editorial Note: written by Levtzion in 2002]

Positions

Bamberger and Fuld Professor of the History of the Muslim Peoples The Hebrew University of Jerusalem (1982-2003)

President, Israel Oriental Society (1998-2003)

Chair, Planning and Budgeting Committee, the Council for Higher Education (March 1997-March 2003)

President, Open University of Israel (1987-1992)

Dean, Faculty of Humanities, The Hebrew University of Jerusalem (1978-1981)

Executive Director, Van Leer Jerusalem Institute (1994-1997)

Academic Chairman, International Center for University Teaching of Jewish Civilization (1992-1997)

Director, Ben-Zvi Institute for the Study of Jewish Communities in the East (1982-1987)

Chairman of the Executive Committee, Israel Oriental Society (1979-1998)

Personal Honours

Honorary Fellow, the Open University, Israel (1995)
Honorary Fellow, Jerusalem Academy of Music and Dance, Israel (2003)
Honorary Fellow, Tel Hai Academic College, Israel (2003)
Honorary Fellow, Shenkar College of Engineering and Design, Israel (tba 2004)
The Bublik Prize of the Hebrew University of Jerusalem (tba 2004)

Education

1957-1960: BA, The Hebrew University, in Islamic History and Arabic
1961-1962: MA, The Hebrew University, in Islamic History
1962-1965: PhD, University of London, School of Oriental and African Studies, History (Islam in Africa)

Hebrew University [Appointments]
    Lecturer, 1965-1969
    Senior Lecturer, 1969-1973
    Associate Professor, 1973-1978
    Professor, from 1978

Visiting Appointments
    Visiting Associate Professor, Northwestern University, Evanson, Illinois (1969)
    Fellow, St John's College, Cambridge (1972-73)

Visiting Professor, University of California, Los Angeles (1975)
Fellow, St Antony's College, Oxford (1977)
Simon Senior Fellow, University of Manchester (1977-78)
Fellow, Center for Middle Eastern Studies, Harvard University (1981-82)
Fellow, Wissenschaftskolleg: Institute of Advanced Studies, Berlin (1996, 1997)
Visiting Professor, Ecole des Hautes Etudes en Sciences Sociales, Paris (1998)
Visiting Professor, Michigan State University, East Lansing, Michigan (2000)

Personal
   Born 24 November 1935, in Israel (then Palestine)
   Parents: Penina (nee Perlow) and Aron (formerly Lubetski)
   Married to Tirtza (nee Gindel)
   Children: Moshe (1964), Osnat (1968), Noga (1970), Avner (1974)

Notes

[1] A moshav was a Jewish village with some collective agricultural assets, yet with private farms and residences. A moshavah was only based on private ownership, unlike a kibbutz which was based on collective, Marxist-style ownership.

[2] Gar'in, literally nucleus, refers to a group aimed at founding a settlement in a certain locality, or future locality, immediately after high school. This was done through the Nahal or Fighting Pioneer Youth, a scheme for Israeli youth that combined active military service with civilian service — especially the promotion of Jewish settlement in Israel.

Meeting with villagers in front of the mosque

Hajj Ibrahim setting up for village interviews

Nehemia Levtzion and Islam in Ghana: Reminiscences

Ivor Wilks

Résumé
Cet article retrace le développement de l'Institut des études africaines au sein de l'Université du Ghana, Legon, à sa création en 1960 et pendant ses premières années. Il relate les étapes qui ont jalonné la transformation d'un sujet cher au nouvel Institut. Ce sujet l'histoire de l'Islam au Ghana et chez ses voisins est peu à peu devenu une enquête sur les matériaux rédigés en script par des musulmans au Ghana. L'article se concentre sur l'importante contribution faite par Nehemia Levtzion à ce projet. Sa recherche a été présentée en 1965 dans sa dissertation de Londres, "The Spread and Development of Islam in the Middle Volta Basin in the Pre-Colonial Period," publiée par la suite en 1968 par Oxford University Press sous le titre **Muslims and Chiefs in West Africa**.

Abstract
This article traces the development of the Institute of African Studies at the University of Ghana, Legon from its inception in 1960 through its early years. It records the steps by which a major concern of the new Institute became first, the study of the history of Islam in Ghana and its neighbours, and second, the investigation of materials in Arabic script written by Muslims in Ghana. The focus of the article is the important contribution that Nehemia Levtzion made to this project. His research was presented in his 1965 London dissertation, "The Spread and Development of Islam in the Middle Volta Basin in the Pre Colonial Period," subsequently published in 1968 by Oxford University Press under the title **Muslims and Chiefs in West Africa**.

Introduction

My claim upon a few pages of this volume has to do with my lengthy association with Nehemia Levtzion as professional colleague and personal friend. I shall, however, begin my piece with reference not to Nehemia but to his wife and constant companion, Tirtza, whose sad death so closely and unexpectedly followed his. Long before I came to know Nehemia, and indeed even before Nehemia knew Tirtza, her way and mine had crossed.

A small café and bar lay at the foot of Mount Carmel, between a large Arab town then named Balad esh-Sheikh but now vanished, and a Jewish industrial settlement, still flourishing, known as Nesher. These places were four or five miles from Haifa, and the year was 1948. I was then a twenty-year old subaltern in the British army, and I and a group of fellow officers met regularly at the café that was conveniently near our camps. We would have to maintain our conversations against the distractions of a gaggle of small girls who giggled and ogled us and vied with each other to gain our attention. And so to the point of this introduction. In 1989, my wife, Nancy, and I stayed with Nehemia and Tirtza Levtzion in their Jerusalem apartment. We usually talked about our time in West Africa and our current researches on Islam in that part of the world. One evening, however, I reminisced nostalgically about Palestine and spoke of experiences there in the months before Israel became independent. I referred to Balad esh-Sheikh and Nesher, and to the café I had frequented. Tirtza, who was a very demonstrative person, literally shrieked. She realized that the café I had described had belonged to her family. She had, she said, played there almost every night, and vividly remembered the soldiers. Cautiously, she added that she thought that she might even remember me! Nehemia decided that of course she did, and pointed out that she and I had always enjoyed a warm relationship since we had "remet"!

Nehemia Levtzion's contributions to the study of Islam in Africa are widely known and acknowledged, and I fully join in the accolades they have received. His earliest work in the field was carried out in the 1960s and had as its focus the Republic of Ghana. These were, I believe, formative years in his intellectual career. Levtzion enjoyed, to use his own words, "the kind hospitality" of the young Institute of African Studies at the University of Ghana, to which he was attached. "I am grateful," he wrote, "to Mr.

Thomas Hodgkin, the Director of the Institute, and to Professor Ivor Wilks, who first invited me to study the history of Islam in Ghana, and inspired me with their enthusiasm" (Levtzion 1968, vii). I fear that I have here sacrificed modesty in order to establish credentials. In this brief memoir, I wish to record, in detail that may otherwise be lost, something of the circumstances of the Institute of which Levtzion was to become an associate in 1963, and something of the contributions he made to its development.

Where Had All the Muslims Gone?

In 1953 I took up a two-year appointment as lecturer in philosophy at what was then the University College of the Gold Coast. It should be kept in mind that, at this time, the Gold Coast consisted of four distinct entities over the affairs of which one Governor presided. These were first, the Colony of the Gold Coast; second, the Colony of Ashanti (now, more correctly, Asante); third, the Protectorate of the Northern Territories; and fourth, British Mandated Togoland. In 1953 through 1955, I lived and taught in the first of these. The majority of my colleagues were designated "European" or "African." The former were for the most part, but by no means exclusively, natives of Britain. The latter came principally from the Colony of the Gold Coast, and most had been educated at one or other of the splendid secondary schools there and had likely "finished" at a British (or increasingly American) university. Thanks to many of these colleagues, my ignorance of my host country began to give way to a modest degree of enlightenment. If I remember rightly it was a political scientist — the redoubtable Joe Price — who first alerted me to the fact that a significant element in Ghana's population was Muslim. Price, however, was mainly interested in the so-called Zongos.

The Zongos were the quarters that existed in all the larger towns, having been founded in the nineteenth and twentieth centuries by immigrants who were, for the most part, from Hausaland and Bornu. In the colonial period, each Zongo had its own court presided over by a chief, the Sarkin Zongo, who was chosen by the people of the Zongo and approved by the British administration. This modest degree of autonomy enjoyed by the Zongo Muslims served at the same time to preserve the general view of them as "strangers" to the Gold Coast. In consequence, they had received virtually no notice from students of the Ghanaian past much before the 1950s. There were, however, other Muslim communities in Ghana the history of which reached back far beyond that of the Zongos, but was even less known. The majority of these lay in what Levtzion usefully termed "the Middle Volta Basin," of which the Protectorate of the Northern Territories of the Gold Coast (henceforth NTs) formed the largest part. Southern Ghanaians thought of this vast area of wooded grassland as the back of beyond, the epitome of remoteness.

In the first half of the twentieth century, many British colonial officers regarded a posting to the NTs as indicative of the Gold Coast Secretariat's lack of confidence in their administrative abilities. Most prided themselves, however, on their prowess as big game hunters. The occasional visitor toured the north, braving the fearfully corrugated laterite roads. They returned to the south with stories of crocodile pools and of sighting of elephants. They described the fearsome plagues of mosquitoes — but seldom mentioned the mud-built mosques that dotted the landscape and often retained something of the beauty, if not the scale, of their medieval prototypes in Timbuktu and Jenne. In 1927, A.W. Cardinall (FRGS) published a travelogue of sorts, *In Ashanti and Beyond*. He had spent over a decade as a colonial officer in the NTs — that is, in the *Beyond* — and informed his readers that there were probably no more than ten mosques in it. Where had all the Muslims gone? Cardinall was later to revise his views, but in 1927 he produced an answer: "for Mohammedanism here," he wrote, "has never made the slightest progress, the Dagomba confederation having been throughout the centuries a firm bulwark against the influence of Islam" (Cardinal 1927, 108). Forty years later Levtzion was to observe: "Dagomba may serve as the best example to illustrate the interaction of Islam and paganism in the Middle Volta States" (Levtzion 1968, 85).

By the 1940s and 1950s, missionaries and anthropologists were the main categories of those happily choosing to work in the north. The former were attracted by the souls to be saved. Conversely, the latter wished to study souls that, as it were, had not yet been saved and so were uninfluenced by Islam (or for that matter, Christianity). Thus, for example, Meyer Fortes and David Tait (personal communications) came to focus their research on the

Tallensi and Konkomba, respectively, and chose to do so precisely because they saw them as relatively "unspoiled" by exogenous religions. In this way, the Muslim communities of the Northern Territories became consigned to an academic limbo. This was to have unfortunate political consequences. In post-colonial Ghana, there was a time when an ill-advised government passed legislation enabling it to expel foreigners from the country. The measure was directed primarily against Muslim immigrants from Nigeria. Northern Ghanaian Muslims living in Accra and other southern towns, however, were harassed and in some cases physically assaulted by mobs of local zealots who warned them to return to their own countries or risk the consequences. It is distressing to reflect that the ancestors of the northerners thus intimidated had in many cases built their mosques and opened their schools within what is now Ghana some four or five hundred years ago. But this is by the way.

In 1955, when the Gold Coast had yet to become Ghana, I was appointed to a position as Resident Tutor in the Department of Extra-Mural Studies of the University College of the Gold Coast, and found myself in charge of all extension work in the Northern Territories and the northern part of British Mandated Togo. I was stationed at Tamale and for three years traveled continuously, organizing classes for the Peoples Educational Association. These were taught in English, the textbooks used were in English, and the topics discussed drawn from Europe (including the USSR) and the USA: for example, notions of democracy from Plato onwards, differences in political party systems, federal and unitary constitutions, and so forth. Needless to say, northern Muslims, other than a few who were fluent in English, did not attend these classes. I did, however, pay regular courtesy visits to local imams and teachers in the Qur'anic schools, and made modest donations towards the maintenance of their mosques. Some of those I visited proudly produced manuscripts they owned. These ranged from quite substantial collections stacked in piles on the floor to just a few items kept in small tin trunks under beds, a location they often shared with small circular vessels with a quite different use. All the manuscripts were in Arabic script but in both Arabic and Hausa language. Many were in a very fragile condition, and it was obvious that they were desperately in need of study. It was also quite obvious that I was not the man to attempt this. I had acquired no more than an embarrassingly basic knowledge of Arabic while in the Middle East and this was, in any case, of little relevance since it dealt almost exclusively with opening and closing valves on petrol pipelines.

Enter the Institute of African Studies, Legon

Peter L. Shinnie had become Professor of Archaeology at the University of Ghana in succession to A.W. Lawrence, a younger brother of (no less T.E. Lawrence of Arabia fame. Shinnie had worked in Arabic-speaking countries and had a good knowledge of the language. In 1960 he laid the foundations for the university's Institute of African Studies, and as acting Director began to make appointments for the academic year 1961-62. Kwabena Nketia was to be responsible for music and arts, I for historical and social studies, and two linguists were recruited to build up materials on Ghana languages. Nehemia Levtzion was to work closely with the Institute, but not until 1963. However, in the interests of keeping the historical record straight, and recording a few interesting facts that might otherwise be consigned to oblivion, I shall draw on my own recollections of the Institute's birth pangs.

Shinnie and those of us gathered around him began prolonged discussions about the form the Institute of African Studies should take. My memory is that we enjoyed a remarkable measure of agreement based on a remarkable effusion of goodwill. I myself urged that a study of the history of Ghana's Muslim communities should be seen as one of the Institute's priorities, and this was accepted. The Institute published a pamphlet, *The Northern Factor in Ashanti History*, which I had drafted at Shinnie's suggestion. It was the first in a projected series intended to publicize the work of the Institute. To my surprise it was reviewed in several journals and became quite widely read. I had not intended this since I had written it hurriedly and certainly did not regard it as other than a preliminary foray in the field. It does enter this story, however. Levtzion was later to tell me that it had convinced him that there was serious work to be done on Islam in the region of the Middle Volta basin.[1]

In 1961 the Institute awaited a full-time Director, Shinnie preferring to remain in his professorship of archaeology. Those of us

Kwame Nkrumah (l), Ivor Wilks (r) (Courtesy of Ivor Wilks and Nancy Lawler)

already appointed were only marginally involved, but we learned that Thomas Hodgkin of Balliol College, Oxford, had many supporters including, most importantly, the President of Ghana, Kwame Nkrumah. I was delighted. Hodgkin was well known for his consummate interest in the Arab world, and this seemed to assure his approval of the Institute's concern with Islam in Ghana. It did. Moreover, he was able to communicate his interest to

Nkrumah, who not only provided generous financial support for the Institute as a whole but was also particularly ready to meet the relatively high costs — by reason of distance — of work on the Ghanaian Muslim communities.

Hodgkin took up his appointment as Director of the Institute of African Studies at a time that was peculiarly difficult. In April 1962 a Secretariat of the Encyclopaedia Africana Project was set up under the auspices of the Ghana Academy of Learning in Accra. The Founding Director of the Project, W.E.B. Du Bois, moved to Ghana, acquired citizenship, and assumed the Directorship of the Secretariat. Hodgkin assured Du Bois that the Secretariat could rely on the cooperation of the Institute of African Studies in the production of the encyclopaedia. There was, however, pressure in some quarters to have the two organizations merged. Matters came to a head when word had it that the Institute was being criticized for recruiting "Europeans" to positions within it.

A meeting with members of the Secretariat was arranged. Du Bois took the chair and his wife, Shirley, and the Deputy Director, A. Hunton, were among those present. Hodgkin was, I believe, in England and Nketia and I spoke for the Institute. We pointed out that our intention was to develop the Institute as an interdisciplinary center of fundamental research focused on Ghana. As such we were concerned with advancing the frontiers of knowledge rather than encapsulating its current state in encyclopaedic form. We also pointed out — one of us "African" and the other "European" — that the Institute should maintain its international character in the recruitment of faculty and admission of students. At the beginning of April 1962, Du Bois issued a statement addressing the matter:

> My idea is to prepare and publish an Encyclopedia not on the vague subject of race, but on the peoples inhabiting the continent of Africa. I propose an Encyclopedia edited mainly by African scholars. I am anxious that it be a scientific production and not a matter of propaganda. While there should be included among its writers the best students of Africa in the world, I want the proposed Encyclopedia to be written mainly from the African point of view by people who know and understand the history and culture of Africans.

And there, the matter rested. Sadly, Du Bois died the following year at the venerable age of 95.

Nkrumah remained a keen supporter of the Encyclopaedia Africana Project but acknowledged that the Institute of African Studies was on a different trajectory of development. Critical to its work on Ghana's Muslims was the appointment of al-hajj Osmanu Boyo as a Senior Research Fellow. I had first met him in 1959 in Bondoukou. Then a septuagenarian, al-hajj Osmanu was well-versed in classical Maliki texts, and spoke Arabic, English, French, Hausa, Juula, and an indeterminate number of other local West African languages (Wilks 2003, 26). He traveled constantly, establishing his credentials with imams and teachers, recording basic information about the structure and history of their communities, and inquiring circumspectly into the contents of their libraries. As he became a familiar visitor, he was frequently able to borrow select items for copying at the Institute. I took a firm decision that originals should not be retained by the Institute, since there was an imminent danger of an international market for them being established in the world of dealers and collectors. The originals were returned to their owners with several copies. This procedure was made possible by the generous gift of a copy machine from the Rockefeller Foundation. This was one of the Xerox Corporation's earliest models, and I cannot resist saying a little more about it. The Institute's staff vied with each other to master the complicated technology. This involved photographing the manuscript to produce a plate, which was then submitted to a number of processes that I can only describe as reminding me of the production of dough in a busy pizza parlor! I seem to remember that the record established by the Institute's operators was to produce a single copy of one manuscript page in fourteen minutes; thereafter, of course, further copies could be turned out at speed.

Hodgkin much facilitated the work of those around him, perhaps most obviously as a result of his being so adept at delegating responsibility to them. He recruited such luminaries as Polly Hill to the regular staff. Among early students who pursued postgraduate degrees at the Institute were ones subsequently to achieved distinction in the African field; the names of R.A. Kea, P.F. de Moraes Farias, T.C. McCaskie, and Charles Stewart spring to mind. There is no doubt that Hodgkin directed the Institute brilliantly. He surrounded himself by those who not only had come greatly to admire him but also were deeply devoted to him. It is particularly unfortunate that no detailed study of Hodgkin in this highly productive period of his career has yet been published. Michael Wolfers' *Thomas Hodgkin: Wandering Scholar* (2007) is appallingly ill informed and quite unworthy of its subject.[2]

On 15 June 1962, I addressed the Muslim Council in Accra through al-hajj Osmanu Boyo. Hodgkin was, I believe, in Britain. I outlined the nature of the Institute's work. "All I had said was true," the Council's spokesman responded,

> ... the Muslims in Ghana had been looked down upon. Now things are changing and many educated people are becoming Muslim. We today are all building on the work of those that are dead. So, in order that our work at the Institute should go well, he was going to give me a list of the malams now dead who advanced the religion of the Prophet in Ghana (Wilks 2003, 27).

We thus obtained the blessing of leading Muslims in Ghana on the Institute's program. In mid-June Thomas Hodgkin, Adu Boahen, al-hajj Osmanu Boyo and I undertook what may be regarded as the first official trip of that section of the Institute concerned with Islam in Ghana (see Wilks 2003, 25-35). We were well received by particularly large gatherings of the faithful in Yendi and Kete Krachi. We became acutely conscious of the very considerable quantity of manuscript material owned by local scholars, and much encouraged by the readiness to allow us to borrow and copy items (see Hodgkin 1966, 442-60; Wilks 1963, 409-17). That is, as the saying goes, the good news. The bad? President Nkrumah's continuing support for the Institute notwithstanding, we still lacked the resources necessary to make more than minor incursions into, if we may mix metaphors, the mother lode.

In point of fact, over the first two years our collection of manuscripts numbered about 350, and I was fond of pointing out to potential supporters that I knew where the next several thousand could be found and consulted. Few of our 350 items were, however, adequately catalogued. The names of authors, titles of works, and so forth were more commonly missing than established, and our longer-range intention of producing English translations of the more important documents was little more than wishful thinking. The Institute had access to teachers of the Arabic language, but not to specialists in the broader spectrum of Arabist studies. It was at this point in time that we were delighted to have a request for affiliation to the Institute from Nehemia Levtzion.

To Come or Not to Come? That Was the Question

Nehemia Levtzion was born in British Mandated Palestine in 1935. He took his bachelor and master degrees at the Hebrew University of Jerusalem in 1960 and 1962 respectively, focusing his studies on Arabic language and literature and on Islamic history. He developed a strong interest in the spread of the religion in Africa, and in 1962 entered the School of Oriental and African Studies in London to work for a doctorate in African History. It was completed in September 1965. Nehemia's generous acknowledgement of support of the Institute of African Studies glosses over a story that may now be put on record to illustrate one sort of political issue that arose.

Levtzion's request for affiliation with the Institute reached Legon at a time when Hodgkin and I had established warm relations with the members of the Egyptian Embassy in Accra. In particular, the cultural attaché, Mahmoud El-Wakkad, had become much interested in Ghana's literary heritage in Arabic, and had brought to our attention a few local manuscripts and had made provisional translations of several of them (El-Wakkad 1961, 1962). The Ambassador encouraged Hodgkin to apply for financial help from Egyptian sources, and perhaps to negotiate an arrangement to exchange scholars. Hodgkin and I made "our" news known to the Ambassador, assuming that he would be delighted to learn of the accession to our strength. Looking back, I find it hard to believe that neither Hodgkin nor I appear to have had any inkling of the perilous state of Egyptian and Israeli relations at that point in time. We seemed to cherish a belief that matters of scholarship in some way transcended those of national interest; that collaboration between scholars should be unaffected by squabbles between politicians. In fact, in the course of 1961 African leaders had begun to align themselves with either the Casablanca or the Monrovia bloc. The former included the Algerian provisional government, Egypt, Ghana, Guinea, Libya, Mali, and Morocco. It should not have surprised us that, when we informed the Ambassador of Levtzion's projected arrival at the Institute, the news was not received with enthusiasm. We felt that the Embassy's attitude towards the Institute was perceptibly cooling. We asked ourselves:

Would Levtzion's appearance threaten our working relationship with the Egyptian Embassy? More alarming still, would it have an adverse effect on our links with the Ghana Muslim Council whose members had assured us of their cooperation?

Hodgkin felt that we should not risk jeopardizing the Institute's Muslim project. He proposed that we write to Levtzion, explaining the problems we faced and suggesting that he might find Nigeria a more suitable research environment than Ghana if only because of its far more extensive literary recourse to the Arabic script.[3] Hodgkin happened to mention the Institute's dilemma to Conor Cruise O'Brien, Vice-Chancellor of the University of Ghana. O'Brien was outraged by the proposed course of action, and told us so in no uncertain terms. And so, it came about that in September 1963 Nehemia Levtzion arrived in Legon, and we duly welcomed him at the Institute.

What's To Be Done? By Whom?

With Nehemia's arrival, the question of how best his work could be coordinated with that of the Institute became one of immediate concern. The problem was that Nehemia's London supervisors, D.H. Jones and H.J. Fisher, on the one hand, and Hodgkin and I on the other, had quite different research priorities. We urged Nehemia to focus his work on the life and times of individual scholars, using their own writings and those of their students and other associates, but supplementing these through interviews with those, including descendants, whose memories reached back to appropriate times. We particularly drew Nehemia's attention to the renowned al-hajj `Umar b. Abi Bakr, who died as Imam of Kete Krachi in 1934 and whose extensive writings on northern Ghana in the late nineteenth and early twentieth centuries were already well represented in the Institute's growing collection. Jones and Fisher, however, had urged Nehemia to undertake what was essentially a survey, and had approved the title of his projected thesis: "The Spread and the Development of Islam in the Middle Volta Basin in the Pre-Colonial Period."

Nehemia had little choice and probably little inclination to negotiate with his London supervisors for a change of topic. He remained committed to the survey. I was somewhat unhappy with this decision since it would duplicate much work that was already in progress, or under consideration, at the Institute. An understanding was reached. The Institute would open its data files, including the Arabic writings, to Nehemia, and would make the services of al-hajj Osmanu Boyo available to him as consultant and advisor. Nehemia would make his own arrangements for the employment of a research assistant and translator.[4] Reciprocally, Nehemia would assist in the development of the Arabic collection, identifying works of particular interest in the libraries of scholars he visited. Al-hajj Osmanu did a splendid job in persuading local community leaders to accept Nehemia as a bona fide researcher, which, of course, he was. In a brief note on what he described as his "Field Study," Nehemia remarks that his "Muslim informants were always very helpful and cooperative" (Levtzion 1968, xxii-xxiv).

Nehemia worked in the Middle Volta Basin, principally in Ghana, from September 1963 to July 1964. In this relatively brief period he visited over a hundred communities, and interviewed about a thousand informants whose testimony became a major source for the thesis. Completed in September 1965, Levtzion's thesis was published as *Muslims and Chiefs in West Africa: A Study of Islam in the Middle Volta Basin in the Pre-colonial Period* (Oxford: Clarendon Press, 1968). At this time, Nehemia was a member of the Institute of Asian and African Studies at the Hebrew University of Jerusalem, and I had left Ghana after the coup of 1966 to join the Program of African Studies at Northwestern University, Evanston, Illinois. Nehemia sent me a copy of the book with a note tucked in the front cover. "Dear Ivor," he had written:

> Neither acknowledgement nor references in foot-notes can tell how much of this book is yours. This I know well, and I am grateful for all I have taken from you (Wilks Papers, Africana Library, Northwestern University).

I found the sentiments very gratifying, but remained ambivalent about Nehemia's decision to carry out such a geographically extensive study. In a report of December 1963, he addressed the problems that he was encountering. "This kind of work," he wrote,

> ... involves much travelling; and I decided to fix as a limit 2 000 miles a month. To avoid visiting every village where there are Muslims I have to choose only those places with an Imam. Though the enquiry is concentrated on the "officers" of the community I try to get as much information about the laymen

as well. The circle of my informants became wider by interviewing the descendants of previous Imams, Naibs and Yarnas (Wilks Papers, Africana Library, Northwestern University).

It will be appreciated why Hodgkin and I had tried to persuade Nehemia to carry out a more modest project. Granted the limitations on his time, we feared that the geographical extent of his inquiry could only be accomplished at the cost of historical superficiality. There is an element of paradox in all of this. A survey of the sort exemplified in *Muslims and Chiefs* in West Africa is surely intended to facilitate and stimulate further research, so that the measure of its success is the rapidity within which it becomes outdated. For example, Nehemia's thirty-seven-page piece on "Islam in Dagomba" was greatly supplemented and in many respects supplanted by Phyllis Ferguson's (1972) 380-page Cambridge thesis (one of the examiners of which was Nehemia himself). Conversely, however, for whatever reasons, much research proceeded at much slower rates. In 1961, for example, I had myself begun a systematic study of Wa in northwestern Ghana, leading Nehemia to footnote his nine-page account of that polity: "Professor Wilks's study of Wa may throw new light on its history" (Levtzion 1968, 139 note 3). It did so, in a 256-page book that did not appear in print for two decades (Wilks 1989). An interval such as this obliged many students to use Muslims and Chiefs as a "pro tem definitive" work (if such a description is permissible). Perhaps the jury should be regarded as still out on this matter. Nehemia and I, however, were not in agreement on a much more fundamental issue. This is no place to enter into detail, but our differences had to do with what I considered to be Nehemia's failure to appreciate the extent to which Islam in the Middle Volta Basin was shaped by the teachings of the sixteenth century Malian cleric, al-hajj Salim Suwari.[3]

In 1962 the translation and publication of a number of manuscripts from Gonja was first projected. These had been accessioned in the Institute's Arabic Collection and Salah Ibrahim, who taught Arabic, made a provisional translation of one item, the *Kitab Ghanja (Book of Gonja)*, that put beyond doubt the great importance of the texts for the historian of Ghana. Seven manuscripts of the work, showing many variant readings, had been accessioned in the Institute's collection in 1962 and 1963. Nehemia located at least two more in 1964 (Wilks, Levtzion and Haight 1986, 52-60). In 1965 he and I agreed to cooperate in preparing an edition of the Gonja texts for publication. Our divergent opinions in no way affected our decision to collaborate, though our often lengthy but not always successful efforts to reach agreement took up a great deal of our time. In 1981 we asked Bruce Haight, who had worked in northern Ghana from 1969 to 1972 and was well known to both us, to join us with responsibility for indexing, preparing maps, and the like, and, if the truth be told, generally to mediate the disputes that I suspect Nehemia and I rather enjoyed. One issue, however, totally defied any resolution, and that was the matter of the writers of the *Kitab Ghanja*. We were agreed that the work was one of the early to mid-eighteenth century, but beyond that our views diverged irreconcilably. We solved the problem in a civilized manner; that is, we agreed to disagree. Each took a few pages to present his case while refraining from attacking that of the other (Wilks, Levtzion and Haight 1986, 61-71).

Notes

[1] The ambiguity in this statement is perhaps resolved in Levtzion (1965, 18); compare Levtzion (1968, xviii).

[2] Wolfers' treatment of Hodgkin's directorship of the Institute of African Studies is particularly disappointing, being based heavily upon social diaries. I found no reference to Hodgkin's personal research interests. He was, in fact, compiling an index of place-names in the extensive writings of al-hajj ʿUmar b. Abi Bakr of Salaga and Kete Krachi. I should also like to put on record that he was much interested in my own work in Wa, and shared with me the expenses of small lodgings adjacent to the central mosque. Unfortunately, ill health prevented his making more than one stay there.

[3] This suggestion was not perhaps as strange as it may seem. I believe that our attention had been drawn to one of Levtzion's early (Hebrew) publications, namely, "The Integration of the Muslim Northern Region into the Federation of Nigeria," *Hamizrah Hehadash* 12 (1962).

[4] Nehemia employed a Dagomba, al-hajj ʿUmar b. Muhammad of Tamale, in these positions, and acknowledged his "invaluable help" (see Levtzion 1968, vii). He had a good knowledge of Arabic but lacked the renown of al-hajj Osmanu Boyo (for which see the dedication to him of J. Hunwick 2003, IV: v). Nehemia may not have realized the extent to which al-hajj Osmanu worked behind the scenes to secure the goodwill of the local Muslims.

[5] There is no mention of this influential figure in Levtzion 1968. For recent accounts of Suwari, see Wilks (2000, 93-115; Robinson (2004, 56, 59, 124-37).

Memories of Nehemia

Martin Klein

Résumé
Cet article est à la fois une esquisse biographique de la carrière de Nehemia Levtzion et une réminiscence. Levtzion a grandi en Israël à l'époque de sa fondation. Il a rapidement choisi d'étudier l'islamisation en Afrique et est devenu le principal interprète de l'histoire de l'Islam en Afrique. Bien que souvent invité pour remplir des fonctions administratives dans le système éducatif israélien, il est resté engagé dans l'étude et la recherche. Les petits congrès tenus à Jérusalem au fil des années tournaient autour d'une manière de repenser les problèmes fondamentaux de l'histoire de l'Islam en Afrique et dans le monde musulman en général. Il s'intéressait particulièrement aux processus de conversion et aux dynamiques de changements. Bien qu'ayant décrit plusieurs variétés d'Islam et divers niveaux d'islamisation, il n'a jamais accepté la notion d'un Islam distinctement africain. Au lieu de cela, il a vu des processus très semblables à travers tout le monde musulman.

Abstract
This article is both a biographical sketch of the career of Nehemia Levtzion and a reminiscence. Levtzion grew up in Israel during the period of its founding. He early chose to study Islamization in Africa and became the leading interpreter of the history of Islam in West Africa. Though often called on to assume administrative responsibilities in the Israeli educational system, he maintained a commitment to scholarship. The small conferences he held in Jerusalem over the years often involved a re-thinking of basic problems in the history of Islam in Africa and in the larger Muslim world. He was particularly interested in processes of conversion and the dynamics of change. Though he described many varieties of Islam and different levels of Islamization, he never accepted the notion of a distinctively Africa Islam. He saw instead processes that were similar throughout the Muslim world.

Introduction

In the early 1960s it was possible to get a reputation in African history not for what one had done, but for what one was trying to do.[1] Nehemia Levtzion arrived in Ghana in September 1963, about four months after I arrived in Senegal; both of us were about to begin PhD research. He was somewhat better prepared for doctoral research because he knew Arabic and had already done research on the history of Islam. He also benefited from the collection of Arabic and Hausa documents that Ivor Wilks had built for the Institute of African Studies (University of Ghana). Levtzion had trained at the School of Oriental African Studies, University of London (UK), then recognized as the most important training institution for would-be Africanists. He also knew what he wanted to do. I had backed into African history when I became dissatisfied with a program in European history. When I returned from Senegal, I began to hear stories about a remarkable young Israeli who was wandering around northern Ghana looking for histories, both oral and written.

Levtzion was born on a *moshav*, an agricultural settlement based on private farms. His father was the secretary and accountant for the southernmost *moshav* in Palestine, in an area where earlier Jewish settlements had been wiped out during a period of Arab Jewish conflict in 1929.[2] He grew up during a period of Jewish struggle against British colonial rule. British soldiers often searched the settlement for hidden weapons and illegal immigrant refugees from the Holocaust who sometimes landed on the coast. His family moved to Tel Aviv after Israel's War of Independence. After high school, he did his military service in the *Nahal*, which combined military training with service to the *kibbutz* movement. This was a period of tremendous idealism and enthusiasm. Israel was very poor and was trying to integrate hundreds of thousands of Jewish refugees from war-torn Europe while creating a society that was socialist, democratic, and prosperous. The *kibbutzim* embodied that idealism. Groups from the *Nahal* would create and form the nucleus of a new *kibbutz*. Though Nehemia was co-opted into leadership roles in the *Nahal*, he asked to be assigned to an ordinary *kibbutz*, where he served in secretariat and tended the sheep pens. He was also active in the Labour Zionist youth movement, Habonim.

Those who served in the *Nahal* did an extra year of service, which means that Levtzion did not enter Hebrew University until almost twenty-two years of age. He studied in the departments of Arabic Language and Literature and Middle Eastern History. He was clearly an outstanding student from the first; he decided early on that he was interested in Islam and, particularly, in processes of Islamization. This interest led one of his professors to suggest that Africa would be a particularly interesting place to study such processes. The Hebrew University was thinking of creating a Department of African Studies. Levtzion was thus sent off to the School of Oriental and African Studies (SOAS) with a fellowship from Hebrew University and the possibility that he would return to create this new department. At the time, SOAS was very much the nerve center for the first professional and university-based studies of African history; Roland Oliver and John Fage were sending students out to the far corners of Africa.[3] SOAS also had a mixture of students, many of them Africans who went on to play an important role in the field. Others came from the United States and the West Indies. In addition, North Americans interested in anglophone Africa often passed through.

Muslims and Chiefs

Though he had done his MA thesis on the medieval empire of Mali, Levtzion decided to write his PhD thesis on Islamization in the Middle Volta region, which contained very different societies marked by traditional levels of Islamization, and the coexistence of Islam and traditional religions. At the time Levtzion began his research, there was no synthesis of the history of the region that he was studying; in fact no histories except some accounts written by colonial administrators and one very important article by Ivor Willks (1961). Wilks had done research and taught in the North, but had only just begun to publish. The rather limited literature available on African Islam concentrated on the medieval desert-side empires. The Middle Volta was, however, more interesting for the study of Islamization because the process was recent and there was a rich fund of oral information. Levtzion and his new wife Tirtza Gindel settled in Tamale, where she found a job teaching high school.[4] He used administrative histories and the documents Ivor Wilks had collected, and then, from his base in Tamale, spent a lot of time wandering first around northern Ghana, then north to the Mossi Kingdom of Ougadougou in Côte d'Ivoire, and finally east to Sansanne-Mango in Togo and Borgu in northern Benin. He claimed to have talked to about a thousand informants. He also dealt with over a dozen societies in four states with documents from three colonial regimes. He worked with an assistant, Hajj Ibrahim, who translated from local languages into Arabic. The two of them generally conversed in Arabic.

These were exciting times in Africa. In general, those of us undertaking research in the decade after West African independence had no one to turn to for models of the processes we were studying; there were no professional histories for us to either rely on or to argue with. We had to do it ourselves. Of that hardy band sent out to Africa in the early 1960s, none was more adventurous than Levtzion.[5] The synthesis he produced was valuable not only for its efforts to understand the process of Islamization, but also for its comparison of state development in a large chunk of the West African Middle Belt. Many of these states had been founded by warriors from the northeast, while others were created by Mande-speaking warriors from the northwest. Both groups soon intermarried with and adopted the languages of the Voltaic inhabitants. Traditions often trace the origin of the state to a marriage between the state's founder and the daughter of a local earth-priest. The gold and kola trades that attracted the warriors also attracted Muslim traders from both the Hausa and Mande regions (Levtzion 1968).

The process, therefore, took place several centuries after the penetration of desert-side societies by Islam. Muslim merchants came by the Volta River early in the second millennium and were important in developing the trade in gold, which in turn contributed to the rise of Mali in the thirteenth century. In Gonja, they were there before the founding of the state. Elsewhere, they arrived later, settling in market towns under the protection of the chiefs and integrating themselves into the culture and political systems of the region. The relationship between the chiefs and the Muslim mercantile community was crucial in the development of the various states, though it operated differently in each one. The chiefs educated some of their sons and often converted to Islam themselves, but many combined Muslim practices with the observance of traditional rituals. Often, there were different merchant communities coming in at different times.

Levtzion's use of oral tradition to reconstruct these processes differed from that being pioneered at the time by Jan Vansina (1965). He had found limited data about the state or the larger community; rather, his informants showed him that the history of Islam was the history of specific families. Furthermore, though he collected documents, many of the societies he was examining were what Jack Goody (1968) has called societies of restricted literacy. This meant that though his training was in interpreting written documents and he was studying Muslims and therefore literate societies, Levtzion was heavily reliant on oral history. His interest in conversion was the reason he was looking at societies in their early stages of Islamization. It was the only time in his career that he relied on oral tradition, but it was a formative experience.

The thesis was defended at SOAS in 1965 and led to a much-anticipated book, *Muslims and Chiefs in West Africa*, published in 1968. The book did not disappoint but was nonetheless controversial, in large part because he spread his net widely over much more than just the Middle Volta.[6] Phyllis Ferguson (1970) criticized it in *Africa* because "extensive coverage has been achieved at the expense of analytic depth"; while in the *American Historical Review*, Louis Brenner (1971) argued to the contrary, claiming that the broad canvas was its strength, permitting both a picture of contrasting patterns and social compromise. In *African Affairs*, John Hunwick noted that Levtzion had proven that "Islam coexisted with and was able to interpenetrate institutions and ways of life without leading in most cases to definitive conversion of the chiefs and hence to any attempt at creating an Islamic state" (1969, 364). Hunwick thought Levtzion's research might illuminate the histories of Ghana, Mali, and Songhay — among his own research interests at the time. Ultimately, "Muslims and Chiefs" provided a window on the rich panoply of political and social development in the Middle Volta and more; it also served as a platform for much further research.

Scholarly Agendas

After completing *Muslims and Chiefs*, Levtzion's interests moved further north;[7] nevertheless, the themes of his first book remained important to his research and publications throughout his life. His next major publication was a return to an expanded version of the subject that had occupied him as an MA student. *Ancient Ghana and Mali* (1973) was the first effort at a synthesis of these historical empires of the Western Sudan since Maurice Delafosse's early colonial *Haut-Sénégal-Niger* (1912) (see also Bovill 1933). Heavily based on the classical Arab geographers and travelers, and the chronicles written by West African scholars, Levtzion also used archeology and oral tradition. Levtzion followed Delafosse and Bovill in their emphasis on the role of the trans-Saharan trade in the development of the medieval empires, but he paid more attention than they had to interaction between Saharan and savanna peoples. The book stimulated a great deal of debate about the medieval empires of Ghana and Mali, and became invaluable to the teaching of West Africa history. The most thoughtful review at the time was that of Paulo de Moraes Farias, who suggested that Levtzion exaggerated the struggle between Berber nomads and Sudanese nomads. De Moraes Farias (1974) saw more cooperation than conflict. He also argued that there was convergence, collaboration, and mutual influence between Muslim and traditional religions. Interestingly, de Moraes echoed the argument of Levtzion's earlier research: he just wanted to push the argument further; he also recognized the importance of the book (see also Willis 1975). Much subsequent research followed Levtzion's lead in describing the evolution of the medieval empires as a part of a long process of development within Africa and as integral to the dynamics of change in the Sahelian region. He continued to be an active discussant in, as well as influence on, this research. In time, it overtook the original work, rendering *Ancient Ghana and Mali* in need of updating. One of the many projects cut short by Levtzion's untimely death was a collaboration with David Conrad, Susan Keech McIntosh, and Rod McIntosh in revising the book. Subsequently, de Moraes Farias accepted an invitation to join the "team."

Levtzion probably gained a special understanding of the dynamics of Islamization from his work with oral tradition; it gave him a picture of the early stages of Islamization not evident in the written sources. The diversity he confronted in the Middle Volta also gave him a feeling for the varieties of Islam and the different patterns of Islamization present not only in Africa, but throughout the Muslim world. His greatest strength as a scholar was, however, his knowledge of Arabic and it was the analysis of historical documents that probably gave him the greatest pleasure. One of his most important works, published in collaboration with J.F.P. Hopkins, was a collection of translations of excerpts from most of the known Arabic sources relevant to West African history (Levtzion and Hopkins 1981). Hopkins did most of the translations, but Levtzion did much of the editing and annotation, in addition to providing the index and glossary. It was a major work that made Arabic language sources up to the sixteenth century available to scholars who did not read Arabic, and it was invaluable to students of all levels.[8]

Nevertheless, his early interest in conversion remained a major theme in his writing, leading to more than a dozen articles in three languages, written over many years. He edited a book on *Conversion to Islam* based on a seminar held at SOAS during 1972 and 1973 (Levtzion 1979). Half of the articles in the book dealt with the Sahara and the African Sahel. The others dealt with other parts of the Muslim world. Levtzion's own contributions were an essay on "Patterns of Islamization in West Africa" ([1971a] 1979) and a wide-ranging introductory essay on the history of conversion. In the African essay, he used his research on the Middle Volta to interpret documentary evidence on what happened several centuries earlier in Sahelian medieval empires. He argued that the *jihads* of the eighteenth and nineteenth centuries essentially displaced memories of earlier processes. In areas not exposed to *jihads*, "Islamic influence has by no means been static during the last three centuries; it has, however, developed along a pattern that may be detected from oral traditions" (Levtzion 1979, 207). He described both the appeal of Islam to merchants and the more qualified appeal to chiefs, who often feel obliged to balance between Islam and traditional religion. In competition with traditional religion, "the Islamization of Africa became more successful because of the Africanization of Islam" (Levtzion 1979, 208). An informed reading of the medieval sources indicated similar patterns. He also analyzed a split within the Muslim community between those who lived with chiefs and those who lived in autonomous Muslim communities. It was an observation he later developed. In his general introduction, he extended his understanding of the process to other Muslim societies, fully recognizing that while in most of the Islamic world conquest preceded Islamization, this not true in Africa. Levtzion's interest in conversion was also reflected in articles he wrote on comparative Islamization and on conversion to Islam after the Muslim conquest of Syria and Palestine (see also Levtzion 1990ab).[9]

Apart from the significance of its content, *Conversion to Islam* (1979) was important in setting a pattern for the many edited books that would follow. Levtzion's collections were usually based on a conference he organized in Jerusalem, and would include a wide-ranging introduction by him (sometimes with a co-editor) as well as a chapter in which he elaborated on the theme of the book. These publications tended to be more coherent than most edited volumes because they were based on scholarly interaction generated by a carefully planned conversation around a question that Levtzion considered both interesting and central.

It was not always possible for Levtzion to immerse himself in texts. There was a demand from the early 1960s for books of synthesis for students, for general readers and for scholars. Many of the books that met this demand came out of SOAS and were edited by Roland Oliver, usually in collaboration with John Fage. Levtzion became, in a sense, the point man on medieval and Muslim West Africa; less than a decade after finishing his thesis, he was the most important scholar working on the history of Muslim West Africa. He did a chapter on "The Long March of Islam in the Western Sudan" for Roland Oliver's *The Middle Age of African History* (1967). He wrote three chapters on Northwest Africa in the multi-volume reference work, the *Cambridge History of Africa* (Levtzion 1975, 1977, 1978), being one of only three authors to have been invited to appear in three different volumes. He also wrote the chapter on the states of the Western Sudan in the *History of West Africa* edited by Ajayi and Crowder (Levtzion 1971b).[10] Later, he edited *The History of Islam in Africa* (2000) in collaboration with Randall Pouwels. A collection with twenty-four authors, it is a large volume that will undoubtedly remain a standard reference work on African Islam for years to come.

Levtzion's research focused on the dynamics of change and, once again, flowed from certain distinctions he had confronted early in his thesis research. One of his most important contributions flowed from a conference he ran in Jerusalem on "Rural and

Urban Islam in West Africa," which led to a special issue of *Asian and African Studies* edited with Humphrey Fisher.[11] The issue is marked by an interaction between Levtzion, Fisher, and Lamine Sanneh on both rural-urban and merchant-scholar relationships (Fisher 1987; Sanneh 1987). There was a tendency up to this time to see Islam as an urban religion and, in Africa, as a religion of the commercial and political elites. Levtzion saw the medieval Sudanic empires as an important support for Islam, but argued that the missionaries of Islam were not the merchants but the scholars. Though scholars and merchants often came from the same families, they differed in ideology and in their interests. It was the scholars who established themselves in rural areas, where they provided religious and magical services for rural populations, as well as establishing schools. The most important schools were in the cities, but religious education became widespread in the rural areas from the early eighteenth century, thereby providing a base for the *jihads* from the mid-1700s through the 1800s.

Two important developments took place in the eighteenth century. First, Sufism became important, particularly in conversion. Levtzion (1987a) argues in his important introduction that there is no evidence of Sufism in Africa before the eighteenth century. It flowered dramatically then because saint worship and the incorporation of local religious practices provided a framework for the incorporation of rural-dwellers into Islam and a deepening commitment among them to Islam. This is the period when Islam acquired a large popular base. Second, the exploitation of slaves on agricultural estates became crucial, providing the leisure men needed to be able to devote themselves to scholarship and eventually to political and military activities (Sanneh 1987). Levtzion's own article in the collection elaborated on this in discussing how merchants and clerics contrasted with and complemented each other. For Levtzion, "merchants served as the carriers of Islam rather than as agents of Islamization" (1987b, 28); they exposed isolated societies to external influence, but it was the scholars who developed Islam. In making this argument, he relied in part on the research of Lamine Sanneh (1979, 1989) on the Jakhanke. Philip Curtin (1975, 75-91) had seen the Jakhanke as traders, but Sanneh argued that they were primarily scholars, that they sought isolated locations and relied heavily on the labor of their slaves.

Interestingly, the ensuing *jihads*, though everywhere rooted in rural areas, often created new urban centers of learning.

This question of rural Sufism led to another book, this time edited with John O. Voll, on *Eighteenth Century Renewal and Reform in Islam* (1987). This work extended his argument on Sufism to the larger Muslim world. Sufism was not new, but its organization and role changed in many Muslim societies. Levtzion and Voll argued that the flowering of Sufism in the eighteenth century took place during a period when great Muslim empires like the Ottomans and the Mughals were in decline. This flowering involved a reforming of Sufi organization and practices and was based on a concern to renew Islamic practice. One of the renewal movements, the Wahabis, was anti-Sufi, but all of the others operated within a reformed Sufi framework. The reform was radical. Where Sufism had hitherto involved a withdrawal from political life, the reformed orders were actively engaged in political life. There was also a movement away from ecstatic practices and towards stricter observance of the *shari'a*. Finally, there was a movement towards more disciplined and centralized organizations within which the leadership played a more dominant role. Within these new *turuq* (or "brotherhoods," "paths"), scholars reached out and offered commoners a more active role than before. Levtzion's (1987c) chapter was a study of the background of the *jihads*, which incorporated the analysis earlier developed of the role of rural Islam. It looked at the role of pastoralists, of both Fulbe and Saharan Islam, and the impact of the decline of the great medieval empires. He argued:

> What Islam had lost in intensity it gained in extension. At the age of the great empires Islam was mainly an urban phenomenon, restricted to scholars, clerics and merchants, stretching out to reach royalty. In the seventeenth and eighteenth century [sic] Islam made inroads into the countryside and won adherents among peasants and fishermen who had hardly been influenced by Islam before (Levtzion 1987c, 24).

This movement involved preaching and writing in vernacular languages. It also involved the development of schools and an increase in literacy in both Arabic and the vernacular. Levtzion's last effort was a book edited with Miriam Hoexter and Shmuel N. Eisenstadt, *The Public Sphere in Islamic Societies* (2002). They

define the public sphere:
> ... as a sphere located between the official and private spheres. While both the official and public spheres work for the common good, the public sphere recruits its personnel from the private sphere, not from the ruler's domain. The public sphere is thus autonomous from the political order, and "its influence rests on interpretations of the common good vis-à-vis the ruler, on the one hand, and the private sphere on the other" (Hoexter, Eisenstadt and Levtzion 2002, 9; Eisenstadt and Schluchter 1998, 10).

The public sphere is based on two characteristics of Muslim society. The first is the *shari'a* and the autonomy of institutions like the *ulema* and the *qadi* that enforce the *shari'a*. The second is the emergence of organizational structures based on mystical practices that were outside the control of the ruler. This conception, which is illustrated by the articles collected in the book, rejects traditional notions of the Islamic state as "oriental despotism." Levtzion's chapter addressed the organization of the Sufi brotherhoods, building on his articles in the two volumes cited above, developed his analysis of organizational change, and argued that the Sufi brotherhoods were more autonomous than the *ulema* because they operated beyond the control of the ruler. By contrast, many members of the *ulema* depended on the ruler and could be influenced by him.

As in much of his later writings, Levtzion's analysis here looked not just at West Africa but at the whole of the Muslim world. He argued strongly that the Sufi renewal and its accompanying use of vernacular literature were found in diverse parts of the Muslim world; he ended with the suggestion that European imperial expansion diverted these movements from internal reform to resistance and may consequently have prevented them from achieving many of their goals. His ability to view Islam in its broad global sweep is an implicit criticism of the idea popular in colonial literature that there was a distinctive "black Islam," qualitatively different from the classical Islam of the Middle East. Though Levtzion dealt with levels of Islamization, he argued that a Muslim was anyone who said he was a Muslim. He did not think there were distinctive racial or ethnic variants, but rather, common processes of change. In essence, he described what Catholic theologians call enculturation, the way in which a universal religion articulated itself within indigenous culture.

The Educator

In spite of our overlapping interests, Nehemia and I did not meet for many years. We were probably often in similar places and even at the same meetings, but somehow never met. We were both, for example, at the founding meeting of the Mande Studies Association in Madison in 1986. It was Levtzion who suggested the use of the acronym MANSA, by which the organization has subsequently been known. Mansa was both an abbreviation of the association's proper name and the Mande term for "king."[12] Our careers had different paths. Though we both dealt with Islam in our theses, I shied away from becoming an Islamicist, never studied Arabic, and moved into the study of slavery. Levtzion was first and foremost an Arabist, though, as we have seen, many of his insights and concerns flowed from his oral interviews in societies of restricted literacy.

He also took on major administrative responsibilities. He was Dean of the Faculty of Humanities at Hebrew University from 1978 to 1981. He was Director of the Ben-Zvi Institute for the Study of Jewish Communities of the East from 1982 to 1987, which involved the study of Oriental Jews. During this period, he did some writing about Jews in the Muslim world. He had already taught a course in the Open University of Israel and, in 1987, was chosen as its President, which led to what he called "The five most fascinating years of my life" (Levtzion 2007, xiv; reprinted in "Introduction," above). He doubled the university's enrolment to about twenty thousand students, established new programmes, and acquired more secure funding. He was Executive Director of the Van Leer Jerusalem Institute from 1994 to 1997. From 1997 to 2003, he was Chair of the Council of Higher Education's Planning and Budget Committee, in which position he was the major intermediary between Israel's universities and the government. He met regularly with the prime minister and presided over increased investment in Israeli training for high-technology fields. Throughout all of these years and in spite of his many responsibilities, he continued to write and to travel — sometimes teaching, sometimes as a visiting scholar.

As Israel's most distinguished Islamicist, Nehemia was also called on to play a public role as an analyst of Islam. He did so as an educator explaining Islam to Israelis. His most important book in Hebrew was a history of Islam prepared for a course he taught at the Open University (Levtzion, Ephrat and Talmon-Heller 1998, 2000). He also wrote on contemporary affairs, most notably a short history of the "Islamic Conference," the major international grouping of Islamic states. Levtzion's (1980) essay set in comparative context the policies the conference pursued toward Israel during the first ten years of the conference's existence. He also spoke of a project on the politics of Islam in Africa, though it never seems to have materialized, probably because he had so many demands on his time. He always wrote about Islam, both past and present, with sympathy and understanding. He wrote about Islam not as an enemy, but as a religion which was very similar to the Judaism in which he was raised.

Through all these years, Nehemia remained a teacher. Naomi Chazan, his first doctoral candidate, described him as a "teacher's teacher ... a fine ... lecturer, and an absolutely superb graduate teacher. He was a dream of a dissertation supervisor" (Chazan, personal communication). With both students and colleagues, he was always approachable and involved with issues that concerned them. He trained most of Israel's best Africanists, though he felt it important that they go abroad for graduate study. His relation to his students was marked by the concern, the breadth of interests, and the depth of learning that shaped his relations with fellow scholars.

I first actually got to know Levtzion in the mid-1990s, when he received a grant to spend a month at the University of Toronto. I was asked to host him, which was one of the most pleasant tasks I have ever had. It was almost no work. He was traveling with Tirtza, who, like Nehemia, had a lively and stimulating mind. Both of them were used to unpacking their bags and settling into new digs. They dealt well with bureaucracies and with the unfamiliar. They were at home wherever they went, open to new experiences, and responsive to new contacts. I did not have to do much to publicize the visit. Lecture invitations poured in from Africanists and Islamicists throughout the city. His work was well known in different quarters. We did, however, manage to have several meals together and to talk about Africa, about history, and about Israel; I also arranged a get-together with my graduate students. In the years that followed, we met from time to time at meetings of the African Studies Association (ASA) and of MANSA. I always enjoyed the breadth of his scholarship and his fine critical mind. In 1998, when I visited Israel for the first time, my wife and I were invited to the Levtzion apartment for Friday night dinner. It was quite a big gathering with several of his children and some in-laws. I remember a very lively conversation, much of it on the many divisions of Israeli society. I think that night I also saw Nehemia as a member of community. He was a world traveler, at home and admired on four continents, and yet very much a part of his Israeli family and community.

We rarely talked politics, though he was clearly a strong supporter of the Oslo agreement. He believed in the possibility of peace. The last time I saw him was at the ASA in the autumn of 2003. He looked very tired, somehow older than our previous meeting at a MANSA conference in the Gambia. This was shortly after Israel decided to try to repress the second *intifada* by force. I asked him what he thought about it. He shrugged his shoulders and with a look of despair, he asked: "What could we do?" I let the subject drop and returned to more scholarly questions. His term at the Council of Higher Education was over and he was looking forward to retiring to the scholarly activities that he loved: there was the revised *Ancient Ghana and Mali* work; he had translation projects planned; he should have pulled together his ideas on eighteenth century reform and renewal. He died, however, in late summer, before the ASA meeting at which he planned a panel on the Ghana and Mali project that was intended to regenerate interest and enthusiasm among those whose research was relevant to the revisions.

We are all used to colleagues who disappear into the upper reaches of academic administration, never to return to the lab or study, except perhaps to write a book on higher education. Nehemia was not like that. He loved his scholarly work. He told Naomi Chazan that that was how he relaxed (Chazan, personal communication). He also enjoyed people. He liked helping young scholars. When I asked my wife how she remembered our encounters, she said she thought of him as a kind and considerate person. MANSA was a small association, probably the least important of those he participated in, but he regularly attended MANSA meetings. He never became too important for his more modest friends. He was also frequently at the ASA. He probably often had business there because he had numerous collaborations, but he enjoyed the academic camaraderie. There is a Yiddish word that has stuck with me, *mensch*. A *mensch* in German is a human being, but in Yiddish it has a connotation of a complete and decent human being. Nehemia was a *mensch*, and a very fine scholar to boot.

Notes

[1] I heard a lot about Ruth Schachter (not yet Morgenthau) and Immanuel Wallerstein, and a bit about Claude Meillassoux, who had only published one interesting article. This was, of course, because very little history had been written. Even published historians like Roland Oliver, Kenneth O. Dike, and Jan Vansina were young and had only begun to publish. We were excited about what we were doing and what colleagues were doing, particularly colleagues who seemed to be on the frontiers of the field.

[2] The introduction to Levtzion (2007) includes a short autobiographical statement made by Levtzion at the request of friends and family at a sixtieth birthday celebration; it is reprinted in this volume. Nehemia was a modest man, who rarely talked about himself or wrote about his life.

[3] The African Studies programs in the United States were just beginning, but SOAS had specialists on different periods and regions. On the creation of the initial team of SOAS Africanists and their first cohort of graduate students, see Oliver (1997, 243-71).

[4] See the "Introduction" to this volume, Nehemia's sixtieth birthday speech, and the memorial piece to Tirtza.

[5] Levtzion's peers at SOAS included Kwame Daaku, David Birmingham, Michael Twaddle, Richard Caulk, Walter Rodney, and Edward Alpers. The founders, however, were the small group trained in London during the 1950s: K.O. Dike, Jacob Ajayi, Adu Boahen, and B.A. Ogot.

[6] This 1965 work is dated today; for most of the states studied, there have since been major in-depth studies. See, for example, Ivor Wilks (1989), J.A. Braimah (1997), and the many works of Michel Izard (1970, 1992) on the Mossi.

[7] He did return to northern Ghana with occasional articles and with *Chronicles from Gonja* (1986), which he produced in collaboration with Ivor Wilks and Bruce Haight. Levtzion translated and collated the documents.

[8] First published in 1981, the *Corpus* was republished in 2000 by Markus Wiener and has been very widely used. Wiener also brought out a selection

from the *Corpus* edited by Levtzion and Jay Spaulding for the use of undergraduates (2003). Levtzion also published about a dozen articles over the years based on fine textual analysis of Arabic language sources (see his CV for references).

[9] See also the articles on conversion re-published in the recent posthumous book edited by Michel Abitbol, one of his first students, and Amos Nadan, his son-in-law (Levtzion 2007).

[10] He also revised this chapter for the 1987 updated version.

[11] Re-published as Nehemia Levtzion and Humphrey J. Fisher, eds. *Rural and Urban Islam in West Africa*. Boulder, Colorado: Lynne Rienner, 1987.

[12] MANSA continues to flourish today, producing regular newsletters and organizing international conferences; see its website at http://www.txstate.edu/anthropology/mansa/index.html (Levtzion's role is recounted on the "History" page of the website.).

Remembering Nehemia: Personal Tributes

Résumé

Quatre collègues et amis de Nehemia Levtzion offrent des souvenirs personnels. Roland Oliver se souvient de l'étudiant en études supérieures d'arabe qu'il a rencontré plus tard au SOAS faisant de la recherche sur le terrain au début des années 1960. Il relève le pas important qu'a fait Levtzion en quittant le confortable domaine maghrébin, choisi généralement par les érudits en études arabes, pour s'aventurer dans le Ghana, au sud du Sahara. William Miles pense à Levtzion comme à un pont entre deux univers d'érudition: L'histoire de l'Afrique et les études juives. En Israël, il a promu une étude respectueuse de la civilisation musulmane par les érudits et institutions d'études supérieures juives; globalement, il a promu un apprentissage respectueux de la civilisation juive. Naomi Chazan elle aussi se souvient de Levtzion comme d'un guide à l'esprit fin et comme d'une âme émouvante derrière les études africaines en Israël dès leurs débuts au milieu des années 1960. C'est un véritable tribut à un érudit doué d'une vision et d'une intégrité exceptionnelles que de retracer son travail et ses qualités de chef. Mais, c'est aussi une histoire de la construction d'un domaine académique en Israël. Les souvenirs que E. Ann McDougall garde de Levtzion sont liés inextricablement à des moments formatifs de sa vie personnelle et professionnelle. A ses yeux, le plus important a été l'influence qu'il a exercée sur sa manière de concevoir le Sahara, les relations Sahara-Sahel et l'Islam par l'intermédiaire de débats et de défis perpétuels.

Abstract

Four colleagues and friends of Nehemia Levtzion offer personal reminiscences. Roland Oliver remembers the young Arabist graduate student he met at SOAS and later encountered doing research in the field in the early 1960s. He remarks upon the important step Levtzion was taking in moving out of the comfortable Maghrebian field in which Arabists normally settled and venturing into sub-Saharan Ghana. William Miles reflects on Levtzion as a bridge between two major worlds of scholarship: African history and Jewish studies. In Israel, he promoted respectful learning of Muslim civilization by Jewish scholars and institutions of higher learning; globally, he promoted respectful learning of Jewish civilization. Naomi Chazan also remembers Levtzion as the shaper, guide and moving spirit behind African studies in Israel since its inception in the mid-1960s. Re-tracing his work and his leadership is a tribute to a scholar of vision and integrity and, at the same time, a history of the construction of an academic field in Israel. E. Ann McDougall's memories of Levtzion are inextricably intertwined with formative moments in her personal and professional lives. Most important is the influence that he exerted on her thinking about the Sahara, Saharan-Sahelian relations and Islam through ongoing debate and challenge.

Roland Oliver

My memories of Nehemia go back to 1962, when he came to the School of Oriental and African Studies in London University as a doctoral student after taking two earlier degrees at the Institute of Asian and African Studies at the Hebrew University of Jerusalem. He was already a competent Arabist, well trained in both the written and the spoken language, and it was a time when most people with these qualifications would have sought a topic for research in the history of the Maghrib; but Nehemia was already clear that he wished to work on the spread of Islam in some part of Africa south of the Sahara, and in due course he settled on the northern province of Ghana and the adjacent parts of Burkina Faso, Togo, and Benin. He spent a full year of field research, interviewing more than a thousand informants chosen from the Muslim clerics of the region. I particularly remember a long talk I had with him during a visit to Ghana in 1964, when he told me that it was his command of Arabic which had aroused the welcome which he had received from these clerics, most of whom knew little Arabic themselves but had a great respect for the language of the Koran. This had made them willing to entrust him with their family genealogies and other traditions, which had enabled him to work out the chronology of Muslim settlement in each ethnic division of his field.

Nehemia's doctoral thesis was published in 1968 under the title *Muslims and Chiefs in West Africa*, and its great contribution was to show that, in its origins, the spread of Islam had been an essentially peaceful process, resulting from the long-distance trade in West African gold, developed first by the Muslim Arabs of the Maghreb and carried southwards from the desert margins by Mande-speaking (Dyula) merchants, who had been the earliest sub-Saharan Africans to convert to Islam. The trade necessitated the crossing of local ethnic frontiers and the establishment of trading settlements in non-Muslim lands. The sense of brotherhood among Muslims was a great support for the traders, whose caravans were accompanied in their travels by Muslim clerics, who soon became the most stable inhabitants of the settlements and those responsible for handling relations with the indigenous rulers, whose good will and protection was obtained by gifts and services, including prayers for healing, for success in warfare, for divination, and the supply of amulets and charms. The rulers themselves were normally reluctant to convert, because they feared the reaction of their subjects, over whom they exercised spiritual as well as temporal authority. But sometimes they went so far as to entrust some of their children to the clerics for instruction.

On his return to Jerusalem, Nehemia was appointed to a post at the Institute of African and Asian Studies and was soon promoted to a professorial chair, which he held for the rest of his career. In his research he now extended his interests northwards across the desert to include the Maghreb, and backwards in time to review the writings of the early Arab geographers. In 1973 he published a slim volume called *Ancient Ghana and Mali*. He also contributed two substantial chapters to the third and fourth volumes of the *Cambridge History of Africa*, covering the whole region from the Maghreb to the fringes of the West African forest, and published in 1975 and 1977. As one of the General Editors of this series, I saw and admired his work, which always arrived on time and required little amendment. Soon afterwards he collaborated with the Cambridge Arabist, John Hopkins, in preparing a *Corpus of Early Arabic Sources for West African History*, published in 1981. What Nehemia saw more clearly than any earlier writer was that none of the early Arabic geographers except Ibn Battuta had themselves crossed the Sahara and that their accounts were based only on hearsay gathered from illiterate sources, such as the Berber cameldrivers of the desert caravans. Such informants might be able to describe the show-business of court ceremonial in the sub-Saharan kingdoms, while entirely neglecting the mechanics of government. They could portray the nuts and bolts of desert travel, but not the extensive network of internal trade of which it was an outgrowth. They knew little of military affairs, or of the relations of the great states of the western Sudan with their lesser neighbours. Nehemia saw clearly how much of our real knowledge of the medieval history of the western and central Sudan comes from the introductory and retrospective chapters of the chronicles written by native Sudanese scholars from the sixteenth century on.

After completing the *Corpus*, Nehemia turned to the planning and editing of two collaborative works which extended his field of interest still further: the first, entitled *Conversion to Islam*, was published in 1979; and the second, *The History of Islam in Africa*, jointly edited with Randall Powels, and published in 2000. This will remain essential reading for students of the subject for many years to come. I did not myself see much of Nehemia during these later years. We had glancing contact at conferences of the African Studies Association (ASA), and once he invited me to visit and lecture at his Institute in Jerusalem, which I was unable to accept, due to a long-term illness in my own family. But I keep the memory of a fine and sensitive scholar and of a singularly gentle and modest person.

William F.S. Miles

In the Hebrew language, *kavod* — respect — conveys a sense of obligation reminiscent of that so strongly entrenched in African culture as well. By highlighting Nehemia Levtzion's contributions in the areas highlighted by the themes of the 2004 ASA meeting (Identity, Language, and Memory, in Africa and the Diaspora) I wish to impart my own measure of *kavod* to one of the foremost Israeli, and Jewish, Africanists.

Who was Nehemia Levtzion? His very name gives us a sense of his origins: Lev Tsion, The Heart of Zion.

The original Nehemia, of the Old Testament, was the wine taster to King Artaxerxes of Persia in the fifth century BCE. (His job, of course, was not to choose the best Bordeaux or Merlot but rather to sip and physically react to any poison that enemies of the king may have slipped in to the royal cup.) One day the King noticed that Nehemia was not looking well. He could have been concerned for his own self, but nevertheless inquired of Nehemia what was ailing him. The prophet responded that Jerusalem ("the city of my ancestors") lay in ruins. Artaxerxes dispatched Nehemia on a mission to restore the welfare of the Jerusalemites, who were then under Persian dominion.

"Our" Nehemia was also a true Jerusalemite, similarly making a mark in Yerushalayim. In his capacity as Dean of Humanities and Bamberger and Fuld Professor of History of the Muslim Peoples at the Hebrew University in Jerusalem, as academic chairman of the International Center for University Teaching of Jewish Civilization, and Director of the Van Leer Jerusalem Institute, like his prophetic namesake, Professor Levtzion contributed immensely to the making of Jerusalem as a center of learning. His contribution in this domain was threefold.

First was his teaching: scholarly, non-politicized study of African history, and especially Muslim African history, to his students at the Hebrew University in Jerusalem. The conference out of which his co-edited *The History of Islam in Africa* (2000) grew was convened at the Van Leer Institute in Jerusalem. Though published only a few years ago, it has already become a standard textbook in the field.

Second was the kind of learning with which historians and Africanists are most familiar: the dissemination, within the global scholarly community, of his scholarship on West African history. In our politicized times, some might have expected the prospect of an Israeli Jew uncovering and interpreting Muslim history to be problematic. Yet Nehemia encountered no such protest or barrier: his scholarly integrity transcended even Middle East tensions.

Third, and probably least known, were Nehemia's efforts to promote Jewish studies, in an interdisciplinary, and international, plane. This included, as he put it in his 1995 contribution to the New York University Press volume *Teaching Jewish Civilization: A Global Approach to Higher Education*, "the development of regional approaches to the teaching of Jewish civilization." *Teaching Jewish Civilization* contains a listing of countries and universities included in the World Register of University Studies in Jewish Civilization, and included seven African nations (Cameroon, Côte d'Ivoire, Congo, Kenya, Nigeria, South Africa, and Swaziland).

Nehemia Levtzion thus integrated two complementary scholarly agendas: on the one hand, respectful learning of Muslim civilization by Jewish scholars and institutions of higher learning; on the other hand, promoting respectful learning of Jewish civilization in non-Jewish universities and by non-Jewish as well as Jewish scholars.

In his life and beyond, Nehemia serves as model for integrative efforts of scholarly exchange between the Jewish and non-Jewish scholarly worlds in general, and between the Muslim and Jewish worlds in particular. It is in this context that I take the liberty of summarizing my own project, which surely bears this Levtzionian imprint: but before doing so, permit me to invoke the first time that I ever met Nehemia.

I was a graduate student at the Fletcher School of Law and Diplomacy of Tufts University when Nehemia was on sabbatical at the Center for International Affairs at Harvard. Just back from Muslim West Africa after two years in the Peace Corps, I was writing a paper on the role of the chiefs under French and British colonial jurisdiction and eagerly attended a talk that Nehemia was giving in the African Studies seminar series convened by Dov Ronen. Somehow, I had the temerity (or chutzpa) to approach this eminent historian and maladroitly ask: "Why would an Israeli be so interested in African history?"

Nehemia misinterpreted my admiration as a challenge and brusquely replied with a variation on "Why not?" "Why shouldn't an Israeli choose this as a field?" he replied in his characteristically powerful manner. "Are not Israelis scholars like anybody else?" I then proceeded to compound my chutzpa by asking Nehemia to read my student paper. (This was a decade after he had already published *Muslims and Chiefs in West Africa* (1968), but I was a bumbling grad student and did not yet know it.) I was incredibly naïve about sabbaticals, professors, and pesky grad students. Remember, he was not my professor, he was not at my school, and he was on leave. Yet Nehemia not only agreed to read my paper, but gave it the benefit of his full critique and commentary. In the ensuing years, I was honored by his friendship.

During my first sabbatical, at the Hebrew University in Jerusalem in 1994, I presented the book *(Hausaland Divided)* (Miles 1994) that expanded from that graduate school paper. Though I was a tenured professor, when Nehemia Levtzion showed up at my talk, I started quaking again. Even among friends, could not Nehemia intimidate by his sheer breadth of knowledge?

My project, one that most bears the influence of Nehemia's integrative scholarly approach, is "Third World Views of the Holocaust" (Miles 2004), "to assess the contemporary relevance of the Holocaust for the non-Western world."

Scholars, writers, and activists hailing from Africa, Asia, Latin America, and the Caribbean focused on the impact of the Shoah on their own thinking, writing, and worldviews. The Symposium belied the preconceived notion that among Third World intellectuals hostility towards Israel and the Jewish world is ingrained and endemic, that sensitivity to the Holocaust is conditional and politically framed, and that there is little sympathetic consciousness of the Shoah among peoples and societies not directly affected by it (Miles 2001).

Including scholars from Palestine and Muslim Mauritius, I wonder what role my emulation of the Africanist "heart of Zion" played in conceiving such a project in the first place. I am confident that Nehemia would have sympathized with at least some of my main conclusions:

1. intellectual globalization includes the Shoah within the emerging universal consciousness of world history;

2. reparations claims for other people's historical injustices derive their moral authority and tactical moorings from precedents established for Holocaust victims;

3. H/holocaust parallelism is a strategy employed by otherwise ignored groups under fire to gain support and sympathy from the West;

4. post-Shoah moral responsibility redounds upon an Israel whose overall legitimacy, despite criticism of certain policies, is respected; and

5. denial of Holocaust (along with fictionalization and self-suppression) is replicated in instances of Third World genocides.

In short, the Third World indigenizes the Holocaust and its legacies in diverse manners.

August 1999 in Jerusalem was the last time I spent with Nehemia, one-on-one. He was very generous with his time, taking me on a tour of his favorite spots in his favorite city. These included the garden overlook near the old United Nations headquarters and the American Colony Hotel in the Eastern part of the city. I distinctly remember being surprised by the unsolicited theological admission he made to me.

> On *yizkor* [death anniversary] for those who are close to me, I say *kaddish*; for High Holidays, I go to synagogue. But I don't go in the whole superstition of it.

I have my own *shulchan aruch* [observance rules]: I don't write on Shabbat. It's something I do for my children, as an example.

The memory of Nehemia unites scholars across disciplines and geographical boundaries. He embodied strong commitment to education in one's homeland, and about one's homeland in the Diaspora. He was the consummate *sabra* — an Israeli-born Jew, named after the desert fruit that is prickly on the outside, sweet on the inside. For sure, no colleague I know called Nehemia "sweet" — but inside, he was certainly a *mensch*, a good man who did good things. We are lucky he was also a scholar.

Naomi Chazan

Nehemia Levtzion was my mentor, patron, colleague, counterpart, and friend for nearly forty years. His story is in many respects that of African studies in Israel during this period. It closely reflects developments in higher education in the country as well. For those of us who were privileged to work with him closely, it is also a major part of our adult lives. The values that guided Nehemia as a human being also informed his work as a scholar, institution-builder, and fellow traveler. He was, and remains, a model of academic rigor and collegiality, efficiency and innovation, scholarly integrity and personal loyalty for those who knew him well and, by extension, for scholars dedicated to promoting humane and superior research on Africa and beyond.

I was Nehemia Levtzion's first PhD student in African Studies. I had just completed my MA in political science at Columbia University and returned to Jerusalem in October 1968 to begin a doctorate in comparative politics. Nehemia, then a young scholar specializing in Islam in Africa, headed the fledgling African Studies Department at the Hebrew University, the first of its kind in Israel. Although he was a historian and my training was in the social sciences, we shared a fascination with the new Africa. He agreed to become one of my supervisors, along with Emanuel Guttmann of the department of political science (an expert in comparative politics with immense interest in, but at the time little intimate knowledge of, Africa).

Serendipitously, I had fallen into the hands of the ultimate dissertation advisor, scholar, and academic guardian. All of these traits were apparent at the time; some I came to appreciate fully only as time progressed.

Nehemia took the task of supervision of his PhD candidates more than seriously. He was an exacting master, holding his students up to the same uncompromising standards he demanded of himself. He insisted on careful, painstaking research, which included the exhaustive scouring of all written sources along with the cautious use of new techniques that he himself had helped hone at the time (most notably in oral history). He demanded meticulous preparation for fieldwork, and followed every step on the ground with interest and, at times, concern. He then read drafts with a fine toothcomb — questioning ideas, querying sources, challenging conclusions, and even correcting sentence structure and spelling. He was, in many ways, a pedant, and gave no slack to his students (and his colleagues) in this regard.

His insistence on detail came together with immense generosity. No matter how busy he was, he was always available to answer a question, deal with a crisis, offer advice, and constantly encourage (as long as his sacred daily siesta was not interrupted by hysterical phone calls). He helped to procure grants as if he were applying for the funds himself. His students were given priority for research and teaching assistant positions. And, when their work was criticized by outside readers, he came to their defense with incredible loyalty, secure in the knowledge that no visible stone had been left unturned in the research process.

I came to recognize and value this wonderful combination of scholarly traits during my six years under Nehemia Levtzion's direct tutelage. My case posed a particular challenge: I was steeped in social science approaches (and jargon) which I defended with the vigor of a young graduate student; I employed survey and interview methods with which he was unversed; I was working on youth and politics in Ghana (which he knew well from a totally different perspective) and the Ivory Coast (with which he had only a rudimentary familiarity); and my background in African history in general and Muslims in Africa in particular was scanty to say the least. Nevertheless, we agreed at the time that I would start studying history and he, in turn, would make an effort to open himself to social science perspectives.

Nehemia's genuine curiosity allowed me to develop independently and to expand my knowledge in new and unexpected directions. He, as he repeatedly acknowledged later on, acquired additional tools and insights while retaining an unwavering adherence to his own (exceptionally high) disciplinary standards. A competent lecturer, he was a superior supervisor. He never imposed his views or predilections; he did, however, insist that I defend mine convincingly. Then, and throughout his career, Nehemia was therefore always the teacher's teacher and the scholar's scholar.

My personal experience during these formative years of African studies in Israel was shared by a magnificent group of graduate students, who began their studies under Nehemia's guidance in the latter part of the 1960s. He nurtured, prodded, and supported the first crop of MA students to pursue third degrees (including Benny Neuberger in political science, Victor Azarya in sociology, and Michel Abitbol in history) and encouraged others who did not go through the program to do the same (Mordechai Tamarkin and Hagai Ehrlich). These scholars later became the backbone of African studies in the country.

In retrospect, Nehemia's critical *cum* collegial approach to his students was symptomatic of his strategy for the development of a robust program in African studies in general. At the outset he and Mordechai Abir, both historians grounded in Middle East history, were the cornerstones of the department. Indeed, the African Studies Department at the Hebrew University was established as an offshoot of the Department of Middle East History and would have doubtless remained so if not for Nehemia's conscious decision to nourish a multi-disciplinary approach to the study of the continent. He actively recruited Africanists in a variety of fields in the humanities and the social sciences, ranging from anthropology and linguistics to economics and literature. He also tried to interest colleagues with limited knowledge of things African to work on African materials. In important respects he was one of the very first to internalize and act on the understanding that strong regional studies depend on a multiplicity of perspectives grounded in a variety of disciplinary departments. That is also why he insisted that all appointment procedures in African studies be carried out jointly with the disciplinary departments — a policy which also proved to be extremely cost efficient.

Nehemia then went on to recruit lecturers and visiting professors to round out the program (most notably Dov Ronen in political science and Mark Karp in economics). He paid particular attention to ensuring a balance between scholars specializing in the different regions of the continent (for years there was a friendly rivalry between those working on West Africa and those with expertise in East Africa and the Horn). Although an avowed Islamicist himself, he also understood that the African experience could not be captured without a deep knowledge of local religions and Christianity (here, too, there developed an intriguing discourse that yielded fascinating debates). Thus, through the careful incorporation of difference, within a few years the African Studies Department, which started at the MA level, flourished as a distinct undergraduate program as well.

From the outset, however, Nehemia went one step further. He created opportunities for constant discussion and interaction first within the framework of informal departmental discussions and then in a more structured manner under the umbrella of the Africa Research Unit at the Harry S. Truman Research Institute for the Advancement of Peace. These gatherings provided a standing forum for airing differing approaches to the study of particular issues and eventually for a variety of unconventional and truly productive collaborations. One of the first debates — in the late 1960s — revolved around the utility of employing concepts of decolonization as opposed to nationalism to describe the transition to independence. Nehemia was a staunch supporter of the nationalism school, while I advocated the then emerging decolonization outlook. Even if gradually (albeit grudgingly), he eventually conceded the relative utility of decolonization and adopted its terminology and conceptual outlooks, he was much more skeptical about critical theories of colonialism and neo-colonialism that were developing at time. He insisted nevertheless on fomenting a constructive intellectual tension, on listening and learning without necessarily agreeing.

Many of the debates at the time were conducted along disciplinary lines, with the more traditional historians pitted against the more iconoclastic social scientists. Each side eventually acquired the tools of the other, accepting the working maxim that "political science without history is rootless; history without political science is fruitless." Some discussions, however, went on to confront disagreements over conceptual frameworks, theoretical controversies, and even methodological dispositions. Nehemia rarely embraced new conventions with alacrity. He nevertheless encouraged their airing. This is why Jerusalem Africanists constantly experimented with innovative ideas and directions and how, over time, they became a funnel for the introduction of some new approaches to understanding historical and contemporary trends on the continent.

These early — earnest yet congenial — sparring sessions laid the groundwork for later research cooperation. They also established a common commitment to African concerns, which gradually evolved into a series of joint workshops, conferences and research projects sponsored by the Department and the Africa Research Unit at the Truman Institute in subsequent decades. Throughout these initial phases Nehemia Levtzion provided the adhesive: he was the teacher and skeptic, supporter and critic, unassuming leader and very much all-around friend who, together with Tirtza, never failed to remember birthdays, celebrate newcomers, and embrace often bewildered spouses.

Indeed, Nehemia Levtzion was very much an Israeli of the old school — erudite, humble, committed, guileless, awkward, and always welcoming. He truly cared about what he was doing and was devoted to extracting the best of himself and those around him. In these very basic respects he was the antithesis of flamboyance and ego-centrism in academe. He was also very self-consciously Israeli — proud of his agricultural upbringing and of his country. That is why he encouraged academic work on Israeli-African relations; that also accounts for the fact that he was less prone to share the progressive political ideas (or applaud the political activities) of some of his colleagues.

By the mid-1970s the patterns established in the early years of African studies in Israel had begun to consolidate, first with the appointment of Michael Wade in African literature and Uri Almagor in anthropology, and then with the absorption of the first group of PhDs (Azarya in sociology, Abitbol in contemporary Jewry and African history, and me, rather belatedly, in political science). The Truman Institute became the research focus: together with sociologist S.N. Eisenstadt annual thematic seminars began to generate exciting results (on African ideologies, on the early state in Africa, on myths and political institutions). Almost each one of these common efforts yielded a series of publications, most written jointly. Some resulted in edited volumes. All the young academics joined hands to produce units in a new course on the "Emerging States of Africa" for the Open University, where Benny Neuberger received an appointment.

Guest researchers were brought in to stimulate and inform — Dick Sklar, Don Rothchild, Victor Low, Tim Shaw, Larry Bowman, Olusola Ojo, Shula Marks, Bill Miles, and many others. Trips to Africa were encouraged along with conference presentations abroad. And new graduates joined the core group (Steve Kaplan in comparative religion, Yekutiel Gershoni in history). Student interest grew at both the undergraduate and graduate levels. And, slowly but surely, in the early 1980s, the first Levtzion generation was tenured.

By that time, the university authorities had begun to appreciate (and take advantage of) Nehemia's demonstrable administrative skills. He was appointed Dean of the Faculty of Humanities, and then head of the Ben-Zvi Institute. He remained, however, always the researcher and scholar. His interest in Islam in Africa yielded more meticulous work on textual materials, as well as broader treatments of rural and urban Islam (another Truman-sponsored conference) and comparative processes of Islamization. Throughout, he never wavered as consultant, frank critic, and standard-bearer.

By the mid-1980s, the Jerusalem Africanists had developed a reputation for cross-disciplinary research and a track record for raising new issues in intriguing ways. At that time, a Tel-Aviv branch had already been formed by Tamarkin and Ehrlich and then buttressed by Gershoni and later by Galia Sabar, the second crop of Levtzion graduates. Daphna Golan joined the ranks of the department in Jerusalem, and new PhD candidates started their dissertations under the supervision of Levtzion's students. This was when some major conferences held in Jerusalem were published, most notably on state-society relations in Africa, Islam in Africa, and civil society on the continent (see, for example, Eisenstadt, Abitbol and Chazan 1988; Rothchild and Chazan 1988; Harbeson, Rothchild and Chazan 1994).

This was also when Nehemia, with his appointment as President of the Open University, first took a protracted leave from the Hebrew University. Although he did continue to teach a bit, his daily involvement in the various research programs was inevitably curtailed drastically. Other Africanists began to branch out as well — Abitbol became provost of overseas students; I was appointed chair of the Truman Institute. The day-to-day activities related to Africa were continued by younger and extremely talented scholars.

By the early 1990s, however, the dual process of success and constriction in tenure-track positions began to take its toll. Nehemia moved on from the Open University to the Van Leer Institute; Michel Abitbol did a brief stint in the Ministry of Education, I was elected to the Knesset. And then Nehemia was appointed Chair of the prestigious Budget and Finance Committee of the Council of Higher Education, essentially the key policy-making and implementation unit for higher education in the country.

We continued to meet — and often to cooperate — but this time in the totally different context of parliamentary hearings and policy debates. The rough and tumble nature of the Israeli political arena was alien to Nehemia's nature. He was often bewildered by, but never bowed to, its machinations — remaining scholarly, substantive, and forthright throughout. He nevertheless did everything in his power to protect the autonomy of higher education and secure its resources in an increasingly hostile political environment.

The fate of African studies proved more precarious. Israeli interest in Africa ebbed in the wake of the new economic boom, changes in the global arena, and the possibility of forging of relations with Asian countries and neighboring states. The African Studies Department that he had so carefully nurtured was on the wane. He himself, however, never faltered, safeguarding precious slots of time for his own research and arranging for at least one month away (mostly in Britain) to pursue his own scholarly interests. His last publications are the product of these stolen moments.

Nehemia's death was in every sense the end of an era. His brand of steady, solid, honest scholarship is no longer as commonplace as it was in the past. His pluralist and enlightened academic entrepreneurship is far from the reigning norm. Even his stubborn caution in the face of new ideas, however enervating at the time, is missed given the rudderless direction of many scholarly developments in recent years.

Most poignantly, the institutional infrastructure that he so laboriously constructed has fallen apart with his departure and with the retirement of other senior scholars. The undergraduate Department of African Studies at the Hebrew University closed its doors just before he passed away; the graduate program was disbanded in 2005. In Tel-Aviv, as well, the Africa concentration is being shut down.

The academic teamwork that Nehemia Levtzion encouraged and oversaw, however, is still very much alive. His students and successors in Israel are now trying to develop a cross-university consortium in African studies to maintain scholarly interest in the continent. A research seminar still takes place in Tel-Aviv and at the Truman Institute in Jerusalem. An annual international conference is convened with guests from abroad. And the tradition of global collaboration still persists. But the inspiration and leadership supplied by Nehemia Levtzion and sustained by his now retired students is sorely missing. His Jerusalem legacy goes far beyond his publications — it embraces a mixture of rigor, curiosity, openness, collaboration, and thoughtfulness. The best tribute to him is to continue in his path.

E. Ann McDougall

In the summer of 2003, I was renovating my house. This meant that after many years and many moves of simply re-filling boxes of papers in the nearest closet, I actually sorted them out. Buried in a thick and ragged folder called "thesis correspondence" was a letter from Nehemia, dated 1981 — a reply to the copy of my thesis I had sent to him for comment. I re-read that three-page, single spaced typed (yes, on a real manual typewriter) letter and remembered, with a smile, the numerous conversations, visits, and "gentle disagreements" that had followed it during the intervening twenty-plus years. I carefully saved the letter.

Two weeks later, Nehemia died. I heard the news, as did probably many people, through an H-Africa announcement. This was quickly followed by e-mails from friends, some of whose voices you will hear below, and a welcome phone call from David Conrad that provided the opportunity to express feelings. While some people had known of his illness, Nehemia had not spoken widely of it; a few colleagues had guessed after meeting him at the previous ASA meeting that something was wrong. But I had not been there and had not heard the concerned comments. It never occurred to me that there would not be another ASA with its accompanying meal or drink with, and inevitable warm hug from, Nehemia.

That letter in 1981 was the beginning. It was how I came to know Nehemia and it set the parameters for both our personal and professional friendship. After complimenting me for my important contributions to the history of Islam, the Sahara, and salt, Nehemia proceeded to take issue with point after consecutive point. Several of these "points" remained issues of debate between us for years to come; we never could agree on the relative importance of "co-operation" as compared to "conflict" along the Saharan desert edges, for example, or the degree to which the "rural" was actually integrated with the "urban" in the Saharan-Sahelian landscape. But his eagerness to debate (and, yes, he did like to win!) was manifested in an invitation to one of his now famous "workshops" held at the Hebrew University in Jerusalem (this one on "rural and urban Islam"). The experience of spending a week in an interdisciplinary discussion group, focusing on what I loved best to talk about, fundamentally shaped and reshaped my approach to everything pastoral, Saharan, and Islamic. As well, it introduced me — a relatively new PhD — to a world of influential and stimulating scholars, most of whom became close colleagues, if not close friends. That week did not, however, in any way dim the enjoyment of finding ways to disagree with Nehemia, and then work for years to fully develop my position. For me, personally, it is this contribution to my scholarship that I most appreciated in our relationship.

There are other "moments" that remain with me as well. There was the time that Nehemia graciously agreed to make a three-day visit to Duke University while I was teaching there as a sessional lecturer. I was so excited and nervous to be organizing such an important event that involved several public talks, as well as the usual informal "hospitality-type" events. After the first of the talks and receptions, we were being driven back to his hotel, going over the schedule for the next day. He pulled out the itinerary and with disarming gentleness pointed out that the title I had publicly distributed referred to Islam in South East Asia whereas his talk, as he had clearly told me on the phone, was to be on "south" Asia. I do not think the word embarrassed quite covers it (thank heavens the darkness in the car disguised my red face). The others laughed a bit nervously, not sure just how our guest was going to continue. They did not know Nehemia. He carried on, barely skipping a beat to say: "But of course, that's not a problem — I can make adjustments to the talk tonight. Don't worry about it!" I have never forgotten his kindness in that moment, nor the fact that he did indeed expand his planned talk so that no one noticed my incredibly stupid mistake.

And on an even more personal note, again, an ASA meeting, one of the first few I had attended — the first person whom I met while waiting to register was Nehemia. "Come and join us for lunch, Ann." Then a warm hug and "How are you?" I said "I'm pregnant." He held me at arm's length, asked me if this was a good thing. Upon my replying in the affirmative, he said, "Well, in that case, I'm happy for you. Congratulations." And then another hug. He was the first person I had been able to tell among my Africanist friends and I was not sure how the news would be received. He remains special for the concern and warmth of that initial response (that was, thankfully, shared by almost everyone else).

Finally, there was that Workshop. Not only was it one of those incomparable intellectual experiences, it was accompanied by an unforgettable welcome to Nehemia's world. My interaction with him, with Tirtza, with friend and colleague, Naomi Chazan and her family — left an indelible mark on a young woman yet to spend anywhere long enough to put down roots, let alone develop the kind of personal and political commitments I felt among these people while in Jerusalem. There are many who knew Nehemia better and many who spent longer in his company than I ever did. But that does not diminish, for me, the role he played in my personal and professional development.

This volume is the only way I know to say "thank you" and reflect back some of the humanity and warmth he left with me and so many others. I only regret that this time there will be no three-page, single-spaced, typed response to my arguments and criticisms, pushing me further and challenging me, as always, to "prove it"!

In Memory of Tirtza Levtzion, 1935-2007

Tirtza Levtzion, nee Gindel, was born in 1935 (the same year as Nehemia), in Nesher, which was at that time a village on the outskirts of Haifa. The family later moved to Haifa and Tirtza attended the Reali High School there.

After military service (as the commander of a unit of Nahal recruits), Tirtza began her teaching training studies at the Teachers' Seminary near Haifa. She subsequently moved to Jerusalem, where she studied History and Geography at the Hebrew University of Jerusalem. In one of the lectures that she attended given by the late Professor Uriel Hed, Tirtza met the man who was to become the love of her life, Nehemia Levtzion. Nehemia at the time was studying Arabic Language and Literature and the History of the Middle East. Tirtza and Nehemia were married in 1961, and remained together until Nehemia's death in 2003. Together they pursued with their careers, visiting London and Africa in the framework of Nehemia's PhD studies, sabbatical leave in the United Kingdom and the United States, as well as senior administrative positions.

But most important of all was the family, which constituted for them a source of strength: first with their four children, Moshe (Shiko), Osnat, Noga and Avner; and following with the expansion of the family. Their genuine love and devotion to their family was felt and noted many of Nehemia's colleagues who were invited to share the Friday night meal with the family.

Tirtza was closely identified with the work of writing research papers, devoting her best years to promoting that subject. In this area she was a pioneer and an innovator, starting at the Rehavia High School, where she established the "Workshop for Preparing Research Papers," providing many pupils with the tools for undertaking academic writing while preparing theoretical papers under the guidance of Hebrew University staff. Tirtza later continued this work in the framework of the Hebrew University, where in 1991 she established the Yuviler Center, training teachers from various sectors of Israeli society (ultra-orthodox, Arabs, and peripheral areas) to supervise the preparation of research papers.

Simultaneously there was cooperation with Palestinian educational institutions. In recognition of her work in education, Tirtza was awarded the Education Prize in 1982 by the President of Israel.

Tirtza was always distinguished by her colorful clothes, which complemented her vibrant personality and youthful spirit. She died early in 2007, leaving two daughters, two sons-in-law, a son, a daughter-in-law, and eight grandchildren.

Tirtza with the teachers of the college where she was teaching (Tamale)

Engaging with a Legacy

Breaking New Ground in "Pagan" and "Muslim" West Africa

David Robinson

Résumé

La carrière de Nehemia Levtzion, interprète de l'Islam en Afrique de l'Ouest a été longue et distinguée, et certaines de ses premières contributions sont d'une très grande valeur. L'article explore tout d'abord l'importance persistante de **Muslims and Chiefs in West Africa** *(1968), analyse de communautés et d'états au sein de la Middle Belt "païenne" du Ghana, et en second lieu, la falsification de documents en arabe, porteuse de sérieuses implications pour le jihad et l'état de Hamdullahi créé dans le Middle Delta du Mali dans "A Seventeenth Century Chronicle of Ibn-al-Mukhtar" (1971).*

Abstract

Nehemia Levtzion had a long and distinguished career as an interpreter of Islam in West Africa, and some of his earliest contributions have the greatest value. This article explores first, the continuing significance of **Muslims and Chiefs in West Africa** *(1968), an analysis of communities and states set in the "pagan" Middle Belt of Ghana, and second, a forgery of Arabic documents with important political implications for the jihad and state of Hamdullahi created in the Middle Delta of Mali, in "A Seventeenth Century Chronicle of Ibn al-Mukhtar" (1971).*

Introduction

Over four decades, Nehemia Levtzion had a great impact on the history of Islam, Africa in general, and West Africa in particular. He is probably best known for three works: his study of old Ghana and Mali (Levtzion 1973), a set of invaluable translations and annotations of Arabic documentation for the "medieval" period of West Africa (Levtzion and Hopkins 1981), and the ambitious *History of Islam in Africa* completed not long before his death (Levtzion and

Pouwels 2000). But some of his finest work was done early in his career. In this article, I wish to look at two such publications, one set in the "Middle Belt" of contemporary Ghana, the other in the savannah of Mali: *Muslims and Chiefs in West Africa: A Study of Islam in the Middle Volta Basin in the Pre-Colonial Period* (1968), a revision of his dissertation; and "A Seventeenth-Century Chronicle by Ibn al-Mukhtar: A Critical Study of *Ta'rikh al-Fattash*" (1971c).

The Historiographical Background

It is important to remember how the history of West Africa and Islamization were understood in the 1960s and 1970s, in both time and space (see Robinson 1985b, 2000b).[1] Thanks to the work of John Spencer Trimingham and others working at the end of the colonial period, the historiography fell rather neatly into an early "medieval" period of old Ghana, Mali, and Songhay, with Hausaland and Bornu thrown in, and a recent period dominated by "*jihads* of the sword" led by Fulbe scholars and warriors. These movements resulted in the establishment of "Islamic" states, often called theocracies, in the same region. These states completed the process of Islamization, which had now reached the majority populations.

Accompanying these emphases was a threefold teleological formula that many of us have worked with in one way or another. Islam was initially practiced by largely commercial minorities, living in trading towns within pagan societies. At a second stage, it was adopted by ruling classes, most spectacularly by some rulers of Mali, Songhay, Kano, and Bornu. Both of these stages fell within, or more accurately started within, the "medieval" settings mentioned above. At a third stage, Islam was accepted by the majority populations, who came under the domination of reformers who used the *jihad* of the sword and Sufi affiliation to bring Islam to the rural areas. This corresponded to the recent period or the eighteenth and nineteenth centuries. At this point Islam was considered the dominant faith and practice in the Western and Central Sudan, and the region was pronounced part of the *Dar al-Islam*. The colonial period that began in the late nineteenth century was of little interest, even though subsequent writing has shown that the pace of Islamization increased significantly during colonial rule. Indeed, it is likely that Islam did not become the majority faith of the savannah region until colonial rule (Stewart 1990ab, 1997).

Accompanying this time frame and these phases was a geography consisting of a number of west-east belts, extending from Sahara to dry savannah to woodland to forest. The best documented was the savannah or Sahelian zone, in which the medieval and *jihadic* states developed. It corresponded to the most important "Islamic" zone of West Africa.[2] Below that were areas of pagan populations and some Christian communities, the product of missionary movements of the nineteenth century.[3] To some extent these bands were the inheritance of an indigenous West African and Saharan religious ethnography (see Hunwick and Powell 2002) formulated by scholars such as Ahmed Baba of Timbuktu (see Robinson 2004, chapter 5).

British and French colonial specialists reinforced these divisions. Northern Nigeria and the savannah zones of French West Africa were Muslim, with some islands of paganism occupied by the Mazugawa, the resistant Mossi and Bambara, and the isolated Dogon. Southern Nigeria, Ghana, and Ivory Coast were non-Muslim territories where Christian missionary activity could be tolerated or even encouraged, while practitioners of Islam were concentrated in cities such as Lagos, Accra, and Abidjan. Levtzion's book is set in "pagan" Ghana (Gold Coast), while his article deals with "Muslim" Mali (Soudan).

Explorations in "Pagan" West Africa

Levtzion was, of course, not entirely free of the constraints of this historiography and geography. In reading *Muslims and Chiefs* (1968) with its careful treatment of the literature, the sources and the area of middle and northern Ghana, one can see the traditional framework. Levtzion concentrates on the "Middle Belt," the zone of woodland between the savannah and forest. In Nigeria "Middle Belt" had a quasi-official designation for the area between savannah and forest, but in colonial Gold Coast it was also important, as the zone between the Mossi in French Upper Volta and the Asante in the south. Levtzion saw his study as showing the ways in which Muslim merchants and teachers practiced the faith, and related to the political realm of chiefs, before the *jihad* movements obscured some of the earlier patterns. In one reading, his work is an archaeological enterprise, a study of the "layer" below and before the culmination of the Islamization process.

But in fact, the work challenged the existing historiographical framework. Muslim communities had been present within Asante and up to the Upper Volta (Burkina Faso) frontier for centuries. They engaged in very complex and varied relationships to the political establishments of northern Ghana. In Gonja chiefs, Muslims and commoners were clearly demarcated hereditary estates. In Dagomba the estates were distinct, but individuals sometimes moved from Muslim to chief or vice-versa. The Muslim communities of Mamprussi tended to guard their autonomy, in some tension with the state, whereas in Wa Muslims and chiefs often joined forces to defend the state against groups of commoners. The spiritual power of all the Muslims was widely appreciated by the chiefs, including the "arch-pagans" of Asante, especially when they mobilized against political and religious threats to their authority.

So the web of relations of Muslims and chiefs was not a prelude to *jihad* or further Islamization, but a stable relationship of great interest in itself. It helped to make understandable the considerable attraction of Islam throughout colonial Gold Coast. Levtzion, with his ability to read and contextualize the Arabic sources, was able to profile the Muslim communities and delineate their complex relations to the larger societies. In his conclusion, Levtzion suggested new directions for research:

> The study of patterns of Islamization is important not only for the understanding of a dynamic process of acculturation in Africa, but also for its significance in the context of the spread of Islam in the wider world..." (1968, 193).

In sum, Levtzion broke down the barriers of the existing historiography and geography of West Africa and set in motion some very powerful vectors of research that have benefited the field and understanding of the last thirty years.

What are some of these directions? The first deals with the sources. Levtzion was the first scholar to pay attention to the Arabic documentation of the "pagan" forest zone, both what could be found in personal and institutional libraries in Ghana and what was located in European repositories. This material indicated that the literacy and piety of Muslims was not inferior to that of the faithful in the savannah, even if they did not deal with the questions of Islamic government.

The second is the development of the "Suwarian tradition," the rationale for Muslims living outside of the *Dar al-Islam* that originated with al-hajj Salim Suwari, the revered scholar who was prominent in the early sixteenth century in the Middle Niger region. In Ghana and Ivory Coast, stereotyped as "pagan" forest zones, the merchant "minority phase" was not a prelude to greater Islamization but a situation of permanence that required a sociology and theology of its own. This tradition is appropriately associated with Ivor Wilks (1968, 2000), whose pioneer works on Suwari and "the transmission of learning" appeared at about the same time as the Levtzion book. But it was Levtzion who read the Arabic correspondence and chronicles; it was he who gave flesh to the tradition and showed it in operation, and who developed the concept of "estates," Muslim, chiefly and commoner, which shifted attention away from the demographics of the historiography and the majority / minority preoccupations of the colonial authorities. A theological "wall" allowed them to construct an interior *Dar al-Islam* of their own.

Closely associated with the Suwarian tradition was the selective appropriation of Islam by the "pagan" population of Ghana, Ivory Coast, and adjacent areas of the forest zone. Clerics prepared — and received generous compensation for — amulets designed for a wide variety of situations of physical health, prosperity, success, and the dangers of war and travel. Muslim ceremonies and themes were incorporated into local rituals. Art historian Rene Bravmann (1983, 2000) carried this vector further than perhaps anyone else in his work on the western fringes of the Akan, on the border between Ghana and Ivory Coast. David Owusu-Ansah (1991, 2000) has developed the rich talismanic tradition for Asante.

Levtzion also helped inspire a generation of researchers to focus on the societies and states of the "Middle Belt," these zones between forest and savannah. Graduate students and scholars at Northwestern, but also at Indiana University and UCLA, examined the estates of Muslims and chiefs, explored the applications of the Suwarian tradition, and looked seriously for Arabic materials. For example, Kathy Green (1984) worked on Kong, the polity in the northeastern corner of what became the Ivory Coast, and the instigator of opposition to Asante on several occasions.[4] John O'Sullivan (1976) worked on Odienne in the northwestern corner, and took it up to the revolutionary changes induced by Samori in the late nineteenth century. Marie Miran (2006) uses the Levtzion framework as background to her study of Muslims in Abidjan. Others have taken the Levtzion idea of estates and applied it further north in the savannah. Emily Osborn (2000 and forthcoming) has examined the region of Kankan, an old Muslim center with a multiplicity of Islamic and non-Islamic corporations. Lucie Colvin (1974) applied the same idea to understand the conflicts of clerics and royals in Cayor, while Tim Cleaveland (2002) uses a similar formula to unpack the social formations of the Saharan town of Walata.

Finally, Levtzion helped break down the existing historiography of Muslim and "pagan" stages, belts and ethnicities in which so much West African research was framed. The Muslims living in Asante, Gonja, Dagomba, Mamprussi and Wa were devout and engaged with chiefs without sacrificing their autonomy. They understood *jihad* as the struggle to sustain their own practice and to witness to the larger community, fully aware that they were not living in the *Dar al-Islam*. They did not represent a stage in a teleological process towards an Islamic state.

Explorations in "Muslim" West Africa

The second work that I emphasize is an exegesis of the manuscripts of one of the Timbuktu histories, the *Ta'rikh al-Fattash* or "chronicle of the researcher." *Fattash* and its companion piece, the *Ta'rikh as-Sudan*, have been available to the wider scholarly community for a century, thanks to the French conquest of Timbuktu and the appropriation of these manuscripts by French Arabists and historians. Maurice Delafosse and his father-in-law, Octave Houdas, provided Arabic editions and carefully annotated French translations of the two chronicles.[5] Together, these accounts have provided the most detailed exposition of the late medieval period of savannah history, notably for the empire of Songhay. The value of the accounts stems in great part from their internal perspectives; they were written and edited by local scholarly families who were contemporary with the events of the sixteenth and seventeenth centuries.[6]

By the title, "A Seventeenth-Century Chronicle by Ibn al-Mukhtar: A Critical Study of *Ta'rikh al-Fattash*" (1971c), we can see that Levtzion framed his article as an exposition of the three manuscripts used by Houdas and Delafosse (1913). It appeared in the *Bulletin of the School of Oriental and African Studies* which devoted considerable space to such solid but circumscribed works. But Levitzion's piece contained a revolutionary charge: he established incontrovertibly that a portion of the chronicle was carefully forged in the early nineteenth century by someone at the court of the Caliphate of Hamdullahi, the Islamic regime of the Middle Niger and a contemporary of the much better known Sokoto Caliphate of Hausaland. Suddenly, he was discussing not only the sixteenth century but the nineteenth, and understanding the West African *jihads* in a new way — as a contest for legitimacy in an area struggling to come into the *Dar al-Islam*.[7]

The Caliphate of Hamdullahi has been regarded as the most thoroughgoing reform movement among the successful *jihads* that completed the main phases of Islamization of the Western and Central Sudan.[8] For John Spencer Trimingham, Hamdullahi represented arrival at the orthodoxy of Islamic practice achieved in the Middle East in earlier centuries. On the basis of the *Fattash* and some French accounts of the early twentieth century, this Islamic authority concluded that the founder,

> Hamadu [Seku Amadu], unlike ʿUthman dan Fodio, proved capable of controlling his Fulbe and showed exceptional administrative abilities. Once his rule was established he organized the state on theocratic lines, appointing an *amir* and a *qadi* to each province, establishing a system of taxation, a *bait-al-mal*, and a form of a military service.... During its short existence the state founded by Shaikh Hamad[u] was the most genuine Islamic state West Africa has ever seen.
>
> At the beginning of the nineteenth century the majority of the Fulbe of the region were still pagan, but they were all required to accept Islam by Shehu Hamadu. Similarly the Bozo and Somono and those Bambara who came under his jurisdiction joined Islam, and in general their conversion was permanent... (Trimingham 1962, 179-80).

Those who have written subsequently have not questioned this judgment (see especially Marion Johnson 1976).

Hamdullahi, in fact, did make very fundamental changes in the social and political organization of the Middle Delta. Under Seku Amadu Bari (reigned 1818-46), the regime forced most of the Fulbe pastoralists to become semi-sedentary and follow established paths of transhumance. It controlled the practices of the merchant families of Jenne, implemented a canonical form of taxation and an extensive system of schools, and dominated the trade caravans of the region. This image in the historiography was strengthened from the 1950s to the 1970s when Amadou Hampâte Bâ et Jean Daget (1955), William Brown (1969), Marion Johnson (1976), and Charles Stewart (1976b) brought the study of Masina into focus alongside the larger body of work on Sokoto. While very little has been done on Hamdullahi in recent decades, the puritan and pristine image articulated by Trimingham is still in place.

What Nehemia did was to lay the basis for a much more troubled and interesting history of the "middle delta" of the river. It had been subject to external domination for centuries — the empires of Mali and Songhay in earlier times, the regime of the Bambara of Segu in the eighteenth century, and to external influence — in particular the networks maintained by the Kunta of Azawad and Timbuktu. Fulbe Ardos controlled the cattle and transhumance, Bambara did much of the farming, Bozo families dominated fishing and river transport, while Marka merchants in Jenne handled trade, but all were subject, to various degrees, to more powerful external forces. There was no local tradition of statehood.

Seku Amadu consequently faced a formidable task as he formulated an agenda for creating a state and a reformed Islamic practice amid competing regional powers. According to the best sources, he sought legitimacy first in the going and growing Islamic power of the time, the regime created around Uthman dan Fodio in Hausaland. By the 1810s Uthman had triumphed over the old sultanate of Gobir, created a new capital at Sokoto, and extended his domain through campaigns in the wider region. These campaigns were led by students and allies equipped with "flags" of authorization. The followers were usually successful, and their new regimes were part of what came to be called the Sokoto Caliphate (Last 1967; Adeleye 1971). Seku Amadu was not a former student, but his envoys secured flags of authorization from Sokoto that were critical for legitimizing his early work of reform, rebellion, and innovation in the Middle Niger.

But Uthman dan Fodio died in 1817, and the Sokoto leadership fell into a succession struggle that was not resolved until 1821, when Muhammad Bello achieved widespread recognition as the caliph. During this period Seku Amadu foreswore his allegiance to Sokoto. He wrote to Bello, invoking a venerable Islamic tradition that the bond could not be sustained when more than one person claimed to rule in the name of Islam (Stewart 1976a). More important was the success that Seku Amadu achieved against his local foes. He defeated the Bambara of Segu at the battle of Noukouma in 1818, triumphed over some rival reformers, pressured influential Fulbe leaders into submission, and created his new capital at Hamdullahi, "in praise of God." At this juncture, in the early 1820s, his ambition and vision went well beyond the confines of a province of the Sokoto regime.

Alongside the ambition came new troubles, troubles that make the exegesis of Nehemia Levtzion all the more important. The opposition from the kingdom of Segu in the southwest diminished, but a more serious internal opposition developed as Seku Amadu and his council in Hamdullahi sought to implement their vision of an Islamic state. The Fulbe Ardos, in particular, chafed at new restrictions on transhumance, family life, and taxation, and they resented the prominence given to pious and learned Muslims.

Serious external opposition came now from the northeast and the Kunta — who saw themselves as the arbiters of Islamic practice in West Africa. The Kunta, led by Sidi Muhammad, son of the reformer and Sufi leader Sidi al-Mukhtar al-Kabir, ran a vast trading and consulting firm with tentacles reaching through the Western and Central Sudan, and they ran much of their operation out of Timbuktu. As merchants they profited from the grain exports of the Middle Niger and the regional trade in salt and tobacco. As scholars they considered themselves to be the experienced and sophisticated interpreters of Islamic practice in the savannah. Hamdullahi, with its strict control of the Middle Delta economy and its ban on tobacco, was a significant obstacle. The Kunta portrayed the new regime as rigid and primitive in its understanding of the faith and law of Islam. They also encouraged rebellion, and played a key role in persuading Ardo Galajo, one of Seku Amadu's most powerful early allies, to pull out his support. Galajo dominated the province of Kunari, a source of grain and avenue for trade, and threatened the capital itself.[9]

Consequently, by the mid 1820s Seku Amadu faced a critical challenge to his fledgling state. As we can tentatively construct it, he prevailed after several years of intensive struggle. He put down the revolt of Galajo, drove him into exile, and established his supremacy over Timbuktu by 1826. At the same time he persuaded Alfa Nuh ibn Tahir, a Masina scholar who had studied with the Kunta, to leave the entourage of Galajo and the counsels of Sidi Muhammad to join forces with him at Hamdullahi. Then and there the scholar — Alfa Nuh — and the reformer and military leader — Seku Amadu — joined forces in one of the boldest manipulations that West African history has ever witnessed. It is this manipulation, in the form of manuscript C, that Levtzion reveals with striking clarity in his article.[10]

Alfa Nuh and Seku Amadu formulated a new introduction to the *Ta'rikh al-Fattash* which made Askiya Muhammad of Songhay the eleventh caliph of the *Dar al-Islam* and provided a prophecy for a twelfth caliph who would emerge at a later time, in the Middle Delta, with the name Ahmad.[11] It placed this prophecy in a declaration made by the famous Egyptian scholar, al-Suyuti, to Askiya Muhammad on the occasion of the latter's pilgrimage to Mecca at the end of the fifteenth century:

> A man of virtue, knowledge and piety, faithful to the Sunna and named Ahmad, will emerge in the islands of Masina, in the one of Sebera. He will belong to the family of scholars of the Sangare. He will inherit from you the title of caliph, as well as your fairness, virtue, generosity, devotion, piety and success.... He will rise higher than you, because he will know more, for you in fact know only the rules about prayer, alms and the main doctrines. He will be the last of the caliphs... (Houdas and Delafosse 1913, 18).

The forgery reinforced this account by making the first author of the chronicle, Mahmud Kati, a companion to the Askiya on his journey. Levtzion, in perhaps his most important contribution in the article, is able to establish convincingly that Mahmud was born in the early sixteenth century and therefore could not possibly have accompanied the Askiya on the pilgrimage of the 1490s.[12] The forgery also included a deliberation that Askiya Muhammad held, on his return from the pilgrimage, with the famous traveling consultant al-Maghili. Al-Maghili confirmed the validity of the statements of al-Suyuti (Houdas and Delafosse 1913, 22-23). Alfa Nuh and Seku Amadu then reworked a number of the extant copies of the chronicle and announced to Muslim rulers in North and West Africa that Seku was in fact the prophesied twelfth caliph of Islam. They almost succeeded in modifying the extant copies of the *Ta'rikh al-Fattash* or destroying those that they could not change.[13]

In this new dispensation, Sokoto and its flags were no longer important. Masina had taken its legitimacy back to the Askiya and a leading Egyptian scholar, and indeed to the foundations of Islam itself. The measure of the success of this effort is the wide acknowledgment of the account in the oral traditions recorded by Amadou Hampâte Bâ in the mid-twentieth century and reflected in *Empire peul du Macina* (Bâ et Daget 1955).[14]

The manipulation dealt with a second issue that went to the heart of the new centralized regime: the control of the people of the Middle Delta. In manuscript C, al-Suyuti authorizes state control of groups of skilled workers. Artisan castes have long been a part of Western Sudanese society, originating probably in the Mande traditions and the Mali Empire, as the work of Tamari Tal (1997) has suggested. They were very much part of the Songhay tradition and the reign of Askiya Muhammad, who considered certain artisans to be serfs, even slaves, and gave them as gifts to important Muslim notables. In the fabricated part of the *Fattash* al-Suyuti gives to Askiya Muhammad and the twelfth caliph control of twelve castes or tribes in perpetuity. This was designed to increase Hamdullahi's control over the Niger boatmen, who played such a crucial role in river transport and the security of the kingdom, and of the slaves, freedmen, and artisans who had helped establish the caliphate. Seku Amadu, as he consolidated his regime, needed to dominate these constituencies and sustain the traditional social hierarchy.[15]

In this seemingly modest article, Levtzion set the stage for a much more fascinating interpretation of the emergence of an Islamic regime in the early nineteenth century. Seku Amadu faced enormous obstacles in the fertile and attractive Middle Delta, with no strong state tradition, at a time of intensifying Islamization and Islamic distinction. He perhaps did achieve, as the Trimingham quotation suggests, more than any of his rivals in the Western and

Central Sudan. Nearby was a strong pagan regime in the form of the Segu Bambara. Inside were strong constituencies accustomed to substantial autonomy. To the northeast lay the formidable network of the Kunta, who prided themselves as the arbiters of faith and practice throughout the Western and Central Sudan. The Kunta considered themselves superior to the state forms of Islam, both the "primitive" one in Hamdullahi and the more "sophisticated" one of Sokoto; they could influence them by provoking revolt or withholding approval. The Sokoto regime, where Seku Amadu turned for initial support, was the rage of Fulbe scholars of the day, and its literary production filled the libraries of would be reformers.[16]

It was in this context that Seku Amadu and Alfa Nuh developed a brilliant tradition of pilgrimage and prophecy which trumped rival claims and buttressed the highly centralized regime that dominated the Middle Niger for several decades. Levtzion prepared the way for this interpretation, which scholars will undoubtedly develop in the years to come.

Conclusion

Nehemia Levtzion made a wide and original range of contributions to enrich our understanding of African history and Islam, and he did so from the very beginning of his public career in the late 1960s. His great value can be seen in the longevity of his work — it continues to be relevant, even as we move well beyond the formulas of Trimingham and his contemporaries. *Muslims and Chiefs* sets the stage for continuing research in the southern parts of West Africa, conceived as multi-religious arenas of conflict and cooperation and not as a "frontier" of Islam. "A Seventeenth-Century Chronicle" opens up the history of the Caliphate of Hamdullahi for an enterprising re-interpreter of the *jihadic* states of the savannah in the eighteenth and nineteenth centuries. It suggests the intensive struggles for legitimation of Muslim communities in a region that was making increasing claims to belong to the *Dar al-Islam*.

Notes

[1] The main author of the "vulgate" of Islam and Islamization in Africa, with a special emphasis on West Africa, was John Spencer Trimingham, who came out of a British missionary background. Oxford University Press

published his *Islam in West Africa* (1959) and *A History of Islam in West Africa* (1962), as well as works on Islam in the Sudan and Ethiopia. The French "equivalents" of this work were Gouilly (1952) and Froelich (1962).

[2] Charles Stewart questioned the artificial division between Saharan and Sahelian zones in 1976.

[3] For a recent reflection on these constructions, see Jean-Louis Triaud's introduction to Robinson and Triaud (1997). For a formulation valid for Senegal, see Robinson (1992).

[4] One could add to this the students trained under Ivor Wilks over the years, all beneficiaries of the work of Levtzion and his occasional visiting professorships at Northwestern.

[5] Houdas (1913) and Houdas and Delafosse (1913). Reprinted editions were published in 1964 by Adrien-Maisonneuve. More recently John Hunwick (1999) has published a new translation and annotation of the first.

[6] The chronicles are the natural complements to the external accounts that Levtzion and Hopkins put together in the *Corpus of Early Arabic Sources for West African History*. They were widely known in Timbuktu scholarly circles, available in some personal libraries, and cited to European travelers such as Rene Caillié, Heinrich Barth, and Felix Dubois. They also entered into the oral traditions of the whole Middle Niger.

[7] The forgery had been acknowledged before in Western sources, beginning at least as early as Felix Dubois (1896, chapter 7), and it was documented in Houdas' and Delafosse's translations. But no one carefully examined what parts were invented and why until Levtzion's article, which sets the stage for a new interpretation of the Caliphate of Hamdullahi and its struggle to establish itself in a highly charged political and religious arena.

[8] See my "Islamic Revolutions in the Western Sudan" (2002b) for a recent summary of the literature and the place of the Hamdullahi regime. The most complete accounts of the Masina phenomenon are Amadou Hampâte Bâ et Jean Daget (1955); William Brown (1969); and Bintou Sanankoua (1990). In the 1970s, Brown drafted a manuscript, "Hamdullahi! Hamdullahi! Watani! A Social and Political History of a Wa Nomocracy ca. 1818-1862 AD," which recast his research and dissertation but has never been published.

[9] The Kunta continued to chafe at the demands of Hamdullahi as late as 1853-54, when they sought to encourage a much older Galajo to come back from exile and lead a revolt against the Caliphate, with Tuareg support. This comes from the explorer Heinrich Barth, who visited Timbuktu as the guest of Ahmad al-Bakkay, son of Sidi Muhammad and leader of the family at the time (Barth 1857 [1965]). Barth had already encountered Galajo in the Gurma region, on land offered by the leaders of the Sokoto regime, and he absorbed the Ardo's version of the reform movement of Seku Amadu (1857, 3: 179-84). For Galajo's support of Seku Amadu and his subsequent rebellion, see Bâ et Daget (1955, chapters 3 and 6).

[10] The evidence for Alfa Nuh's key role in the forgery is circumstantial but very strong. He wrote the letters to the rulers of the Maghrib and West Africa announcing Seku Amadu's accession as the twelfth caliph of Islam (see the Umarian or Archinard collection in the Bibliothèque Nationale de Paris, 5259, ff. 74-78; they can also be found in the Fonds Gironcourt of the Institut de France). Nuh's defection from the court of Galajo to that of Hamdullahi is well attested in the traditions of Masina (Bâ et Daget 1955, 111-14).

[11] The ten others had already served, according to this prophecy: five in Medine, two in Cairo, one in Syria, and two in Iraq (Houdas and Delafosse 1913, 17). Presumably, four of the Medine caliphs were the "righteous" administrators who succeeded after the death of Muhammad. Syria and Iraq rulers presumably refer to the Umayyad and Abbasid regimes, or particular caliphs in them.

[12] Mahmud Kati is the figure usually associated with *Ta'rikh el-Fattach*, but in fact the chronicle was written by several members of his family over three generations, including his grandson Ibn al-Mukhtar, who figures in the title of the Levtzion article. See Levtzion (1971a, 573-76), and Houdas and Delafosse (1913, xvii-xvii), where they advance a date of 1468 for the birth of Mahmud Kati.

[13] Felix Dubois (1896, 301-04) recounts an interesting tradition where the "original" copy of the *Fattach* controlled by a descendant of the Kati family was seized by a delegation from Hamdullahi, but was lost when the canoe capsized on the way back to the capital. We get a sense of the celebrity of the caliphate in the 1820s when Abd al-Karim, a Tijaniyya scholar of Futa Jalon and teacher of al-hajj Umar, journeyed to Hamdullahi to witness the achievement (Bâ et Daget 1955, chapter 11).

[14] See especially the first chapter, focused on the pilgrimage of Askiya Muhammad, his conversations with Arabian and Egyptian intellectuals of the late fifteenth century, his appointment as the eleventh caliph of the Islamic world, and the prophecy of a twelfth caliph by the name of Ahmad. It is striking to see how the Masina oral traditions, which form the basis of Bâ et Daget (1955), have absorbed the forged version of *Fattash*. Sanankoua (1990, 57-65) repeats the same understanding of Hamdullahi's legitimacy. Brown (1969, 6-7) has an interesting commentary on the uniformity of the oral and written traditions of the Middle Delta. The tradition was not widely accepted in Timbuktu and other places outside of Masina.

[15] Levtzion (1971a, 590-91), where he cites a letter from William Brown dated 17 November 1969. The relevant passages of the published *Ta'rikh el-Fattach* are 19-22 of Houdas and Delafosse (1913). The *Ta'rikh* mentions twenty-four "tribes" or castes, but only spells out the identity of twelve of them.

[16] See Robinson (1985a, chapter 9) for a comparison of the regimes created by the *jihads* of the eighteenth and nineteenth centuries.

Neo-Sufism: Reconsidered Again

John O. Voll

Résumé

Le Néo-Sufisme est un terme utilisé par les intellectuels, tels Nehemia Levtzion, pour décrire un ensemble de mouvements de la renaissance islamique à la fin du dix-huitième siècle et au début du dix-neuvième. Au début des années 1990, certains critiques en sont arrivés à considérer ce terme comme la représentation d'un consensus conceptuel erroné, puisqu'on n'avait pas compris les mouvements Sufi. Au début du vingt-et-unième siècle, un ré-examen de cette critique a abouti à la conclusion, dans l'analyse de cet article, que la critique soulève d'importantes questions mais a besoin d'être modifiée à la lumière de récentes études. Les organisations Sufi de cette période sont considérées comme "nouvelles." En ce qui concerne le contenu, certains aspects des conceptualisations du "néo-Sufisme" sont confirmés, mais de telle manière que s'impose une modification, d'une part des premières descriptions relativement simplistes données par le prétendu consensus, d'autre part, des lignes dures de la critique. La recherche de Nehemia Levtzion joue un rôle important dans ce révisionnisme.

Abstract

Neo-Sufism is a term used by scholars, including Nehemia Levtzion, to describe a set of movements of Islamic renewal in the late eighteenth and early nineteenth centuries. By the early 1990s, the term came to be viewed by some critics as representing a conceptual consensus that was erroneous in its understanding of Sufi movements. At the beginning of the twenty-first century, a reconsideration of this critique leads to the conclusion, in this article's analysis, that the critique raises important issues but needs to be modified in view of recent scholarship. The Sufi organizations of the period are seen as being "new." In terms of content, certain aspects of the

---

This article is based on a presentation made as a part of a Roundtable on "Engaging with a Legacy: Nehemia Levtzion and Islam in Africa" at the 2004 annual meeting of the African Studies Association in New Orleans. I greatly appreciate the insights from the discussions in that panel.

"neo-Sufism" conceptualizations are confirmed, but in ways that require modification of both the relatively simplistic early descriptions in the so-called consensus and the stark lines of the critique. Nehemia Levtzion's research is important in this revisionism.

Introduction

Movements of Islamic revival and reform are an important part of Islamic history. Scholars approach the study of these movements in different ways, and sometimes debates develop concerning distinctive interpretations of the processes of Islamic renewal. At the beginning of the twenty-first century, such debates are important in policy analysis, as extremist Muslim movements capture headlines. Fierce debates rage over effective responses to terrorist groups claiming to be part of an Islamic resurgence. Unfortunately, much less attention is given to Muslim movements of renewal and reform that are not associated with violence.

In broader historical terms, many movements of Islamic renewal have played important roles in the histories of states and societies across the Muslim world. Many such movements are associated with Sufi *tariqahs* or brotherhoods. Some scholars identified such Sufi organizations in the period of the eighteenth and early nineteenth centuries CE as "Neo-Sufism." Nehemia Levtzion was among this group of scholars and he wrote a number of studies examining the characteristics of Neo-Sufism (Levtzion 1986, 2002).[1] The interpretation of movements of Islamic renewal within the conceptual framework of Neo-Sufism resulted in a critique providing a critical analysis of the conceptual construct. This critique was drawn together in a comprehensive article by R.S. O'Fahey and Bernd Radtke, "Neo-Sufism Reconsidered" (1993). More than a decade following the publication of this article, it is useful to "reconsider again" the issues involved in the conceptualization of eighteenth and nineteenth century Islamic renewal movements as a part of the discussion of the scholarly legacy of Nehemia Levtzion. While this "reconsideration again" will not involve the dramatic headlines relating to movements at the beginning of the twenty-first century, it can provide important insights into the development of scholarly understanding of such movements within a broader historical framework.

The Concept of Neo-Sufism

The development of the concept of "Neo-Sufism" as an identification for a certain type of Sufi organization in the eighteenth and early nineteenth centuries is relatively simple. Already in the nineteenth century, Western scholars examining Muslim activist movements noted the importance of Sufi *tariqahs* within the groups of the most successful renewalist movements. French scholars, many of whom were associated with colonial administration and concerned with issues of security, provided elaborate descriptions of a new, activist style of Sufi brotherhood. Because of the geographic concentration on North Africa of French interests in the Muslim world, most of these analyses emphasized brotherhoods active in North and West Africa. Some of the most important of these studies were those by Louis Rinn (1884), A. Le Chatelier (1887), and the co-authored volume by Octave Depont and Xavier Coppolani (1897), written in the late nineteenth century. These volumes provided descriptions of virtually every major *tariqah* operating in North and West Africa, giving special attention to "pan-Islamic" and possibly militant aspects of their activities.

In the analyses of Islamic activist movements early in the twentieth century, similar attention was given to Sufi brotherhoods whose origins were in the traditions later identified as "Neo-Sufi." A good example is the discussion by Lothrop Stoddard (1921) following World War I. He identified "Pan-Islamism" as an important element in world affairs in the 1920s when major movements opposed to European imperialism were being defined. In his view, "Pan-Islamism" had been uncoordinated during the early nineteenth century, but the "beginnings of self-conscious, systematic Pan-Islamism date from about the middle of the nineteenth century" when the movement was shaped by the effective organization of major Sufi brotherhoods, especially the Sanusiyya, which was one of the most visible orders at the time because of its resistance to Italian imperialism in Libya (Stoddard 1921, 52). At the same time, the director of intelligence in the Anglo-Egyptian Sudan, C.A. Willis, wrote a "speculative" report in 1922, which was to provide a "general resumé" of Muslim political propaganda and movements. The report provides a wide-ranging summary of Islamic movements that might be security risks, ranging from the very local (a teacher in Nyala in western Sudan) to grand Pan-

Islamic schemes in which Willis portrays Mustafa Kemal [Ataturk], the Sansusis, Saad Zaghloul's Egyptian nationalists, and others as part of a large pattern of resistance to the West. Again, Sufi *tariqahs* played an important part in the framework of his general analysis (Willis 1921, 1922).

Whether or not the label of "Neo-Sufi" is appropriate for the activist orders of the late eighteenth and nineteenth centuries, these brotherhoods were a significant force in the Muslim world. However biased, Eurocentric, and imperialist the French scholars and others may have been, the attention that they gave to the well-organized orders of the nineteenth century was not misplaced. Sufi *tariqahs* provided the organizational base for many of the most efficient movements of opposition to European imperialist expansion in the nineteenth century, from Algeria to the Caucasus to Southeast Asia (Voll 1999).

Attention continued to be given to the reformist-renewalist brotherhoods during the twentieth century. O'Fahey and Radtke (1993, 55-57) provide a useful history of the development of the concept and the usage of the term. The concept that there was a special type of Sufi order emerging at the end of the eighteenth century developed before the term "Neo-Sufi" was applied to that style. One of the key scholars in this development was J. Spencer Trimingham, most of whose work concentrated on the history of Islam in Africa. In his local / regional studies, he noted the emergence of activist, *tariqah*-based movements of renewal and reform in the late eighteenth and nineteenth centuries, and much of this analysis was summarized in his wide-ranging historical survey of *The Sufi Orders in Islam*, containing a major chapter on "Nineteenth-Century Revival Movements" (Trimingham 1998). This view was also presented by H.A.R. Gibb, who noted that in "India, in Central Asia, and in most of the outlying lands, there were Sufi revivals during the nineteenth century," and that in the early nineteenth century, "the most striking of these newer developments was the formation of reformist missionary congregations on a strict orthodox basis, but organized on the lines of the Sufi *tariqas*" (1953, 130-31).

The idea of a style of Sufism that involved an activist sense of renewal and reform had developed over a long period of time. It remained for Fazlur Rahman to provide a label for the many different tendencies and movements that had been noted by people like Trimingham and Gibb. O'Fahey and Radtke identify Fazlur Rahman as the "first to employ the term" Neo-Sufism (1993, 55). Fazlur Rahman used this term in the first (and subsequent) editions of his general introduction to Islam as a useful way of referring to "Sufism reformed on orthodox lines and interpreted in an activist sense" (1968, 254). In broader historical terms, Fazlur Rahman used the term for a general response to popular religious practices and theosophies that could be more clearly understood within the limits of a more-narrowly defined interpretation of Islam, reconciling the populist Sufi legacy with "orthodox Islam." Rahman argues:

> ... the moral motive of Sufism was emphasized and some of its technique of *dhikr* or *murâqaba*, "spiritual concentration," adopted. But the object and content of this concentration were identified with orthodox doctrine and the goal redefined as the strengthening of faith in dogmatic tenets and the moral purity of the spirit. This type of neo-Sufism, as one may call it, tended to regenerate orthodox activism and reinculcate a positive attitude to this world (1968, 239).

In Rahman's analysis, this development had important specific consequences:

> Besides the changes wrought in the doctrines and practices of the old established Sufi orders through this new development, certain new brotherhoods with an entirely fresh orientation came to be formed in the nineteenth century, such as the Sanusiya in North Africa and the Muhammadiya in India, which were strictly orthodox in *spirit* and practice and differed radically from the traditional objectives of the old orders (1968, 202 [emphasis in original]).

These new brotherhoods have become, in subsequent scholarship, most closely identified with the term "Neo-Sufism."

The term began as a way of identifying a cluster of organizations and developments in the eighteenth and nineteenth centuries. It was more a term of descriptive convenience than a proposed theory of Muslim renewal movements. In that mode, it entered historical discussions of movements throughout the Muslim world. By the mid-1980s, it was possible to examine the general subject in a more organized manner. Levtzion took the lead in convening a year-long (1984-85) study group on the socio-political roles of the *ulama* in Islam at the Institute for Advanced Studies of the Hebrew University in Jerusalem. Then he and I organized an International Colloquium on "Eighteenth Century Renewal and Reform in Islam" in June 1985; debates were vigorous about the nature of Neo-Sufism and whether or not there was a group of phenomena to which the label could be applied. The result of the Colloquium was a 1987 volume of the same title (Levtzion and Voll 1987a).

The article by O'Fahey and Radtke (1993) marked the important next stage of the debate over Neo-Sufism and in the early 1990s it became formalized. O'Fahey and Radtke felt that something called "the neo-Sufi consensus" (1993, 56) had emerged, although it should be noted that many of the scholars identified as being creators or part of the consensus were unaware that such a formal school of thought actually existed. The scholars in this so-called consensus school had largely used the term as a convenience rather than thinking that they were establishing a particular theory that could have a label. Nevertheless, in many ways, that article represented a summation of debates about Neo-Sufism.

Subsequently, scholars like Albrecht Hofheinz (1999) and Mark Sedgwick (1998) studied specific topics related to the "Neo-Sufism debates" but there has been no broad interpretative summary of the particular issues raised by O'Fahey and Radtke, even though much important work has been done. Instead, heated debates relating to movements of revival in Islam shifted to other topics in the context of the 1990s with arguments about the "Clash of Civilizations" and the nature of Muslim militancy in an era of increased terrorist activity.

In this current stage of scholarship, it becomes useful to revisit some of the debates of the early 1990s. As O'Fahey and Radtke put it,

> To summarize the neo-Sufi consensus point-by-point: new "Reformist" Sufi orders arose in the eighteenth and nineteenth centuries. These orders differed markedly from the pre-existing localized often clan-based brotherhoods (1993, 56).

They then provided a summary of what they felt were the nine main characteristics of Neo-Sufism, especially as it had been described by Trimingham ([1971] 1998), Voll ([1982] 1994), and B. G. Martin (1976). O'Fahey and Radtke's framework, in turn, provided the basis for objections to the so-called consensus defining Neo-Sufism by others in the field.

Objections: Neo-Sufism is Not New

The first basic objection to "Neo-Sufism" was terminological — "Neo-Sufism" means that there was "new" Sufism. The argument has been that the characteristics discussed in the "consensus scholarship" involve many things that are elements of continuity and are not "new" to Sufism at the end of the eighteenth century. The critique of the so-called consensus, as presented by scholars like O'Fahey and Radtke in their article, maintained that Neo-Sufism was not "new" at all. In light of recent scholarship, this assessment of the lack of "newness" requires reconsideration since, at least in terms of organizational structures "Neo-Sufi" organizations are seen as, in fact, being "new." Levtzion continued to argue strongly for the novelty of the developing organizations as he had in his early discussions of Neo-Sufism. For example, in his chapter in *The Public Sphere in Muslim Societies*, Levtzion argues: "In the eighteenth century, brotherhoods transformed from old patterns of decentralized diffusive affiliation into larger-scale organizations, more coherent and centralized" (2002, 114). In other words, in the late eighteenth century and the early nineteenth century, a new kind of Sufism was really emerging.

It is in terms of organization that the newness of the developing *tariqahs* has been most strongly supported by recent scholarship. O'Fahey (1990), in his authoritative study of Ahmad ibn Idris, one of those teachers most frequently identified as a "Neo-Sufi," examined the organizational dimensions of the new brotherhoods. He distinguished issues relating to intellectual content from those dealing with organization. O'Fahey states:

> I have preferred to use, without prejudicing its intellectual content, neo-Sufism to mean a new organizational phenomenon that appeared in certain areas of the Muslim world in the late eighteenth and early nineteenth centuries. In these areas, new orders were established that were relatively more centralized and less prone to fission than their predecessors; they introduced into areas where they proselytized new forms of social organization, often based on autonomous agricultural communities, *zâwiya* or *jamâ'a*; recruited *en masse*, and later

were politically active (1990, 4-5).

The newness of the organizations created by people called Neo-Sufi has been emphasized by a number of recent studies. O'Fahey and Radtke themselves note that at least some of the organizations discussed in the "Neo-Sufi consensus" represented significant innovations. They note, for example, that a student of Ibn Idris, al-Sanusi, "created in Cyrenaica a network of institutions which in design and function were totally new to the society in which they were implanted," while other Idrisi students in Sudan incorporated "pre-existing religious centres into a new supra-community *tariqa* network" (O'Fahey and Radtke 1993, 76, 79). Knut Viker argues that this institutional newness was a conscious part of the program of Muhammad al-Sanusi as he set out to establish his mission in Cyrenaica:

> Al-Sanusi set out from Mecca to realize an organizational ideal; although the spiritual contents of the ideal were to spread the teachings of Ibn Idris, not his own, he was looking for geographical space to establish something new in terms of institutions (1995, 144).

Similarly, a comprehensive study of Sufi brotherhoods in Sudan during the nineteenth century by Ali Salih Karrar (1992) distinguishes between the older decentralized orders in Sudan and "centralized brotherhoods" that began to come to Sudan in the early nineteenth century. The two centralized orders that Karrar discusses are the Sammaniyyah and the Khatmiyyah, which he says "were part of a general revivalist or reformist movement which reached its climax during the second half of the eighteenth and the early nineteenth centuries" (1992, 42). Karrar notes that the "many strands within the reform movement" included "a number of new Sufi *tariqas*" and some strands included Naqshbandi teachers in South Asia as well as the brotherhoods that came to Sudan (1992, 42-43).

In terms of organization, new kinds of brotherhood structures emerged. Despite the assertions by some scholars that "Neo-Sufism" was not really new, recent scholarship indicates important innovations in structures. Whether the new organizations are called "Neo-Sufi" or something else, there was something new happening during the eighteenth and early nineteenth centuries.

The Issue of "Union with the Spirit of the Prophet"

In the concepts and content attributed to the Neo-Sufis, the so-called "Neo-Sufi consensus" has been most thoroughly criticized. Most of the early discussions were part of broader surveys of Islamic history and they did not go in depth into the writings of individual teachers and scholars involved in the activities described. As more research has been done on the content of the teachings and writings of individuals associated with the development of Neo-Sufism, the discussions have gained a wealth of detail that moves beyond earlier simplistic generalizations. One such generalist interpretation was articulated by Gibb, among others — namely that Ahmad ibn Idris "rejected entirely the Sufi doctrine of union with God, substituting for it, as the goal of the mystical life, mystical union with the spirit of the Prophet" (1953, 131). This assertion may have originated in the analysis of an Italian Orientalist, C.A. Nallino, and was repeated in many accounts of the development of Neo-Sufi thought (Sedgwick 1998, 48).

O'Fahey and Radtke put bluntly the basic argument against this position:

> ... the idea that Ibn Idris substituted union with the Prophet for union with God is nonsense. For him, as for Sufism since its inception, the *imitatio Muhammadi* was a means, a way to the union of God — not a substitute (1993, 70).

This is an interesting assertion of the unchanging nature of the major goals of Sufi devotion, regardless of the era or context. They note that two of Ibn Idris's students in the early nineteenth century discuss the "'passing away' in the Prophet," that is, having some mystical union with the Prophet, as only one stage in the broader mystical processes of "passing away:" the first stage is "passing away" in the spiritual guide or teacher, the second is passing away in the Prophet, which is described as simply a step toward "passing away" in God (O'Fahey and Radtke 1993, 70).

Subsequent research suggests that this issue is not simply a choice between two clearly defined positions. Vikør notes an important passage in the writings of Ibn Idris's student, al-Sanusi, that Nallino cites as supporting the "union with the Prophet" hypothesis. However, Vikor argues that the passage from al-Sanusi does not suggest a special union with the Prophet, saying that in Vikor's reading of the text,

... it is also clear that there is no question of a union with the Prophet in the same way as one experiences union with God. The text clearly and repeatedly refers to meeting the Prophet, standing face to face with him as it were, in the most physical sense. It even refers to the *muhammadi* asking the Prophet for guidance, thus bringing the encounter on to a completely different level to that of the mystical union with the divine (1995, 234).

However, other recent scholarship would suggest that students of Ibn Idris were talking about more than simply meeting with the Prophet and asking for advice. Albrecht Hofheinz, in his analysis of the teachings of Muhammad al-Majdhub, a Sudanese student of Ibn Idris, states that al-Majdhub notes the special cosmic role of the Prophet in the life of the Muslim believer. Hofheinz points to the fact that this is specially defined in al-Majdhub's *mawlid* (poems honoring the Prophet on the traditional birthday):

The fact that Majdhub was the most prolific of the first generation of Sudanese *mawlid* authors indicates the central importance he assigned to the Prophet in shaping the ritual life of the community of his followers. This central role of the Prophet is also reflected in the content of Majdhub's *mawlids:* the Eternal Muhammad becomes the focal symbol of Islamic identity. The *mawlids* deal with his birth — that is, his coming into this world — and with his unique relationship to God (1999, 391).

This more cosmic description of the Prophet and his place in the universe may reflect a long-term significance for the concept of union with the spirit of the Prophet. Valerie Hoffman argues that "annihilation in the Messenger of God" is a long-standing part of Sufi thought. Hoffman argues that rather than this concept being "a distinctly 'neo-Sufi development,'" it has a long history and is firmly rooted in the influential writings of the medieval Sufi teacher, Ibn al-`Arabi (Hoffman 1999, 351-52). Specifically, in Hoffman's view,

... the practice of annihilation in the Messenger by Sufis in the tradition of Ahmad ibn Idris represents neither an innovation nor a rejection of Ibn `Arabi ... [A]nnihilation in the Messenger is linked with the doctrines of Ibn `Arabi concerning the Muhammadan Reality and did not originate with modern Islamic reformism (1999, 365).

At the same time, she emphasizes that Sufism in general and the place of the Prophet in Sufi piety is not static. In fact, Hoffman notes: "Scholars have long noted that the Prophet Muhammad assumed increasing importance in Sufi thought and practice over the centuries" (1999, 351). This position may provide a basis for modifying the older competing views. Hoffman concludes: "The practice of meditation on the Prophet may have undergone changes and appears to have gained in importance in recent centuries, but it is not a radical departure from pre-modern Sufi tradition" (1999, 365). From this perspective, the changing place of Muhammad in Sufi devotional conceptualizations at the beginning of the nineteenth century may not represent a radical innovation warranting the label "Neo-Sufism." At the same time, the ideas and approaches of people like al-Majdhub clearly do reflect the continually changing nature of devotional orientation and the place of the Prophet Muhammad in the teaching and devotions of *tariqahs* at the beginning of the nineteenth century. Sufism's vision of the Prophet was not static. The developments in the practice of meditation on the Prophet in the eighteenth century may not have been a "radical innovation" but these meditational practices were different from earlier ones. This mode of Sufism is not simply a continuation of practices and beliefs unchanged from medieval times.

Neo-Sufism and Ibn al-`Arabi

Hoffman's discussion of "union with the spirit of the Prophet" notes another part of the debate about Neo-Sufism raised by O'Fahey and Radtke. One of the nine characteristics of Neo-Sufism as defined by their "consensus" is: "Rejection of Ibn al-`Arabi's teachings, especially his doctrine of *wahdat al-wujud*" (O'Fahey and Radtke 1993, 57). Part of O'Fahey and Radtke's persuasiveness on this point reflects a rhetorical reductionism in their description of the "Neo-Sufi consensus." They describe scholars in the "consensus" group as being more absolute in their statements about the Neo-Sufi position on Ibn al-`Arabi, but the presentation of the so-called consensus position is usually more nuanced. For example, my description of Mustafa al-Bakri, a teacher often mentioned by the "consensus scholars" as important in the Islamic revival involved with "Neo-Sufism," states that "Al-Bakri thus combined the *tariqah* of Ottoman respectability [the Khalwatiyyah

Tariqah] with the *reinterpretation* of the Sufi theology of Ibn al-`Arabi and the more activist mood of the Naqshbandiyyah" (Voll 1994, 39-40). Another source cited as reflecting the Neo-Sufi consensus, Levtzion and Voll, state:

> Some of the major figures in the eighteenth-century revivalist networks of scholars ... were still under the influence of Ibn al-`Arabi. There was, however, a shift away from the approach and mood of Ibn al-`Arabi (1987a, 9).

These analyses present a picture in which Ibn al-`Arabi is being reinterpreted, but still has influence. This critique of the "Neo-Sufi consensus" tends to concentrate on the tradition of Ahmad Ibn Idris. In talking about Ibn al-`Arabi and Neo-Sufism, O'Fahey and Radtke base their critique almost exclusively on a discussion of the Idrisi tradition. They note "a suspicious if not negative view of Ibn al-`Arabi" among the "Neo-Sufis," but then simply state that "the writings of the neo-Sufis *of the Idrisi tradition* are so clear that again one must wonder how this cliché [about rejecting Ibn al-`Arabi] arose" (1993, 71 [emphasis added]). The response to this implied question is simply that the the Idrisi tradition is not the only manifestation of what the scholars were discussing when they described "Neo-Sufism." Examination of movements other than those in the Idrisi tradition can provide a broader base for drawing conclusions about the nature of "Neo-Sufism" and its views of the teachings of Ibn al-`Arabi.

This gap in the critique is most visible when O'Fahey and Radtke discuss the concept of *wahdat al-wujud* ("unity of being"), a concept central to the tradition of Ibn al-`Arabi. Some discussions of "Neo-Sufism" note that this concept had been rejected by the renewal movements included in broader discussions of "Neo-Sufism." However, O'Fahey and Radtke simply state: "The term itself is never used" (1993, 72), citing this absence only with reference to writers in the Idrisi tradition. This ignores the major traditions, frequently discussed in examinations of Neo-Sufism, associated with the Naqshbandiyyah tradition of the Indian scholar-teacher, Ahmad Sirhindi (1564-1624).

Sirhindi, called the "Renewer *(mujaddid)* of the Second Millennium," presented an alternative to Ibn al-`Arabi's concepts of *wahdat al-wujud* and this position was continued among "Neo-Sufi" activists in the Mujaddidi tradition into the nineteenth century. Some scholars have argued that Sirhindi "criticised the doctrine of *wahdat al-wujud* and showed that it was incompatible both with the Shari'ah and the experience of difference which the Sufi ultimately realises" (Ansari 1986, 6). However, some recent scholarship argues that this position exaggerates or misreads the positions of Sirhindi, and that the vigorous opposition to Ibn al-`Arabi's *wujudi* conceptualization is actually the product of later activists in the Mujaddidi tradition of the Naqshbandiyyah. Dina Le Gall, for example, expresses agreement with the argument presented by Hamid Algar that

... the notion of the Naqshbandiyya's hostility toward him [Ibn al-`Arabi] must originate in later (and in his view exaggerated) readings of the criticism of Ahmad Sirhindi, and more generally in a later sensibility that casts observance of the *sharia* as inconsistent with theosophical speculation (2005, 126).

This historical revisionism that reinterprets the role of Sirhindi and his positions regarding Ibn al-`Arabi and *wahdat al-wujud* does not contradict the descriptions of Neo-Sufism. Instead, it provides some interesting support for those descriptions by arguing that the opposition to Ibn al-`Arabi's conceptualizations did not emerge in the sixteenth and early seventeenth centuries, but rather is the product of Mujaddidi Naqshbandis in the late eighteenth and nineteenth centuries. In other words, the "kind of historiographical anachronism" (Le Gall 2005, 126) that attributes these views to Sirhindi is a product of Sufi activist narratives in the period when Neo-Sufism was said to be developing. In important ways this confirms that at least among some of the so-called "Neo-Sufis," there was a rejection of some of the teachings of Ibn al-`Arabi, including the concept of *wahdat al-wujud*.

Similarly, there was an anti-*wahdat al-wujud* tradition among renewalist Sufi teachers in Southeast Asia, like Nur al-Din al-Raniri (died 1658) and Abd al-Ra'uf al-Sinkili (died about 1693). One of the major debates in Muslim intellectual and devotional circles in Southeast Asia involved opposition to the *Wujudiyyah*. Al-Raniri made a distinction between two different *Wujudiyyahs*: the *Wujudiyyah* of Ibn al-`Arabi, which he accepted as valid, and that of al-Raniri's near contemporaries, like Hamzah Fansuri, who, in spite of being scholars in the Ibn al-`Arabi tradition, he attacked as invalid (Riddell 2001, 120-21). In his religious writing, he "tried in particular to refute the writings of the Wujûdîyah movement" (Maier 1995, 3: 29).

A collateral aspect of the description of Neo-Sufism by scholars of the "consensus," which O'Fahey and Radtke did not discuss, was the place of Abu Hamid al-Ghazali in Neo-Sufi thought. Some scholars involved in developing the "Neo-Sufi consensus" thought that "Neo-Sufi" thought tended to give attention to and view with favor Sufism as articulated within the traditions of the thought of al-Ghazali. Albert Hourani was one of the first contemporary scholars to suggest that during the eighteenth century there was significant attention given to the teachings of the twelfth century Sufi intellectual, Abu Hamid al-Ghazali. When Hourani wrote about the dynamics of eighteenth century Muslim intellectual developments, he noted the tensions between the scripturalist traditions of Ibn Taymiyyah, an influential fourteenth century legal scholar, especially as articulated in Wahhabism, the strict puritanical eighteenth century movement, and the mystic traditions associated with Ibn al-`Arabi. Hourani noted the work of Murtada al-Zabidi, an Indian-born scholar who was a major intellectual figure in eighteenth century Cairo. Hourani suggested that al-Zabidi may have written his major commentary on a significant work of the medieval scholar-mystic, al-Ghazali, as a way of combating the extremes of Wahhabi-style thought:

> For the conflict of Wahhabism and Ibn al-`Arabi, he substituted the tension, more easily bearable, between Wahhabism and Ghazali [and] the revival of interest in Ghazali gave a new lease of life to the more moderate form of mysticism (1961, 57).

The "Neo-Sufi" position was different from the contemporary Wahhabi stance. It did not totally reject Sufism as a whole and did not even, among most of the "Neo-Sufis," reject the Sufi discourse as articulated by Ibn al-`Arabi. Instead, as Levtzion and Voll argue,

> ... movements of renewal often took place within the context of a reformulated Sufi tradition ["Neo-Sufism"] which often still utilized the terminology of Ibn al-`Arabi but also reflected a renewed interest in the works and style of thought of al-Ghazali (1987a, 9).

The place of al-Ghazali's thought in Neo-Sufism, in the presentation of the "consensus," did not, in other words, totally displace Ibn al-`Arabi. Instead, Ibn al-`Arabi may no longer have been as uniquely central as he had been in the conceptualizations of a number of the major earlier Sufi traditions.

Neo-Sufism and Vernacular

Levtzion added a dimension to the discussion of movements of Islamic renewal in the eighteenth and nineteenth centuries that is frequently ignored: the use of local languages and vernaculars in presentations of programs of Muslim renewal. Soon after the 1985 colloquium on eighteenth-century Islamic renewal, Levtzion presented a paper at the 1986 annual meeting of the British Society for Middle Eastern Studies on "Eighteenth Century Renewal and Reform in Islam." In this paper, he noted that, as Islam spread into areas outside of the Middle East, vernacular presentation of the faith became increasingly important. From South and Southeast Asia to West Africa, by the end of the eighteenth century Islamic reformers increasingly used vernaculars, opening "new ways of diffusing the teaching of Islam" (1986, 7-8).

Almost two decades later, after significant research on many parts of the Muslim world, Levtzion reported:
> Looking for common features of Sufi movements across the Muslim world I have observed that written Islamic literatures in the vernacular languages appeared simultaneously all over the Muslim world in the seventeenth and eighteenth centuries, and that the predominant literary genre in all the vernacular literatures was the mystical verse (2002, 115).

This process enabled urban-based scholars to communicate more effectively with rural people and the broader population of believers outside of the Arabic-speaking world.

The increased utilization of vernacular in presenting reformist teaching reinforced the changing style of *tariqah* organization:
> Changes in rituals emphasized the hierarchical and centralized nature of the reformed *tariqa* and the expanded role of the shaykh. Brotherhoods offered larger scope for the participation of the common people in their ceremonies, facilitating the recruitment of new adherents (Levtzion 2002, 117).

This process also permitted the reformed brotherhoods to have greater impact in the public arena:
> The discourse of the public sphere in Muslim societies addressed social and political issues, and in order to reach the

illiterate it was written in the vernacular languages. In this way, written Islamic literatures in the vernacular languages developed simultaneously all over the Muslim world in the seventeenth and eighteenth centuries (Levtzion 2002, 117).
Levtzion noted the significance of this process, tying the development of vernacular Sufi literature to activism: "A new Muslim leadership emerged that articulated the grievances of the masses, criticized the rulers, and contributed to the radicalization of Islam" (2002, 117).

Conclusion

When one reconsiders Neo-Sufism, the picture is not as clear as it seemed to O'Fahey and Radtke (1993). Their critique of what they called the "Neo-Sufi consensus" raised important issues and provided very important correctives to what had become widely-accepted but simplistic generalizations about Islamic renewal movements. Since that time, new scholarship has shown that the debate can no longer be understood as a simple choice between accepting or rejecting the conclusions of the "Neo-Sufi consensus." The movements and organizations that were labeled Neo-Sufi turn out to be not as "new" or different from earlier Sufi movements as early discussions of so-called "Neo-Sufism" might have led one to expect. Only in terms of organizational changes is there now agreement that new types of Sufi brotherhood structures did, in fact, develop at that time.

In conceptual terms, the old picture of Neo-Sufism, especially as defined by O'Fahey and Radtke, requires revision. The old idea of Neo-Sufis replacing "union with God" by "union with the spirit of the Prophet" needs redefinition. However, the idea that themes like "annihilation in the Prophet" were gaining importance in the eighteenth and nineteenth century is not best refuted by simply calling it "nonsense." Refutation by rhetorical overkill works neither for advocates nor opponents of the "Neo-Sufi" consensus. Instead, the importance of the concept of the Prophet Muhammad in the organization and devotional life of Sufi groups like the followers of al-Majdhub in Sudan need to be taken into consideration as this issue gets redefined.

Similarly, the attitude of the "Neo-Sufis" toward Ibn al-`Arabi and his teachings needs to be reconsidered. It should be noted that scholars actually involved in defining the "Neo-Sufi consensus" arguably did not state as strongly as O'Fahey and Radtke suggest, that Neo-Sufis rejected the teachings of Ibn al-`Arabi. However, by their concentration on the Idrisi tradition, O'Fahey and Radtke ignored aspects of Neo-Sufism that other scholars included in their consideration of this issue. Again, looked at in this broader context, the issue appears best understood not in "either/or" terms but in a careful redefinition of the elements involved. Ibn al-`Arabi was not necessarily rejected but he may not have had the priority and prominence by the eighteenth century that he had in previous iterations of Sufism. This may be reflected in the growing attention we see being given to the perspectives of al-Ghazali by at least some Sufi teachers during the eighteenth century.

The rise of vernacular religious literature and its role in the radicalization of some groups within the Muslim world as articulated by Levtzion, on the other hand, suggests new lines for discussion of Islamic renewal movements. In particular, his placement of these movements within the conceptual framework of "the public sphere in Muslim societies" can be helpful for understanding twenty-first century movements as well as their eighteenth-century predecessors.

The debate over the validity of the concept of "Neo-Sufism" and the actual historical nature of the movements that were labeled "Neo-Sufi" is important for understanding the dynamics of the eighteenth- and nineteenth-century Muslim world. However, at the beginning of the twenty-first century, it is useful to revisit this debate. Such a revisiting can provide suggestions for ways to understand the new movements of Muslim activism. It reminds us, at a minimum, that simplistic generalizations need to be continually reconsidered in the light of new research and new understandings of the meaning of "renewal." Beyond that, the debate about Neo-Sufism emphasizes the importance of looking at the actual modes of organization and the intellectual content of movements of renewal, whether they are in the eighteenth or the twenty-first century.

Notes

[1] See, also, the works of other scholars, like Fazlur Rahman and J.S. Trimingham, which represent what is described as "the neo-Sufi consensus" in R.S. O'Fahey and Bernd Radtke (1993).

Linking Translation Theory and African History: Domestication and Foreignization in *Corpus of Early Arabic Sources for West African History*

Dalton S. Collins

Résumé

Le **Corpus of Early Arabic Sources for West African History,** édité par Nehemia Levtzion et J.F.P. Hopkins compile et traduit en anglais de nombreuses sources arabes, vitales à la construction de l'ancienne histoire ouest-africaine. Cette compilation est, à juste titre, vite devenue essentielle aux érudits désireux de s'engager sur le terrain des premières perceptions et descriptions arabes de l'Afrique de l'Ouest. Cependant, depuis la publication du Corpus, de nouveaux développements dans les domaines des philosophies du langage et de la théeorie de la traduction ont montré qu'il existe une multiplicité de méthodes et de motivations de traduction, ainsi que de nombreuses alternatives possibles d'interprétations et de traductions de textes, Cet article déclare que les historiens utilisant le Corpus devraient être conscients des effets que certaines stratégies de traduction ont sur le texte traduit, de manière à placer le Corpus dans une certaine perspective et à suggérer la valeur à lui accorder grace une lecture mieux informée.

Abstract

The **Corpus of Early Arabic Sources for West African History,** edited by Nehemia Levtzion and J.F.P. Hopkins compiles and translates into English many of the Arabic sources vital to the construction of ancient West African history. This collection has quickly and deservedly become essential to scholars wishing to engage with early Arab perceptions and descrip-

---

This article was originally a paper funded by SSHRC. An earlier draft was presented at the 2007 International Translation Day Conference, University of Alberta. I would also like to thank Anne Malena and E. Ann McDougall, both of the University of Alberta, for comments and suggestions on earlier drafts.

tions regarding West Africa. However, since the publication of the Corpus, developments in philosophies of language and translation theory have shown that there are a multiplicity of methods and motivations for translation, and many possible alternative interpretations and translations of texts. This article argues that historians who utilize the Corpus should be aware of the effects that various translation strategies have on the finished translation, in an attempt to put the Corpus in perspective and to suggest the value we might bring to it through a more critical reading.

Introduction

Arabic sources are vital to the reconstruction of West African, especially medieval West African history. The *Corpus of Early Arabic Sources for West African History*, edited by Nehemia Levtzion and Cambridge Arabist J.F.P. Hopkins (Levtzion and Hopkins 1981), presents many of them as excerpts translated into English. There is a measure of comfort in knowing that someone has decided what, among all these sources, is all-important for West African history. However, comfort is often rife with danger. Since the publication of the *Corpus* in 1981, developments in philosophies of language and translation theory have shown that there are benefits to be found in multiple readings and alternative interpretations and translations of texts; as historians, we have not yet addressed these developments in full. A complete deconstruction and analysis of the theories and methods that shaped the creation of this seminal work would constitute many years of scholarship — and may not, in the end, justify the effort. However, I am arguing that it is useful at this point to make some preliminary remarks based on current debates within the field of translation studies, in an attempt to put the *Corpus* in perspective and to suggest the value we might bring to it through a more critical reading.

Accompanying the excerpts drawn from lengthy, often obscure manuscripts or printed reproductions of early Arabic texts are biographical sketches of the sixty or so Arab authors the editors have chosen to feature, useful linguistic, ethnographic, and historical information, a glossary of unfamiliar African and Arabic terms, a bibliography, and detailed indexes. The original purpose of the *Corpus*, as articulated in 1956 by the University College of Ghana, was to compile a book consisting of English translations of Arabic sources important to the history of Ghana, with detailed commentary regarding associated linguistic, geographical, historical, and ethnographical information.¹ As the project took shape, its geographical framework came to refer not only to the modern state of Ghana, but to West Africa in general. In keeping with both era and goals, the translations gave priority to a literal over a poetic translation, while allowing for frequent interruptions in the way of parentheses and footnotes. In creating a work accessible to relative beginners in the field, yet useful for veteran scholars, the editors attained their stated purpose. Initially, the main complaint against the *Corpus* was its price, and the 2000 paperback edition both silenced that criticism and cemented the *Corpus* as a seminal representation of ancient and medieval West African voices.

In many ways, the *Corpus* was ahead of the curve. By combining Levtzion's vast knowledge of West Africa with Hopkins' skill as an Arabist, the *Corpus* transcended the abilities of individual translators. It is doubtful that either Levtzion or Hopkins could have produced such a prolific work alone. Yet, innovative and thorough as they were for their time, they did not engage with some of the relevant issues that translation theory had raised even as early as the 1970s. Most notably absent, given the subject matter of their work, were issues deriving from translators' concerns about the role of the foreign and the Other in texts, about the contradictions between exoticising and domesticating translation and representation strategies, and about the impact of the authors' own "foreignness" on their portrayal of the subject matter, quite independent of the additional "layer" of interpretation provided by them as translators. Given that the *Corpus* was comprised of views of West Africa by Arab travellers, traders, and arm-chair geographers who were quite foreign to both the human and geographical terrain about which they wrote, and that they were subsequently interpreted by translators whose Otherness was accentuated by many centuries of time and space, these issues are not inconsequential matters for those of us who would use the *Corpus* as our principal window onto medieval West Africa.

Cultural Studies of Translation Strategies

The development of methods for the construction of critical readings of texts has occurred in many fields — gender studies, postcolonial studies, and linguistics among them (see for example, Butler 1990; Said 1993; Fairclough 1989), and textual analysis has become embedded in many disciplines. It seems obvious that a diligent historian using translated materials would want to know something about the translator and what informed his or her work. This poses a problem for those using the *Corpus*. While we know something about Levtzion's background, methods, and involvement with this project,[2] his role was primarily to add cultural and historical context to the translations produced by his colleague. Conversely, we know next to nothing about Hopkins — next to nothing of his motivations, methods, and theoretical alignment expressed in the *Corpus* or in any of his other extant work.[3]

This relative silence around the central translator is exacerbated by the relative lack of discussion of methodology in the book's introduction; it does not, in any case, seem to engage cultural theories of translation. It is true that the scholarly importance of "cultural studies" has grown exponentially since the 1981 publication of the *Corpus*; the field, however, had been given impetus even at this early date by Edward Said's (1978) (in)famous work on "orientalism." The cultural emphasis that has grown since the early 1970s is a rebellion against colonialist and ethnocentric scholarship, both past and present. Within this cultural turn, attention is paid to representations of the Other and to how these representations relate to our construction of the Self. The Other is distinguished from the Self through difference, that is, through aspects with which we do not self-identify. The injection of "cultural studies" into translatology and work dealing with the connections between language and culture has added a new dimension to the extant dichotomy between source and target language / culture. This cultural dimension to the translator's always-present dialogic dilemma asserts that a translation can move the reader towards the author through the text, or can bring the text nearer to the target audience.

In 1813 Friedrich Schleiermacher coined the term "foreignizing translation" to describe the translator's act of bringing the reader towards the author (Venuti 1995, 19-20). Lawrence Venuti expands on this notion, drawing on the Nietzschean negation of the Other through the "master narrative," and Emmanuel Levinas' attempts at formulating an alternative understanding of knowledge by disrupting the hegemony of the Same. In Venuti's system, the "foreignizing translation" can be a restraint against the violence of translation, especially "domesticating translation" and the "transparent discourse" in translation that causes the translator's disappearance. Venuti sees an "ethics of difference" in translation as a route to heterogeneous cultural communities and as "a form of resistance against ethnocentrism and racism, cultural narcissism and imperialism, in the interests of democratic geopolitical relations" (Venuti 1995, 20; Venuti 1998). Put another way, Venuti sees intercultural communication as the road to a multicultural utopia. Furthermore, in his view, translators constitute a vanguard force, providing creative interpretations of the target text that draw attention to the text's difference, both culturally and linguistically.

Ovidi Carbonell draws our attention to an alternative to this dialectic: Bakhtinian dialogism. Mikhail Bakhtin holds that language acquires meaning through "dialogue," a two-way speech act that occurs in a specific context. In this way, a combination of interpretations of the utterances of the Other is used to create a unique and context-specific image of the Other (Van Leuwen 2004, 17). Instead of a binary relation between Self and Other, a constellation of relations between aspects of Self / Other can be conceptualized.

This dialogic construction of the Other is easily positioned within the source / target dichotomy. As language acquires meaning through a dialogue, a translation, as an intercultural act of language, can present the author of the source with or without agency and legitimacy. A representation of the Other is constructed by any translation, but can be presented as truly Other, or as an expected stereotype.[4] In this way, power and domination enter the dialogue. A translator has the power to present the translated as a resistance to domination by pre-existing hierarchies of knowledge or to dominate the translated, and the systems of knowledge symbolized by them, through incorporating them into the knowledge systems of the target language.

Carbonell accuses Venuti of forgetting that "any approach to the Other responds to the intrinsic need to know and dominate through knowledge" (2004, 29-30, 38). In his own work, Carbonell revisits Schleiermacher's terms, and uses the reader's identification with the text and construction of Others and Sames as his avenue of approach. A text with which the reader identifies is "domesticated" by the reader, while a text that lacks familiarity is "exoticised." Exoticism results from either an ignorance of the Other, or from a conscious strategy that retains images and effects from the source text, instead of replacing them with "authorized knowledge" such as that which informs dominant target values (Carbonell 2003, 151). Such identification is not easy or stable, nor do all readers share it (Carbonell 2006, 53-57). Of course, a translator enters this dialogue by creating a text that mediates between author and audience, further complicating this process.

Carbonell and Venuti agree on the existence and importance of recognizing Others and Selfs in translated texts, but disagree as to the purposes to which this recognition should be put. In a sense, their disagreement is yet another episode of translation theory pitting the reader against the translator, with Venuti urging the translator to subvert the dominant paradigm and Carbonell seeking ways for the reader of translations to better utilize it and recognize the way Others are articulated. The dialogue between Carbonell and Venuti is telling, supporting a Bakhtinian constellation of multiple possibilities in the ways in which shades of Other and Self can be interpreted from texts

Translation theory does not hold all of the answers, but may assist in the crystallization of questions within the exoticizing / domesticating framework. Since the earliest postulation of the source / target dichotomy,[5] translators have searched for a solution to the problem, a synthesis for the dialectic. Derrida saw a "relevant" translation as one that successfully displays the qualities of the text through source language equivalence, while remaining faithful to the quantity of the source text. That is, one should elucidate the quality of the source text to the fullest, while keeping the word and page count as near as possible. In characteristic fashion, Derrida (2001, 425-27) admits the impossibility of a perfect translation of this type, and leaves the solution to practicing translators.

Al-Khafaji returns Derrida's dilemma to the source-target dichotomy, characterizing the quantity / quality conflict as one between an "adequate" relation to the source language and an "acceptability" within the target language. In his explanation of this phenomenon he alludes to the quantity / quality debate simply as a matter of style (al-Khafaji 2006, 40-41). The most common solution to the polarization of translation studies seems to be the invention or redefinition of theoretical binary opposites. Translators set boundaries for themselves, attempting to escape one dialectic by creating another.

An alternative to this approach is Bakhtin's dialogism. As language acquires meaning through a dialogue, a translation, as an intercultural act of language, can present the author of the source with or without agency and legitimacy. A representation of the Other is constructed in one of two ways by any translation. It can be presented as truly Other, or as an expected stereotype. In this way power and domination enter the dialogue. A translator has the power to present the translated as a resistance to domination by pre-existing hierarchies of knowledge or to dominate the translated, and the systems of knowledge symbolized by them, through incorporating them into the knowledge systems of the target language. In a dialectic approach, the Other is exoticized or domesticated; though both domestic and foreign elements often exist in a translation, the dialectic approach imposes a definitive category on the representation of the Other. Dialogism allows the Other to be observed from more than one perspective. Though ultimately the Other must be foreign, the interpretation of this foreignness by the reader is multifaceted.

These theories clearly did not inform the translation of the *Corpus*, yet they open up new vantage points, particularly poignant for those looking for data that may have been marginalized by dominant Western paradigms. They reveal a deep-seated opposition between the source and target cultures and languages, with the translator acting as a mediator. What is important is that the reader understands that this mediation cannot but do violence to the source, either by ignoring the unknown, the Other, or by attempting to know the Other, in effect dominating it through the process, and incorporating it into the target's system of knowledge. The violence of this mediation is intensified in a colonial or post-colonial context. In fact, it could be argued that all interlinguistic translations inflict such violence in one form or another. Recognition of this violence is a necessary aspect of recognizing the myriad possibilities for meaning inherent in the dialogic relationship between source and target texts.

There are many different ways in which the Other is represented in translation, and each highlights different aspects of

Otherness. However, there is no way to remove the violence from translation of the Other. The Other cannot be known or expressed — once expressed, it ceases to be Other. Some translation strategies do attempt to deal specifically with the Other as it is represented in the translation process. Each of us has socially established images of Others, be it Arab, African, or Martian, and these Others are assumed to behave in certain ways with which we either identify — or not. Exoticizing translations generally reproduce the images and ideas that an audience already holds of the culture and its society, removing the "problem" by taming and dominating it (Carbonell 2004, 29, 38).

The Translation of the Corpus

Traditional knowledge systems played a major role in the history of the translations that make up the Levtzion and Hopkins' *Corpus*. The editors paid close attention to, and made extensive use of, existing translations of these Arabic sources. In turn, now unknown administrators, under the auspices of colonial powers, performed the majority of these earlier translations, for distinctly colonial purposes, in dominant colonial languages. As a rule, and consistent with the larger lens through which subjects were viewed, these equivalents of colonial ethnographies exoticised and simplified the lives of Africans as they had been earlier described by Arabs; these intersecting prisms, separated in time and culture, further complicated the basic process of re-presenting the Other and determining the degree of exoticisation that would shape the *Corpus'* methodology, albeit unconsciously. There is an additional problem that our "re-reading" through translation theory poses. While Levtzion and Hopkins did a remarkable job of selecting and compiling what they saw as "the" most important excerpts for West African historians from the Arabic sources, the excerpts are just that: they immediately lose context and cohesion because of the fact that they are excerpts. In their original, these excerpts were each, individually, part of a particular narrative. And a narrative requires a social context in order to be fully received. The reader imposes categories, discourses, and stereotypes onto the context and text to create coherence, but the greater context of the larger text is lost. Thus, the reader of the *Corpus* is forced to assimilate texts into the dominant values of his/her culture, without the context of the original author or language, and without the manifest intertextuality that could be found in larger works but is often missing (or embedded in a footnote) in the *Corpus*.

An example is Al-Masudi, whose tenth century excerpt occupies pages 31-32 of the text. His rare interest in social and cultural history (that is, rare among his peers) is not mentioned in the *Corpus*; rather, emphasis is given to his economic and political information about "silent trade" in the context of gold commerce, because this is an issue that has long fascinated historians.[6] This lack of context reflects the prevalence of a dominant paradigm that emphasizes politics and economics over social and cultural information in both classical Arab and colonial scholarship — and, not surprisingly, is reflected in the *Corpus*. The removal of texts from context is further compounded by Levtzion and Hopkins' literalist and foreignizing translation strategies, which give many excerpts, including al-Masudi, a disjointed and exotic feel. By translating the texts nearly word for word, Levtzion and Hopkins exoticize the texts with a rhythm and flavour that is unfamiliar to English-speakers. In Schleiermacher's terms, they set out to "foreignize" the text for its readers by retaining a literal flavour. However, they simultaneously undermine this attempt by domesticating the text with transliterations and Anglicisms. Put another way, lack of consciousness about the debates over "exoticising" and "domesticating" texts, over the question of bringing the reader to text or the text to reader means that, methodologically speaking, their translations are inherently contradictory.

We can perhaps see this issue reflected even more clearly by comparing the Levtzion and Hopkins translation with its French counterpart, *Recueil des sources arabes concernant l'Afrique occidentale du VIII au XVI siècle*, published by Joseph Cuoq in 1975.[7] These two works share the same issues arising from translation into and, in many cases, through colonial languages (in West Africa, French was equal to or greater than English in terms of colonial linguistic power). Comparing them, therefore, can, in some instances, raise some critical questions around meaning, identity, and representation. It is not my intention to analyse or categorize Cuoq's methods of translation, nor to compare these methods and theories to those of Levtzion and Hopkins. French and English translation theories rarely co-mingle. Generally speaking, however, one may ask similar questions of both sets of translations, and of their translators. The vast cultural differences between the English, French, Moroccan Arabic, and Modern Standard Arabic languages make variations in their respective dominant paradigms of translation strategies all the more likely and complicated.

Even very slight variations can mean different things within the realm of Othering. Levtzion and Hopkins report that Al-Yaqubi, a tenth century CE Abbasid functionary writing from Egypt, described the inhabitants of the town of Zawilla as Ibadi Muslims[8] and traders in "black" slaves (Levtzion and Hopkins 2000, 22). Cuoq translates this passage into French with a nearly identical meaning, except that the slaves are *"al-sudani"* — "from the Sudan" (1975, 48-49). The difference is small, but a great deal of Othering comes into play.

If the slaves are referred to as Sudani, then al-Yaqubi may be saying that the Ibadis, not being "true" Muslims themselves, are enslaving their own people. If al-Yaqubi refers to the slaves as "black," (al-AswaDi) however, he may be conveying the meaning that these longtime Muslims do not prey on their own kind, but on those Others from far away. That is, he may be describing those from Zawilla and their slaves as constituting a single group, "Other" from himself. Alternatively, he may be constructing three groups: Arabs (himself), Berbers (Zawilla Muslims), and blacks (al-AswaDi). This is significant because al-Yaqubi was writing in the late ninth century CE, during the very early years of Saharan Islam, and he might well have tried to distance himself from the long-persecuted Ibadi groups. One word cannot reveal al-Yaqubi's perspectives regarding Ibadites, Zawillans, and African Muslims on the fringes of Islam, yet the problem does indeed lie within this "one word." Which word — Sudani or *AswaDi* — did al-Yaqubi use? And here the problem further complicates itself. Most scholars turn to Cuoq or Levtzion and Hopkins for the answer; the original Arabic manuscripts are not readily accessible even to those few who have the necessary linguistic and calligraphic training to use them.

Though Levtzion and Hopkins did not engage formally with translation theory, they did identify at least one issue that was, in fact, part of that theory. In the section on transcription, the editors noted the difficulties involved in translating certain words, that may have been Arabizations of Berber words, or vice-versa, or they could have been false cognates — words that sound alike in different languages but do not share a meaning. Another problem arises with the concept that certain words "sound like Arabic." The authors of the excerpts within the *Corpus* were predominantly not West Africans, but rather of North African or Middle Eastern birth. Their understanding of the diverse dialects of Arabic and local languages found in West Africa during this period must have been understandably limited. Ultimately, these early Arabic authors performed a translation of foreign, West African concepts into the Arabic language and thought process that was coherent to them. The addition of the second level of translators (those from Arabic to English) distantly removed from the original context of the works could mean that many inter-linguistic possibilities have been missed. This method gives another false sense of security to scholars, both those familiar with Arabic and those who are not.

The power of the translator is heightened in direct proportion to the degree of difference between the language, culture, and knowledge systems being drawn into play. In the case of English and Arabic that "difference" is powerful indeed. Textual analysis informs recent translation theory and is especially salient for this discussion. The masterful patchwork that is the *Corpus* is a text in itself, made up of individual "sub" texts. Texts, pieces of discourse, need to be studied in a social context, as argued above. The text's social activity occurs through cohesion, coherence relations, and thematic patterns that allow it to be part of a discourse. The coherence relations and thematic patterns are dictated by context and in turn give texture to the text. These textual and contextual features are largely language and text-type specific. This becomes problematic because Arabic and English display very different techniques for creating cohesion and coherence relations, even within the same discourse-type. Additionally, the structural norms of texts also vary across language and text-type — Arabic and English are cultural worlds apart in both norms and techniques for the creation and interpretation of texts (Jabr 2001, 306).

An example of this extreme dissimilarity is Arabic's use of lexical repetition to fulfill important rhetorical and textual roles. By contrast, English rhetoric discourages repetition, except as a figure of speech (al-Khafaji 2006, 39). Translators of Arabic into English have, as a norm, avoided lexical repetition, and these norms have tended to be followed closely (Ben-Ari 1998, 2). The debate continues as to whether repetition is a merely matter of style and therefore "optional," or if it is a necessary and integral element that the translator must retain to achieve "equivalence" with the source text. In the case of the *Corpus*, Arabic lexical repetition does not appear in the translation; though the translators attempt to maintain a literalist style, this omission reveals the domesticating nature of the translations.

Levtzion and Hopkins domesticate through more explicit strategies of translation. Their use of punctuation, Anglicizations, and transliteration are telling examples. Though punctuation is used in remarkably similar ways in English and Arabic, Arabic language studies have historically ignored it as ornamentation or used it haphazardly and poorly, belittling its importance (Ghazala 2004, 230-31). In translating from Arabic to English, we are reminded that punctuation was likely not a consideration at all for medieval Arabic scholars, who used it for purposes of style, if at all. Yet the *Corpus* is liberally flavoured with punctuation, in standard English usage. Here, another potential foreignization (the exclusion of punctuation altogether if that is the case in the original Arabic, or the inclusion of punctuation representative of the relationship of *difference* between the Arabic and English renditions) is lacking from the *Corpus*, though it claims to be meant for students who "will wish to know as far as possible what the Arabic says in detail without any regard for the quality of English" (Levtzion and Hopkins 1981, 3) and attempts to maintain other foreign elements.

It seems that Levtzion and Hopkins approached this project with the intention of presenting a foreignizing translation, which retained, as much as possible, the quality of the original. However, they fail at this translation strategy because the tools at hand for a translator, particularly during the 1950s, were those of domestication and the transparency of the translator. Likely, the editors were not aware of the "mixed messages" that these foreignizations and domestications deliver to the reader, confident in the translation theories and strategies of the colonial period, but not pushing translation theory beyond.

Many of the translation strategies used in the *Corpus* break down the text into apparent English equivalencies that allow it to be incorporated into Western terms of reference. One problem this introduces is the "Anglicization" of certain Arabic words. "Emir," "khatib," "qadi," and others Arabic words are singled out as "common [and] are treated as anglicized" (Levtzion and Hopkins 1981, xiii). This Anglicization disrupts their relationship with Arabic and creates a false assimilation into English, domesticating the Arabic language for the reader. Similarly, as with any system of transliteration, the method used in the *Corpus* is in itself a further example of domestication: representing Arabic characters with Latin characters is an obvious translation of the Other. Apparent or near equivalency between characters is invariably a false equivalency, an attempt at translating the untranslatable.

Finally, a word needs to be said about the extensive endnotes and annotations that historians see as giving such value to the work. The Corpus can be a difficult read; extensive endnotes were intended to assist the reader through difficult passages as well as to contextualize them historically. Elsewhere, they were principally inserted to add cultural "flavour" to what might otherwise have been dry or obtuse passages. These foreignizing translations were not merely "annotated," as Levtzion and Hopkins would have it; they were successfully domesticated with the insertion of detailed endnotes. Drawing on post-colonial analysis, one can go further and argue that these notes provided an ethnocentric and colonial "lens" for our reading of the translations that imperceptibly perpetuated the earlier paradigms that had long coloured Western perspectives of the "Arab-Other."

Levtzion and Hopkins' attempts at fluency and transparency counteracted each other and further obscured the translation methods used in the *Corpus*. The translations prioritize a literal translation over poetics (itself often an important part of the styles of the original authors), but contain frequent interruptions in the way of parentheses and footnotes, as well as an inconsistent adherence to Arabic syntax. The literal translation can be seen as having two general results. First, it promotes transparency and is an obstacle to fluency by retaining, as much as possible, the original diction and syntax. However, the second result of this literalism hurts transparency by ignoring poetics and other aspects of style and rhetoric that contribute to the context effect of the original Arabic text. Here it adds to the fluency of the translation by detracting from foreign language norms that contributed to the construction of the source text. The goals of communicating both transparency and fluency are, in this case, mutually exclusive.

Conclusion

The creation of the *Corpus* was a long and difficult process. The excerpts themselves required approximately twenty-five years to translate. By emphasizing the manuscript irregularities, important and challenging though they may have been, over the conceptual difficulties involved in such process, the *Corpus* editors caused the translator to vanish.[9] The translation is presented as equivalent to the original, which it can never be. Though they drew readers' attention to problems raised by the lack of vowelization and diacritical points in the original Arabic documents, they did not engage with some of the issues emerging from post-colonial studies and language on the one hand, and could not have anticipated the evolution of translation theory with its embedded debates and unresolved issues, on the other (Levtzion and Hopkins 1981, xii).

Every act of communication, translated or otherwise, presupposes an agent. The translator may or may not present the original author of the translated text as agent. Part of the inescapable violence that translation does is to appropriate and integrate the original author into the translator's agency (Carbonell 2006, 49). Even in a literalist translation such as the *Corpus*, with all of the editors' attempts to preserve the original authors' agency and present a transparent translation, this appropriation and exoticism occurs. What the Arabic means *per se* cannot be rendered perfectly into English. A translator interprets and "re-presents," in this case, presenting again in English what was originally presented in Arabic. The translated text is unavoidably presented in a different context than the source text — starting with language, but also including time, intention, and audience. A key difficulty for translation has been the repeated attempts to find ways to make this "re-presentation" transparent. Efforts to make the translator invisible, such as those under taken by the *Corpus* editors, and theories that favoured allowing the source text to "shine through" the target language in a pure and embryonic state have shaped normative translation theory until fairly recently (Venuti 1995).[10]

Though Levtzion and Hopkins must have been aware of the

relevance of such post-colonial discussions as those generated by Said's "orientalism," if not other postmodernist approaches to language embedded in nascent cultural studies, to translation processes, they apparently chose not to engage them either in their early work or in the more recent edition. The work of Venuti and Carbonell, among others, goes much farther than the scholarship that existed during the preparation of the *Corpus* but similar questions were being asked and acknowledged by the time the re-edition was planned (Jakobson 1959; Steiner 1975, among other examples before 1981).

The creation of the *Corpus* was motivated by efficiency and accuracy. To minimize the student's exertions, the *Corpus* excluded the Arabic texts, attempted to make itself accessible to both the trained Arabist and the beginner, and published a paperback edition. However, it did not push the boundaries of previous study as much as it displayed them. The *Corpus* is a valuable tool, but it must be used with the context of its creation in mind. While we do not need to re-translate it, a fuller awareness of its limitations is necessary. Though many of the categorical Others represented here have been recognized, few have been represented, made visible, given voice.

The *Corpus* deserves the accolades bestowed upon it. As Steven Straight (1981, 46) observed, no translation will ever achieve equivalence with the source text to the degree desired by all readers. The translations that make up the *Corpus* succeed as a historical reference because of the teamwork between an Arabist and a West Africanist. This combination of expertise and awareness of some of the limitations involved with such a project has created an accessible and useful tool for the scholar. However, as a translation, the *Corpus* today is vulnerable to the scrutiny of translators more deeply immersed in the conceptual and theoretical questions of the process.

Though there is little doubt that with the *Corpus*, Levtzion and Hopkins advanced the field of West African history in providing access to selected medieval Arabic sources, the time for alternative readings of this work is upon us. The effect of cultural studies on translation theory is not a neat and easy package to apply to West African history as I have attempted to explain, but there seems no better place to begin than with this pillar of cross-cultural research and legacy of Nehemia Levtzion's devotion to African history.

Notes

[1] The University College of Ghana (now the University of Ghana) commissioned a book consisting of translations into English from Arabic sources concerned with historical Ghana. John Fage drew up a list of materials on the basis of Youssouf Kamal's *Monumenta Cartographica Africae et Aegypti* (1926-51).

[2] See, for example, his autobiographical sketch in this special issue of *CJAS*.

[3] The translations were begun in 1956 by Witold Rajkowski. He had completed a draft of "about a third" of them when he passed away in 1957. J.F.P. Hopkins took over in 1958 and presented "most of the translations" to the University of Ghana in 1963. Then, after a long hiatus, Nehemia Levtzion joined the project and he and Hopkins worked on it throughout the 1970s (Levtzion and Hopkins 1981, vii-x).

Besides an article and a dissertation for each, Rajkowski and Hopkins have left little evidence to show their ideological, theoretical, and methodological views and approaches. The fact that so little is known about the translators makes it easy for younger scholars to attribute the *Corpus* solely to Nehemia Levtzion. Though the majority of the preface, introduction, and notes seem to speak with Levtzion's voice, we must remember that the *Corpus* constituted a group project. No two translators work the same ways, and Rajkowski's translations must have had some influence on Hopkins' finished product. The fact that many of the translations were in various stages of completeness further complicates our lack of information about Hopkins' methodology.

[4] The idea of a stereotyped Other is paradoxical. To stereotype is to domesticate and assimilate, to remove all power and agency of the Other.

[5] The earliest mention that I have seen is Cicero, circa 46 BC. See Venuti (2004a, 13).

[6] De Moraes Farias (1974) gives a review of the evidence for "silent trade."

[7] In terms of this study, Cuoq (1975) is not entirely the *Corpus*'s "counterpart," because it leaves both translation and annotation in the hands of one scholar. It does have other strengths, such as excerpts that are not contained in the *Corpus* and an emphasis on the French historiography of West Africa, as well as Cuoq's vast knowledge of both the sources and the region concerned.

[8] Al-Yaqub was Shi'ite, the dominant sect in Egypt during his lifetime. Ibadi Muslims were a minority group, whose persecution had often led to their relocation to less orthodox climes. See Lewicki (1960ab, 1971).

[9] Venuti (1995) chronicles the translator's tendency to disappear from the radar, especially in the context of the North American publishing industry.

[10] The works of Gayatri Chakravorty Spivak, Ovidi Carbonell i Cortes, and Lawrence Venuti display some of the new questions being asked by translation theorists.

*The **Ancient Ghana and Mali** Project*

Reconceptualizing Early Ghana

Susan Keech McIntosh

Résumé

*Peu avant sa mort, Nehemia Levtzion avait entrepris un projet visant à réviser son livre, **Ancient Ghana and Mali**, à la lumière de nouvelles études. La publication originale datait de 1973. Il proposait de revoir complètement les origines et les débuts des régimes de type soudanais comme au Ghana, pour tenir compte de récentes découvertes archéologiques et des disciplines qui s'y rattachent. Dans cet article, quatre sujets sont évoqués (variabilité climatique, interactions entre sédentarité et mobilité, dynamique externe / interne, et variabilité dans l'organisation), sujets au centre du rapport de 1973 rédigé par Levtzion sur les origines du Ghana et les implications des résultats de recherches à ce jour, pour nous permettre une meilleure compréhension des débuts de la consolidation politique du Sahel.*

Abstract

*At the time of his death, Nehemia Levtzion had initiated a project to revise **Ancient Ghana and Mali** in the light of new scholarship since its original publication in 1973. He proposed that the question of origins and early development of Sudanic polities such as Ghana should be thoroughly reconsidered with regard to findings from research in archaeology and related disciplines. In this article, I discuss four topics (climate variability, sedentary-mobile interactions; external / internal dynamics; and organizational variability) central to Levtzion's 1973 account of Ghana's origins and the implications of research results to date for our understanding of early political consolidation in the Sahel.*

Introduction

Ancient Ghana and Mali was a landmark volume, unique in its mastery of the Arabic texts coupled with its compelling picture of the ancient western Sudan that was accessible to specialists and students alike. The idea of updating Ancient Ghana and Mali as a project incorporating history, archaeology, and oral tradition had been on Nehemia Levtzion's mind since 1993, when he approached me about a possible collaboration at the MANSA meetings in Bamako, shortly after I met him for the first time. Two years later, David Conrad, Rod McIntosh, and I met with him in Jerusalem for a week-long set of meetings to reconceptualize *Ancient Ghana and Mali* within a new multi-disciplinary and multi-authored format. He started our brainstorming session by giving us a set of the reviews of *Ancient Ghana and Mali* and saying: "we must address all the criticisms of the first edition, indicating where new evidence supports the critics and where it does not." It was characteristic of his formidable scholarship that he was much more interested in seeking out the best-supported argument than in shoring up a prior interpretation that had lost its luster or been superceded by new information. In this article, I look at what we have gleaned from archaeology and related fields since 1973 that can help us understand the emergence of Ghana, as well as the other early polities of Takrur, and Kawkaw, by the later first millennium CE.

At the time that Levtzion wrote *Ancient Ghana and Mali*, archaeology was still a rare undertaking in West Africa. As a basis for outlining historical processes that culminated in "the emergence of `empires' or amalgamation of kingdoms" by the later first millennium CE, he had little to rely on outside of rock art, oral tradition, historical projection, plus Munson's work at Tichitt. He identified two themes of historical importance — interaction and confrontation between camel-herding nomads and sedentary cultivators, and participation in the trans-Saharan trade — as central to state formation in the Sudan. He cited the importance of horses and cavalry to the maintenance of hegemony and control of the trade routes. As Levtzion summarized the process,

> The development of agriculture, the introduction of iron and cavalry all contributed to social, economic, and political differentiation by the beginning of the Christian era. Some forms of more elaborate political organization, perhaps small chiefdoms, emerged. About the middle of the first millennium AD, the increasing pressure of the Saharan nomads and the growth of trans-Saharan trade acted as stimuli for political reorganization on a larger scale in order to present a unified force against the nomads, and to achieve a wider and more effective

control over trade (1973, 14).

In the thirty-five years since this account was published, some of its assertions have been supported and others amplified or revised by new evidence. The conceptual structure of analysis has also changed. Both historiography and archaeology have taken a markedly critical turn, resulting in the rejection of typologies (chiefdom, state, empire) that obscure the significance and extent of organizational variability among cases lumped under a single rubric. Simple, linear, cause-and-effect scenarios have yielded to far more complex understandings that emphasize human agency, contingency, and historical context at multiple scales. This creates significant challenges for the reconstruction of historical process in the Western Sudan, since the recovery of archaeological detail for the relevant first millennium time period in no way matches the requirement for richly textured, local sequences from many sites that current archaeological theorizing requires. In the discussion that follows. I focus on four topics that are central to the reconceptualization of early Ghana:

Climate Variability: In contrast to the relatively static climatic backdrop of events in *Ancient Ghana and Mali*, research has documented the significance of climate variation in recent and historical periods and its manifold impacts on Sahelian societies.

Sedentary-mobile Interactions: Levtzion focused on conflictual interactions of Berber nomads and Sudanese agriculturalists as a key to historical process in the Western Sudan. This dichotomized view masks a far more complex situation. One aspect of this is the interaction of seasonally mobile populations of Sahelian cattle herders and agropastoralists with camel herders and their role in the early organization of trade.

External / Internal Dynamics: Stimulus or diffusion via the trans-Saharan trade has figured in many accounts of the emergence of complex societies in the western Sudan. I consider the evidence for the antiquity of this trade and the movement of gold across the desert. I then outline some of the archaeological research that has provided insights into the internal dynamics involved in the historical process of early polity formation.

Organizational Variability in Early Polities: *Ancient Ghana and Mali* invoked chiefs, kings, vassals, and empires uncritically. Typologies of political formations have been under sustained review in archaeology. Interest now focuses on identifying and understanding variability in the forms and developmental trajectories of complexity as an outcome of historical, not evolutionary, processes.

Climate Change, Subsistence, and Mobility
Since 1973, considerable evidence has accumulated on the nature and effect of variable climate patterns on population movements and the distribution of sedentary and mobile populations over time. *Ancient Ghana and Mali* recognized that the late Holocene desiccation of the Sahara had produced the present desert's general configuration by the fifth century BCE. However, it attributed later extensions of desert conditions into the Sahel to human activity, such as overgrazing.[1] Subsequent research on African climate has revealed continuing variations in African climate that include broad shifts in environmental zonation lasting centuries[2] and local patterns of change of shorter, decades-long duration (Nicholson 1996). These permit a more nuanced view of regional opportunities and challenges for human populations and their subsistence and trade pursuits during the last 2 500 years. Although the shift from grassland to desert within the present-day Saharan zone had already taken place by 4000 BP, rainfall fluctuations over longer and shorter terms during the past 2 500 years ensured that its southern boundary was never fixed. Increased mean rainfall at times shifted the zone in which rainfed millet / sorghum agriculture was possible broadly northward for periods of a century or longer. Conversely, the period from 300 BCE to 300 CE was very dry with some exceptionally arid peaks during which, for example, the flow of the Senegal River was so low that sea water flowed inland for three hundred kilometres c.2000-1900 BP, and collectors of oysters and cockles in the Senegal Delta region moved farther south (Monteillet *et al.* 1981; Mbow 1997, 115). The evidence for subsistence disruption and population movement at this time is widespread.[3]

The return of wetter conditions after 300 CE, and continuing until at least 1000 CE, when rainfall became increasingly erratic, coincided with the expansion of camel-herding Berbers and then Arabs across the desert. George Brooks (1993) discussed the range of opportunities and challenges offered by these latitudinal swings in isohyet position. One other important aspect of climate deserves more attention than it has generally received by historians, however: the highly localized nature of significant fluctuations in moisture at a decadal scale (R. McIntosh 1998, 69, 79) Sharon Nicholson (1986, 1994) has marshaled a variety of data to demonstrate the magnitude of variations interannually in West Africa. At interdecadal time scales, she has posited phase-like regularities in continent-wide rainfall that she has grouped into six recurring modes or "anomaly types" (Figure 1). Mode 1, for example, with dry conditions over virtually all of West Africa, describes the conditions associated with the Sahelian drought.

If these precipitation modes are a long-standing feature of

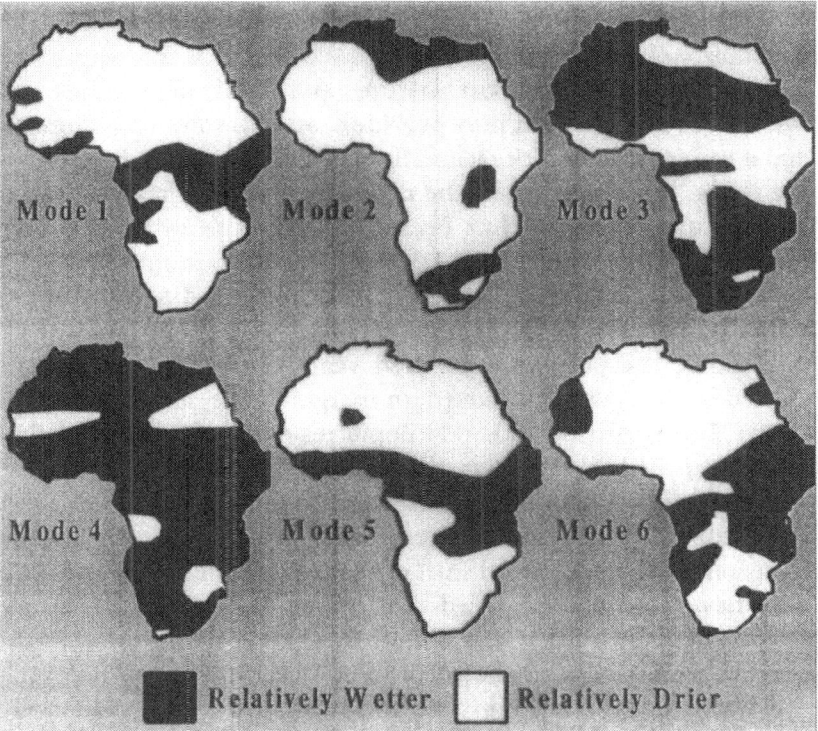

Figure 1 Continent-wide rainfall variations grouped into recurring modes or "anomaly types" Source: Nicholson (1986, 1994)

African climate, then simple reconstructions of north-south isohyet movement will not adequately capture the complexity of past climate shifts that affect decision-making, desert travel, trade, and subsistence on a decadal scale. Local histories and detailed archaeological sequences become essential for reconstructing these short-term events that would have presented a mosaic of shifting opportunities and constraints on populations. At present, we have few of these.[4] Until these are available, it would be prudent to keep firmly in mind that unpredictable short-term climate shifts, as well as longer-term trends may have played out in a variety of ways in different places at different times. Spatial displacements as well as disruptions in trading systems and infra-structural institutions may have been among the most common consequences. Equally, we must be cautious about extrapolating indisputable evidence for change in one region to other, more distant parts of Africa.

The Sahara, then, if defined only by rainfall and vegetation, is a constantly changing entity. Even at its driest, it is interrupted by highlands that may support pastures and fields, depressions and fossil river systems that may provide seasonal water and biomass, and a water table that occasionally lies close to the surface, creating oases. Pathways across the desert have always tracked water and pasture, and have thus been confined to a few main routes historically (Mitchell 2005, 137) (Figure 2). Certain routes may be favored or not at particular points in time depending on shifting rainfall regimes or political circumstances.

Within the past four hundred years, ecological zones have shifted broadly, with the southern margin of the desert moving c. 1600 CE to a position 250-300 kilometres north of its position 250 years later (Webb 1995) (Figures 3 and 4). The Sahelian cattle zone and savanna agricultural zones were similarly displaced, with significant variability at interdecadal timescales, as already mentioned. The northward shift of ecological zones from 300-1000 may have at times exceeded that of the 1600 CE shift, before retreating southward at the end of the first millennium. Ninth-century wells in the northern Hawd at Tegdaoust were shallow — the water table was high; but two centuries later, wells were substantially deeper.[5] The "Big Dry" (R. McIntosh 1998, 72) from 300 BCE-300 CE would have seen a southward shift significantly

Figure 2: Map of early Saharan trade routes, areas, and sites mentioned in the text

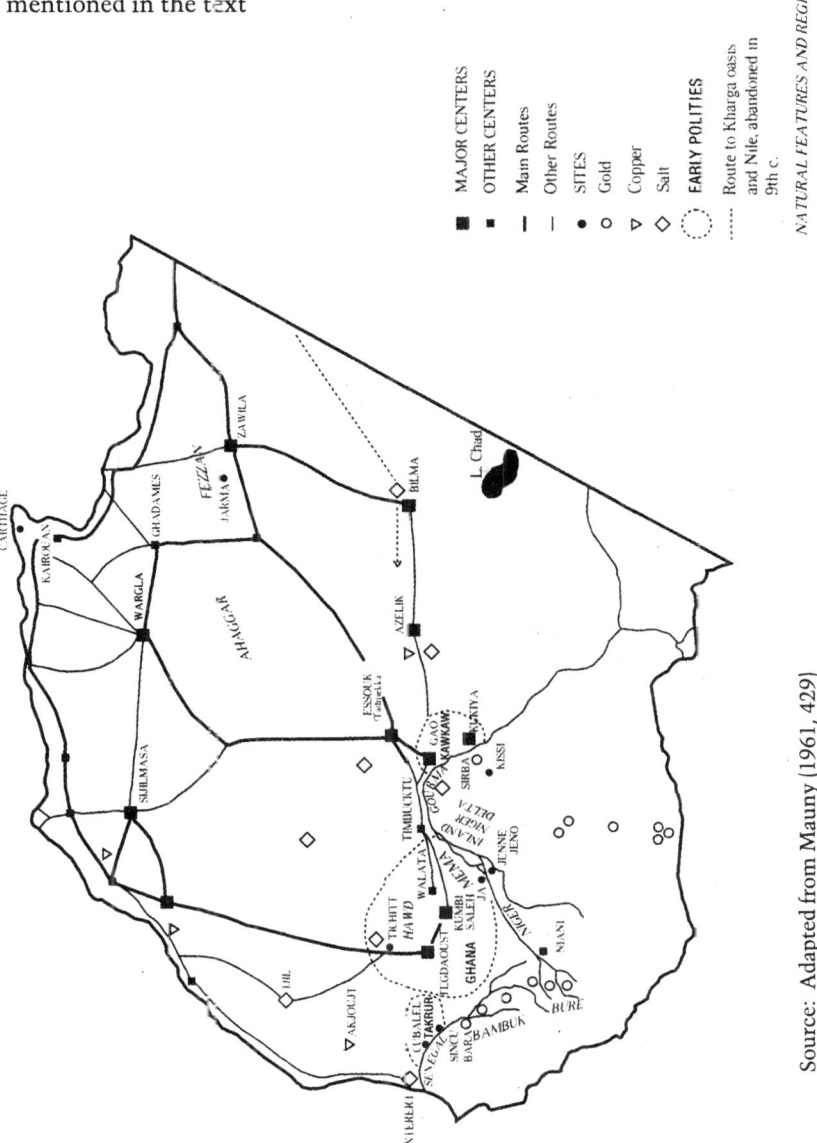

Source: Adapted from Mauny (1961, 429)

greater than that at 1850, and exceeding even the desert expansion associated with the Sahelian drought of the 1970s. In contrast to the relatively fixed environmental tableau that Levtzion envisioned, paleoclimatic work on recent periods has made us aware of

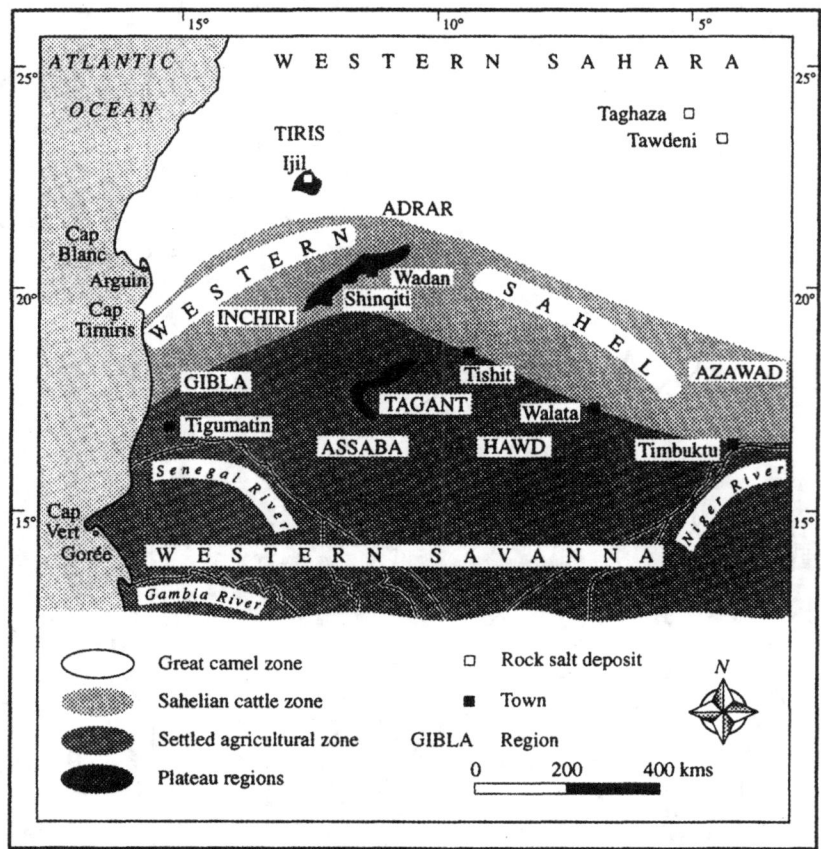

Figure 3 Approximate location of ecological zones, c.1600
Source: Webb (1995, 6, Map 1.1)

the dynamism of climate at various scales of time and geography in West Africa. Ecological shifts of this magnitude create an ever-changing landscape of challenge and opportunity for human subsistence and economic systems incorporating different degrees of mobility.

Nomads and Sedentaries

Levtzion characterized the Sahel broadly as a zone of interaction and confrontation between camel-herding Sanhaja nomads and sedentary agriculturalists. The binary opposition implied here — between mobile and sedentary economies, between camel herders

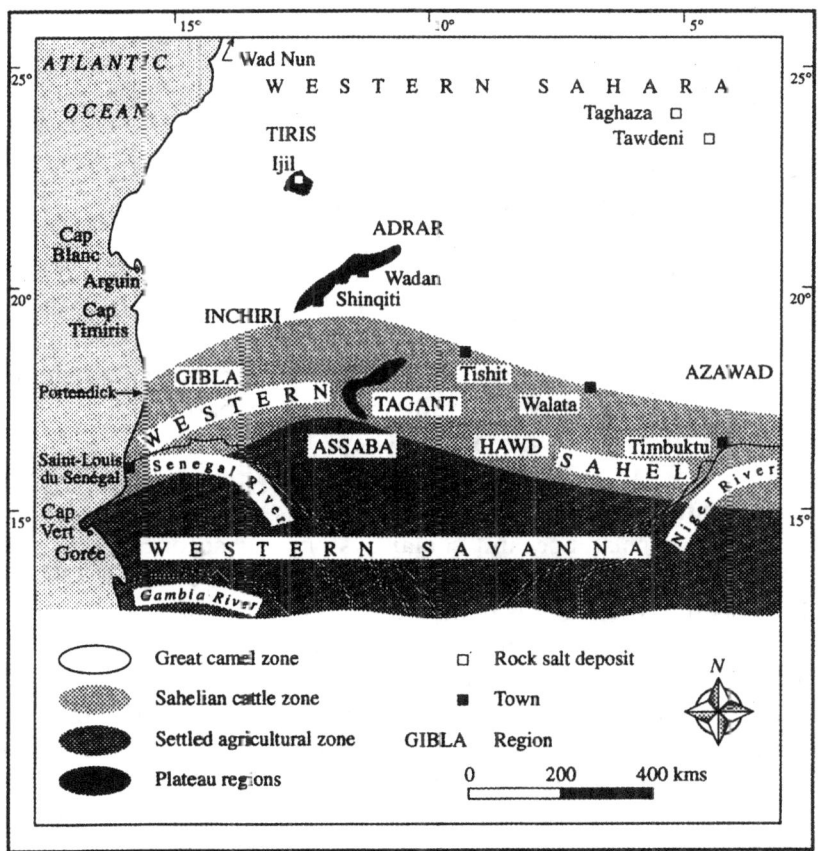

Figure 4 Approximate location of ecological zones, c.1850
Source: Webb 1995, 10, Map 1.2)

and farmers — does not do justice to the complexity of the Sahelian system as it evolved over time, however.[6] Historically, the Sahel has been dominated by stock herders and horse-breeders with varying degrees of seasonal mobility. Until 2000 BCE, Sahelian herders with domestic cattle and ovicaprids also collected wild cereals, which permitted a degree of seasonal sedentism in high biomass regions, including the Hawd basin around Tichitt. Domesticated cereals, beginning with millet and fonio, were added to the herding-collecting economy in the Sahel from 2000 to 1000 BCE. Pastoralism was thus succeeded by agropastoralism, which maintained considerable flexibility in subsistence strategy by seasonal mobility and exploitation of a diverse portfolio of wild and domestic plant resources. The sedentary farmer, fully committed to domestic cultivars, that emerged fairly early in the history of agriculture within Old World temperate zones (Near East, China, Indus, the Balkans) was rare to nonexistent in the first millennia BCE and CE in West Africa. The greatest commitment to year-round sedentism was made in the Mema and Inland Niger Delta, where *tell* (mound) settlements were created by first millennium BCE and CE communities that fished and hunted, but also raised stock, and cultivated domestic rice, millet or fonio (see Takezawa and Cissé no date; Bedaux et al. 2003; S. McIntosh 1995).[7] By contrast, recurrent seasonal, agropastoral settlement remained the pattern throughout the first millennium CE in parts of the Middle Senegal Valley. I have argued elsewhere, however, that in both the Middle Senegal and Niger, mobility was maintained in different ways and to different degrees as part of a risk-management strategy built into subsistence and social systems to accommodate the interannual uncertainties of rainfall and flood (S. McIntosh 1999b). Sedentism in the Sahel is relative.

For the first millennium CE period for which we seek insights concerning socio-political development in the Sahel, then, we must envision a range of economies that incorporate different degrees of mobility. Camel-herders enter the picture and begin transforming the desert economy during or after the Big Dry.[8] That severe climate downturn was almost certainly devastating to cattle herds in the Sahel, probably resulting in huge losses and wholesale abandonment of formerly occupied areas, as previously mentioned. The wide-ranging nature of human responses and social dynamics that attend such contractions of ecological zones in the Sahel is brilliantly laid out for a much more recent period in southern Mauritania (1600-1850) by James Webb (1995). While the historical factors at play in the first and, later, second millennia CE were very different, Webb's analysis points to the number of interacting elements that must be considered relevant to any attempt to reconstruct shifts in Sahelian economy and political structure in the face of environmental change. His work is a counterpoint to more reductionist approaches that attempt to link specific events and ecology (see McCann 1999). He provides a richly historicized account of change in multiple facets of pastoral and agricultural systems, counteracting any tendencies to view the social and economic relations that underpin them as intrinsic and unchanging.[9] From his analysis, we can extract a variety of elements relevant to investigating historical processes of ecologically-mediated change in the Sahel (Table 1).

Table 1. Variables implicated in historical processes of political and economic change in West Africa

Political Economy
    Resource availability
        Raw materials, Foodstuffs, Luxuries, Labor, Pasture, Water
    Organization of resource exploitation
    Control of resource access and/or distribution
Interaction
    Hostile: Raiding, Warfare
    Collaborative: Specialization and interdependencies, Political alliances, Gift exchange, Mutual aid conventions, Trade networks and diasporas, Clientship
Technology
    Subsistence systems, Transport, Tools and Weapons
Cultural values
    Wealth, Power, Ethnicity, Rights

Responses to the Big Dry likely had some social, political, and economic consequences, which then had fundamental significance for responses to the climate upturn after 300 CE. This is the long-term chronological framework within which the question of Ghana's and Takrur's early development must be considered. As a broad generalization that has notable exceptions, archaeological research on first millennium sites has neither theorized nor implemented an approach that investigates more than one or two of the elements in Table 1. Many of the necessary determinations — such as the presence of slave labor, or subsistence intensification — require specialized investigations that must be built into a research plan. It is unfortunately the case that even the most basic studies, for example of plant and animal remains, have often been neglected in the past, partly due to the paucity of appropriate specialists, including archaeozoologists and archaeobotanists.[10] Where such analyses have been undertaken, a significant presence of cattle and ovicaprids in the economy has been documented (Law 1980).[11] At most sites, the cattle and sheep are in the size range of modern stock that transhume. In these cases, considerable seasonal mobility is likely. The stock at early Jenne-jeno are an exception: the sheep / goats are small, even dwarf, a trait that historically correlates with animals that are not well-adapted to lengthy transhumance. No faunal analysis has been reported for Kumbi Saleh, and only a small sample has been published from Tegdaoust, but historical evidence suggests that cattle and ovicaprids were important elements of the local economy at the end of the first millennium.

Another important element that has begun to come to light is the presence of horses in the first millennium CE. In *Ancient Ghana and Mali*, Levtzion rightly emphasized the importance of horses in the political economy of early Sudanic polities. Subsequently, Law argued that horses could not have been effectively used in warfare prior to the adoption of stirrups and bridles in the thirteenth century.[12] However, horses would have increased the ability of horse-breeding groups to trade, raid, and collect tribute from other groups, even without this technology. In archaeological sites along the Middle Niger between the seventh and tenth century CE, (ninth to tenth century Jenne-jeno and Tango Maare Diabel in the Gourma and at Akumbu in the Mema as early as the seventh century) we find horse bones and statuettes of horses with riders (S. McIntosh 1995; Togola 2008). They ride bareback (Figure 5). These are the small ponies that al-Bakri noted in the royal capital in the eleventh century (Levtzion and Hopkins 1981, 80-81). Horse burials in elite tombs are present along the northern Middle Niger in the eleventh century (R. McIntosh 1998, 225). Horses would have created a highly competitive regional environment (they are hard to monopolize), with many groups enjoying the same trade-and-raid capacity. Thoroughbred Arab horses at various later points in time became an item of prestige trade, with stallions owned only by chiefs (Law 1980; Webb 1995).

Given this economic profile from surrounding regions, we can propose with great confidence that livestock trade and production would have been of major importance in the Hawd during the wet period from 300-1000 CE, thanks to an abundance of excellent pasturage for horses and cattle and proximity to the earth salts at

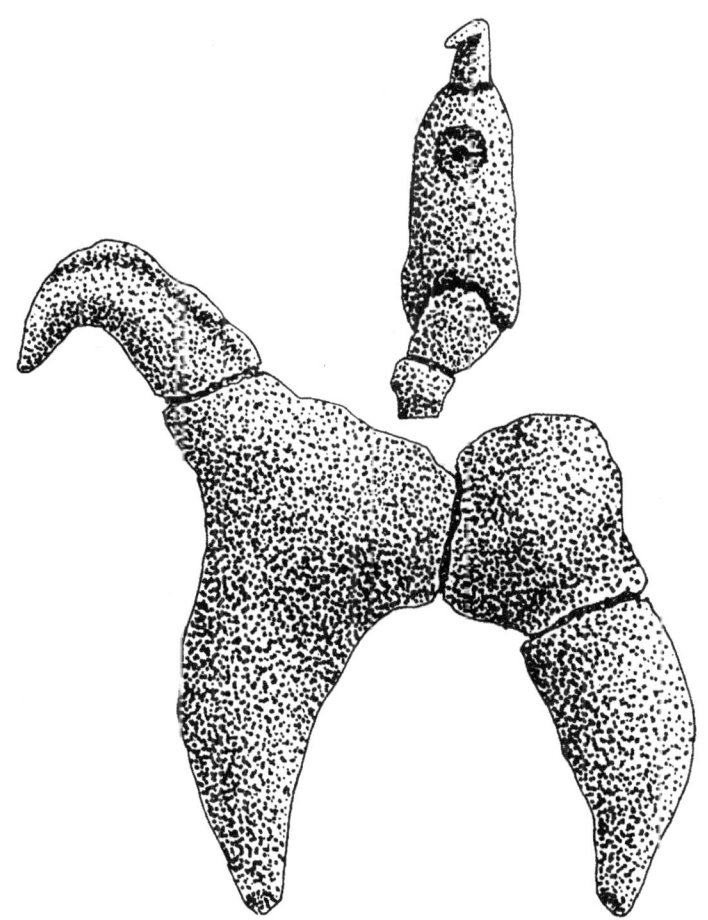

Figure 5 Equestrian terracotta figurine recovered from excavations at Tongo Maaré Diabel, Mali
Source: MacDonald and MacDonald (2000, 141)

both Tichitt and Walata. The cattle zone at that time would have extended north into the Adrar. Throughout the cattle and agriculture zones, a diverse landscape of herders, agropastoralists, and mixed farmers would have positioned themselves with regard to local opportunities.[13] If Ghana first staked a claim to regional importance in the southern Hawd / Awker, where al-Bakri situates it in the tenth-eleventh century, a glance at Google earth imagery of the town of Kumbi Saleh may suggest land-use potentials.

Kumbi Saleh is located along a schist outcrop lined with seasonal lakes and channels. To the south, field systems can be seen in the moist depression that borders the rock outcrop. This was the agricultural and dry season pastureland that supported Kumbi. During the rainy season, herds would have to be driven northward, both for salt and to avoid disease, depending on how plentiful rainfall was at the time. As economic networks developed, cattle and salt would have moved to southern markets seasonally. We thus have to conceptualize Ghana as having significant component of seasonal mobility, with some portion of the population involved in transhumance and movement of herds to markets. Whether this involved distinct ethnic groups, like the Peul, or certain age or specialist groups within the general population, is not known. As already mentioned, the systems we see in the Sahel today developed over time in response to particular historical conditions, making them impossible to project confidently into the past.[14] The key point is that conceptualizing Ghana as "sedentary" misses the extremely significant, seasonally mobile, herding component of its economy. As we shall see in the next section, early in the first millennium CE, this herding element may have been responsible for the development of trade networks bringing copper and salt to the Sahel and savanna, onto which the gold trade was later grafted.

Trans-Saharan Trade

In *Ancient Ghana and Mali*, Levtzion evaluated the available evidence and concluded that the volume of trade carried over the desert was insignificant before the introduction of the camel (9).[15] The superiority of the camel over bullocks and donkeys for desert transport is well-known: "it can survive without water or fresh grazing for eight to ten days, or twice as long as a donkey; the strongest draft camels can carry two hundred kilograms of freight, or one-third more than the donkey or bullock," and the camel alone can negotiate the hazardous footing of desert erg (Webb 1995, 11). Levtzion proposed that as Sanhaja Berbers acquired enough camels in the third or fourth century CE, they pressed southwest, connecting a pre-Arab trade in which gold was the principle staple with the Mediterrannean sphere (1973, 6-8). The question of the chronology of regular trans-Saharan commerce in gold continues to be debated.

Recent documentation of a regional Garamantian trade

network in the course of recent work by British and Italian teams in the Fezzan has re-opened the question of direct, organized trade between the Mediterranean and the Sudan in the first millennium BCE. Liverani suggests that the trans-Saharan itinerary recorded in Herodotus V.181-185 in the fifth century BCE is a major source documenting the beginning of trans-Saharan trade involving salt and gold. He outlines a regional system linking the Fezzan with Tripolitania, Cyrenaica, and Egypt in the north and the Ahaggar Mountains and the Niger River to the south, with the Garamantes at the very heart of the system (Liverani 2000).

One of the major difficulties with this hypothesis is the paucity of evidence for North African or Garamantian goods south of the Tropic of Cancer prior to the second half of the first millennium CE. Mattingley (2003, 85, 358) suggests that items mentioned by Herodotus, Pliny, and Strabo in regard to the Garamantes — salt, horse breeding, date cultivation, ivory, ebony, and hunting Ethiopians (for slaves?) — hint at a trade with low archaeological visibility. However, glassware and glass beads (some locally manufactured) were common at the Garamantian capital, Jarma, in the first four centuries CE. The popularity of these items after the eighth to ninth century CE farther south is abundantly attested at sites such as Awdaghost, Kumbi Saleh, Gao Ancien, Gao Saney, and a wide range of others. Why would a lightweight, desirable trade item such as glass beads not move along trade routes in earlier centuries? Only a very few glass beads have been recovered from contexts demonstrably earlier than the eighth century. Three of these came from early levels dating to 250 BCE-200 CE at Jenne-jeno and three from Ja (S. McIntosh 1995; Haskell, McIntosh and McIntosh 1986, 52; Bedaux et al. 2003, 263-77). Why are there so few early glass beads in comparison with the explosion of beads after 700-800 CE? One likely possibility is that they are moving via hand-to-hand gift exchange or barter at this early date, rather than as commodities in an organized trade.

Postulating an early salt trade of any magnitude, as Liverani does, is problematic without evidence for camels. While he rightly suggests that the faunal sample that has been analyzed for this time period is small, camel is not present in the voluminous first-millennium BC faunal samples from Jarma (Mattingly 2003, 354). Nor is there any evidence yet for his hypothesized rise of new polities at the southwestern end of the trade route, along the Niger Bend and in the gold producing regions as a consequence of the early trade. Archaeological surveys along the Niger Bend around Timbuktu, Gourma Rharous, and Gao (S. McIntosh and R. McIntosh 1984; Togola, Cisse and Fane 2004) and in the Falemme Valley near the Bambuk goldfields (Thiaw 1999) and around Niani, close to the Bure goldfields (Filipowiak 1979) have not produced any obvious evidence of such a development in the first millennium BCE. Admittedly, however, only a small portion of the goldfields has been surveyed. Currently, the case for regular, organized trade in the first millennium BCE between the Sahel and the Mediterranean via the Garamantes remains thin, but new archaeological evidence may change that assessment at any time.

There is, however, considerable evidence for a variety of regional exchange systems throughout the southern Sahara and Sahel at that time. As different systems intersected, some goods, such as our few early beads, perhaps, may have been able to travel considerable distances. Stone beads also traveled in the first millennia BCE and CE from Saharan and Sahelian sources (such as the Hombori uplands in the Malian Gourma) and are regularly recovered from Late Stone Age and Iron Age archaeological deposits. From 500 to 1 BCE, copper from Akjoujt in western Mauritania moved north and south over distances of up to four hundred kilometers (Deme and McIntosh 2006; Vernet 1993). Copper from Azelik in Niger moved within a similar radius (Grebenart 1985). In both cases, the populations engaged in exploiting and moving copper were mobile pastoralists or agro-pastoralists who would also have had a vital interest in the salt deposits found in the same region. In both cases, copper (and salt?) exploitation ceased at the end of the first millennium BCE, coincident with the onset of the harshly arid conditions described above. How cattle herders who had moved far to the south of Saharan sources managed to procure the salt for their herds is a matter of considerable interest. They likely reoriented trade and transhumance towards more southerly sources — the amersals of the Gourma,[16] and coastal salts at Nterert, for example.[17] The earliest unambiguous evidence we have for the re-establishment of links between desert and Sahel / savanna is the presence of copper at Jenne-jeno by the fifth century CE, which marks the likelihood of desert salt trade as well (S.

McIntosh 1995). I have argued that the visible items of trade at Jenne-jeno, such as stone and iron, from the earliest deposits, and later copper, and still later, gold, were exchanged against local commodities such as grains and dried fish. No comparable clues to an exchange system were detected during the first eight centuries of the first millennium CE at nine sites excavated on the Middle Senegal, however. There, copper apparently was not imported again until after 850 CE (McIntosh, McIntosh and Bocoum, forthcoming). Evidence for exchange with the north is also forthcoming from Kissi, located in northeastern Burkino Faso, where cowries, copper, wool fabric, and glass beads have been recovered from the sixth and seventh century warior burials (Magnavita 2003).

Another clue to interaction networks is provided by the distribution of polychrome painted pottery with red slip, and black and white paint, from the Middle Niger in the fourth to fifth century CE at Jenne-jeno, Ja, and extensively in the Lakes region and the Mema, as well as Gao by the seventh century CE. For earlier or contemporary polychrome, we must look north and east to Berber sites, including Garamantian period tombs (Mattingley 2003, 229).[18] Polychrome pottery has not been documented along the Middle Senegal. The available evidence to my mind supports the idea that regional trade systems were established along the Middle Niger and interlinked with other regional systems north and south of the river to form extensive inter-regional exchange networks within one or two centuries after the end of the Big Dry around 300 CE. The expanding use of the camel encouraged this development and made possible the transport of substantial cargoes of salt, copper, and semiprecious stone for beads, among other goods, from the desert to the river, where boats carried foodstuffs to exchange.

One recurring question is when gold began to move along these exchange networks and reach North Africa. Liverani believes that the trade, organized by the Garamantes, was active in the first millennium BCE (Liverani 2000). Garrard marshaled impressive evidence from North African mint strikes to suggest that the reactivation of the Carthage mint to strike imperial gold after 296 CE until it closed in 695 was made possible by a new, probably West Africa source reaching North Africa during that period (Garrard 1982). He proposed that this source was then taken over by the Arabs, who minted West African gold at Kairouan. Sutton argued that, on the contrary, the historically documented, early, eastern routes from Ifriqiya via Air could have no connection with gold from the western parts of West Africa that are assumed to have been the earliest source (Sutton 1983). Indeed, Blanchard indicates that from 300 to 620 CE, the main source of gold in the eastern Roman Empire (including N. Africa) were new production centers in Armenia and the Caucasus, until their seizure in the seventh century by the Persian Sassanids (Blanchard 2001). By 625, the Sassanids dominated the known world gold supply and the Byzantines experienced an acute gold shortage.[19] The Arab conquests changed everything. They broke the Sassanid monopoly on gold and caused huge amounts of the metal to enter the monetary system through massive taxation on Gothic and Byzantine churches in North Africa, plundering of Pharaonic gold in Egypt, and "dishoarding" of Sassanian gold treasure. They also secured the Nubian gold route. The price of gold at Medina plummeted as a consequence (Blanchard 2001).

Recent trace element analyses of gold coins minted in North Africa during Byzantine, and Arab dynasties from Ummayad (661-750 CE) to Almohad (1147-1269 CE) support Blanchard's argument. Byzantine gold was recycled for early Arab mint strikes until the Aghlabids (800-909 CE). At that time, a new chemical fingerprint, consistent with extremely pure West African gold lacking platinum trace elements, appears in Aghlabid dinars (Guerra et al. 1999; Gondonneau and Guerra 2002). Coin molds recently excavated from ninth century contexts at Essouk-Takmekka in Niger have gold droplets still adhering (Nixon 2007). Chemical studies are currently underway. At present, then, evidence for a trans-Saharan gold trade prior to 750-800 CE is lacking. Source areas in Burkina Faso, such as Poura and Sirba, have not been fingerprinted, however, so an earlier trade in West African gold may yet be documented.

In evaluating the archaeological evidence that can be mobilized to interpret the factors that contributed to the emergence of Ghana in the first millennium CE, it is evident that the points of clarity are few in number and limited in contextual detail. Only one locale identified with one of the very earliest political entities mentioned by Arab chroniclers — the Middle Senegal Valley — where the sites of Walade, Cubalel and Siwré are thought to be in the general area of Takrur, and Sincu Bara may be in the region of Sila — has revealed archaeological deposits dating to the first millennia BCE and CE that have been excavated and described. For the Hawd / Awkar and the Gao / Tilemsi region, there are no excavated and described deposits that have produced radiocarbon dates in the first millennium earlier than the sixth-seventh century. Some of the best detail currently available on the period from 500 BCE to 1000 CE comes from the Mema and the Inland Niger Delta — two areas that were far from the proposed political center of Ghana at Kumbi Saleh. From these brief glimpses into the past, however frustrating in their limited sample size, we are able to see that various commodities were moving considerable distances between Sahara and Sahel at different points in time, without any compelling evidence of regular organized trade with the Mediterrannean sphere prior to 700 CE. The early influence of northern (and eastern?) Berbers is, however, suggested by the popularity of polychrome (white / cream, black, red) pottery along the Middle Niger after about 200 CE, which seems to correspond with the re-establishment of exchange systems disrupted by the extreme aridity of the Big Dry from 300 BCE to 300 CE. Recent analyses of the lead isotope ratios of the copper from Kissi, recovered from contexts dated from the fifth to the seventh centuries CE have demonstrated similarities to Moroccan or Tunisian ore sources. But T. Fenn (2008) has been careful to note that additional analyses of West African ores are needed to make sure there is not a local ore source with similar lead isotope ratios.

Along the Middle Senegal Valley (MSV), the re-appearance of copper after 800 CE foreshadows a development of new types of pottery heavily influenced by the material culture at Tegdaoust. After 900 CE, the pottery of both Tegdaoust and the MSV share an emphasis on red-slipped wares with prominent ribbed cordons and little or no painted decoration.[20] These two different ceramic domains (painted *versus* slipped and ribbed) suggest different sets of cultural interactions and influences and merit considerably more study. At present, the Hawd-MSV connections seem to develop relatively late. Prior to these connections, the MSV sites remain quite small and undifferentiated with a very limited material culture repertoire through much of the first millennium CE. Without further research to explore different sectors of the MSV and to extend the excavated sequence into the tenth century and beyond, there is little more we can say about the development of Takrur. The Middle Niger presents quite a contrast, with sites such as Jenne-jeno and Ja reaching considerable sizes early on and displaying a diverse material culture reflecting influences and interactions over a wide area. Although these sites are, as previously noted, distant from the political center of Ghana, they provide insights into the systems of trade and interaction in the first millennium CE that may have been linked to Kumbi Saleh. At Kumbi Saleh itself, however, the present paucity of excavated deposits dating prior to the ninth century CE severely constrains our interpretations of its chronological depth and development.

Political Organization

Given the state of the evidence just outlined, any discussion of the development and political organization of early Sudanic polities must be both theoretical and speculative. Two post-*Ancient Ghana and Mali* developments that are especially important for this effort are the documentation of indigenous inter-regional trade and town growth in the early first millennium CE and an increased understanding of the organizational variability of complex societies. These make it possible to theorize the internal dynamics of emerging Ghana and also to contemplate a range of possible organizational structures for the historical Ghana of al-Bakri that move us away from uncritical analogies with kingdoms and empires in other, better-known parts of the world.

Ancient Ghana and Mali was written at a time when accounts of emergent African complexity were couched almost exclusively in terms of external dynamics or stimulus. Diffusion, borrowing or emulation, and variants of the Hamitic hypothesis were variously proposed to account for the appearance of early polities in West Africa. Levtzion parted ways with the more extreme versions of external stimulus accounts and focused on interregional interaction — nomad-sedentary conflict and trans-Saharan trade — as the key dynamic. He identified the "more advanced culture of the sedentaries" as an important influence on the organization of the early state, "even if we admit — according to traditional and sometimes documentary evidence — that some of the early dynasties in the Sahel had nomad ancestors" (Levtzion 1973, 8-9). His timeline for the beginnings of political reorganization in the Sahel, stimulated by the trans-Saharan trade in gold, extended back to the centuries preceding the Arab conquest of the Maghrib.

Today, we can make an alternative argument for political developments at that time based on local trade systems that linked desert and savanna, but did not necessarily extend to North Africa. With copper as the durable marker of exchange networks that were operating by the fifth century CE, we can postulate a set of interlinked networks that moved comestibles (such as dried fish, grains, and stock on the hoof) among environmental zones, and raw materials (stone, iron ore or blooms, copper) and salt from source areas. I have argued elsewhere that the participation of Jenne-jeno in these networks was a significant factor in the rapid growth of the town by the mid-first millennium (S. McIntosh 1995; R. McIntosh 1998). The dynamics involved were internal, as occupational specializations developed to increase productive output and organize exchange, as well as external, with a variety of possible scenarios for inter-regional interaction and trade (see Table 1). The early development of Ghana may also have been spurred by a similar set of factors. The exchange networks of the fourth to seventh centuries developed and expanded at a time of transformation in the desert, with the growth and expansion of camel herds, which offered both transport and military advantages.[21] In the cattle zone, where the most direct interaction between camel nomads and stock herders and agropastoralists occurred, the use of horses for raiding and other military ends may have increased in response, and negotiations over pasture and water and passage along communication routes would have resulted in conflict or accommodation.

Somewhere within these murky centuries, Ghana likely established a strategic advantage in the trade networks that provided a key to its ability ultimately to link together the trade in salt coming from distant sources in the north, and in gold, from equally distant sources in the south. Within the vast area between the Senegal and the Niger in the Soninke heartland, various groups and polities must have competed for access to salt and copper, and eventually, gold. What enabled Ghana to prevail and remain the foremost polity associated by Arab chroniclers with gold for four centuries?

Ibn Hawqal made it clear that Ghana ensured the flow of salt in the tenth century from the Sanhaja of Awdaghust by means of political alliances and gift exchange between rulers to secure goodwill

(Levtzion and Hopkins 1981, 48). In contrast to salt, for which there were a small number of discrete sources and a restricted number of Saharan routes, gold was mined over a large area and could potentially move along a large number of savanna pathways. How did Ghana succeed in attracting gold to its market and routes rather than those of competitors? It is quite clear that gold production was highly decentralized and not under Ghana's control (Perinbam 1988, note 4). So the organization of procurement at source markets and shipment north must be a key element. The early development of a Soninké trade diaspora — well before the first mention of ethnically distinct merchants (the Banu Naghmarata) by al-Bakri — is one mechanism by which the savanna trade in gold could be organized (Levtzion and Hopkins 1981, 82).

The trade diaspora concept, as developed by Ronald Cohen (1971), describes a trading group that emigrates to market centers along trade routes, specializes in trading particular commodities, and remains ethnically distinct from the host community. Trade diasporas provide a way to organize long-distance trade where physical and economic security are lacking, and communication and transportation are difficult (Stein 2002). Such diasporas have been a characteristic of the Mande-speaking zone of West Africa, historically. Even supposing that first millennium trade was organized by Soninke merchants, however, we are still left wondering why trade flowed preferentially to Ghana, over other, competing Soninke towns and markets, particularly early on, before Ghana's political reach became extensive. Were diaspora merchants attached to great families with links to the ruler of Ghana?[22] Alternatively, ritual may have provided the link. From al-Bakri's account, we know that the ruler of Ghana was a ritually powerful leader, associated with the ancestor cults of previous kings (Levtzion and Hopkins 1981, 80). He was also, according to Youssouf Tata Cissé, the mystical brother of Bida, the serpent in the Epic of Wagadu with power over both rainfall and gold (cited in Kesteloot 1994). Diabé Cissé, the first king of Ghana and the first to be invested with sacred regalia, was the offspring of a water *jinn* and Dinga, mythical founder of the Soninke clans of Wagadu. Diabé's twin brother was Bida (R. McIntosh 1998, 254-55). Is it possible that gold flowed to Ghana preferentially because of a belief that the ruler's intermediation in the serpent / ancestor cult was essential not only to fertility and the production of rain, but also the productivity of the gold mines? Kesteloot has suggested that variants of this serpent cult of Wagadu origin were widely adopted as royal cults and were associated with the emergence of both the Takrur and Wolof polities (Kesteloot 1994). One of these variants in which kingship and serpent worship are linked was described among the Zafqu by al-Bakri. Levtzion and Hopkins suggest that the Zafqu were Soninke, perhaps Diafunu (Levtzion and Hopkins 1981, 78).

Despite the fact that archaeology has to date brought us no closer to identifying the early and perhaps shifting location of Ghana's capital, we have been able to look at a variety of archaeological evidence and to suggest possible scenarios for the early emergence of the polity that encompass both internal and external dynamics. The mobility of early Ghana's pastoral sector, its involvement in inter-regional trade in copper and perhaps salt provided the initial basis for the development of the political economy. Ghana's ability to enter and ultimately dominate the gold trade was perhaps due to three main factors: skill in crafting alliances with the Sanhaja leaders who controlled salt, elaboration of a religious ideology linking gold production and sacred kingship, and the organization of a trade diaspora by merchants with ethnic and perhaps clan links to the ruler. They would have been important purveyors of the royal cult ideology.

By the time of al-Bakri's description, the political economy had grown enormously through levies on trade, and tribute. The actual political organization of Ghana is less clear, however. *Ancient Ghana and Mali* employed a variety of descriptive terms that suggested misleading correspondences with the European warrior kings of the Middle Ages, such as dominions, vassal chiefdoms, king, and kingdom. West African rulers had quite different concerns: securing trade routes rather than conquering territory, procuring goods and followers rather than land. They also had quite different cultural concepts of power, as Assombang reminds us: "the concept of power and authority in Africa has more to do with the ability to engage or contain occult forces than with military force, administrative authority, or economic control" (1999).

Levtzion appeared to take at face value statements by al-Bakri that Tunka-Menin, whose reign began in 1063, "wielded great power and inspired respect as the ruler of a great empire," leaving

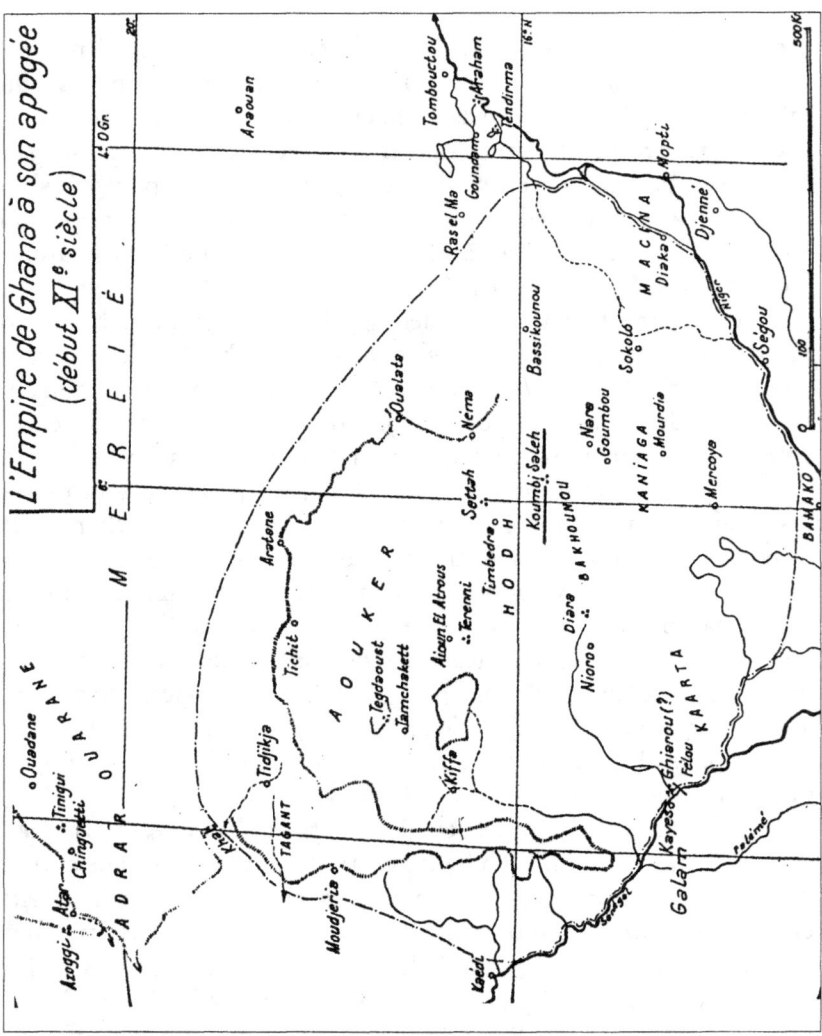

Figure 6. The Empire of Ghana at its apogee
Source: Mauny (1961, 510)

unasked the questions, "what was the source of the power and how was it manifested?" and "what is an empire?" Willis cautioned in his review of *Ancient Ghana and Mali* that such usage "frequently shrouds in further obscurity the very peoples and institutions he would expose to view" (1975). R. McIntosh has presented a model for Ghana as a "slowly consolidated confederation of many small polities that stood in varying relations to the core, from nominal tribute-paying parity to fully administered" (1998, 255-56). This reconstruction reflects recent archaeological theorizing about the origins of states out of an earlier landscape of small polities. Although Mauny's reconstruction (1961) of Ghana at its height (see Figure 6) is often used to illustrate Ghana throughout its existence, this projection back in time denies an ongoing historical process that must have involved periodic struggles to consolidate trade territories, subdue rivals, and expand influence. We still have much of that process to discover archaeologically. The necessary research will involve excavation of first millennium deposits throughout a wide area of the Mema,[23] Hawd, Tagant, and the vast expanses to the south, between the Senegal and Niger Rivers, looking for patterns of imported prestige goods (as proxy measures for the size and penetration of the political economy), shared material culture (as a guide to patterns of interaction), and changes to settlement systems (as indicators of changing social / political organization). We can only hope that as archaeology shifts emphasis from its long-running concern with evolutionary sequences in areas of pristine state development to the documentation of variability in early state development, the Western Sudan will at last attract the attention of enough archaeologists to get the job done. For the time being, our reconsidered view of early Ghana remains dominated by darkness and lack of evidence in many of the areas most central to our concerns.

Notes

[1] McCann (1999) notes the growing influence of anthropogenic models for "desertification" from the colonial period in the 1930s to the Sahelian drought of the 1970s and 1980s. By the early 1990s, considerable evidence to challenge the human degradation hypothesis had become available.

[2] Brooks (1993) considers these longer-term shifts.

[3] Extensive, first millennium BCE agropastoral systems that exploited inter-dunal depressions in Western Mauritania during the wet season and pasturage further south, closer to the Senegal river, during the dry season were likely disrupted (Deme and S. McIntosh 2006). The associated exploitation of Akjoujt copper by these pastoralists over a period of several centuries ceased by the end of the first millennium BCE (Vernet 1993). The near cessation of Saharan rock art depicting horses may also date to this period. In the Hawd, the known archaeological sequence around Tichitt ends about 300 BCE and resumes further south after 500 CE at Tegdaoust (Munson 1980).

Further east, sites in the Mema appear to have been abandoned at this time as the region dried up. Iron-using populations moved farther south along the Middle Niger into the eastern Inland Niger Delta, settling permanently at Jenne-jeno as water levels dropped in the period 200-0 BCE (S. McIntosh 1995).

[4] McCann (1999) makes a similar point:
> There have been few if any attempts explicitly to link questions of climate to micro-level studies of communities, villages, or ethnic groups.... Studies ... on a national or regional scale on the basis of inter-annual patterns of climate impact provide little or no foundation for establishing a precise relationship between the effect of climate on social, economic, and political life locally.

[5] Devisse (1983, 382) postulates a dramatic decline in the water table to date to the eleventh to twelfth centuries CE.

[6] A point also made in McDougall (1983). De Moraes Farias (1974) also lodged an objection, noting the over-emphasis on conflict in this formulation.

[7] It is also possible that bush meat and fish were procured via exchange of grains and milk with hunters and fishing groups.

[8] Camel is documented in the Middle Senegal Valley around 200-400 CE. MacDonald and MacDonald (forthcoming).

[9] McDougall (1985) also articulated concerns with "sufficiently historical conceptualizations" of pastoral and sedentary peoples through time, to counteract the tendency to dichotomize them.

[10] This situation is changing, fortunately. There are several excellent archaeozoologists and archaeobotanists currently working on West African material. German archaeobotanists working under Katharina Neumann at Frankfurt have in recent years been especially instrumental in theorizing the development of Sahelian agriculture from an initial, Neolithic period with one or two cultivated cereals (millet, rice) and a variety of wild plants, to a secondary, Iron Age phase, in which sorghum, pulses, and other domesticates were added (Neumann 2003). The development of the full West African savanna agricultural complex has obvious implications for both increased sedentism and the production of surplus for trade.

[11] In the Middle Senegal, these occur in the context of episodic occupation by agropastoralists who also hunt local antelope and do a bit of fishing. The offtake of both cattle and ovicaprids suggests culling practices designed to maximize herd size, rather than meat or milk productivity (MacDonald and MacDonald, forthcoming). The fauna from first millennium deposits at Akumbu in the Mema indicates the dominance of cattle and ovicaprids, with hunting of antelopes and some fishing also contributing to the subsistence economy (Togola 2008). Fish constitute a much larger component of subsistence at Jenne-jeno throughout the first millennium, but cattle and

ovicaprids are significant as well (S. McIntosh 1995).

[12] The discovery of an arab-type bridle at Koumbi Saleh in a context dated to 530 _100 BP confirms that this equipment was being used within a calibrated date range of CE 1285-1525 (2 Sigma). See Berthier (1997, 78-79).

[13] Camel herders likely entered this area just prior to or at the beginning of this period; and must be envisioned as part of this landscape, at least seasonally. A definite camel bone has come from deposits dated from 200 to 400 CE at Siwré in the Middle Senegal Valley (MacDonald and MacDonald, forthcoming). Although *Ancient Ghana and Mali*, like most historians, saw camel nomads moving southward from North Africa, Bulliet (1990) has proposed a spread from east to west through the Sahel, based on the distribution of saddle styles and other evidence.

[14] With regard to the development of the Fula / Peul cattle herders, the earliest historical confirmation that we have of their distinctive pastoral (as opposed to agropastoral) identity is the 1339 map of Angelino Dulcert, on which "Felle" and "Tochoror" are identified in the region of the Middle Senegal Valley, today inhabited year round by the agropastoral Tukolor, and seasonally by the Fula

[15] See Bulliet (1990) for a slightly different interpretation.

[16] Excavation at the four-metre high tell of Tango Maare Diabel in the Gourma revealed a building sequence in tauf and mud brick beginning in the first century CE, and an agropastoral occupation (K. MacDonald, R. Hutton-MacDonald and T. Togola 1998).

[17] Salt sources as per Mauny (1961, 322 [Figure 66 Distribution of mineral salts in West Africa]).

[18] The commonest painted Garamantian style is red on white bichrome, however, a combination that is rare in the Sahel.

[19] Heraclius, Roman Emperor over North Africa at the time of the Arab conquests, had to appeal to the Church to lend him, at interest, gold and silver plate so that he might mint money to finance a military response to Sassanid incursions by the emperor Chosroes (Baynes 1913).

[20] Painted decoration is absent at the Middle Senegal sites (S. McIntosh 2001); it is present at Tegdaoust only in early levels, where it may point to links with Kumbi Saleh, which produced some ribbed sherds with red and white paint in early levels (see Berthier 1997, 64-65; Devisse 1983, 257).

[21] On this military use of camels somewhat later, see McDougall (1983, 272).

[22] For a later period, Ralph Willis (1975) argued that the Juula and perhaps the Wangara were attached to great families. He disagreed with Levtzion's interpretation of them as independent, itinerant traders.

[23] The late Tereba Togola fimly believed that the capital of Ghana would ultimately be revealed to be one of the huge tells in this region (see R. McIntosh 1998, 167, 258).

Captain of "We Band of Brothers": An Archaeologist's Homage to Nehemia Levtzion

Roderick J. McIntosh

Résumé

Lorsqu'il a invité les archéologues à collaborer à la révision de son si cher **Ancient Ghana and Mali,** *Nehemia Levtzion a confronté l'asymétrie souvent admise, pourtant rarement testée dans le pouvoir explicatif entre l'histoire documentaire et l'archéologie. D'autres ont traité les spécialistes de la préhistoire comme, au mieux des serviteurs, et au pire des cas, des hommes de science parvenus. Levtzion a explicitment rejeté plusieurs admissions qui rendaient les nombreuses histoires de l'Afrique pré-coloniale tout à fait inintéressantes aux yeux des spécialistes de la préhistoire: (1) que les données archéologiques offrent, dans le meilleur des cas, une toile de fond et un contexte, (2) que l'état de hiérarchie est l'unique structure intégrative viable lorsque les peuples sont stratifiés économiquement et politiquement, et (3) que les changements culturels en Afrique ne font que refléter les modèles déjà observés ailleurs, rien d'autre. Levtzion s'est entouré d'une force diverse de spécialistes, "frères d'armes," pour continuer sa bonne guerre contre ceux qui persistaient à dédaigner les belles réalisations de l'Afrique.*

Abstract

By inviting archaeologists to collaborate in the revision of his beloved **Ancient Ghana and Mali,** *Nehemia Levtzion confronted the oft-assumed, yet-rarely tested asymmetry in explanatory power between documentary history and archaeology. Others have treated prehistorians as, at best, handmaidens and, at worse, scientific parvenus. Levtzion explicitly rejected several assumptions that render many histories of pre-colonial Africa uninteresting to prehistorians: (1) that that the data of archaeology provide, at best, background and context, (2) that the hierarchical state is the only viable integrative structure when peoples become stratified economically or politically, and (3) that culture change in Africa simply replicates patterns already known from elsewhere, and no others. Levtzion enlisted a plural force of specialists, a "Band of Brothers," to continue his Good Fight against those who would distain Africa's accomplishments.*

ENGAGING WITH A LEGACY: NEHEMIA LEVTZION (1935-2003)

What a thrill and an honor, and how curious it was to have been invited by Nehemia Levtzion to collaborate in the revision of his beloved *Ancient Ghana and Mali* (1973). Susan Keech McIntosh, the other archaeologist invited, and I were curious, of course, because archaeology had been minimally represented in Nehemia's original. (This reflected, of course, the nascent state of the discipline in the Western Sahel as of 1971, the date by which the manuscript was completed and shipped off to the publisher.) Oral traditions were only marginally more present. We were, naturally, delighted (and not surprised) to learn that the other scholar invited to collaborate was David Conrad, with his obsessively encyclopedic command of Mande corpus of traditions. Much had changed since the 1973 publication date.

Ancient Ghana and Mali, after all, was grounded largely in the Arabic sources, most of which were external to the continent, most second-hand, third-hand, or even more hands removed. Nehemia's twenty-four principal sources, from Ibn al-Hakam at the end of the ninth century to Leo Africanus (CE 1526) were not, frankly, very sympathetic to the peoples of Africa. Even the locally-written *tawarikh* of Timbuktu (al-Sa'di's *Ta'rikh al-Sudan*, 1655, and al-Mukhtar's *Ta'rikh al-Fattash*, 1665) were subject to a heavy editorial and canonical hand.

Yet Nehemia was able not only to put together a masterful synthesis of the history of the Western Sudan. He abstracted two (in his words) "Radical Propositions." These both were quite revolutionary for the times, which, as you will remember, were the birthing days of African history as a scholarly discipline. The first Radical Proposition: that states were first created at the frontier, at the intersection of expansive, militaristic (Saharan) nomads and "more advanced"[1] sedentary peoples of the Sahel. The up-to-then rarely-questioned Arab Stimulation model by which the civilizing traits of complex society (towns, long-distance trade, states) were brought across the Saharan wastes by early Arab traders, these effects radiating southwards to the benighted lands of the Lamlam, by stimulus diffusion, from commercial entrepots such as Tegdaoust or Tekkada.

Nehemia's second Radical Proposition came from his own life experience as a first generation Israeli, participating first hand in the birth of a state alternative to and liberated from the Statism model of Europe. His belief was that each society was capable of inventing its own, signature state structure and that the post-Independence history of the Third World would be a proliferation of experiments in political economy and state legitimations every bit as novel and individual as Israel. The Core and Periphery (or shadow) vision of world history: by which some inventive societies were the "culture creators," and other societies passive and (to historians and prehistorians alike) uninteresting "culture-recipients." Fundamental to that individualism of the emerging post-Colonial states would have been the deep-time experiences of the people, their communities, and their societies. Hence, Nehemia's belief that by compiling a history such as *Ancient Ghana and Mali* he would be aiding the abetting of the true, post-Colonial liberation process.

In his mind, at the time of his invitation to the three of us, the revision of *Ancient Ghana and Mali* would be largely a process of writing history from non-historical sources.[2] He thought there would be little change to the interpretation of the Arabic sources. Yes, there had been some critiques of *Ancient Ghana and Mali* since its publication, and these were to be addressed, as appropriate, in the revision. But few new and no radically different Arabic sources had come to light since. What was new was to come from the oral traditions and from archaeology.

However, just how new could the revised *Ancient Ghana and Mali* be if the interpretation of the texts essentially was not to change? Were the contributions of archaeology and of oral traditions simply to be supplemental, or would they be allowed to contribute their own Radical Propositions, altered perspectives not only on the world written about by the Arab chroniclers, but also about the explicit and implicit filters those authors brought to the task of compiling knowledge into, for the most part, world geographies and world histories?

And this, then, is the origin of the title of this homage to Nehemia Levtzion — he created an ambiance at the several preliminary meetings about the revision (at several professional meetings, in Jerusalem and in Houston, Texas) in which we four truly felt us to be "We Band of Brothers."

We few, we happy few, we band of brothers;

For he today that sheds his blood with me
Shall be my brother.[3]

We were warriors together, differently armored and armed to be sure,[4] engaging together as equals to fight the three enemies of interdisciplinary collaboration and respect. The first enemy has already been alluded to (and it is one that archaeologists feel very touchy about): "The Handmaiden Problem." Can archaeology ever truly be a co-equal investigatory tool when dealing with peoples, or periods for which historical documents exist? Or will the "real histories" of such periods or peoples always be generated by the documentary sources, the stuff unearthed from the ground (or, for that matter, recorded in the memories of descendants) simply adding flavor? I, for one, always felt a brother in a band captained by an historian with a respect for my craft.

The second enemy was the "Empire Problem." Implicit in the first rendition of *Ancient Ghana and Mali* was a search for states: beyond *chercher le chef* to *chercher l'empereur*. But what if archaeology provided examples of complex societies, or large areal expanses of economically (and politically) integrated peoples — without the expected multi-tiered, hierarchical state apparatuses (S. McIntosh 1999a; R. McIntosh 2005)?[5] What if the oral sources strongly suggest that advanced political forms existed in the Sahel or savanna in direct disagreement with explicit statements in the Arabic sources? Might the eye of these sources have been so occluded by their Mediterranean Basin experiences and expectations (or by racialism) that radically different forms of government were simply not recognized? "We Band of Brothers" together abandoned the field of empire-envy, into a short foray with "Over-Kingdom" (Nehemia's suggestion, with a twinkle in his eye), to settle finally on "Polities." (The *Ancient Ghana and Mali* revision will be entitled *Emerging Polities of the Western Sudan: Ancient Ghana and Mali.*)

And it was against the third enemy, the "Eclipsed Grand Narrative Problem" (Feierman 1974; S. McIntosh 1999a),[6] that Nehemia's captaincy of our Band shone with brilliance. What pulls together the contributions of an "alternative" historian (Conrad), a traditional text-driven historian (Nehemia himself) and two archaeologists when narratives such as Core-Periphery or Stadial Progressivism (primitive band organization to chiefdoms to states and, finally, to empire) no longer adequately describe the history of the Western Sudan. Africa does very well at breaking down universal narratives. The problem for us four was to find what replaces these to ensure consistency to the narrative? (For the answer to this question, you will have to buy the book).

Having introduced this motif (with apologies to William Shakespeare's *Henry V*) of "We Band of Brothers," and before ending with a preview of the "Antecedents" chapter(s) of Child-of-*Ancient Ghana and Mali*, I did want to contrast Nehemia's embrace of archaeologists with another depiction of prehistorians and their trade that has enormously distressed all Africanist archaeologists. And we had thought we were far beyond this, certainly so by 1995, the date of the offending publication: Jan Vansina's curious article, "Historians, are archaeologists your siblings?" This caricature of archaeology as practiced in the 1960s — how utterly discouraging. How sad when one is stereotyped by a respected colleague as a wayward servant (Robertshaw 2000), a mere handmaiden, and as a scientistic neo-evolutionary lick-spittle.

I had always (perhaps with intolerable pride) boasted to prehistorian friends specializing in other areas that africanist historians and archaeologists had a special relationship, a common mission to destroy the myth of "unrewarding gyrations" — as evidenced by the *Journal of African History* being a high-status publishing organ, equally, for archaeologists. Now, we are told that all archaeologists can hope ever to do is to "give resonance to documentary evidence by placing it against its background" (Vansina 1995, 398). It sounds like mere Hand Maidenism to me.

More than that, "Siblings" appears to be a reminder of Terence Ranger's "golden rule that a historian should trust an archaeologist no further than he can throw a trench" (1979, 522; Stahl 1993, 248). Vansina (1995, 396) inventories the several sins of prehistorians, cardinal moral failings responsible for the "mutual incompatibility," the "major dissonances at the juncture" (1995, 370), of the two disciplines:

(1) Stewardesque multilineal neo-evolutionism (yet S. McIntosh's *Beyond Chiefdoms* [1999a] is almost a cult classic among opponents of neo-evolutionism?);

(2) Reductionist determinism (especially environmental) (*The Way*

the Wind Blows [McIntosh, Tainter, and McIntosh 2000] is an explicit search for a new climatic and landscape approach between determinism and the opposite extreme, purposeful ignorance);
(3) Models (those incubi of Satan Science);
(4) Extrapolation (by which he probably means uniformitarianism and reliance for explanation upon ethnographic or ethnohistorical examples);
(5) Nothing to limit the free range of imagination.

But Vansina's greatest archaeological sin is his last: Lack of historical Specificity and Contingency. Can he really be unaware of the decade-long embrace in prehistory of the Braudelian paradigm of the *longue durée* — as a device to reconcile the "low frequency" time-scales of the archaeologist with the "high-frequency" time-scale of most historians? Can Vansina really not know of the deep ambivalence, within archaeology, about the identifiability of agency and contingency? It is worth quoting Christopher Hawkes (1947):

> ... do we not ... think of ourselves as more scientific than historians? Or at least that the immensity of historians' material, and the turbidity caused in it by the frettings and struttings of so many historical human individuals, must prevent their seeing the wood for the trees — I mean, the men, as trees walking. Whereas with us, we tell ourselves, the most scientific and therefore the best, because the purest, kind of archaeology is the prehistoric kind, where individuals are nameless and unknown, and so cannot disturb of studies by throwing any of their proud and angry dust into our eyes (quoted in Evans 1998, 400).

In effect, Africanist archaeologists have just had a front-end-loader-full of dust thrown into their eyes.

How terribly sad that Nehemia Levtzion was never able to respond to Vansina, with his signature poignant good humor, to diffuse the situation. Perhaps he could have explained why he invited two archaeologists to join the rewrite of his beloved *Ancient Ghana and Mali*? Perhaps he could explain why, in joint discussion about that project, he consistently looked to archaeology (and oral sources) for a mutual, utter rethink of the book. Nehemia clearly did not expect from the archaeologists merely a prologue and a bit of backdrop to the revision. So, I will spend the rest of my time talking about the three-part logic of my "Antecedents" section of the new *Ancient Ghana and Mali* — and why I hope that it will go beyond the white-bread, descriptive *longue durée* narratives of much recent archaeological writing.

There will be description — I hope not too turgid — of long-term currents of change in climate, of soils and vegetation zones, of hydrologies, and gold, copper, and iron sources. These will form the First Aspect of the Antecedent chapter. This description of the bio-physical sphere will complement a reconstruction of the general social and economic transformations leading, by first-millennium CE, to the first of the historically-mentioned polities (Ghana and Takrur) — changing demographies, settlement organization and subsistence practices, emergence of specializations (including the explosively innovative West African metallurgies) and attendant craft corporations. But this chapter is equally about people dealing with change and with the special challenges confronting those who will become the Mande. Whence the signature deep-time trajectories of Resistance and Resilience at the juncture of contingency and long-term (low-frequency) eco-social[7] change of Mande history (Chang 1962). How, to give one example, can one even begin to understand the perversely heterarchical emergence of political and social complexity in the mid-first millennium AD without an appreciation of the opportunities bestowed by the overall rainfall optimum (millennium-scale) and, at the same time, of the special challenges of the abrupt cycling of Sharon Nicholson's (1980, 1986) six climate modes (at the decadal and century scales)? This is not mindless reductionist determinism. This is not mere backdrop. This is about real people developing a highly successful tradition of Resistance and Resiliency, with all the attendant mental and material armaments, to deal with change.

And here, I hope, we will have an exploration of the *longue durée*, that dialectical relation between culture and geography. *Longue durée* is best described by Olivier and Coudart as "as if on a bridge over the rapidly flowing river of time, [we are] ... as much interested in the movement of the waters as in the process of resistance which creates the whirlpools and the eddies of the waters" (1995, 362). The meander and flow of Ghana and Mali's histories (and Takrur and Songhai) are sounded at the confluence of our principles of Resilience and Resistance and historical contingency (just as Stephen Jay Gould reminds us that the course of evolution is charted at the intersection of evolutionary principles [mutation, natural selection, and drift] and the contingency of individuals within populations] (Fletcher 1992, 35).

Thus, my Antecedent section will be partially about the biophysical and social evolution of the Ghana and Mali landscape. But it will go far beyond that to explain Mande as a deep-time physical and occult Landscape of Power. I hope this, my Second Aspect, can go beyond even the exciting writings on sacred landscapes coming from the "forest of kings" of the Maya (Schele and Freidel 1990). First, archaeologists now generally take it as a given that all landscapes are deeply transformed by millennia of human action and human symbolic appreciation. Landscapes are palimpsests of long-term social history and of social memory (DeCorse and Chouin 2003). Even so "history-bereft" an archaeological problem as the emergence of early pastoral economies and identities out of hunter and gathering antecedents in southern Africa has been transformed by a new appreciation of negotiated cultural landscapes (Smith *et al.* 1991; Sadir 2003). When young Sunjata travels the *nyama*-laiden places of the Mema or Do and Kri, harvesting occult knowledge, he is navigating a sacred landscape. When Fakoli brings back a piece of the Black Stone of Mecca, he is creating the Mande Occult Landscape: contingency and deep-time principles of social memory.

So Vansina disdains archaeologists for only having "mute artifacts" (1995, 370), unlike the historian who deals with "messages" from the past. But what were the landscapes of ancient Ghana and Mali if not messages from deep-time, there to be read and acted upon by the successful Mande hero and heroine?

Lastly, my Third Aspect of the Antecedent chapter is to introduce a hoary old favorite of mine: Symbolic Reservoir (R. McIntosh 1998, 4-17). That roiling reservoir, bounded by permeable membranes, of symbols, rituals, beliefs, ideologies, legends and the like, into which individuals dip to extract the instruments of sectional advantage. Historical agency and deep-time principles are again at the confluence. How can one possibly understand canons of Mande legitimation and invention of tradition (what David Robinson calls the construction of the Western Sudanese Imperial Tradition) (Robinson 1985; R. McIntosh 1998, chapter 10), how can one understand the accommodation of corporate heterogeneity at urban centers such as Jenne or Dia without an appreciation of the workings of Mande as a Symbolic Reservoir? Vansina (1995, 384) claims that archaeologists cannot directly contribute data on human thought, ideology, ritual gestures, or practices of social organization. Yet interpretation of Great Zimbabwe, a context now utterly depauperate of primary archaeological material, has been transformed and advanced by the (sometimes acrimonious) debates about symbolic manipulation between the prehistorian Tom Huffman and the historians David Beach and Eugenia Herbert (Huffman 1996, 2000; Beach 1980; Herbert 1995). Nehemia embraced this concept of Symbolic Reservoir — and I think he looked forward to playing with the idea in his own narrative of the new *Ancient Ghana and Mali*. Great pity.

I had always thought that Africanist archaeologists and historians had a special, almost martial calling. I had always thought of us as a "Band of Brothers." I do not believe for a moment that Nehemia ever thought of us prehistorians as wayward servants. He may have been captaining the particular band revising *Ancient Ghana and Mali*, but I never sensed contempt for the troops. I fully agree with Roland Fletcher's warning: "Large-scale processes do not determine small-scale processes, nor can they be reduced to small-scale ones" (1992, 35). Understanding as he did the interplay of processes and events at different time-scales and causal-scales, Nehemia led us in the good fight.

What fight? We may be battling against the monolithic explanations and contempt for Africa of *Guns, Germs and Steel* (Diamond 1997), but it is a noble battle. We may be fighting a global arrogance of "The Coming Anarchy" (Kaplan 2000), but it is the Good Fight. We are, after all, contesting with as venerable a foe as Hegel:

> For [Africa] ... is no historical part of the world; it has no movement or development to exhibit.... [Africa] is still involved in the conditions of mere nature ... only as on the threshold of the World's History (1956, 98-99).

How discouraging: I always thought we were all together in the battle to enlarge all of humanity by demonstrating, at all time-scales and time-depths, the enormous, giddy precociousness and expansive innovation of the African continent. I always thought I would be accursed if I were not at the fight, not that I would have to hold my manhood cheap because of the weapons I carry (be they as humble as Marshalltown trowels and Hubco soil-sample bags). I deeply feel the absence of my Captain.

Notes

[1] Personal communication with Nehemia Levtzion, 1999.
[2] It must be said that Nehemia always harbored a touch of ambivalence about oral sources. We archaeologists were always thankful we did not have to stare down that skeptical eye!
[3] Saint Crispin's Day Speech, from William Shakespeare's *Henry V.*
[4] I cannot resist: I ended my talk at the 2003 African Studies Association meetings in Boston with the too, too theatrical admonishment:
> Archaeologists Arise! Brandish your razor-sharp Marshalltown trowels; armor yourself with bucket and screen; beat the flotation drums; and gird your loins with Hubco soil-sample bags! And Brother historians, let loose your argent arrows of agency!

[5] We argue that this was the case at the time of the earliest cities in Mali's Middle Niger (R. McIntosh 2005; S. McIntosh 1999a).
[6] That is, how to put together a unifying narrative, in the spirit of the original *Ancient Ghana and Mali*, with the breakdown of universal narratives. See S. McIntosh (1999a, 1-30), after Steven Feierman (1974).
[7] Borrowed from Kwang-Chih Chang (1962) who dealt with analogous high-frequency, low-frequency issues in Chinese prehistory.

From the *Banan* Tree of Kouroussa: Mapping the Landscape in Mande Traditional History

David C. Conrad

Résumé

La vision du monde des Mande d'Afrique de l'Ouest relie les éléments spirituels du mythe, de la légende et de la magie à des aspects remarquables du paysage, dont la dimension fonctionnelle est éclairée par un ensemble de travaux sur le "mapping indigène" entrepris par des anthropologues consacrés à l'étude des peuples indigènes américains. Les efforts pour interpréter la perspective des Mande sur leur propre histoire se sont concentrés sur les acteurs et leurs actions aux dépens de l'environnement physique à l'intérieur duquel ces évènements se sont déroulés. Bien que reconnaissant les risques encourus à se fonder sur des évènements dont les dates d'introduction dans le discours sont inconnues, cet article déclare que dans certains cas, certaines références au paysage iconique peuvent servir à tester l'exactitude des textes épiques Mande. Une comparaison entre les références topographiques des Mande aux exemples venant du folklore des Premières Nations révèle un besoin universel dans la tradition orale de faire un lien spatial entre passé et présent.

Abstract

The West African Mande worldview links spiritual elements of myth, legend, and magic to conspicuous landscape features, the functional dimension of which is illuminated by a body of work on "native mapping" by anthropologists looking at Native American peoples. Efforts to interpret the Mande people's perspective on their own history have focused on the actors and their deeds at the expense of attention to the physical environment in which events occur. While acknowledging the

---

An early version of this article was presented at a roundtable (in which Nehemia Levtzion was to have been a participant) titled "Fadenya or Badenya? Archeology and History as Siblings in the Up-Dating of Ancient Ghana and Mali" at the 46th Annual Meeting of the African Studies Association, Boston, Massachusetts 1 November 2003. I want to thank Kassim Koné for reading the final draft.

risks of relying on elements with no known date of introduction into the discourse, this article argues that in some cases iconic landscape references can be used to test the accuracy of Mande epic texts. Comparison of Mande topographical references to examples from Native American folklore demonstrates a universal concern for relating the past and present spatially in oral tradition.

Four principal historical topics engage the interest of the *jeliw* (professional bards) who have been responsible for Mande oral tradition through the centuries. The most conspicuous concerns are kinship, power and authority, the physical landscape, and spirituality. These are snugly interwoven in the oral discourse to illustrate the fabric of Mande history and culture according to those who tell the story. Within the vast corpus of Mande oral narrative that includes several epic traditions, the collective discourse now usually identified in the non-Mande world by the name of its central character Sunjata, provides a wealth of information on Mande views of the predominant themes, which are, in fact, inseparable. Extremely complex kinship patterns and mores combine with issues of power and authority to include perceptions of the ancestors as larger-than-life builders of state and society, pride of descent from those heroes of the distant past, and shaping of cultural values based on the ancestors' deeds, all of which are bound together with a pervasive spiritual consciousness.

These elements formed (and to a considerable degree still form) the basis of a Mande social structure characterized by specific standards of status and identity, which on one level determined acquisition of power that enabled the establishment of the foundations of political structure. Conspicuous natural features comprising the spiritual landscape include virtually all water sources — not just streams, rivers, ponds and lakes, but also certain wells and subterranean aquifers, all of which are linked either physically or symbolically by the River Niger (Brett-Smith 1994; Fairhead and Leach 1996, 138-39). Of similar import are particular hills and mountains, great trees standing alone or as parts of groves and forests, unusual rock formations, caves, and termite mounds. Individual manmade structures as well as entire villages, towns, and urban *quartiers* are enhanced, secured, and sometimes threatened by proximity to spiritually significant landscape features occupied by denizens of the supernatural world. Spiritual integration into the culture's

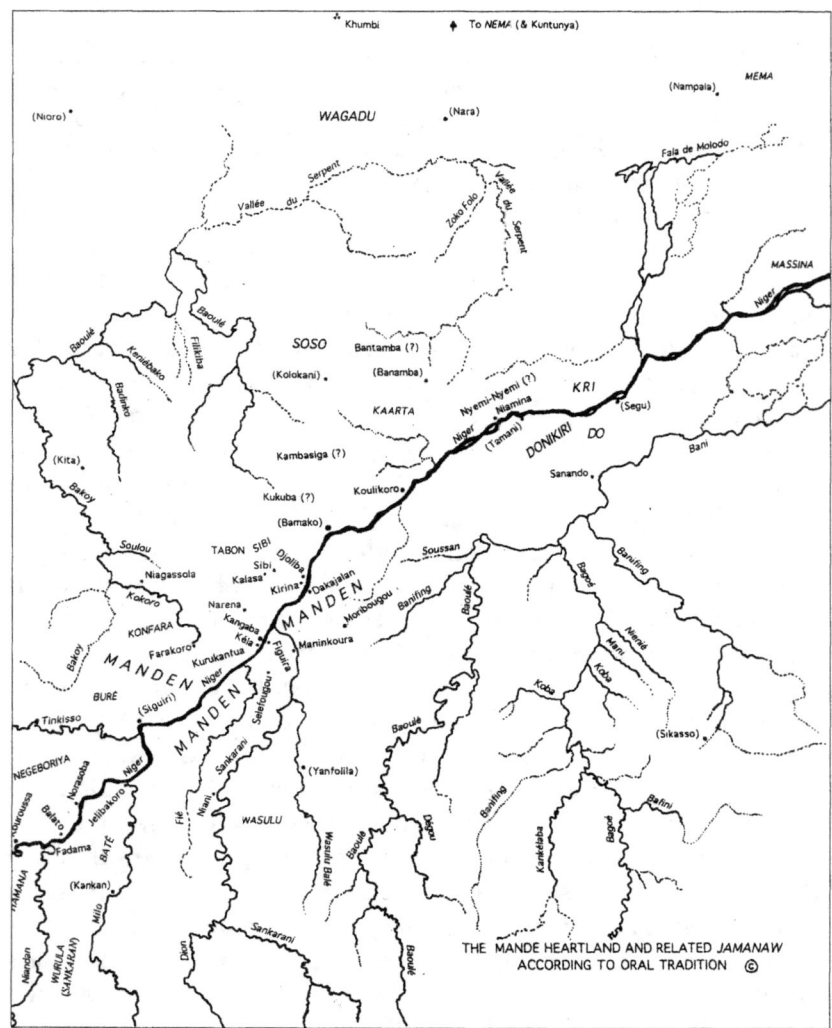

Map A

economic foundation is reflected in initiation society proceedings and seasonal celebrations of hunters, fishermen, food collectors, and farmers (Cashion 1982, 180-95 [hunters]; Conrad 2001, 1-30 [fishermen]; Wooten 2000 [farmers]; Fairhead and Leach 1996, 171-73 [hunting, fishing, and farming]). All human relationships including matters determining political power and authority are framed according to both individual and community command of occult powers. The spiritual elements of myth, legend, and magic with iconic links to conspicuous landscape features are part of the soul of Manden, and no historical inquiry could be complete without acknowledging their importance.[1] The functional dimension of conspicuous landscape features in the Mande worldview is illuminated by an extensive body of work on the subject of "native mapping" that has been described by anthropologists looking at Native American peoples, among others.[2] According to Margaret Wickens Pearce (1998, 158), "native mapping" was developed in non-archival societies to meet needs where the forms of the maps may not resemble conventional European cartography. Increasingly flexible definitions of mapping have been devised to encompass different cartographies. According to one of these, maps are described as "graphic representations that facilitate a spatial understanding of things, concepts, conditions, processes or events in the human world" (Harley and Woodward 1987, xvi). Expanding on this "to enlarge the discussion to representations that may not be graphic," Pearce defines maps as "representations that facilitate a spatial understanding," and mapping as "the process of creating and interpreting these representations." Such mapping, Pearce says, "may produce a wide variety of forms depending on the particular cultural context, and the historical period in which the mapping takes place" (1998, 159).

The kinds of mapping references that occur in oral tradition were noticed during research on Native American use of toponyms for place naming and for recording history. Anthropologists, historians, and linguists studying widely diverse native groups of North America have concluded that toponyms mentioned in oral traditions describe sites either in terms of their physical appearance, the way in which the land is used, people using the land, or a story or historical event that occurred in that place (Basso 1996 [Western Apache]; Bragdon 1996 [the Ninnimissinuok and other native peoples of New England]; Cruikshank 1990 [Athapascan peoples of the Northwest Territories]). They have concluded that the site-specific nature of local place-names, similar to ones familiar to us in Mande oral tradition, recreate the landscape as an ecological and spiritual map that is "read" through both the recitation of place names and experience. "Thus, the recitation of place-names is a mnemonic device for recalling the landscape" (Pearce 1998, 159).

Oral tradition addressing pre-imperial Mali is replete with

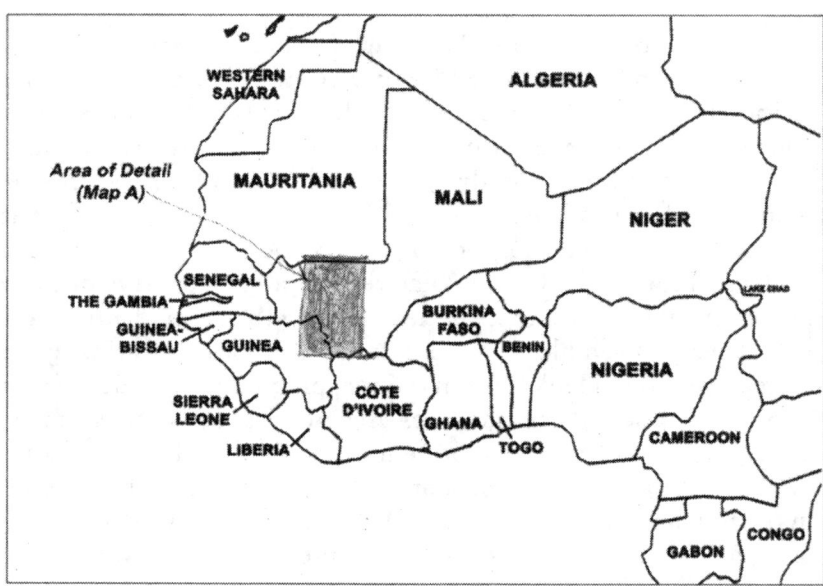

Map B

references to specific natural landmarks including mountains, rock formations, open spaces (such as large outcroppings of tabular bedrock, Bamana / Maninka: *fugaw*), and bodies of water (such as the Niger and its tributaries, but also any lake, pond, or spring) that are readily recognizable in the modern landscape. Specific village sites of the ancestral homes of individual clans or lineages are also part of the common currency of oral discourse. Many villages and towns have apparently risen, flourished, fallen into ruin, and been reincarnated with the same name at locations both near to, and far from the originals. Others simply lie in ruins with only the name surviving, although the name itself is often distorted and barely recognizable in mnemonic praises that are sometimes incorporated into the names of legendary characters like Sunjata's father and others discussed below. Traditions of migration woven into the oral discourse identify specific ruins or surviving villages as ancestral homes, ritual locations, or as being adjacent to major battle sites, but they also mention entire regions as temporary dwelling places of populations in transition.

Episodes describing transformative experiences associated with key locations serve a mnemonic or cognitive function (Cruikshank 1990, 55). Mande pilgrimage tales, like the infant

Fakoli's journey to a series of sacred places with his foster mother Tenenba Condé (Tassey Condé in Conrad 2004, 112-14),[3] preserve the names and significance of historical sites. The names of these sequential locations are charged with the kind of spiritual power represented by the Mande equivalent of Frances Harwood's (1976, 789) rosary bead analogy, that is, the knots in a *tafow* string that manifest the incantations called *kirisiw* (Brett-Smith 1994, 135-36).[4] Moreover, Harwood's reference to "a pilgrimage replicating the sequence of sacred geography" (1976, 789) aptly describes the spiritual significance of life-altering power journeys made by Fakoli, Sunjata, Al-Hadj `Umar Tal (Laye Umaru), and other heroes of Mande discourse.

In the general corpus of the Sunjata narrative, while the hero's journey into exile begins with a flight from mortal danger, it shortly becomes a walkabout through the symbolic landscape during which he debuts his heroic stature and heralds the coming of a new era in Mande history. Sunjata's peregrinations involve a series of visits to various Mande *jamanaw* (chiefdoms) where he participates in the oath-swearing ritual *sigifili* (or *sifili*) (Conrad 1997; Conrad 1999, 89, 121-23, 183-85; Conrad 2004, 180-81).[5] On these occasions he (that is, the *jeli* telling the story) evokes the names of his ancestors and attests to his own honor, integrity, and legitimacy, implying that he is the ultimate candidate for leadership (Johnson 1986, 156-59; Ly-Tall, Camara and Diouara 1987, 41-42; Cissé and Kamissoko 1988, 109-10; Jansen, Duintjer and Tamboura 1995, 98-99; Mamadi Diabaté in Conrad 1999, 83; Demba Kouyaté in Conrad 1999, 184). The journey into exile involves a pilgrimage similar to Fakoli's, a traditional hunter's quest *(dalimasigi)* (Cashion 1982, 240-43) for knowledge and protective medicine *(basi)* to sacred sites like the cave in the Kamissoko *jamana* of Kirina and the great stone arch above the Kamara *jamana* of Sibi-Tabon. Here again, Sunjata proclaims his own pedigree through publicly sworn oaths. The trope is particularly conspicuous in a variant by the Condé bards of Fadama where Sunjata assumes the character of an iconoclastic rebel going from place to place in the company of his sorceress mother Sogolon who initiates a brazen, challenging visit to the stronghold of Sumaworo himself. At each location on the journey Sunjata methodically violates the sacred taboo *(tana)* of his host, thereby demonstrating firm control of occult forces *(nyama)* that would kill any ordinary man (Jeli Mori Kouyaté in Conrad 1999, 58-59; Mamadi Condé in Conrad 1999, 119-24; Demba Kouyaté in Conrad 1999, 183-85; Tassey Condé in Conrad 2004, 118). Whether the trope involves boastful oath-swearing[6] or brazen *tana* destruction, the bards' message is essentially the same: an irresistible, commanding agent of change is announced, as the super hero *(danama yirindi)* (Tassey Condé in Conrad 2004, 86, 146) marches through the sacred landscape giving notice that a time is approaching when the pre-imperial *jamanaw* and their formerly autonomous rulers will be subject to a new order.

Aside from miracle myths of the colonial era involving fanciful flights to Mecca and Paris (Conrad 1981, 843, 853-54; Robinson 1985a, 34-35; Brett-Smith 1996, 33; Diop 2000, 43), travelers of Mande epic do not usually travel fantastic distances, in unrealistic directions, or on impossible routes. They are not journeying into mythical space, but to "spatially anchored" (Basso 1984, 32) locations that have by all accounts always been sacred in Manden, and in fact still are, despite the centuries-old presence of Islam. Exploring the mapping practices of "indigenous, non-archival cultures" of southern New England, Margaret Wickens Pearce could have been describing the Mande perspective when she wrote: "the web of place-names on the land comprises a map that orders physical, economic, and cultural information in a spatial framework, and which may be accessed through the combination of oral recitation and direct experience" (1998, 160). When *jeliw* describe the peregrinations of central characters like Fakoli and Sunjata, there is very little to quarrel with in terms of the juxtaposition of individual *jamanaw* and practicality of distances traveled. A bard's personal acquaintance with topographical markers cited in his own narrative varies from one to another. Some *jeliw* confuse the correct sequence of stops on the journey, but others are accurate, and there is nothing fantastic about the distances traveled, with only days or weeks between destinations (Ly-Tall, Camara and Diouara 1987, 43-47; Cissé and Kamissoko 1988, 109-123. Jansen, Duintjer and Tamboura 1995, 98-110; Mamadi Condé in Conrad 1999, 123; Djanka Tassey Condé in Conrad 2004, 112-17).

The Mande sacred landscape serves as the stage and dramatic backdrop for episode after episode of the great epics, especially

Sunjata and the epic of eighteenth-century Bamana Segou. Efforts to interpret the Mande people's perspective on their own history have tended to focus, quite understandably, on the actors and their deeds, perhaps at the expense of sufficient attention to the physical environment in which the momentous events occur. Based on anthropological documentation of relationships between Native American Hopi traditional history and ancestral village ruins, Peter Whiteley argues against long-standing apathy to "the perils of ethnographic analogy" (2002, 408) and supports archaeological use of indigenous oral traditions. Contrasting Southwest American archaeological methodologies with classical archaeology, Whiteley acknowledges that the interpretation and explanation of ancient Greek or Trojan sites rests on contemporary textual references and other archival information. Nevertheless, he argues that this reflects the oft-recognized prejudice in favor of written records however problematic they might be, as opposed to the densely coded historical reports of oral tradition. But simply because oral traditions are densely coded and do speak simultaneously in a variety of cultural registers (cognitive, natural-historical, psychological, religious) as well as the directly historical, this is no grounds for simply ignoring their historical value.

In light of anthropologists' findings on "native mapping" of the American Southwest and elsewhere, the relative accuracy of some topographical references in Mande epic discourse is of particular interest. While taking into account the well-known and commonly acknowledged risks involved in relying on elements with no known date of introduction into the discourse, it seems worth considering that in some cases the landscape might be profitably used to test the accuracy of Mande oral traditions. In any case, comparison of Mande topographical references to some examples from Native American folklore clearly demonstrates a universal concern for relating the past and present spatially in oral tradition. Keith Basso found that the locations of early events in Western Apache "historical tales" are recalled according to distinctive features in the landscape such as clusters of rocks and groves of trees. The land of Manden has, for example, many counterparts to the Western Apache location known as "big cottonwood trees stand spreading here and there" (Basso 1984, 37). Several great trees of Manden are dwelling places of *wòkilòw* (Conrad 1990, note 544) and other spirits both dangerous and benign, and, along with other prominent landscape features, they mark the interface between the natural and supernatural worlds.

The *banan* tree (*Ceiba pentandra* [Malgras 1992, 172-73] also known as kapok, silk-cotton, [French: *fromager*]) of Manden ranks as one of particularly strong spiritual import, with an appearance in a Bamana creation myth where it is said to be regarded as a link between Earth and sky (Zahan 1963, 117). In one tradition a village called Jomabanan, or "sacred *banan* tree," was the location of a great *banan* to which people journeyed for communication with the spirit world (Conrad 2002, 99). As a landscape icon in Mande oral tradition it is also of political and economic significance in the mnemonic lines: "From the *banan* tree of Kouroussa to the region of Samanyana" (or a variant), "Starting under the *banan* tree of Kouroussa and ending at Yirikurunje, everybody knows about it" (Conrad 1990, 190 note 3625, 301). For another bard, the *banan* serves as a temporal marker tacitly acknowledging that trees are more ephemeral than mountains and caves:

It is all called Kouroussa, Kouroussa.
....
In early times all the trees [there] were *banan*,
But I cannot say that about today.
Those *banan* trees have fallen (Jeli Mori Kouyaté in Conrad 1999, 68).

A mystical, protective tree linked to both good and bad spirits, the *dubalen (Ficus thonningii)* (Malgras 1992, 298-99) stands as a towering sentinel shading Mande villages' central dancing grounds where major events are held. In Bissandougou, Guinea, the enormous *dubalen* at the village's center was surely present when the nineteenth-century empire-builder Almami Samori Touré established his headquarters there in 1874. Under the *dubalen* of Bissandougou on 2 June 2000, local youth observed the centenary of Samori's death in exile with a performance about him and his *sofa* warriors. Mande epic narrative contains frequent references to important events that happened under a *dubalen* in the village *bara* or an eminent person's family compound (Tayiru Banbera in Conrad 1990, 106, 177, 181, 188, 225, 266, 281, 293 and Conrad 2004, 70).

The *balansan (Acacia albida)* (Malgras 1992, 244-45), which some French scholars associate with a Bamana creation myth (Ganay 1949, 182; Dieterlen 1951, 16; Zahan 1963, 38; see also Belcher 2005, 414), has particularly strong occult associations with Segou, former capital of the late seventeenth and eighteenth-century Bamana Empire. As one bard expresses it, the old Bamana city is "Segou of the *balansan* trees":

Four thousand *balansan*,
And four hundred *balansan*,
And four *balansan*,
And one small humpbacked *balansan*.
Not every native understands their significance,
To say nothing of a stranger (Sissoko Kabiné in Kesteloot 1972, 1: 33, 2: 21, 4: 47; Baba Cissoko in Dumestre 1979, 63; Sory Kamara in Dumestre 1979, 185; Tayiru Banbera in Dumestre 1979, 267, 361; Tayiru Banbera in Conrad 1990, 44, 199, 266, 283).

For local people, those mystical trees symbolize the treachery and intrigue for which the seventeenth- and eighteenth-century Bamana Empire is famous, and Segou's reputation as a risky place for strangers carries through to modern times (Dieterlen 1951, 37-39; Kesteloot 1972, 1: 22, 3: 38 note 18; Dumestre and Kesteloot 1975, 21; Sissoko Kabinè in Dumestre and Kesteloot 1975, 109-11; Dumestre 1979, 63 note 1; Conrad 1990, 45 note 25).

The rivers of Manden are also frequently mentioned topographical markers, and a frequently heard example of mnemonic place location occurs in the epics of both Bamana Segou and Sunjata. Referring to the *jamana* known to the bards variously as Dòdugu or Dò ni Kiri (Dò and Kiri), they consistently describe it as straddling the Niger somewhere in the general vicinity of modern-day Segou. In the epic of Bamana Segou, the mnemonic lines describe that kingdom's components:

Segou is a group of four villages,
Marakadugu is a group of nine villages,
Dòdugu is a group of twelve villages,
Six of them on one side of the river and six on the other side (Tayiru Banbera in Conrad 1990, 135 [the line-order here is slightly altered for convenience].

In the Sunjata epic, references to Dòdugu or Dò ni Kiri include the phrase "the twelve towns of Dò, the six towns *behind the river* [my italics], and the four towns of Kiri" (Demba Kouyaté in Conrad 1999, 162, 187; Tassey Condé in Conrad 2004, 23, 27). The references to Dò are ambiguous and hence problematic, but they offer potentially useful clues to solving the ongoing difficulty of identifying the location of Dò. The mysterious land of Dò (Dòdugu) is referred to as being in several places, and the specifics of its connection to a place called Kiri are not yet resolved. Moreover, in references to the Condé-Diarra rulers of Dòdugu, tradition consistently associates it with Sankaran. The effort to justify this through archival sources is daunting (Bühnen 1994, 10-12), and the goal might be better served by striving to decipher the mnemonic oral mapping by *jeli ngaraw* (the most knowledgeable bards). When the *jeliw* speak of the Buffalo Woman, her sister Sogolon, and the Condé / Diarra rulers of both Dòdugu and Sankaran, do they mean to indicate that the two were part of the same *jamana*? One of the above-quoted passages about the four, nine, and twelve villages associated with Dòdugu continues, again stressing key patronymics and a conspicuous landscape feature:

Great Naminyan Konté[7] of Sankaran, *wulu wala*!
Sogolon Konté will not destroy a calabash full of Jata.
If people speak of Koné, Koné,
The Koné came from Sankaran.
Sankaran, Sankaran, where is Sankaran itself?
Sankaran is far away near Kankan,
Kankan in Guinea.
Sankaran is between here and the West.
This town was christened by Baji Sankalan.
When wind touches the river water and pushes it toward shore,
It is said there are waves in the water.
Sankaran town took its name from this (Tayiru Banbera in Conrad 1990, 49).

As Margaret Wickens Pearce expresses it, "Every toponym describes a site either in terms of its physical appearance, the way in which land is being used, the people who use the land, or a story or historical event that occurred at that place" (1998, 159). The mnemonic lines referring to Sogolon of Dò, a *dutigi* (chief) called Sankalan, the windy river, and naming of Sankaran come, not from a variant of the Sunjata epic, but from the Bamana epic of Segou, and they might well help us to understand *jeli* perceptions of the relationship between Dòdugu and Sankaran.

If the more famous topographical sites of Manden are regular features of epic narrative, traditional "mapping" of historical markers is by no means limited to the *jeli* (bardic) repertoire. Rural Mande populations in general, along with the neighboring peoples of the Sahel to the north and forest to the south, regard their environment in a manner similar to Keith Basso's Western Apache, with their historical recollections through distinctive features like groves of trees (Basso 1984, 49; Basso 1988 104-05). To illustrate this point, we can take examples from the research of James Fairhead and Melissa Leach in the forest zone of southeastern Guinea, and Roderick McIntosh in the Malian Sahel.

In their path-breaking study of the "course, pattern, and causes of vegetation change" in the forest-savanna mosaic near Kissidougou in southeastern Guinea, Fairhead and Leach (1996, 4) discovered that instead of being remnants of a once vast forest, the "forest islands" or large groves in which many Kissi villages are located, were created by human settlement. In addition to first-hand observation of forest island growth around recently established village sites and air photograph evidence, Fairhead and Leach were able to rely on "forest island histories" emerging from oral testimonies in thirty-eight villages. From these accounts they learned that several Kissi villages with forest islands are called "Tineni" ("in the savanna"), which reinforces their inhabitants' claims that they were founded in savanna, and indicates the growth of forest around them rather than forest destruction as had been previously supposed (Fairhead and Leach 1996, 79).

Continuing with our Western Apache example in relation to local Mande lore, Basso emphasizes Apache maintenance of "a complex array of symbolic relationships with their physical surroundings" (Basso 1984, 49), which echoes Roderick McIntosh's efforts to establish a deep-time chronology for peoples of the Middle Niger (including proto-Mande ancestors) for the period around 3000 to 300 BCE. McIntosh stresses that deep-time core values and an ancient vision of the landscape as a natural, symbolic, and occult phenomenon are intimately linked to the Middle Niger peoples' vision of their landscape. McIntosh sees the Mande landscape as one "that enables all its aspects (the bio-physical landforms, the human actors traveling over and modifying the landscape, and the occult power elements ...) to be understood as a self-organizing whole" (R. McIntosh 2005, 136; also R. McIntosh 1998, 16-17; R. McIntosh, Tainter, and S.K. McIntosh 2000, 157-71). In the late 1970s, during a survey of the ruins of ancient satellite communities near the present-day city of Jenne in the Middle Niger Bend area, the McIntosh's research team noticed that at one particular location they were not receiving the kinds of genial greetings and handshakes usually forthcoming from curious onlookers. Instead, passersby would avoid setting foot on the site, avert their eyes, and hurry on their way. The researchers eventually ascertained that the satellite settlement called Kangousa was an ancestral site of three lineages of Somono fishing families who were also ironworkers, despite the usual distinct separation of the two occupations. The local mental map of that satellite community was clearly marked with the legendary warning that anyone not from one of the three Somono lineages who set foot on the site without permission would be struck by a silver hammer flying through the air (R. McIntosh 2005, 108-09).

In Mande epic tradition, spatial conceptions are embedded in place names that are used "as situating devices and conventionalized instruments for locating narrated events in the physical settings where the events have occurred" (Basso 1984, 32). As noted above, topographical markers that anchor episodes of the Sunjata epic punctuate the Mande landscape. One of the most socially and politically meaningful of these is the great natural stone arch of Kamanjan *(Kaman donda)*, a striking example of the kind of site for socially important events that "were carefully selected for their symbolic contributions to action" (Bragdon 1996, 126). The natural stone arch on Tabon Mountain looms above the modern road running north to Bamako and south to the Guinea frontier on a route paralleling the Niger River that was clearly traveled since time immemorial. The stone arch's mnemonic references are contained in praise names of Kamanjan, the ruler of of Sibi-Tabon, who is one of the most prominent of the charismatic ancestors of Manden. Kamanjan is praised as both Tabon Wana Faran Kamara and Sibi Wana Faran Kamara (Quiquandon 1892, 312; Zeltner 1913, 41, 44; Diabaté 1970, 33; Ly-Tall, Camara and Diouara 1987, 59; Jansen, Duintjer and Tamboura 1995, 118; Sanassy Kouyaté in Conrad 1999, 34). In the epic, Kamanjan's spiritually charged *jamana* is almost invariably associated with rites of passage, and the references are not confined to Sibi and Tabon. Nearby is the village of Kalassa, distinguished by the rock formation Nienkema Kourou ("Anvil of Manden"), scene of the Kamara ancestor's torchlight rituals involving the recognition and initiation of groups of worthy male youth *(kamalenw)* expected to become the next generation of distinguished farmers, hunters, and warriors (Cissé and Kamissoko 1988, 191 note 3; Jeli Mori Kouyaté in Conrad 1999, 63; Tassey Condé in Conrad 2004, 169-70).[8]

The iconic landmark of Kirina, another historic Mande *jamana*, is a cave that is home of the Kònò or "Great Bird" society. According to oral evidence, each *jamana* sent a representative to an annual water ceremony of renewal at Kirina, which featured sacrificial offerings made at the cave of the ancestors (Zeltner 1913, 36; Cissé and Kamissoko 1988, 17; Tassey Condé 1994, TS lines 15644-15701). For people of the Niger River port of Koulikoro, the mountain known as Nyanankulu at Koulikoro where Sumanguru / Soumaworo is said to have disappeared after his defeat by the army of Manden contains several sacred sites harkening back to epic events (Johnson 1986, 176; Ly-Tall, Camara and Diouara 1987, 64; Cissé and Kamissoko 1988, 175; Jansen, Duintjer and Tamboura 1995, 160). Near Kangaba, famous for one of the *kamablonw* (council houses of Manden) is the large open space called Kurukanfuga Gbara where Sunjata is alleged to have held a public assembly after the victory over Soso (Niane 1960, 133; Niane 1965, 73; Kanté 1994; Tassey Condé 1994, TS lines 14,536-14,681; Jeli Mori Kouyaté in Conrad 1999, 65).

The name of the ancient *jamana* of Nègèbòriya is mnemonic, reflecting its economic foundation. The domain of Fakoli's father Mansa Yèrèlènkò Koroma (Tassey Condé in Conrad 2004, 95), Nègèbòriya translates roughly as "place of iron outflow." The exact location of Nègèbòriya is not yet clear, but the best guess at present is southwest of Konfara, beyond the Tinkisso River in the general area of today's Norasoba. In this case, one would seek to verify its location through a combination of local oral testimony and archeological survey confirming and dating the presence of extensive ancient slag heaps, early deforestation, and other signs of intensive iron production.[9]

Another of the place-names of great historical significance in

Mande epic tradition is Dakajalan, said to be the place where Sunjata spent his early years, to which he returned from exile, and which served as his headquarters during the war with Soso. Dakajalan's location is firmly implanted on local elders' mental map, but as a place so closely associated with the activities of the Mali Empire's larger-than-life founding hero and possibly his burial (Cissé and Kamissoko 1988, 301; Conrad 1994, 376; Jansen, Duintjer and Tamboura 1995, 161), it has the status of a strictly protected sacred site. There was no mistaking the determination of a knowledgeable local elder to guard that secret when an eminent Malian scholar once asked for Dakajalan's location and the elder threw his hands in the air, declaring: *Cela est trop grand pour ma bouche* (Cissé and Kamissoko 1988, 4).

Anthropologists looking at other parts of the world have argued that place names are not just decorative embellishments, but structural markers that divide the traditional texts into cognitive units and spatially anchor stories so they can be recalled by remembering the land (Harwood 1976, 785-89; Cruikshank 1990, 55). In Mande epic tradition, one of the most significant and often-heard mnemonic passages occurs in the familiar praises for the Soso *mansa* Sumaworo, whose identity is wrapped in praises citing the four principal towns or provinces of his domain: Kukuba, Bantamba, Nyèmi-Nyèmi, and Kambasiga (Montrat 1958, 92; Kaba 1974, 12; Diabaté 1970, 35; Johnson 1986, 150; Ly-Tall, Camara and Diouara 1987, 49-50; Cissé and Kamissoko 1988, 135; Jansen, Duintjer and Tamboura 1995, 157-60; Fayala Kouyaté in Conrad 1999, 47; Mamadi Condé in Conrad 1999, 121; Tassey Condé in Conrad 2004, 98). What better example could there be in Mande discourse, of Peter Whiteley's "densely coded historical reports of oral tradition" (2002, 408)?

Among knowledgeable Mande informants of northeastern Guinea and southwestern Mali there is no confusion or doubt regarding the location of the thirteenth-century Kingdom of Soso. The heartland of the ancient Kingdom of Soso centers on the village of Sosso (local spelling) north of the town of Banamba in the Beledougou region of Mali. However, in an article called "In Quest of Susu" for which Stephan Bühnen conducted a commendably thorough archival investigation, he falls prey to some errors in the printed sources that lead him to the erroneous conclusion that

Sumaworo's Soso was located in the region of the Upper Niger and Futa Jalon. One of the problems in Bühnen's hypothesis stems from his mistaken impression that Sumaworo's *jamu* or patronymic of Kanté was one and the same with that of the Condé (Koné, Konté) rulers of Sankaran (Bühnen 1994, 13).[10] Bühnen, a thorough and conscientious researcher of the archival sources, was apparently unable to spend time on the ground meeting informants and visiting the places in question. Had he done so, he could not have committed the errors responsible for the implosion of his hypothesis.[11] Be that as it may, it seems fair to say that there has not been enough attention given to messages imbedded in iconic praise lines like Kukuba, Bantamba, Nyèmi-Nyèmi, and Kambasiga.

Despite some scholars' refusal to believe there is any significant time-depth to the collective *jeli* memory, it is ill-advised to discount the Mande people's own knowledge of historical locations like that of Soso. They recall that Soso formed an interface between the small Soninke states like Kaniaga and Mema that succeeded Wagadu / Ghana to the north, and the Mande chiefdoms to the south. Geographical references from the Condé *jeliw* of Fadama's reservoir of knowledge convey their belief that the southern frontier between Soso and Manden was just north of today's Bamako, in the location of present-day Kati. The northwestern line of Manden extended roughly from somewhere below Kati near present-day Bamako, down to Kouroussa in Guinea (Tassey Condé 1994, TS lines 4726-31).

The cumulative oral sources, local knowledge, and topographical markers convincingly locate the Soso heartland above the left bank of the Niger north of Banamba in what is today's Beledougou region of Mali (Vidal 1924, 321).[12] According to the mental map maintained by the Condé *jeliw* of Fadama, it extended from the area of Kati all the way to the land of Dodugu in the general area of today's Segou (Tassey Condé 1994, TS lines 4726-31). Through their uniformly consistent references to Sumaworo's extensive holdings, the bards indicate that prior to Soso's defeat by the army of Manden, Soso commanded much greater territory than any single chiefdom among the Mandé *jamanaw* to the south, and they emphasize that its expansion was accomplished through conquest (Johnson 1986, 151; Ly-Tall, Camara and Diouara 1987, 49-50; Cissé and Kamissoko 1988, 135; Tassey Condé 1994, TS lines 4682-

85; Jansen, Duintjer and Tamboura 1995, 158; Fayala Kouyaté in Conrad 1999, 47; Demba Kouyaté in Conrad 1999, 175).

To non-Mande ears, few details about Soso's towns and provinces emerge from the narrative; indeed, it has generally gone unnoticed that there is any useful information contained in references to Sumaworo's state. The four sequential place names in the mnemonic line "Kukuba, Bantamba, Nyèmi-Nyèmi, Kambasiga" are usually about all that one hears, but one hears them often (Montrat 1958, 92; Diabaté 1970, 35; Johnson 1986, 150; Ly-Tall, Camara and Diouara 1987, 49-50; Cissé and Kamissoko 1988, 135; Jansen, Duintjer and Tamboura 1995, 157-60; Fayala Kouyaté in Conrad 1999, 47; Mamadi Condé in Conrad 1999, 121; Conrad 2004, 98), and they probably merit more attention than they have received. A son of Babu Condé, the bard of Fadama who was described by Laye Camara (1980) as *le maître de la parole*, provides a glimpse of what might lie behind Sumaworo's praise lines. According to his perception, which may or may not involve semantic confusion with present-day locations, Sumaworo's walled "kingship house" *(mansayaso)* was strategically located at Kukuba ("Big Kuku"), atop the mountain overlooking the Niger River in the place now known as Koulouba above present-day Bamako. Kukuba is alleged to have been Sumaworo's *kèlèmansa* town, the base of his military campaigns (Tassey Condé 1994, TS lines 9232-34).[13] More centralized was the fortified town of Bantamba which is said to have contained Sumaworo's principal war medicine *(kèlèbasi)* and his fiery oracle called Nènèba (Tassey Condé 1994, lines 5551-55, line 12224; Conrad 2004, 119).[14] Whether it is a local invention owing to the similarity of names or a legitimate part of tradition, the Fadama bards identify Bantamba with today's Banamba. This is in the general area of what people of today's Beledougou region of Mali identify as the heartland of old Soso, with their point of reference being the village of Sosso (local spelling) north of the town of Banamba.

In several of the published variants the curious sounding name of the Soso province or town that Tassey Condé and other Guinean *jeliw* pronounce as "Nyèmi-Nyèmi" or "Nyami-Nyami," has been transcribed as "Niani-Niani," implying a perceived connection between Sumaworo's praise line and the town of Niani on the Sankaran River (Johnson 1986, 150; Ly-Tall, Camara and Diouara

1987, 49). Without providing any justification for doing so, a few writers specifically identify the praise reference as referring to Niani (Montrat 1958, 93 note 13; Diabaté 1975, 59 note 114), but this is inconsistent with topographical references and specific events described in the overall corpus. The most reasonable possibility appears to be that the bards are referring to Niamina, located within the perceived Soso boundaries southeast of the alleged location of Bantamba, on the left bank of the Niger. The double utterance in the praising could derive from the fact that, as Youssouf Cissé points out, there was another Niani near Niamina (Cissé and Kamissoko 1991, 12). The praise could have originated as something like "Niani-Niami," which is actually what it sounds like on the tongues of many *jeliw*. Wâ Kamissoko mentions these two locations as part of Sumaworo's domain in conjunction with a place called Niamanko, a major initiation site for young blacksmiths of Soso (Cissé and Kamissoko 1991, 12). The place apparently referred to as Nyèmi-Nyèmi was just downriver from Koulikoro, another important riverside town said to have been within the territory of Soso, and the one to which so many variants claim Sumaworo fled upon his defeat by the forces of Sunjata (Quiquandon 1892, 315; Arnaud 1912, 171; Zeltner 1913, 32; Vidal 1924, 324; Doumbia 1936, 352; Diabaté 1975, 82; Johnson 1979, 187; Johnson 1986, 176; Ly-Tall, Camara and Diouara 1987, 64; Cissé and Kamissoko 1988, 211; Cissé and Kamissoko 1991, 22; Jansen, Duintjer and Tamboura 1995, 160; Diabaté in Conrad 1999, 89).

Mande scholars have largely overlooked one important mnemonic reference to a place-name, apparently because it has been concealed within one of the names of Sunjata's father. There appear to be several topographical references contained in the father's various appellations. In 1918, a Diabaté *jeli* of Kéla reluctantly told a colonial official who was looking for Mali's so-called "capital" that it had been located on the left bank of the Niger between Niagassola and Narena (Montrat 1958, 91). That *jamana* is said to have extended up to the location now occupied by the town of Narena (Tassey Condé 1994, lines 115-120, 3461-76),[15] which might account for an alternative name, Nare Famaghan, by which its *mansa* Maghan Konfara is also known (Delafosse 1912, 2: 166; Zeltner 1913, 7; Doumbia 1936, 349; Diabaté 1970, 39; Diabaté 1975, 31; Johnson 1986, 107).[16] Recently, Jeli Babu Condé affirmed the Fadama bards' historic view (back at least four generations) that Sunjata's father was at Narena when he was looking for a wife, and that this is where Sunjata was eventually born.[17]

Setting aside for now the possible Nare Famaghan-Narena connection, let us direct our attention to the Maghan Konfara variant. Readers of D.T. Niane's *Sundiata* know Maghan Konfara as Maghan Kon Fatta, according to Niane's early transcription of what he heard (Niane 1965, 4-5, 16-17). In what is nearing a half-century since Niane's pioneering effort, many additional variants of the epic have emerged, and in recent decades the name has more often been heard and transcribed as something closer to Maghan Konfara. As part of one of the names of Sunjata's father, Konfara (also Kounkana [Quiquandon 1892, 306], Konkaya [Leynaud et Cissé 1978, 147], Konkanya [Ly-Tall, Camara and Diouara 1987, 36], Konkannya [Cissé and Kamissoko 1988, 43-44], Kunkanyan [Jansen, Duintjer and Tamboura 1995, 52]) apparently indicates a place south of Sibi and Kirina, the name of which is mentioned by many *jeliw*. The title *maghan* is synonymous with *mansa* (chief, king, ruler), hence the praise name "Maghan Konfara."[18] The bards of Fadama specifically claim that Konfara was part of the *jamana* of Sunjata's father. Many *jeliw* also refer to Sunjata's father as Farako Manko Faran Konkèn or a variant thereof (Zeltner 1913, 44; Vidal 1924, 320; Monteil 1924, 62 note 1; Humblot 1951, 111 note 1; Diabaté 1975, 24; Johnson 1986, 107; Ly-Tall, Camara and Diouara 1987, 23; Cissé and Kamissoko 1988, 43; Cissé and Kamissoko 1991, 59; Jansen, Duintjer and Tamboura 1995, 52; Sanassy Kouyaté in Conrad 1999, 25; Fayala Kouyaté in Conrad 1999, 40; Mamadi Condé in Conrad 1999, 101; Demba Kouyaté in Conrad 1999, 168) along with the more rhetorically convenient Maghan Konfara (Ly-Tall, Camara and Diouara 1987, 27 note 1; Tassey Condé 1994, lines 119-20). According to the Fadama bards, Konfara and the *maghan's* town of Farako (or Farakoro) were in the area of the Kokoro River, which is in accord with the geographical context of events described in the tradition. The Kokoro flows just south of present-day Niagassola, home of the Kouyaté bards who, as all Mande specialists know, have special status as guardians of the shrine of the Soso *bala* because their ancestors were the spokesmen and musicians for Sunjata's family. The distinction between the places called Konfara and Farako / Farakoro is not entirely clear.

However, one of the most detailed oral sources specifically refers to the "land of Konfara" and speaks of Sunjata's father being in "Farakoro" (Tassey Condé in Conrad 2004, 13). Even a variant of the epic devoted to eighteenth-century Bamana Segou contains mnemonic lines stressing Farako / Farakoro's importance in tradition addressing the thirteenth century:

> At that time the *mansa* of Farako was very powerful at Farako. In those days there was a *mansa* at Farako (Tayiru Banberain Conrad 1990, 13).

The mentally mapped location and related references to Farako / Farakoro in the oral discourse suggest that a possible site of at least one of the residences of Sunjata's father was a village near the Kokoro River. At the very least, it seems this location should now be included in the ongoing discussions regarding the supposed importance of Niani as a seat of Mande power on the Sankarani River.[19] The bardic emphasis on Mande rulers' wealth from Sunjata to Musa and Sulayman (Al-`Umari in Levtzion and Hopkins 1981, 270-71; Ibn Battuta in Levtzion and Hopkins 1981, 290-91; Tassey Condé in Conrad 2004, 9) is consistent with Konfara's location on the northern edge of the goldfields that extend southwestward above present-day Siguiri.[20] In a passage from the Condé bards of Fadama, the name of Sunjata's father is closely linked with the region's gold fields, which at their greatest extent are commonly known as Buré:

> For us to give you many details about Manden, (Naamu)
> With which part of Manden will we start? (Naamu)
> We will start with Sunjata's father, (Naamu)
> Who is Farako Manko Farakonken. (Naamu)
> The name of Ma'an Sunjata's father is, (Naamu)
> Manko Farakonken of Konfara. (Naamu)
> Do you know where Konfara is? (Naamu)
> It is on the frontier between Guinea and Mali,
> At a place now known as Kourémalé. (Naamu)
> The swampy area,
> Where the Kourémalé people dig their gold mines,
> Is known as Konfara. (Naamu)
> The father of Simbon was named after that, (Naamu)
> But his real name is Maghan. (Naamu)
> He is Maghan Konfara (Tassey Condé in Conrad 2004, 4-5).

Konfara is specifically said to have been located in a swampy region near the present-day town of Kourémalé (on the Guinean side of the border with Mali). In an initial step to test the validity of specific but rarely heard topographical references in oral discourse by the Condé bards of Fadama, I went looking for Konfara in the company of the archeologist Susan Keech McIntosh on 28 June 2005.[21] With the help of a guide graciously provided by the Chef de Cercle of Doka, we found an extensive area of ancient gold diggings locally known as Konfara in a location corresponding to the above-quoted passage from Djanka Tassey Condé. Pending later revelations and convincing material evidence to the contrary (intensive archeological investigation is urgently needed), listening to the bards' recitation of these place-names as mnemonic devices for recalling the landscape indicates that Farako / Farakoro may for now be tentatively identified as the town,[22] and Konfara (or Konkanya among others) as one of the names of the *jamana* or chiefdom of Sunjata's father.[23]

No claim is being made that because the correct location of Konfara and its gold workings are mentioned in oral discourse recounted by the Condé bards of Fadama, this necessarily constitutes an accurate historical reference in epic tradition. For one thing, there are many cases of multiple locations in Manden with the same or similar names (though usually not with a specific identifying element like gold workings). Moreover, it has long been recognized that one of the great weaknesses of oral tradition as potential source of historical evidence is that there is rarely, if ever, any way of knowing when specific references were first inserted into the narrative. The Farakoro / Konfara references in epic narrative are among several Mande place-names of particular interest because there appears to be some potential for eventual archeological verification.

In many instances, local topographical references, or "mapping" of the Mande landscape, are common knowledge. In the more conspicuous cases such as, for example, the natural stone arch on Tabon Mountain, anyone familiar with the Kamanjan Kamara (Tabon Wana Faran Kamara) episodes of the "Sunjata" tradition is more or less aware of that topographical marker's iconic significance. With regard to more isolated, less conspicuous landmarks such as the ancient settlement of Kangousa described by

Roderick McIntosh, in some instances awareness of their significance may have been lost altogether, perhaps appearing in oral discourse unrecognized at worst, and unidentifiable at best. Still others seem purely apocryphal, as in the case of the multiple alleged locations of the sunken canoe *cum boliw* that transported the mythical pilgrim Fajigi up the Niger upon his return from Mecca, becoming "sacred sites" in various places.[24] As David Henige reminds us, "landforms are dynamic, appearing and disappearing, and changing appearance at varying rates" (2007, 248). Even locations with genuine historical potential like the "island of gold" known as Wangara / Palolus (S. McIntosh 1995) or a battleground location like Dakajalan (Conrad 1994) can meander like the landscape features that supposedly mark them.

Nevertheless, thanks to the work on "native mapping" by anthropologists working with Native American peoples among others, it seems unwise to dismiss the possibility of historical accuracy or at least some degree of significance simply because the topographical references occur in oral tradition rather than archival sources. On the level of scientific historical accuracy, the goal of verifying by archeological evidence some obscure place names of potentially great historical significance mentioned in Mande oral tradition is surely worthwhile. Having said that, it must be stressed that proven cases of site accuracy in Mande oral tradition cannot be expected to validate events described in the epic. As David Henige points out, an insidious aspect "of site-identification exercises is the ease with which the arguments move beyond any evidence relating to a particular site and subsume larger-scale claims" (2007, 251). In the case of the Iliad, asks Henige: "Does being able to assign Troy to a particular place *ipso facto* increase the likelihood that stories about it from ancient times are true?" (2007, 239). Similarly, in the Sunjata epic, if, for example, archeological investigation somehow revealed that the above-mentioned torchlight rituals at Kalassa were held there in the thirteenth century, this would not definitively confirm their purpose as described in oral tradition, nor would it prove that Faran Kamara and/or Sunjata ever had anything to do with them.

On a more modest level, the aspiration of "some degree of significance" is addressed by anthropologists like Renato Rosaldo, who insists that oral sources should be regarded as "cultural documents that organize perceptions about the past, and not containers of brute facts." As Rosaldo expresses it, the "facts" in oral tradition are "culturally mediated," so stories that people tell about themselves should be "conceived less as documents to be restored than as texts to be read" (1980a, 97). To Julie Cruickshank's list of "Homeric poems, Icelandic sagas, Tlingit oratory, [and] Tagish life stories" one might add "Mande epic tradition" where she remarks that "the issue of how much historical accuracy [they] contain is really beside the point if we understand their contribution as providing social memory however adequate or inadequate" (Cruikshank 2002, 18). However, one can perhaps be more optimistic with such fertile ground as Mande epic tradition to plow, and I would argue that it is not unreasonable to aspire to more than varying degrees of adequacy. If, as mentioned at the beginning of this paper, the most conspicuous concerns of Mande oral tradition are kinship, power and authority, the physical landscape and spirituality, all snugly interwoven to illustrate the fabric of that culture's history according to its bards, it seems well worthwhile to continue studying that culture's historical consciousness as the medium through which oral testimonies present the shape of the past (Rosaldo 1980a, 97).

Notes

[1] This is the subject of a work in progress, tentatively titled "Sorcery and Pilgrimage in West Africa: The Mande Quest for Spiritual Power."

[2] I want to thank Tom Bassett and Roderick McIntosh for help in locating these sources.

[3] In some cases, references to this source will be to the original transcript (TS) because the passage in question is not included in the book. Interview transcripts include:

Condé, Tassey. Recorded at Fadama, Guinée, February 1994.
Diabaté, Mamadi. Recorded at Kéla, Mali, March 3, 1976.
Dioubaté, Adama. "Ancestors, Sorcery and Power in Manden." Recorded by Fatamata Doubaya Kamara at Siguiri, village of Tondo, Guinée, 1986.

[4] The knots are material representations of the incantations called *kirisiw* (alternatively *kilissiw, klissiw*). See Brett-Smith, 1994, 135-36.

[5] The ritual is described in detail in Conrad (1997). Specific examples are found in Mamadi Diabaté (in Conrad 1999, 89), Mamadi Condé (in Conrad 1999, 121-23), Demba Kouyaté (in Conrad 1999, 183-85), and Tassey Condé in Conrad 2004, 180-81).

⁶ In some variants Sunjata personally visits Sumanguru / Soumaworo before their battles, in others he sends a messenger, but the verbal confrontation *(da la kèlè)* between opposing leaders / heroes prior to armed conflict is a standard motif that often recalls a historical place-name (Ly-Tall, Camara and Diouara 1987, 58; Cissé and Kamissoko 1988, 165-69; Conrad 1990, 306-07; Jansen, Duintjer and Tamboura 1995, 150; Mamadi Condé in Conrad 1999, 146-47; Demba Kouyaté in Conrad 1999, 195-96).
⁷ When translating this we heard "Konté," which is a variant pronunciation of Condé and Koné, not to be confused with Kanté, the *jamu* of Sumaworo of Soso. For detailed explanation of this passage see Conrad (1990, 49-50).
⁸ According to the Kalassa *dugutigi* (chief), the youth there still held torchlight rituals (interview 22 December 2005).
⁹ Relevant oral testimony was recorded at Norasoba by the author in 1994, and the archeological survey was part of the planned itinerary of a trip by the author with the archeologist Susan Keech McIntosh, 27 June-1 July 2005. However, owing to the sudden illness of a research assistant, that part of the research was postponed to a later date.
¹⁰ This error is traceable to the fact that Condé / Koné / Konté are all variants of the same *jamu* (confirmed by Dr. Kassim Koné). All three are also known as Diarra (or Jara), but this extended family identity *(jamu)* is unquestionably distinct from the Kanté.
¹¹ This is not the place for a comprehensive discussion of the Bühnen article, but one feels compelled to note that one consequence of not distinguishing between the Konté (Condé) *jamu* of Sunjata's mother and the Kanté identity of Sumanguru, is that Bühnen engages in an elaborate, implausible discussion of how the relationship between Sunjata and his Konté (Condé) relatives is characterized by ambiguity: matrimonial allies on the one hand (Sogolon Condé is Sunjata's mother), and "temporal or continuous enemies" on the other with (Sumanguru Konté [sic] as the archetypal enemy (1994, 12-13). This does considerable violence to some of the most fundamental and ancient family relationships comprising the fabric of Mande society. At one point, Bühnen styles the Susu Konté [sic], that is, Sumanguru, as "maternal uncle" of the "nephew" Malian Keita, that is, Sunjata, which aside from being patently wrong, flies in the face of the entire corpus of tradition on Fakoli Koroma (see especially Conrad, 1992). Moreover, the notion of Sunjata and the Condé as mere "matrimonial allies" greatly understates the depth and significance of the Sunjata / Sogolon relationship, which accurately reflects Mande social custom in being far more important than the one between Sunjata and his father.
¹² Vidal's informants (1924, 321) were in agreement with my own of recent decades (See Conrad 2002, 99).

[13] One of the lists of Sunjata's battles against Sumaworo includes Kuku (See Zeltner 1913, 45).

[14] For possible corresponding references see Doumbia (1936, 349) and Diabaté (1975, 74). Wâ Kamissoko names Toufinna as the residence of Sumaworo's genies (Cissé and Kamissoko 1991, 12).

[15] According to Adama Dioubaté, the ancient name of Narena was Mènèmu, and he stresses that "it belonged to the Konaté," which was the *jamu* of Sunjata's father (1986, line 1154).

[16] See also where Niane combines the names and titles as "King Naré Maghan Kon Fatta" (1965, 6).

[17] Interview at Kankan, Guinea 1 December 2007.

[18] In the great bard Wa Kamissoko's opinion, "Fara-Koro Makan-Kègni" was a man of distinction, but he was not a *mansa* (1988, 303).

[19] The association of Sunjata's father with one location of course does not eliminate the possible significance of other places. Arguments to the contrary notwithstanding (such as Conrad 1994), the persistent *jeli* references to a town called Niani should not be ignored. A potentially rewarding PhD dissertation topic would be for someone to explore the degree of feedback that must have emerged from the 1960 French edition of Niane's *Soundjata* and its references to "great Niani," which are quite common, such as Demba Kouyaté's remark (using pronunciation characteristic of bards in southeastern Guinée) that Sunjata's father was Falakolo Manken, and that he "built the wall of Nianiba" (Conrad 1999, 168).

[20] Along with Siguiri, Kourémalé remains a base of the gold mining industry in today's Guinée.

[21] This was immediately following the 6th International Conference on Mande Studies 20-26 June 2005. The decision to visit Konfara was influenced by a reference in one of the conference papers to *"Konfra, un village d'orpailleurs situé à sept kilomètres de Kurémalen"* (Camara 2005, 9).

[22] This Farako is not to be confused with the current one in Mali, near Segou.

[23] Any non-Mande tendency to think in terms of single, definitive names for individual chiefdoms *(jamanaw)* could well be misleading, as is suggested by alternative praise-names for Sunjata's father that signify different places (or alternative residences?).

[24] Kouri near Narena (Monteil 1924, 270); Nora near Siguiri (Traoré 1947, 24); Tikko on the Niger (Dieterlen 1951, 92).

Developing "Themes": History of Islam in Africa

Christians and Muslims in Nineteenth Century Liberia: From Ideological Antagonism to Practical Toleration

Yekutiel Gershoni

Résumé

Le Libéria a été établi, entre autres, comme nation chrétienne avec pour mission de propager l'Évangile sur le continent noir. Cette intention, potentiellement, causerait une collision inévitable entre les colonisateurs et cette autre religion monothéiste importée qui avait des siècles durant, déjà fait du prosélytisme dans de vastes régions d'Afrique de l'ouest, je veux dire l'Islam. Cet article analyse le processus par lequel la dure réalité a battu l'entreprise chrétienne, transformant l'antagonisme idéologique initial en une coopération pratique. Il discute aussi de l'initiative visant à formaliser les relations entre les deux religions à l'intérieur d'un cadre politique et les raisons de son échec. S'appuyant sur des sources disponibles, l'article retrace la pénétration de l'Islam d'abord, et plus tard, au dix-neuvième siècle, de la Chrétienté au Libéria, et analyse les conséquences de l'affrontement entre ces religions.

Abstract

Liberia was established, among others, as a Christian nation that would spearhead the spreading of the gospel to the black continent. This endeavor had the potential to bring about a collision between the Liberian settlers and the other imported monotheistic religion that had already been proselytizing in large areas of West Africa for centuries, namely Islam. This article analyzes the process by which the harsh reality defeated the Christian enterprise, turning the initial ideological antagonism into practical cooperation. It also discusses the initiative to formalize the relations between the two religions within a political framework and the reason for its failure. Relying on available sources, the article traces the penetration first of Islam, and later, in the nineteenth century, of Christianity into Liberia, and analyzes the consequences of the encounter between these religions.

Introduction

Liberian history is unique for several reasons: the only place in Africa where freed African American slaves settled in an organized fashion, it was also the only colony established and controlled by an American public company, the American Colonization Society (ACS). And of course, it became the first black independent republic. It can additionally be argued that it is exceptional, at least within West Africa, with respect to the development of its domestic Christian-Muslim relationships.

Liberia was not the cradle of Christianity in West Africa. By the time Christian African American settlers started arriving in what became Liberia in 1822, neighbouring Sierra Leone, a British Crown colony since 1807, was already a center of Christianization in the region. However, most of the missionary zeal stemming from Sierra Leone was aimed at recaptured non-Christian Africans who had been brought to the colony after having been freed on the high seas by the British Royal Navy. The black settlers from the United States, and the white agents who accompanied them to Liberia, arrived with plans for wide-ranging proselytism among local, native Africans. Indeed, Liberia was established as a Christian nation that would spearhead the spreading of the gospel to the black continent. This endeavour seemed destined to collide with the other foreign monotheistic religion that had already been proselytizing in West Africa for a millennium — namely, Islam. That this confrontation did not occur as one might have expected provides the context for the following inquiry.

As my research to date has focused on Liberia's political history, I was surprised to find in my first foray into this field that there has been little academic attention devoted thus far to the issue of Christian-Muslim relations in the region. This neglect is probably due to Liberia's image as being an overwhelmingly Christian state, in addition to its perceived position on the outer "periphery" of Islamic West Africa. However, Islam has not merely been present in this area for close to two centuries, it has long been an important cultural, economic, and political factor in Liberia's history.[1] Focusing on the relations between the Christian black settlers and the local Muslim population in Liberia, this article attempts to remedy this academic neglect and provide a context for better understanding of the local role of Islam. It analyzes the process by which a harsh reality defeated Christian zeal, turning initial ideological antagonism into practical cooperation. It also discusses the proposed initiative to formalize relations between the two religions within a political framework, and the reasons for its subsequent failure. The first section traces the penetration of Islam and Christianity into Liberia during the nineteenth century, while the second analyzes the consequences of the encounter between these religions. My aim here is to show the far-reaching effects of Christian-Muslim relations in Liberia on the country's political history, as well as their significance in the social dynamics of this first "black republic."

Nehemia Levtzion dedicated much of his fruitful and inspired academic life to tracing, tracking, and explaining the spread of Islam in Africa. Liberia was one region he did not explore. It is my hope that this article will address the lacunae and, moreover, because it is written from the viewpoint of a political historian, add a different perspective to the grand historical narrative of religious evolution that has become Nehemia's legacy.

Muslims in the Forest and Christians on the Coast

In the third decade of the nineteenth century, when Christian freed slaves from America established themselves in the coastal area, Islam was already practiced in the hinterland where it influenced some of the forest and coastal segmentary societies in the North East and West of what later became the republic of Liberia. In his research on the spread of Islam in West Africa, Levtzion showed how Muslim traders, followed by Muslim clerics, were responsible for spreading Islam from North Africa, through the Sahara, to the savannah and *Bilad ai Sudan* ("land of the black people"). These traders were drawn to the savannah by gold, slaves, and kola nuts that they bartered for salt, copper, glass, and other manufactured European / North African products. Africans who wanted to participate in the Muslim-monopolized trade were aware of how crucial it was for them to join its commercial diaspora. This diaspora not only shared a common religion and language, it used "a common legal system, the Sharia, a personal, extraterritorial divinely ordained law, that added to the mutual trust among merchants" (Levtzion 2000, 64). These African traders were Manding speakers known variously as Juula, Wangara, and Malinke. Several African kings were also eager to convert to Islam following their encounter with these Muslims. Muslims seemed capable of accomplishing religious-magical feats beyond the power of the local priests; Africans became convinced that Allah's power was superior power (Levtzion 2000, 64-65). By the end of the fifteenth century, Islam had become an influential presence along the trade routes of the savannah region. The discovery of gold in the Akan forest of today's Ghana drew Mande-speaking traders to the area; by the eighteenth century, these Juula appeared in what was later to become North Eastern Liberia where they were referred to by local people as "Mandingo."

The Mandingo learned the language of the people among whom they settled and married local women. Yet they maintained their Muslim identity and refused, for example, to allow their own women to marry non-believers, fearing that children born from such marriages would be brought up in the father's pagan faith. Furthermore, they ensured their own children's Muslim identity by setting up Muslim schools and encouraged Muslim community life by bringing in clerics and building mosques (Konneh 1996b, 145). Their dominant role in commerce was another factor that contributed to the spread of Islam. The proved material success of Muslim traders in the savannah provided an incentive for non-Muslims to accept the faith. As one Mano told Augustine Konneh,

> The people [Mandingo] are different from us, but they like us and care for us. We never knew about trade but they taught us. If the people are good, their religion also must be good and I will join it (1996b, 143).

The Mandingo's successful performance also enabled them to hold an important position in constructing a trade confederation. Under the leadership of Mandingo traders, a loose trade confederation known as the Condo confederation was established. This included the Gola, Loma, Vai, and Dey people, all of whom lived along the trade routes that connected the forest to the coast. By the early nineteenth century, the political and religious rule of the Mandingo extended from the North Eastern forest region to the coast (Liebenow 1987, 27, 37).

As in the savannah, the presence of Muslim traders in the forest region was not the only factor that contributed to Islamization. Indeed, the presence of Muslim clerics who followed the traders was crucial: while the traders spread Islam among the local population, the clerics, using their spiritual knowledge, converted headmen and chiefs.

The local chiefs' belief in the spiritual ability of the Muslim clergy is evident in a local tradition that describes how Islam first came to the town of Boporo. The local chief purportedly asked a Mandingo Muslim holy man to provide spiritual protection for the town against its enemies; as a reward, he provided him with a portion of land and his sister as a wife (Konneh 1996a, 35). Boporo eventually became an important forest trading center. Another such local tradition comes from Bakemi. Muslims first came to the trade centre of Bakemi (probably the contemporary Bakhomah, located between the trade centers of Musadu in the savannah and Boporo in the forest), when the local chief summoned a Muslim scholar to pray for his rule over his neighbours. A competing version of the story has the scholar summoned to expel an evil spirit from the town (Fisher 1971, ix-xiv) — in each instance, it was the power of the Muslim scholar that has been remembered as key to the arrival of Islam by local communities.

Indeed, chiefs and headmen in general who were impressed by the Mandingo holy men's spiritual capabilities often asked them to settle in their villages. Once settled, these Muslim clerics, known in the forest area as *karamoko*, usually became farmers and integrated into the local community by marrying local women and establishing families. In many instances, they also received permission to instruct the chief's sons in the Qur'an. Soon, more children would be attracted to the *karamoko*, and a Muslim school would emerge. Its teaching included the Arabic alphabet and introductory verses of the Qur'an (Konneh 1996a, 32).

The penetration of Islam into the forest region and the coast was, therefore, undertaken by peaceful means: the influential presence of Muslim traders and spiritual services offered by Muslim clergy. The commercial benefits the local people enjoyed and the integration of traders and clergy within the local society greatly facilitated acceptance of the newcomers and their religion. This gradual, peaceful, and non-coercive spread and integration of Islam was a catalyst to the co-existence of local culture and Islam. This coexistence is evident in the usage of Arabic script to write vernacular languages and in the translation of the Sharia and the Hadith into these languages (Konneh 1996a, 32, 37). Among the Vai people (even today), local traditions remain integrated into their Muslim faith; the traditional sacrifice offered to keep the rain away before the rice fields are burned is still performed — now it is offered to Allah and performed by the Imam (Holsoe 1967, 41).

Such harmonious coexistence was made possible mainly because the Muslim clergy who spread their faith in the Liberian hinterland were members of the Qadiriyya *tarîqa* (brotherhood). The Qadiriyya, an ancient Sufi brotherhood founded in Baghdad in the twelfth century, penetrated West Africa from across the Sahara from the seventeenth century. Built on a theoretical foundation of tolerance, the Qadiriyya brotherhood emphasized spiritual purification of the self, the interpretation of the fundamental principles of Islam through mystical experience and the importance of charity (Margoliouth 2008). This, then, became the essence of Liberian Islam.

While Islam entered North Eastern Liberia somewhat haphazardly with the Mandingo traders and commerce arriving by land, African American settlers from across the Atlantic Ocean brought Christianity to South Western Liberia; moreover, these settlers came expressly to spread Christianity methodically, according to a plan. In 1816, the American Colonization Society (ACS) was formed in Washington DC with the aim of locating a suitable place on the West African coast where freed slaves from the United States could be settled. These settlers first established themselves in Cape Mesurado in 1822 and formed the Liberian colony; Monrovia became its capital. The colony, which was first controlled and financed by the ACS, turned into an independent republic in 1847, ruled by the settlers and their descendants, who became known as Americo-Liberians. The ACS planned to base the colony they were founding on the Western model of a Christian society. It was hoped that Liberia would, on the one hand, serve as an asylum for all blacks living in the United States, and on the other, bring about the regeneration of the entire African continent by spreading Christianity and Western values among Africans.

The settlers' and the society's agents' enthusiastic confidence in the ideals underpinning their effort allowed them to underestimate the practical difficulties they were to encounter when trying to realize these ideals. Not only did they harbour the naive conviction that the local population would accept them with open arms, they were also quite ignorant about local peoples and conditions in general, and about Muslim communities in particular.

Indeed, for them, all native Africans, including Muslims, were "heathens" who had to be converted. Rev. Samuel J. Mills and Rev. Ebenezer Burgess, the two agents sent by the ACS in 1818 to locate a suitable place for the settlement, referred to the task of regeneration in their official report to the society, expressing the ideals that later served as spiritual guidelines for the black settlers and their government:

> The altars on these mountains, which the natives had dedicated to devils, are falling before the temples of the living God, like the image of Dagon before the ark. The time is coming when the dwellers in these vales, and on these mountains, will sing hosannahs to the Son of David. Distant tribes will learn their song. Ethiopia will stretch forth her hands unto God, and worship (Alexander 1969, 101).

To implement these ideals, several proposals were considered. For example, in 1827 and again in 1861, plans were drawn to establish, with the assistance of American missionaries, a network of schools among the settlements and African villages that would spread Christian and Western education (Ashmun 1827, 10; Benscn 1863, 77). Another plan was to extend the settlement effort from the coastal area, where it was concentrated, to the interior forest. Known as "civilized" settlements, these planned settlements were to be inhabited by black immigrants who would then transmit Christian and Western values in predominantly African areas.

Trade, which served as a powerful tool in the spread of Islam, was not considered by the ACS as an auxiliary in spreading Christianity or in establishing an economic base for Liberia. In fact, the black settlers, victims of the slave trade themselves, strongly objected to the trade in human beings which was one of the most profitable forms of commerce at the time. From its inception, Liberia, which had adopted the slogan "The Love of Liberty Brought Us Here," saw itself as spearheading the local abolition of the slave trade and of slavery. As part of that effort, the Liberian Militia actively interfered in the hinterland's slave trade. In 1832, Liberians marched against a local chief on the St. Paul's River, and, in 1839, a Liberian column raided Boporo, the center of the Condo confederation, and burned it down (B. Anderson 1971, xii-xiii). The ACS envisioned the growing of staple and cash crops as the main economic occupation of the settlers, most of whom had worked as agricultural slaves in the Southern plantations of the United States. Indeed, Liberia encouraged the cultivation of cash crops such as cam wood, used for the dye industry, sugar cane, and coffee, all of which were supposed to generate a significant source of income for the government.

The establishment of a black political entity based on zealous Christian ideology seeking to replace the existing religions was to be accomplished by the continuing arrival of Christian settlers from the New World and by ongoing material support from the ACS. The next section will look at how the Americo-Liberians dealt with the failure of both these hopes to materialize.

From an Ideological to a Realistic Approach

There was a wide gap between the grandiose ambitions accompanying the establishment of Liberia and the founders' ability to realize them. The colony, and later the republic, was a weak state that lacked the material and human resources to really attempt the fulfillment of the ideals upon which it had been founded. For example, the above-mentioned plans for schools all over the country yielded only a few establishments, founded solely by the Christian mission from the United States. The grander plan never materialized due to the lack of qualified teachers, administrative staff, and financial resources. The trickle rather than the expected flood of black immigrants from the New World undermined the ambitious plan of establishing a chain of settlements to transmit Christian and Western values into the hinterland. Eventually, that specific plan led to the establishment of only three settlements from 1857 to 1869, and even these were relatively close to the coast.[2]

A further reason for failure was the economic system planned by the ACS that never materialized and, consequently, was unable to support the envisaged national government. Either the chosen cash crops were available from more efficient growers elsewhere, or market fluctuations decreased the anticipated crop value, or both. Gradually, many of the settlers gave up on the idea of cultivating and started looking elsewhere for their economic fortune. The location of the Americo-Liberian settlements offered them the possibility of venturing into trade, in spite of the ACS's earlier concern about looking to commerce as an answer. These coastal settlements, backed by the authority of the Liberian government, were well situated to compete successfully with European merchants in controlling trade depots that connected the sea with the forest and savannah.

Developing trade as their main economic activity, however, was neither an easy nor a simple task. Americo-Liberians had already tried to establish direct contact with major hinterland trade centers. In 1858, Seymore and Ash, two Americo-Liberians, tried unsuccessfully to reach the savannah. Benjamin Anderson, former secretary of treasury in the government, was more successful when in 1868, and again in 1874, he made the journey via Boporo to the capital of the western Mandingoes, Musadu. These explorers' main concern was to investigate local, mostly Mandingo, trade practices along the way, in the hope of encouraging further trade.[3] But as they soon found out, their attempts were opposed by ethnic groups both along the coast and in the hinterland; indeed, the Mandingo were more concerned about the Americo-Liberians encroaching on their control of trade than with their missionary efforts. In 1850, Bowen, an American Baptist missionary, visited Boporo; its ruler allowed him to open a school in the town but would not permit him to carry any of his goods into the interior (Bowen 1857, 78-80; Fisher 1971, xiii).

If trade were to infuse much needed oxygen into the stifled Liberian economy, cordial and trustful trade relations with the various ethnic groups, particularly the Mandingoes who controlled such an extensive and complex trade network, were absolutely necessary. However, in addition to local ethnic resistance, Liberian opposition to the slave trade remained an obstacle. It began to generate disruptive reactions from those whose business interests were threatened; in 1860, warriors from the Condo confederation went so far as to attack the capital Monrovia (Konneh 1996a, 38). With the economic survival of the state on the line, the Liberian government chose to forgo its ideological position against the slave trade and slavery, and to cooperate expediently with the locals. This explains why Liberians in the Grand Cape Mount region of Robertsport (1887) and Schieffelinville (1885) turned a blind eye to the widespread use of slaves for farming and porterage in the area.

Moreover, though they refrained from directly participating in the slave trade, Americo-Liberians eagerly integrated into Grand Cape Mount's local trade networks, fully aware of their roots in human trafficking (D'Azevedo 1962, 54-55). In the most recent reflection of this nineteenth-century compromise of ideology, Liberia allowed domestic slavery in the republic until the 1930s.[4]

The harsh realities they encountered weakened the Americo-Liberians' principles, not only their objection to the slave trade but also their desire to spread Christianity. Indeed, their disappointing attempts at proselytizing inevitably led them to compare their failure with the "Mohammedan" success in establishing their own religious structures. Americo-Liberians acquainted with Muslims could not but look at that success with an admiration tainted by jealousy. Edward Wilmot Blyden (1832-1912) took it upon himself to find out why the Muslims had succeeded where the Christians were failing. An outstanding scholar and politician, Blyden was an ordained minister, teacher, and school principal; he later served as professor at, and then president of, the Liberia College. He also served as Secretary of State and Minister of the Interior and Education, later becoming Liberia's first ambassador to Great Britain. Blyden was widely considered the most learned African of his generation. He acquainted himself with Muslims by touring Muslim centers throughout West Africa and even the Middle East, and deepened his knowledge of the Muslim world through research and learning. Indeed, he was the only high official in Liberia who studied and taught Arabic.[5] An admired scholar of Islam, Blyden was asked to present lectures abroad. His publications gained popularity, astonishing scholars in England who could not believe such erudite papers had been written by a black African (Lynch 1970, 74).

Blyden's interest in Islam was not merely academic. From his research he drew several pragmatic conclusions that he tried to implement in his religious and political endeavours. The first was the need to emulate Muslims' successful proselytizing; the second was to integrate Liberia and the British colonial territories into a "modern trans-tribal West African nation," wherein Muslims and Islam would play an important unifying role.[6] The Muslims' numerical strength and their widespread influence in West Africa made them a central constituent of Blyden's plan for a unified West African state; a strong alliance between them and African

Christians was a necessity. According to Blyden, the way to achieve that alliance was by education and by fostering a mutual sense of belonging to a common West African community. The former could be achieved by a chain of schools in which Muslims would be exposed to "Western" education, while Christians were enlightened about Muslim culture. Blyden hoped that the latter could be accomplished by convincing Christian Africans to give up their European heritage and find pride in a comprehensive African identity. In so doing, Blyden was adopting the settlers' original idea of establishing a chain of schools in the hinterland, but adapting it to his own vision. Instead of serving as a means to spread Christianity, these Muslim-Christian schools would enable children of both religions to learn together, developing a sense of common destiny and identity.

Blyden's attempts to encourage healthier Muslim-Christian relations through education achieved only partial success outside his home country, namely in Sierra Leone and Nigeria (specifically, Lagos). In Lagos, where he had been nominated Agent of Native Affairs, he had some success in convincing Muslim leaders to send their children to a "Western" school established in 1896. By the time that he left the country at the end of 1897, three more schools of this kind had opened. From 1887 to 1895, while in Sierra Leone, Blyden provided private English lessons to Muslims. These efforts were later formalized during his tenure as Director of Mohammedan Education for the British administration from 1901 to 1906. However, although Blyden reported to the British governor that his endeavour was successful (Lynch 1970, 203, 235-36), in his home country of Liberia Muslims remained reluctant to send their children to such schools, fearing that their children would succumb to Christianity. Nor did he have full support from other prominent Liberians. President Joseph J. Roberts (1809-76), for example, remained fully committed to the superiority of Western education and therefore strongly objected to Blyden's plan to teach Arabic at Liberia College. Moreover, many Americo-Liberians did not trust Muslims and agreed with the above-mentioned Anderson, who had traveled to Musadu in search of trade agreements and described Muslim clerics as "needy, cunning and mischievous" (B. Anderson 1971, 70). Muslims were seen mainly as competitors, and in addition to the more evident cultural and religious antagonism fuelling fear that Islamic education in any forum was antithetical to the spread of Christianity, Americo-Liberians feared the Mandingo competition in hinterland trade (Konneh 1996a, 46). Eventually, in 1871, just as Blyden was about to start a chain of schools in Liberia, he was driven out of the country by political rivals for the next four years (Lynch 1970, 52).

While the plans that had accompanied Liberia's founding were relinquished, the ideology that saw the Christian religion as superior to, and incompatible with, Islam remained in place. Moreover, Christianity and Western values became ideals by which Americo-Liberians identified themselves in opposition to the local population. Indeed, any African who wanted to integrate into the Americo-Liberian socio-political structure was required to become a "civilized" Christian. Christianity became an efficient "enforcer" of group solidarity within the community. Political leadership and religious leadership went hand in hand: the preacher's pulpit was often a springboard for political advancement, and prominent politicians could claim, almost by right, high office in religious organizations. This remained common among Americo-Liberians until very recently (Liebenow 1987, 81-82).

Conclusion

An organized Christian onslaught into an area where Muslim communities and schools were already present could have led to violent clashes between the adherents of the two religions. However, a few insignificant skirmishes notwithstanding, large-scale violent confrontation did not occur. Neither of the potential adversaries had the strength or motivation to lead a religious war. Indeed, even Almamy Samori Turé's large-scale *jihad* in the region in the last decades of the nineteenth century was warfare aimed at the French colonialists, not indiscriminately at Christians. Samori, who carried the title of *amir al muminim* (commander of the faithful), did not attack the Liberian Christian republic (Wilks 2000, 107).

Muslims in the region did not attempt to create a centralized Muslim state or empire before the arrival of Samori; Muslim political entities were small-scale, scattered and engrossed in trade, not in pursuing political ambitions. Moreover, Islam in that region did not generate the kind of highly learned *ulamas* who could discern the gap between orthodox and locally practiced Islam, and who might have devoted themselves to a process of purification of Islam as had happened in Hausaland (northern Nigeria) and in the Upper Niger regions of Senegal, Guinea, and Mali. It was the holy wars predicated upon this process that led to the formation of Muslim States or *caliphates* in these areas. In short, in nineteenth century Liberia, Islam was never politicized.

Christianity, on the other hand, was always political. Liberia's foundation was based on the commitment to spread Christianity and Western values, and Christian missionaries were actively engaged in converting Africans. However, the ideals that had underpinned the establishment of the country were never implemented. The lack of human and material resources and the accompanying failed economic system forced the Americo-Liberians not only to accept the existence of ethnic groups and communities that rejected Christianity and Western ideals, but also to acknowledge their own economic dependence on a successful cooperation with these groups.

Blyden's efforts to lead both Christians and Muslims to work together for the formation of a unified West African state never took root in neither Liberia nor, indeed, anywhere else in West Africa. He was never able to convince his contemporaries to embrace his ideas. Moreover, the same lack of human and economic resources that chronically stymied the Americo-Liberians' plans also hampered the implementation of his own elaborate and complex initiative. However, it might be argued that even had these resource issues been manageable and contemporary Christian Africans thereby convinced of his views, it is still by no means certain that his plan could have materialized. Success would have been heavily dependent on active Muslim cooperation and this seems to have been decidedly lacking; there was not one Muslim thinker or spokesman who envisioned a "modern transtribal West African nation." Moreover, Liberia never became the kind of major political and economic power that could have motivated Muslims from the hinterland to embrace the notion of a modern West African state, let alone convince them to be part of it. As a consequence, the Christian and Muslim communities remained culturally, socially, and politically separated throughout the nineteenth century. Only in the second half of the twentieth century, as a result of changes in the international order and, ultimately, drastic changes in the political situation of Liberia itself, have Muslims started to integrate into the Liberian cultural, social, and political structures (Konneh 1993, 53-55).

Notes

[1] Among those that did look into Islam in Liberia, and at times even at Christian-Muslim relations, the most important is Benjamin Anderson's description of the journeys he undertook to Muslim towns in the forest and the savannah in the last quarter of the nineteenth century, which is probably the earliest account of Islam in Liberia. A complete edition of his reports was published in 1971, accompanied by a very insightful introduction by Humphrey Fisher. Anderson was followed by his contemporary and fellow Liberian, Edward W. Blyden, who published from 1887 a series of essays on the topic of Islam, including Islam in Liberia (1887ab [1967 and 1971]). Other contributors to the study of Islam in Liberia are Augustine Konneh (1993, 1996b) and M. Alpha Bah (1991). The former published comprehensive studies of the main Muslim group in Liberia, the Mandingo, while the latter wrote on Islam in Liberia and Sierra Leone.

[2] Careysburg, east of Monrovia, which was founded in 1857, Brewersville, and Arthington up the St. Paul River, both founded in 1869.

[3] Benjamin Anderson's (1971) account was considered one of the best geographical descriptions of the Liberian hinterland at the time, although the veracity of his reports was questioned mainly by French writers, who went as far as claiming he never even reached Musadu.

[4] The League of Nations Commission's Findings, Suggestions and Recommendations (Guannu 1972, Appendix 7: 179).

[5] Blyden published extensive research on Islam. His most comprehensive scholarly work on the topic is *Christianity, Islam and the Negro Race*, published in 1887 (reprinted 1967 and 1971). It is comprised of fifteen papers, four of which deal directly with Islam. Two more of Blyden's articles about Islam were published in a separate collection of his essays *Black Spokesman* (1971).

[6] See Hollis R. Lynch, "Introduction" to Blyden (1971). In this article, I only elaborate on the second of these "conclusions." For Blyden's explanation of Islam's advantages over Christianity as a religion for Africans see chapter "Edward Wilmot Blyden (1832-1912) and the paradox of Islam" in Curtis IV (2002, 21-43).

From the Colony to the Post-colony: Sufis and Wahhâbîsts in Senegal and Nigeria

Irit Back

Résumé

On a observé des conflits et des affrontements entre Soufis et Islamistes à travers l'histoire islamique au Moyen-Orient, dans le nord du Caucase, et dans le sous-continent indien. Dans ce contexte, deux cas observés en Afrique de l'ouest sont d'un intérêt particulier. Dans le Sénégal colonial, les influences Wahhâbî étaient communes, et durant les années 1950, elles ont même semblé offrir une alternative à l'hégémonie du Soufisme dans la colonie du Sénégal. Pourtant, durant la création et le développement de l'état post-colonial, la centralité du Soufisme a apparemment repoussé l'influence des Wahhâbistes. En revanche, au Nigéria, l'influence des Wahhâbîyah était marginale pendant la période coloniale et les Soufis tarîqas ont maintenu leur statut auprès des foules et continué de les séduire; à partir des années 1960, les influences Wahhabî ont graduellement diminué le pouvoir du Soufisme parmi les musulmans nigérians. Cet article se propose d'explorer et de comparer la dynamique qui s'est établie entre les Soufis et les Wahhâbîstes au Sénégal et au Nigéria, de la période coloniale à la période post-coloniale. Dans la mesure où le Sénégal et le Nigéria représentent les colonies et post-colonies francophones et anglophones, l'analyse du développement historique d'héritages coloniaux différents clarifiera les similarités et différences apparentes dans les relations entre Soufis et Wahhâbbîstes dans ces deux sphères d'influence.

Abstract

Conflicts and encounters between Sufis and Islamists have persisted throughout much of Islamic history in areas such as the Middle East, the North Caucasus, and the Indian sub-continent. In this context, two cases from West Africa are particularly interesting. In colonial Senegal, Wahhâbî influences were common, and during the 1950s, they even seemed to pose an alternative to the hegemony of Sufism in the colony of Senegal. Yet in the creation and development of the post-colonial state, the centrality of Sufism has apparently confined the influence of the Wahhâbîsts to the margins. In Nigeria, on the other hand, the influence of *the Wahhâbîyah was marginal in the colonial period and the Sufi tarîqas maintained their status and appeal to the masses; from the 1960s onwards, Wahhâbî influences gradually diminished the power of Sufism amongst Nigerian Muslims. This article explores and compares the dynamics that developed between Sufis and Wahhâbîsts in Senegal and Nigeria, from the colony to the post-colony. Inasmuch as Senegal and Nigeria represent the Francophone and Anglophone colonies and post-colonies, analyzing the historical development of different colonial heritages will clarify the apparent similarities and differences in relations between Sufis and Wahhâbîsts in these two spheres of influences.*

Introduction

Conflicts and encounters between Sufis and Islamists have been evidenced throughout much of Islamic history in areas such as the Middle East, the North Caucasus, and the Indian sub-continent (Sirriyeh 1999). During the nineteenth century, a major shift in their relations seemed to appear. Growing contact with western imperialism, and the decline of the great Islamic empires such as the Ottoman, the Safavid, and the Mughul, gave birth to the creation of reform movements that could be categorized as "Islamic modernism." Such were the *Salafia* of the nineteenth century, which, in contrast to the *Wahhâbîyah* movement, introduced a more ambivalent attitude toward practical and theological aspects of Sufism, usually trying to put them on a sounder, rational, moral basis. Yet, in spite of the differences of the various reform movements of the late nineteenth century and the beginning of the twentieth in their attitudes toward Sufism, it can be claimed that they posed a substantial challenge to Sufi *tarîqas* in various areas and societies, under different colonial rules.

Amongst Islamist currents, relations between the *Wahhâbîyah* and Sufism were characterized with tensions and conflicts. Muhammad B. `Abd al-Wahhâb (1703-92), the founder of the *Wahhabi* movement, was a Sufi adept in his youth, but later came under the influence of the writings of Ibn Taymiyya (661-728); he had spoken out strongly against beliefs and practices such as *tawassul* (intercession), saint veneration, and grave cults. The *Wahhâbîyah* under `Abd al-Wahhâb strongly opposed Sufi practices such as visiting the tombs of saints for God's favour, introducing the name of a prophet, a saint, or an angel into a prayer, and seeking intercession from any being but God, practices defined as bid'ah (innovation; derivation from acceptable teaching and practice). The *Wahhâbîyah* became the dominant political force in the Arabian Peninsula from the middle of the eighteenth century (see al-Yassini 1995). Later, during the twentieth century, its influence on attitudes towards many aspects of Sufi practices and thought was enormous.

With the rise of Islamist influences in the last quarter of the twentieth century, the relations with Sufism appear to have become tenser, characterized by frequent conflicts and encounters. This phenomenon has also characterized African Islam, especially since the 1970s, with the strengthening of relations between African Islam and the broader world of Islam (Rosander 1997, 1-27). In this context, two cases from West Africa are particularly interesting. In colonial Senegal, *Wahhâbî* influences were common and during the 1950s, they even seemed to pose an alternative to the hegemony of Sufism in the colony of Senegal. Yet in the creation and development of the post-colonial state the centrality of Sufism has apparently confined the influence of the *Wahhâbîsts* to the margins. In Nigeria, on the other hand, the influence of the *Wahhâbîyah* was marginal in the colonial period and the Sufi *tarîqas*[1] maintained their status and appeal to the masses; from the 1960s onwards, *Wahhâbî* influences gradually diminished the power of Sufism amongst Nigerian Muslims.

This article aims to explore and compare the dynamics that developed between Sufis and *Wahhâbîsts* in Senegal and Nigeria, from the colony to the post-colony. Senegal and Nigeria represent the Francophone and Anglophone colonies and post-colonies. As such, analyzing the historical development of different colonial heritages will clarify the apparent similarities and differences in relations between Sufis and *Wahhâbîsts* in these two spheres of influences. The challenges of modernity to the spiritual as well as material authority of the Sufi *tarîqas* and the *Wahhâbîsts* movements, and their confrontation with and adaptation to the changing realities of the colonies and the post-colonies, will be analyzed through examining different aspects, such as their bargaining with the local and national governance, and relations between leaders and their adherents. In this context, several fundamental questions will be discussed. First, are the practices, institutions, and intellectual traditions associated with Sufism in West African Islam disappearing with the appearance of "modernity," as was predicted, for example, by Clifford Geertz (1968) and Ernest Gellner (1983)? Second, in the cases of shift from the popular devotional practices of Sufism to the "legalist" form of Islam (as represented by the *Wahhâbîsts*), which aspects of modernization and globalization influenced this change? To which audiences did it appeal? Finally, where Sufism is explicitly constructed as "modern" or compatible with modern life, how is that achieved, particularly in the face of the rising challenges of Islamism and *Wahhâbîsm*?

The Roles of Sufism during the Colonial Period

As in other parts of the Islamic world, Sufism in West Africa played a vital role in expanding the boundaries of *Dar al-Islam*. As Nehemia Levtzion (2002, 110) claimed, "It was through the *shaykh* and the tomb, rather than through the *'alim* and the mosque, that Islam reached the common people." Indeed, the local *shaykhs* were usually more accessible to the common follower than the established community of Islam. The power of *baraka* (blessing) of the *shaykh* was influential both in the worldly affairs of the common followers and in their spiritual world. Moreover, on many occasions the *shaykhs* voiced the people's grievances against oppressive and corrupt regimes.

The penetration of Sufism, and its adaptation to local social, religious, and political structures of Western African societies, was not essentially different from similar processes which occurred in other parts of the Islamic world. These developments characterized the penetration and the deepening roots of universal *tarîqas* such as the *Qâdiriyya* in the sixteenth century and the *Tijâniyya* in the eighteenth century (Vikor 2000). Yet, during the eighteenth and nineteenth centuries, the course of development of Sufism changed dramatically, both within the larger world of Islam and in West Africa. These changes occurred on the eve of the colonial conquest of Africa, thus they had a major effect on the colony and its relations with the Sufi *tarîqas*.

Prior to the eighteenth century, the simultaneous affiliation of the Sufi believer (even his *shaykh*), to several *tarîqas* was not a rare phenomenon in West Africa. But during the 1700s, the call for exclusiveness in the believer's affiliation was spreading throughout the Sufi world; the *tarîqas* had become larger, centralist, tighter.

These developments were associated in some cases with the militarization of these formerly social organizations. Such was the case with the emergence of the *jihad* movement of ʿUthman dan-Fodio (1804-1807), which was the foundation for the establishment of the Sokoto *caliphate* (see Hiskett 1994). Although Sufism was not a central theme motivating this movement that struggled against local corrupt Islamic authorities and aimed to create a *caliphate* ("community of believers"), Sufi practices and affiliation to the *tarîqa Qâdiriyya* played a decisive role both in recruiting new believers (Muslims as well as non-Muslims), and in consolidating the *caliphate*.

The affiliation of the Muslim believers to the Sufi *tarîqas* was very common in the territories that eventually created the colony of Senegal during the colonial period, within the *quatre communes* and beyond. Since the late eighteenth century, this area also experienced the spirit of the *jihad* movements, such as the movement of *al-hajj* 'Umar Tal. In contrast with the *jihad* movement of ʿUthman dan-Fodio, 'Umar' Tal's movement had recruited its *muqaddam* (agents) on the basis of their exclusive affiliation to *tariqa Tijâniyya* and their commitment to destroy "paganism." During his military campaigns against local forces, 'Umar' Tal had developed an exclusivist interpretation of affiliation to *tariqa Tijâniyya* as incompatible with the other affiliations. In the last decades of the nineteenth century this spirit of *jihad* was directed against European expansion into the Senegalese hinterland. The last territory in the colony of Senegal to be conquered by the French in the early 1890s was the "Tokolor Empire" that was established as the result of Umar' Tal's movement — an event that preserved the image of Umar' Tal as the ultimate anti-colonial fighter in Senegalese national memory (Robinson 2000a, 20-25).

During the last quarter of the nineteenth century, both the French and the British were struggling to expand their rule from coastal regions into the West African hinterland. Their first encounters with the different interpretations of Sufism had tremendous impact on their attitudes toward the Sufi *tarîqas* during the period in which they established colonial control. Sufi *tarîqas* were one of the components of the colony with which the colonial authorities had to negotiate. Both the British and the French had some previous knowledge of Sufi *tarîqas* from their occupation of the Indian sub-continent and Algeria (respectively).[2] Generally, Sufi *shaykhs* were considered as belonging to the non-radical component of the Muslim community and, as such, were viewed as potential collaborators. Yet, colonial policy toward the Sufi *tarîqas* was changing according to their relations with other forces within the Islamic communities, as well as their estimated potential for radicalism and creating unrest in the colonies.

The boundaries of the Sokoto *caliphate* almost overlapped those of the northern part of the colony of Nigeria, which was created in 1914 through the merger of the protectorates of Northern and Southern Nigeria. As the northern part of the colony was the model for the creation and the establishment of Lord Lugard's "dual mandate" or "indirect rule,"[3] many of the institutions, identities, and practices, which were prevalent in the Sokoto *caliphate*, were maintained during the colonial period. The policy of the "dual mandate" in northern Nigeria was originally directed towards leaning on the more established political forces within the Muslim community, first and foremost of which was the *Masu Sarauta* ("the possessors of governance"), generally the descendants of the Sokoto *caliphate*. As most of the elite and their followers belonged to the *tariqa Qâdiriyya*, the British administration considered them part of the "Native Administration," that is, part of the mechanism for the establishment of peaceful cooperation (Hiskett 1984, 285-88). Moreover, *tariqa Qâdiriyya* was considered "a peaceful sect," as compared to the more radical *tariqa Tijâniyya*. The British fear of the *Tijâniyya* originated both from the influences of the French attitudes toward this *tarîqa* and from its image as a pan-Islamic organization (to be discussed later). Generally speaking, the British perceived their Muslim subjects in Northern Nigeria as "good," as long as they could be isolated from "outside influences." They saw the *Qâdiriyya* as a local organization, to be contrasted with the more universal character of the *Tijâniyya*, in turn considered as having the potential to "radicalize" the stability of the colony.

The occupation of wide-scale territories inhabited with various Muslim societies, both in North and West Africa, urged the French to define their "paths of accommodation" with the different forces within the Muslim societies (Robinson 2000a, 75-96). In contrast to Northern Nigeria where "indirect rule" adapted the Caliphate's hierarchical and centralized pattern of traditional governing, the diffused and segmentary patterns of domination in the Senegalese hinterland forced the French authorities to abandon their preference for direct and centralized models of domination and to lean towards local Muslim leaders for support. During the first two decades of the twentieth century, French governors and local administrators identified the advantages of cooperation with local *marabouts* — leaders of Sufi *tarîqas*. In the process, assumptions about their potential for creating radical unrest in the colony shifted towards attitudes viewing them as the cornerstone for establishing the new order of the colony, as exemplified in the case of the *Murîdiyya*.

Whereas in northern Nigeria the two major players were the established *tarîqas* of the *Qâdiriyya* and *Tijâniyya*, the course of development of Sufism in Senegal saw the phenomenon of the creation of a new *tarîqa* during the colonial period. The *Murîdiyya* was founded in 1886 by the Senegalese *shaykh* Ahmadu Bamba Mbacké, who was born in the middle of the nineteenth century to a well-established *marabout* family in eastern Baol. He developed a new Islamic pedagogy based on the commitment to learning that was linked to action, work, and loyalty; he began to consolidate the foundation of the community *murids*, the "seekers after God." Initially, *shaykh* Bamba was perceived by the French as a potential risk to the establishment of their rule in the hinterland of Senegal, especially due to his criticism of the practice of power. Although Bamba's criticism was directed mainly against the local political establishment, France's perception resulted in his enduring two periods of exile, first to Gabon (1895-1902) and later to Mauritania (1903-07) (Cruise O'Brien 1971). Yet, already during the last exile period, relations between the *tarîqa* and the colonial authorities were gradually improving, mainly due to a mutual recognition of the utility of cooperation. As David Robinson concludes:

> For the administration, the Murids offered a major solution to the problems of social control. Former warriors could be demobilized; former slaves could be incorporated as followers and clients. The labor power of both groups could be turned to the growing of peanuts, millet and other work.... It was Bamba and the Murids who completed the transformation of the old disintegrating regime into the new colonial order (2000a, 226-27).

Besides analyzing the *tarîqas'* ability to bargain with the local and national governments during the colonial period, it is important to examine the dynamic of Sufi *tarîqas* through their adaptation to processes of social change. Processes such as large-scale urbanization and changing economic patterns were accompanied by feelings of alienation and confusion amongst large segments of the population. The Sufi *tarîqas* were able to respond to these changes, both spiritually and practically. Joining the *tarîqa* provided the follower with a feeling of belonging and a sense of coping with the new and dramatic challenges of the colonial period. The leaders of the *tarîqas* were perceived as mediators who could voice the people's grievances against the colonial authorities. In this sense, it seems that the *tarîqa Murîdiyya* was adapting best to the changing realities of the colony. The emphasis on the premise that physical work leads to spiritual salvation, the ability of the *tarîqa* to recruit new followers from the rural areas, and the pragmatic attitude toward the integration of African traditional customs with orthodox Islamic practices and beliefs, all contributed to the rising popularity of the new *tarîqa* and its economic success.

In spite of *Murîdiyya* success, the *tarîqa Tijâniyya* was able also to maintain its status and enlarge its membership. After the colonial occupation of Umar Tal's *Tijâniyy* Empire, two new branches of this *tarîqa* began to thrive and attract followers. The formation of the communities of the followers of *el-hajj* Malik Sy (first in Cayor, then in Tivaouane) and the followers of Abdoulaye Niasse in Kaolak were proving the ability of the *tarîqa* to create new urban Sufi centres. The institution of the *daaira* reflected the ability to cope with changing political and social realities. As Leonardo Villalon argues,

> The institution of the *daaira*, which is almost certainly of Tijan origin, emerged as a central component of Senegalese religious organization. And what is most important to note here is that the adaptation of religion took place in accordance with the imperative of interacting and responding to the evolving state structures which the French were erecting during this period (1995, 203).

Another outcome of the colonial period was the creation of improved infrastructures such as communication and media. These changes produced new opportunities for the *tarîqas* to expand beyond the local level and attract new followers.[4] The impact of the improved infrastructure on the flow of ideas was demonstrated by the case of the *Tijâniyy shaykh* Ibrâhîm Niass, who was born in Senegal in 1900 and became one of its *muqaddam*. From the 1930s to the 1950s, Niass helped spread the message of the *Tijâniyya* throughout West Africa, including through the branch of *Jamâ'at al-fayda* that was established in Kano, Northern Nigeria. This branch rapidly became very popular, not only in the northern part, but throughout the colony (Hiskett 1984, 286-88). The activities of the North African cleric Sherif Alowi, who helped establish the first specifically *Tijâni* mosque in Kano in 1925 and influenced many prominent leaders within the *tarîqa* in Northern Nigeria was another expression of this kind of influence (Reynolds 2001, 613-16).

External influences of Sufi theology and practices motivated a large-scale intellectual revival, which helped to establish the image of the *Tijâniyya* in Northern Nigeria as a dynamic and innovative *tarîqa*, an image which in turn appealed to a larger audience (Umar 1999, 367-71). Yet, the major power remained in the hands of the *tarîqa Qâdiriyya* that was closely identified with the traditional political establishment of the north. During decolonization, the *tarîqa* went through a process of politization and its leaders were identified mostly with the conservative and regional Northern Peoples' Congress (NPC). The rising popularity of *tarîqa Tijâniyya* was considered to be a threat to the political hegemony of the NPC. Thus, on the eve of independence, the relations between the two major *tarîqas* in Northern Nigeria were characterized by competition about their appeal to their followers and their influence on the political sphere.

In spite of occasional eruptions of tensions between *tarîqas*, it can be argued that, during the colonial period, Sufi *tarîqas* were fortifying their position both by attracting new followers and negotiating with the colonial authorities. After World War II, they were also able to create a successful cooperation with emerging local political elites. Thus, while in Northern Nigeria the Sufi *tarîqas* remained just one component of the various identities that comprised the fabric of Muslim society, in Senegal they became the cornerstone of the newly established order during the decolonization phase after War World II. Only during the 1950s was this centrality challenged by the emergence of *Wahhâbî* influences.

Wahhâbîsts and Sufis during Decolonization and Independence

One of the main factors influencing the relations between Sufis and *Wahhâbîsts* in Senegal and Nigeria was the attitudes of the colonial authorities toward the *hajj*. The return of African Muslims in Mecca, the Holy City where the *Wahhâbî* doctrine had been official since the conquest of the Hijaz by `Abd al-`Aziz ibn Sa`ud in 1925, was one of the main causes of the spread of *Wahhâbîs* doctrines in West Africa. The attitudes of the colonial regimes toward the *hajj* changed in different periods according to its beliefs concerning the potential threat of this pilgrimage. Yet, generally it could be argued that although the French authorities were alert to the radical potential of *Wahhâbîs* influence, they helped both materially and spiritually to make the pilgrimage possible for their Muslim subjects as part of their efforts to establish an image as a pro-Muslim colonial power. Thus, through the route of the *hajj*, French territories in West Africa were fertile ground for the spread of *Wahhâbîs* influence (see Kaba 1974). The British authorities, on the other hand, were less bothered with the potential challenges of the *Wahhâbîyah*. Their main fear was concentrated on the possibility of the penetration of Sudanese *Mahadists* influences among Nigeria's Muslims. Most Nigerian pilgrims traveled by foot, thereby passing through Sudan; in many cases they stopped to work in the cotton fields, sometimes for years, to help finance their pilgrimage. These fears, combined with Britain's general goal to isolate Muslim Nigeria from outside influences, resulted in a policy aimed at restricting both the number of pilgrims to Mecca, and to limiting, as far as possible, the duration of their stay abroad (Reynolds 2001, 609-12).

The establishment of *Ittihâd Thaqâfi al-Islâmî* (ITI) in 1953 by Cheikh Touré in` Dakar revealed the influences of *Wahhâbî* doctrines and practices (Loimeier 1994). Since its creation, the ITI's attitudes had been marked by a clear anti-*maraboutage* stance:

> The ITI's attacks against the marabouts, who were singled out and stigmatized as the chief perpetrators of the backward development of the Senegalese society, led to a conflict between the ITI and a number of marabouts who, from their part, inter-

preted the Islamic Reform movement as a threat to their influence on state and society. In its activities and campaigns, the ITI drew strong support from the urban youth who rejected the established system of Islamic education and the concept of maraboutage. In their eyes, maraboutage came to mean unconditional surrender to the authority of a marabout (Loimeier 2000, 172-73).

The ITI challenge to the Sufi *tarîqas* in Senegal showed itself both at the practical and ideological level. At the more practical level, the organization's ability to adopt modern organizational forms such as effective administration, together with its abilities to offer effective tools for coping with the challenges of the 1950s, were appealing to new audiences such as the urban youth. These capabilities were revealed through the establishment of a network of Arabic schools that, in contrast to the *maraboutic* schools that taught only the Qur'ân (and that by rote), also taught Arabic and Islamic sciences, as well as French and general sciences (Loimeier 2000, 173-75). At the ideological level, the ITI constructed its image as an anti-colonial movement, exploiting especially the characterization of Sufi *tarîqas* as colonial collaborators.

The organization's appeal to a growing audience was based not only on its more modern and radical image as compared to Sufi *tarîqas*, but also on its image as "more Muslim." This reflected its claim of offering a more extensive Islamic education and its demands for a cessation of the missionary activities of the Catholic Church, total suppression of the importation of alcoholic beverages, and the institution of Muslim courts (Kaba 1974, 292-300). This image was communicated not just amongst educated elites able to participate in the intellectual discourse of the organization, but also among illiterate audiences. The struggle against "un-Islamic" Sufi practices, such as the production and the belief in the power of amulets *(gri-gris)*, was transformed into an artistic expression through theatre plays in Wolof, which could reach audiences not able to understand French or Arabic. To the literate audiences, *Le Reveil Islamique* the ITI's monthly periodical, published many overtly "anti-Sufi" articles as part of their politicization campaign (Loimeier 2000, 175).

In a similar way to the developments in Senegal, anti-Sufi responses in Nigeria also grew initially through changes in the educational sphere. These influences were recognized first within the new Muslim elites educated in Kano Law School (renamed School for Arabic Studies [SAS] in 1947). In this school, and in others which later followed its prototype, a new Muslim elite was emerging, one influenced by broad traditions of both Muslim and Western scholarship. Many of its graduates had opportunities to join the modern British bureaucracy and even to pursue advanced studies abroad. The criticism of Sufism amongst the teachers, students, and graduates of this school was both theological and political. At the theological level, SAS's students, teachers and graduates criticized what was perceived as Sufi superstitions. New national poetry spread the call for "the kind of Islam practiced at the time of the Prophet, which was simple, clear and free from superstitions and other accretions" (poem by Sa`ad Zungur, quoted in Umar 1999, 371). Just as Wolof had been adopted by the ITI to disseminate anti-Sufi propaganda in Senegal, Nigerian critics utilized the local vernacular to penetrate "the masses" — this new poetry was in Hausa. At the political level, the criticism was directed mainly toward the tight cooperation between the British authorities, the traditional leaders of the North, and the leaders of the Sufi *tarîqas*, which they named the "sacred alliance."

In both Nigeria and Senegal, the first years of independence witnessed a remarkable shift in relations between Sufis and *Wahhâbîsts*. This shift was the result of many factors, but it can be argued that the ability to create effective alliances within the newly independent states was one of the more decisive. While in Nigeria Sufi hegemony was diminishing in the face of the rising power of *Wahhâbî* influences, in Senegal Sufi *tarîqas* were able to reconstruct their power through marginalizing them during the 1950s.

In the Nigerian context, the shift in the relation between Sufis and *Wahhâbîsts* was mainly due to the influence of a single figure — Abubakar Gumi (died 1992). His anti-Sufi attitudes began to form while he was a student at SAS and were reinforced through his further education in Sudan. Yet these attitudes matured mainly during the late 1950s, when he represented Northern Nigeria in the Muslim World League in Saudi Arabia. During this period his doctrinal orientation became pronouncedly *Wahhâbî* and, as a result, anti-Sufi (see Tsiga 1992). In 1962 Gumi was appointed the

Grand Qadi of Northern Nigeria. From this influential position he was able to reach large audiences.

Gumi was one of the first influential figures in independent Nigeria to recognize the potential of mass media for spreading anti-Sufi views (see Umar 1993). He used both established media channels, such as Kaduna television and radio stations and the Hausa newspaper *Gaskiya ta fi kwabo*, as well popular means such as audiocassettes and soft-cover booklets.

Yet, in spite of the growing popularization of his anti-Sufi views, his political alliances were evidencing some cracks. Although he was closely associated with the Premier of Northern Nigeria (*Saradauna* of Sokoto), the latter began to show signs of discontent with Gumi's intensive activities, concerned that they would result in major divisions among Muslims in northern Nigeria. As a result, he initiated the establishment of a new Sufi *tarîqa*, the *Usmanniya*. Through using the name of Uthman dan-Fodio, the well-known *jihadist* leader of the nineteenth century, the *Saradauna* intended to create Sufi *tarîqa* that would bridge the theological gaps between the different Sufi *tarîqas*. In addition, the *Saradauna* saw Sufism as part of his own Islamic identity and heritage — he had personally prayed in tombs belonging to al-Jilani (in Baghdad) and al-Tijâni (in Fez). It was only after the assassination of the *Saradauna* and the transition of Nigeria from democracy to military rule in 1966 that the route of Gumi's anti-Sufi struggle became clear once again

Until 1962, it seemed that the case of Senegal would follow the route of Nigeria, and that the power of Islamic reformism would exclude the hegemony of the Sufi *tarîqas*. In the first years after independence, the ITI retained its glory as the anti-colonial fighter and the organization that was struggling to revive the Muslim character of Senegalese society. Moreover, it enjoyed the support of Mamadou Dia, Senegal's first Prime Minister. Socialist Dia found that through the alliance with ITI he was able to contest the *marabouts'* claim to be the sole representative of all Muslims, and thus was able to motivate socialist reforms. He even nominated Cheikh Touré as chief of the *section de presse arabe* in the Ministry of Information, an influential position that provided Touré with the ability to control the contents of many organs of the media. In addition, the new government responded to other demands of the

ITI, such as equal recognition for examinations of their *Écoles Franco-Arabes* with those of governmental schools.

In December 1962, Prime Minister Dia was accused of involvement in a coup attempt against President Senghor. The overthrow of Dia was followed by the immediate destruction of the ITI's privileged position. Senegalese President Léopold Sédar Senghor openly declared his support for the Sufi *tarîqas* as a reward for their loyalty to him during Dia's attempted coup (Creevey 1968, 64). During the 1960s, many of Senghor's gestures were designed to prove the commitment of the Senegalese government to the *tarîqas*. In July 1963, Senghor initiated the Great Mosque of Touba (see Ross 1995), the sacred site of *tarîqa Murîdiyya*, a symbolic act directed at the rising power of the youngest *tarîqa* in the new state (*Dakar Matin* 9 et 12 juillet 1963). As for *tarîqa Tijâniyya*, Senghor emphasized the international appeal of the *tarîqa*, both by reconstructing the Islamic messages of Ibrâhîm Niass to other audiences throughout Africa and by sending *Tijâniy* students to acquire further education in Islamic institutions abroad. He even used the historical connections between the *Tijâniyya* in Nigeria and Senegal as a lever for strengthening relations between the two states.[5] Besides creating effective alliances between the state and the Sufi *tarîqas*, Senghor was also able to control the development of the Islamic reform movement, in particular through the establishment of the *Fédération des Associations Islamiques du Sénégal* (FAIS), a parent organization which was able to control most of the Islamic activities in Senegal (Loimeier 1999, 348-49). Yet, in spite of the effectiveness of this alliance in the first decades of the independent state, by the late 1970s, even it was not able to resist the spirit of change that was penetrating West African Islam.

Islamic Radicalism and Sufi Responses in the Post-colony

One of the forces that had a tremendous effect on the creation of the post-colonial space in West African Islam was the revolution in media and communication in the second half of the twentieth century. As John Hunwick sees it,

> African Muslims, no less than Muslims elsewhere, are reaching out on both the intellectual and material planes to their co-religionists through a series of Islamic organizations and

networks, both official and unofficial. Through the press, radio and TV, cassette tapes, books, the fax machine and above all the rapid travel facilities in the jet age, ideas are being exchanged between Sub-Saharan African Muslims and members of the global community to an extent and with a rapidity that were unimaginable during the colonial period. Fax machines connect Muslims in Kano and Dakar to others in Cairo and London; radio broadcasts are beamed to Sub-Saharan Africa from Tripoli, Cairo, Riyadh or Teheran; cassette tapes of sermons and speeches can be duplicated in minutes and distributed cheaply; Muslim-run magazines and newspapers published in Paris, London, Beirut and Cairo are read in African countries, and African authors publish their books and pamphlets in English in London, in French in Paris and in Arabic in Beirut and Cairo (1997, 29-30).

One of the main effects of the globalization of media and communication was the facilitation of the penetration of Islamism[6] into West Africa. In general terms, the events of the 1970s, and especially the rupture of diplomatic relations between Israel and sub-Saharan countries after 1973, helped to reinforce the relations between Africa and the Arab world. This was manifest both at the diplomatic level, through tighter cooperation between the African Unity Organization and the Arab League (see Boutros-Ghali 1994), and through greater involvement of African Muslims in various pan-Islamic organizations (Hunwick 1997, 28-52). At the same time, the fortification of the *Wahhâbi* identity of Saudi Arabia and the Islamic revolution in Iran in 1979 led to processes of Islamic revival and politization in many West African societies. The implications of the process of Islamization of West Africa on the relations between *Wahhâbîsts* and Sufis affected both. Some of these Islamist influences, such as those related to *Ayatollah* Khomeini's period, were more favourable to Sufism (Sirriyeh 2000, 250). Yet, in the places where Saudi Arabian influences were strong, *Wahhâbîs* influences were marginalizing Sufism. This can be clearly demonstrated by developments in Nigeria since the 1970s, especially in regard to Gumi's anti-Sufi campaign.

In the theological sphere, Gumi's most articulate critique against Sufism was published in 1972 in his *al-'Aqîda al-sahîha bi-muwâfaqat al-sharî'a* (the true belief according the Shari'a). His main criticism was directed against the concept of the *walâya* (status of friend of God, of one who enjoys divine patronage) of the Sufi *shaykh*. He claimed that every God-fearing Muslim is a *walî* (friend of God, connotation of patron when referring to God). His criticism was directed toward the *Tijâniyya*, especially regarding *al-Tijâni's* claim of having received a special *wird* (litanies, often unique to *tarîqa*, bestowed at initiation) and exclusive guarantees in a live encounter with the Prophet Muhammad. These ideas were elaborated on later by Gumi himself and also by a number of other thinkers, the most well-known of whom was Dahiru Maigari (Umar 1999). These publications, which were published both as academic books in Arabic and as booklets in local languages, helped to spread the concept of Sufism as *bid'a* — incompatible with the *sharî'a*.

At the organizational level, Gumi was influential in establishing the Nigeria pan-Islamic organization *Jama'at Nasril al-Islam* (JNI-Association for the Victory of Islam) in 1962. Although the attitudes of the organization were clearly anti-Sufi, it was only at the beginning of the 1970s that circumstances were ripe for the establishment of a mass organization to spread these messages. Although the effects of oil exploitation were evident already through the 1960s, the major implications of this resource discovery became clear only about a decade later. They included an abrupt entrance into a macro-capitalistic economy and the exclusion of a wide stratum of Nigerian society from oil revenues. Legacies of inadequate governing were evident in successive military and civilian regimes, which in turn perpetuated a culture of intolerance, violence, and violation of human rights. In the general atmosphere of domestic despair and a malfunctioning state, Islamists' messages such as revivalism could be easily absorbed amongst the Muslim masses. One of the results was the establishment of hundreds of Muslim associations and societies *(jamâ'as)*, whose followers and supporters have grown in number consistently since the 1970s.

One representative of such an organization was the *Jamâ'at izâlat al-bid'a wa-iqâmat al-sunna* (the Society for the Eradication of Innovation and the Establishment of the Sunna, known as *yan izala*), established in 1978 in the city of Jos (capital of Plateau State). Its patron was Abubakar Gumi who gave his blessing to his disciple Isma`ilia Idris to establish this organization. Many of the organization's activists were graduates of Arabic schools.[7] The movement's messages were spread through the media — newspapers, radio programs, brochures, and audiocassettes. The mobilization of hundreds of thousands of followers and supporters in less than a decade was proof of the effectiveness of the message and of its efficient distribution (Loimeier 1997). In comparison to the JNI, the *yan izala* actions against the Sufi *tarîqas* were much more radical, and included publicizing lists of their followers. As a result, violent clashes between *yan izala*'s supporters and the Sufi *tarîqas* followers spread during 1978-79.

The responses of the *tarîqas* to the challenges of the reformist Islamist movements, mostly inspired by *Wahhâbîsts*, were both theological and organizational. In 1977 they established two organizations — *ungiyarb jama'atu halus-sunnati* and *kungiyar dakarun dan-Fodic* (see Hiskett 1994) which aimed to coordinate the activities of the Sufi *tarîqas*, and demanded that Gumi moderate his anti-Sufi declarations. At the theological level, various Sufi thinkers published books, articles, booklets, and pamphlets in which they tried to refute the Islamists' claims that Sufism was un-Islamic and *bid'a*. Muhammad Ainûma, for example, tried to portray al-Tijâni as a holy man who acted for the revival of the *Sunna* and the elimination of *bid'a*. Answering the critics of Sufism, Muhammad al-`Âshir Shu`ayb claimed that it was not grounded on formal rationalism but on the intuitive illumination which God placed on its servants (see Umar 1999, 378-82). Nevertheless, practices, institutions, and intellectual traditions associated with Sufism were gradually disappearing in the face of the Islamist, *Wahhâbî* challenge characterizing post-colonial Nigeria.

Post-colonial Senegal seems to have experienced the reverse process — Sufi influences marginalized *Wahhâbi* influences. As Christian Coulon (1979) shows, the system of *maraboutic* collaboration with the colonial state continued in a mutually beneficial exchange system even after 1960. The cohesiveness of the *tarîqas* was preserved and this enabled them to function as a civil society, maintaining a balance between state and society that prevented unchecked authoritarian excesses. Indeed, the relative political stability and efforts for democratization seen in Senegal were exceptional in the history of post-colonial Africa. Yet it must be noted that this collaboration was in many ways "cohabitation without affection" (Villalon 1995, 213-19). Many perceived *maraboutic* power as an obstacle to the true development of Senegal. As was the case in Nigeria, since the 1970s the political system has been under stress as persistent economic decline and political frustration produce protests and wide dissatisfaction. But whereas in Nigeria most of the anti-Sufi activities developed in *Wahhâbi*-inspired circles and organizations, in Senegal, the challenges to the dominance of Sufi *tarîqas* were generated mostly from within.

Senegal could not remain isolated from global influences such as the rise of Islamism. Since the mid-1980s, these influences were expressed by growing criticism of the secular orientation of the Senegalese state, especially under the *laïcité* policy of President Abdou Diouf (1981-2000).[8] The Islamist influences were articulated in the emergence of *Dahiratoul Moustarchidina wal Moustarchidaty*, a movement established in 1973 in Tivaouan by Moustapha Sy, a young *marabout* from an important *Tijâni* lineage. Apart from its call for the adaptation of Islam to modern life and the reduction of the secular character of Senegal, the *Moustarchidine* turned to attracting new urban audiences from both the educated elites and the unemployed, increasingly alienated masses.[9] During the 1980s, the organization developed as a successful mass movement, hierarchically structured. Although the *Moustarchidine* were using Sufi practices and structures to mobilize the masses and establish their reputation, they were simultaneously challenging the relational *status quo* between the political realm and the Sufi *tarîqas*. Following a public attack on President Abdou Diouf during the 1993 presidential campaign, the group's political involvement escalated into violent protests throughout 1994; the *Moustarchidine* thereby emerged as the first serious consecratory political movement built on a religious base in Senegal (Villalon 1999, 129-34).

It is reasonable to expect that anti-Sufi attitudes will be expressed more explicitly in Islamist organizations established outside the boundaries of the Sufi *tarîqas*. Yet, analyzing the activities and ideologies of one of these organizations leads to other possible conclusions. *Jamâ`t `Ibâd al-Rahmân* (JRI) turned out to be a particularly active and successful organization among the

Islamist organizations in Senegal during the 1980s. The organization openly cultivated contacts with Islamist countries such as Saudi Arabia, Libya, and Sudan. Through financial assistance from these allies, it was able to establish networks of mosques, nursery schools, and schools throughout the country. Although these activities presented a challenge to the dominance of the Sufi *tarîqas*, the organization's leadership continued to take part in all of the great Sufi celebrations and festivities as a public demonstration of its close relations with tarîqa leaders.

Wahhâbîsts and Sufis at the Turn of the Century: A Comparative Analysis

In analyzing the relations between state-religion and the different forces within Islam in post-colonial societies, major differences between the developments in Nigeria and Senegal are apparent. First, large-scale natural resources such as oil were not discovered in Senegal, so the scope and intensity of processes of economic and social change were less brutal. As a result, the creation of the post-colonial space in Senegal was not followed by the acute confrontations and encounters within the Muslim community that Nigeria experienced. Second, in contrast to post-colonial Nigeria, which has been dominated for almost four decades by military and/or military-civilian rulers, Senegal has been practicing various forms of democracy since the mid-1970s. One of the consequences of democratization was the development of relatively pluralistic and non-violent public discourse. The central emphasis was on the unity of Muslim interests rather than on a secularization of state and society.

Yet, it seems that in the transition between the colony and the post-colony, one of the main factors to analyze with respect to relations between different currents of religion, is whether they constitute a majority or minority within the independent state. This issue is particularly relevant when analyzing the relations between Sufis and *Wahhâbîsts* in Senegal and Nigeria. In contrast with Senegal, where the majority of the population is Muslim, Nigeria divides almost equally between Muslims and Christians. Muslims' position as a minority within the Nigerian state contributed to a lack of unity within their discourse. During the 1970s and 1980s, Nigerian Muslim discourse was characterized by rifts and confrontations, as described above. For example, during 1977-78, *Wahhâbîsts* attempts to inspire political leaders to implement the *Shari'a* failed due to their inability to create a unified front with the leaders of the Sufi *tarîqas* (Mahmud 2004, 87). However, with the turn of the century, recent developments concerning the implementation of the *Shari'a* point to the possibility of creating a new alliance between Sufis and *Wahhâbîsts*.

In September 1999, the governor of Zamfara declared his intention to adopt *Shari'a* as the state's legal system. During the next two years, another twelve states in the predominantly Muslim North declared the same intention. These declarations were not coincidental. They occurred after successive dictatorships and the opening of political space to permit a gradual return of democracy to Nigeria. The traditional hegemony of the Muslim North, re-established following the civil war in 1970, was threatened by the victory of Olsegun Obasanjo, a southern Christian. The moves toward implementation of *Shari'a* and the ensuing debates were significant factors shaping the emergent religious sphere in Nigeria:

> In these debates, each religion is ascribed its own particular concept of "good" politics, together with the right to seek the recognition and institutionalization of its symbols in the country's polity. It could, in fact, be argued that the present debates are of scholarly interest not primarily because they revolve around the possible coalescence of religion and politics, for this is nothing new in human history nor is it unique to Nigeria. The debates are significant because of the *new vocabularies being used*, which, depending on perspectives, could either help launch Nigeria in a new cultural and moral direction, or precipitate its political fragmentation (Ilesanmi 2001, 531 [emphasis added]).

The debate over the implementation of the *Shari'a* in Nigeria is not only one between Christians and Muslims; it also divides the Muslim community. In this sense, a major shift seems to characterize the dynamics between Sufis and *Wahhâbîsts*. For the first time since the 1980s, the *Wahhâbî*-inspired *yan izala* and the Sufi *tarîqas* leadership, together with the traditional leadership of the North, are presenting a united front in their claim to the "right" of *Shari'a*.

In Senegal, on the other hand, recent developments seem to be showing cracks in what appears to be the unchallenged pact between Sufis and Islamists. The rise of Islamism in recent years, especially in scholarly and intellectual circles, is raising a debate concerning the nature of Sufism. Although it is not a direct attack on the Sufi *tarîqas*, it tries to formulate a new discourse concerning its potential role in twenty-first century Muslim society. Thus, in a June 2003 lecture on "Sufism and the State," Sidi Lamine Niasse, editor and founder of the important media group *Wal Fadjri*, made a distinction between three aspects of Sufism, illustrating his points with key historical figures of Senegalese Islam. The third aspect, the one represented in Senegal by 'Umar Tal, the nineteenth-century *jihadist* leader who resisted the French conquest, is one of militant resistance. This type of Sufism, he suggested, is the appropriate Sufi response when confronted with political aggression, and every indication suggests that such is the nature of the times in which we are living (Villalon 2004, 69). This kind of remark could be interpreted as criticism against Sufi *tarîqas'* inability to cope with the challenges of the modern era in the spirit of Islamic reform — a criticism echoing in many respects the ITI's attacks against the *marabouts* in the 1950s.

Conclusion

Referring to the transition from the colony to the sovereign national state, Ernest Gellner concludes:

> The scripturalist style of faith is modernisable; the tribal and saintly one is *not*. The scripturalist version can be presented as a national ideology; defining all Moslems in a given territory as one nation. It is also possessed of an international ideological dignity: petty hereditary saints and their market-place profane festivals lack it. What a nation uses for attracting tourism it cannot also invoke for workday and serious identity. Better far to see the old tribal forms as corrupt aberrations, which had been introduced or encouraged by the foreign occupying power (1983, 58).

In the transition from the colony to the post-colony, it seems that while the dynamics between Sufis and *Wahhâbîsts* in post-colonial Nigeria fit to some extent with Gellner's analysis, those in post-colonial Senegal seem to contradict it. In post-colonial Nigeria,

Wahhâbî-inspired leaders and movements undermined the dominance of the Sufi *tarîqas*, both theologically and organizationally. In Senegal, on the other hand, during the post-colonial era, the Sufi *tarîqas* were able to maintain and even fortify their colonial status in the face of threatening *Wahhâbî*-inspired organizations; they cooperated with various Islamist currents, including the *Wahhâbî*-inspired, and contained them. Thus, while it can be claimed that in post-colonial Nigeria Sufism reflected its image as anti-modernist and even anti-nationalist, in the setting of post-colonial Senegal Sufism has made some of its greatest gains and become almost synonymous with the Senegalese state.

Recent events, however, point to the possibility of changing dynamics between Sufis and *Wahhâbîsts* — in Nigeria, a rapprochement between these two forces, in Senegal, a more radical interpretation of Sufism. Rather than conforming to Gellner's prediction, these dynamics invoke Achille Mbeme's concept of the "post-colony," that is, a nation made up not of one "public space" but of several, each with its own logic yet liable to become entangled with other logics (Mbembe 2001, 104).

As acknowledged from the outset of this paper, conflicts and encounters between Sufis and Islamists are not unique to the history of Islam in Africa; they are global phenomena. Therefore, future research could benefit the analysis addressed here by extending the parameters of comparison; for instance, looking at post-colonial Africa in light of the experiences of post-Soviet territories.[10] Such "global" comparisons can potentially contribute significantly to our analyses of interactions between different ideological, theological, and social forces in the many and varied spaces occupied by contemporary Islam.

Notes

[1] An incidence of a *tarîqa*, Sufi order or brotherhood. I will use here the English plural of the Arabic term.

[2] See, for example, reports of the Algerian Bureaux Arabes established in 1844, as analyzed in Harrison (1988, 16, 37).

[3] This model was created and implemented mainly by Lord Fredric Lugard, High Commissioner of the Protectorate of Northern Nigeria (1902-06) and Nigeria's General Governor (1912-19). For a detailed description of this model see Lugard (1923).

⁴ For the effect of the colonial period on the Sufi *tarîqas* in the Indian subcontinent, see Buehler (1997).

⁵ One of the examples was the selection of Nigeria's first ambassador to Senegal -*al-hajj* Adu Bayero, head of the *Tijâniyya* in Northern Nigeria, that was designated to emphasize the historical relations of the *tarîqas* in Senegal and Nigeria. See: Omole (1987).

⁶ Amongst the various terms defined Islamism, such as renaissance, revival, renewal, awakening, protest, fundamentalism, and rejuvenation. I will use the term here in the sense of radicalization and politization of Islam. For a comprehensive discussion in these terms, see Sela (2002).

⁷ These schools were aimed to spread the knowledge of Islam, in its *Wahhâbî* form, amongst the masses; see Riechmuth (1993).

⁸ On the debate concerning the uses of the term "anti-religious" versus "secular," see Loimeier (1997, 349).

⁹ One of the main reasons for the alienation of various sectors in the Senegalese society was the deteriorated economic conditions during the 1970s and the disappointment from the consequences of the democratization process, see Villallon (1999).

¹⁰ For example, in the Republic of Dagestan contemporary conflicts between Sufis and *Wahhâbîsts* resemble in some aspects the developments witnessed (above) in Nigeria during the 1970s and 1980s (Zelkina 2004).

The Philosophy of the Revolution: Thoughts on Modernizing Islamic Schools in Ghana

David Owusu-Ansah and Abdulai Iddrisu

Résumé

Cet article examine la répugnance historique pour l'éducation séculaire dans les communautés musulmanes du Ghana et l'enthousiasme croissant du Ministère de l'Éducation ghanéen, soucieux de transformer les écoles coraniques par l'introduction de disciplines séculaires. La popularité des écoles coraniques persiste dans certains lieux — que ce soit sous les arbres, dans des cours, ou au coin des rues—où les étudiants récitaient le Coran, enseignement pertinent seulement parce que fondamentalement religieux. L'article déclare que les fondements philosophiques contemporains de l'enseignement islamique devraient être basés sur le précepte islamique sur l'éducation qui veut assurer non seulement la taqwa ou peur d'Allah mais une foi inébranlable chez les étudiants afin que les efforts de modernisation visant à incorporer l'enseignement technique et scientifique dans les écoles coraniques deviennent acceptables. L'article conclut que les changements structurels et pédagogiques constatés à la Makaranta ou écoles de récitations dépassent le cadre des réconciliations philosophiques et emploient à bon escient les avantages combinés des enseignements islamique et séculaire pour le bien de la nation.

Abstract

This article examines the historical distaste for secular education within the Muslim communities of Ghana and the growing enthusiasm of Ghana's Ministry of Education in transforming Qur'anic schools to integrate secular subjects. The popularity of the Qur'anic schools has remained as places—either under trees, at courtyards, or at street corners—where pupils simply recited the Qur'an, relevant only because it is fundamentally religious. The article argues that the contemporary philosophical foundations of Islamic education ought to be based upon the provision of Islamic learning that ensures not only taqwa or the fear of Allah but also renders students' faith unshakeable for the modernization efforts of incorporating technical and scientific learning at the

Qur'anic schools to become acceptable. The article concludes that the recent structural and pedagogical changes taking place at the Makaranta or recitation schools go beyond philosophical reconciliations to harnessing the combined benefits of Islamic and secular education for the good of the nation.

Introduction

In 1987, the Ghana Education Service established the Islamic Education Unit and charged it with the responsibility of attracting Islamic schools to accept secular teachers and secular curricula in their schools. The corollary of sustained government effort to streamline Islamic education was the increasing number of Muslim schools accepting the program nationwide. Hitherto, the perception had existed that Ghanaian Muslims favoured Qur'anic religious learning over secular education. In fact, it is often argued that Muslims oppose and mistrust Western education because of its potential as a Christian converting agent. However, the establishment of an Islamic Education Unit in Ghana with supervisory responsibilities over Muslim-operated secular learning institutions implies that a good number of modern Islamic schools have been established in the country to warrant government regulation. Thus, judging by these developments and given the thought that Ghanaian Muslims have long been opposed to secular education for their children, the progress made by both local Muslims and the Ghana Islamic Education Unit in transforming Muslim schools is revolutionary. It is argued that only in the context of the Muslim position on secular education and of the importance of religious instruction to the community that their ultimate and courageous embrace of modernized education could be appreciated.

The Narrative

Rev. Dr. Edward Blyden, who worked in Liberia and later in Sierra Leone in the 1880s, argued in his *Christianity, Islam and the Negro Race* (1887ab [1967 and 1971]) that the provision of Western education for Muslim children was an important step in their conversion to Christianity. As a world religion and because it was a religion of the Book, Islam stressed the art of reading and writing (Blyden 1887ab [1967 and 1971], 62). Being the Christian missionary he was, Blyden held the view that Islam was inferior to Western culture; he saw it as only fitting that the civilizing process introduced through Qur'anic-based reading and writing be completed at Westernized schools so as to imbue Muslim children with Christian and European ideals.

Usually, Muslim children spend considerable time memorizing and reciting Qur'anic verses, hence the term *Makaranta*.[1] David Skinner identifies these recitation schools as places "where pupils learned the Arabic alphabets, recognized Arabic words, [and learned] how to recite the Qur'an, and the fundamental concepts and rituals of Islam" (1973, 503). Ivor Wilks also observes in his work on the learning traditions of the Dyula of West Africa that the Qur'anic school was "where students learned to copy religious passages" and the "talented and well-taught pupils rapidly acquired a command of Arabic" (1968, 166), engaged in the study of grammar and syntax, and even started reading the basic works of Maliki law. For Wilks, the introduction of Muslim children to the rudiments of religious learning was indeed the very foundation of *tajdid* or renewal and reinvigoration of the Muslim community. It was not surprising then that Mande traders, whose activities took them to the non-Muslim communities of West Africa, made sure that such schools were established at their numerous trading settlements. Lamin Sanneh (1976) affirms the importance of clerical association to these schools — the fundamental importance of the programs, whether conducted under a tree, at a courtyard, or at street corners, was religious.

Blyden held mixed views about Islamic education. As a Caribbean-American of African descent, he was impressed by the ability of Black Muslim children in Sierra Leone to memorize and recite large portions of the Qur'an — a clear sign that African children could be educated. But as a western-educated Christian missionary, he was convinced of the benefits of the Judeo-Christian civilization. He was equally convinced that Muslim religious education did not prepare students for life in the modern world. Appointed first Director of Mohammedan Education for Sierra Leone in 1903 and charged with the task of spreading Western-styled schooling, he was determined to persuade Sierra Leone Muslims to accept arithmetic and English language instruction in their schools. What Blyden failed to do was to encourage a progressive transformation of the numerous Qur'an schools in Sierra

Leone into what Ghana created in the late 1980s — the integrated English / Arabic school. Had he seized this opportunity, he might have killed two birds with one stone — teaching religious knowledge while introducing secular education. For Blyden, the preferred arrangement was for Muslims parents and leaders to encourage children to attend Christian / Western schools so that their wards would be introduced to the advantages of Western civilization.

The benefits of Western education for Africans were articulated over two hundred years prior by the Portuguese, the Dutch, and later by the English whose trading posts dotted the Gold Coast. Information from the Portuguese imperial instruction to the Governor of the Elmina Castle in 1529, observations from the Dutch Charter of 1621, and pieces of note from British Royal Company correspondence all make explicit mention of the need for the early European merchants to organize educational programs at their forts as Castle Schools where "qualified African children" were to be provided instructions in reading and writing as the basis for the introduction of the Christian religion. Historian C.K. Graham (1971, 1) noted that Africans who received this Western education, usually mulatto children, were employed in the European commercial firms on the Gold Coast as interpreters and clerks. Kenneth Gordon Davies (1957, 280) similarly observed in his history of The Royal African Company that the trading company was in such a great need of African agents that it hired teachers and established a school at Cape Coast Castle in 1694. But lessons were limited to Christian religious instruction, and this was of course seen as important insofar as it introduced students to European culture. Due to limited funding and other problems, Castle schools educated only a small number of "qualified Africans." However, the establishment of schools was invigorated in the late eighteenth and especially the nineteenth centuries when several Christian missionary societies took interest in spreading the gospel through education. All Christian Missions societies — the Basel, Presbyterian, the Wesleyans, the Bremen, and the Catholics — that operated in the Gold Coast then were all committed to the introduction of basic western education. Even though the administration of these mission-controlled institutions remained under denominational control, government policy toward the introduction of Western schools was formulated to ensure uniformity of educational standards. In the British Gold Coast, the Education Ordinance of 1882 ensured colonial grants to Christian mission programs that were evaluated as providing efficient instruction.[2] Of course, the role of missionary societies in the "civilization" of the native was officially recognized under Article VI of the 1884-85 General Act of the Conference of Berlin (see Fetter 1979, 34-38). In fact, not only were Christian organizations to be protected but their missionaries were charged by the Conference to improve the condition as well as the moral well-being of the native. For that matter, a new British Education Ordinance of 1887 that called for improvements in the mission school curricular for the training and certification of teachers, as well as for the provision of practical instruction for pupils, was consistent with the general philosophy of the Berlin Act, as well as its provision calling for the moral improvements of Africans.

The place of Christian missionaries in the establishment of Western schools in the Gold Coast was tangible and 132 of such programs had been established in the country by 1901 (see Wright 1905). At the end of World War I, the Basel Mission alone had established over 176 schools nationwide. All the missionary educational institutions in the British Gold Coast favoured educating girls as much as boys at separate boarding grammar schools, but until the governorship of Sir Gordon Guggisberg in 1919 the focus of colonial government-supported education was more on elementary education rather than secondary schools. Courses taught to these students included the reading and writing of the English language, the local Twi and Ga languages, arithmetic, history, geography, and Bible studies. Greek and Latin were courses taught at the grammar school. Despite the rapid growth of Western schools, the great majority of missionary educational institutions were located to the southern portion of the country — a reality that was affirmed in the Phelps-Stokes Commission Report on Africa (1922 and 1925). As a fact-finding delegation of the Foreign Missions Conference of North America, the Phelps-Stokes Commission was charged to review the state of education in Africa (see Wilson 1963, especially chapter 3). In addition to recognizing Bible knowledge — as well as writing and arithmetic — as important bases for imbuing western values to students, the commission recommended the introduction of science and practical training to the curriculum of missionary African schools. Education, it was argued, must serve the practical economic needs of the people. From 1923 to 1948, the Education Conference of Missionary Societies in Great Britain and Ireland also submitted its memorandum on Africa education to the Office of the Secretary of State for the Colonies (see Hardymen and Orchard 1977). The Secretary of State responded to those recommendations by appointing an Advisory Committee to study and report on Native Education. Despite its advisory status, the committee made several major policy recommendations that covered such topics as mass education, citizenship education, and the provision of guidelines for the overall development of education in the colony.

The Phelps-Stokes Commission observed casually that Western education in the Gold Coast needed to extend to the predominantly Muslim Northern Territories. In the report of the Education Conference of Missionary Societies of Great Britain and Ireland, however, no mention whatsoever was made of the historic role of Qur'anic schools in the provision of religious knowledge to the colony's Muslim children. For all intents and purposes, the dissemination of knowledge at the Christian missionary-operated schools became synonymous with the term "education." On the basis of colonial government requirements that the schools meet set standards, Western schools were thus recognized as institutions of enlightenment, and their programs thus claimed all the characteristics of the famed rationalizing movement. Since pupils who attended formal Western schools were more likely to adopt aspects of Western culture and therefore have better chances of securing non-traditional employment because of their ability to read, write, and understand European languages, Western education was seen as being synonymous with progression, innovation, practicality, and civilization. Qur'anic school children, on the other hand, who possessed knowledge of Islamic religious subjects, were deemed illiterate and lacked the rational attributes of formal education.[3] The distinction was therefore made between Western schools as promoters of human reasoning and Islamic Qur'anic teaching was viewed as the instrument of traditionalism.

By the 1930s, Muslims in the Gold Coast fully associated the role of Western schools as vectors for the spread of Christianity. European cultural values were seen as synonymous with Christian values. Even when the stated goal of Western schooling was the "enlightenment" of its subjects, the underpinning Christian philosophy directly challenged the goals of Qur'anic instruction (see Galadanci 1993). This contest between Islam and Christian education was best articulated from a Muslim point of view in the 2003 writing of the Nigerian Muslim scholar M.A. Bidmos. He criticized Western secular learning and argued that any educational philosophy that made the attainment of material gains central to its goals was inadequate in scope. Bidmos put it more radically when he asserted that the transformation of Muslim children through Western schooling was a capitalist agenda that sought to expand European commerce and to incorporate the old world into a new world order in which Muslim children are regulated under new cultural values. Thus, according to Bidmos, despite their institutional affiliation to Church organizations, Western-operated schools "lack(ed) in morality, normality, and decency." On the other hand, Qur'anic education was thoroughly religious and started from the basic premise of recognizing God (Allah) as the Creator of the universe and all that is within it. The primary philosophical objective of Islamic education was the acquisition of knowledge about the Creator — the purpose, therefore, is to deepen spiritual knowledge as a means to facilitating closer relations between the created and God (Bidmos 2003).

Louis Brenner (1995) illustrates that the content of Islamic education that facilitated this closeness to God and thus informed Muslims of their daily religious obligation is provided to students at two distinct but related levels of learning. *Zahir*, or the basic content of instruction that was available to the general Muslim population at the *Makaranta* schools is distinguishable from the *batin* — hidden and private — form of learning that those who became Muslim clerics received. *Zahir* learning included such basic things as learning how to write and identify Arabic alphabets as well as memorizing simple verses from the Qur'an. *Batin* knowledge, on the other hand, included information on astrology, numerology, and several other subjects of expertise. In the nineteenth century, for example, the *Tafsir al-Jalalayn* of al-Mahalli (died 1459) and of al-Suyuti (died 1505) were among the content materials introduced to advanced or *Ilm* students at Bunduku, Kong, Buna (now in the Côte d'Ivoire), and at Wa, Banda, and Salaga in Ghana. Additionally, the *Kitab al-Shifa*, a very important book on the life of the Prophet by Iyad b Musa b. Iyad al-Sabti (died 1149), the *Risala* of Ibn Abi Zayd al Qayrawani (died 996), as well the *Muwatta'*, the well-respected comprehensive body of discussion on Muslim law as presented by Imam Malik b. Anas (died 795), were studied. The dispersion of Mallams across the West African region, especially in the eighteenth and nineteenth centuries, ensured the distribution of Muslim specialists under whom advanced students could study.

On completing a particular program, students received testimonial *(isnad)* in which the *silsila* or the list of names of teachers under whom a student was instructed as well as the content of books completed were recorded. Wilks concluded from his Volta Basin research that the Dyula discouraged younger candidates from pursuing *batin* education because their

> ... ulama preferred to recruit only from those who ... [had] already shown evidence of piety and of social responsibility. It was not uncommon to meet students who were over 50 years [old] and even in their sixties (1968, 168).

There were, however, those exceptionally bright youthful *batin* students such as Limam al-Hajj Ibrahim b. al-Hajj Muhammad Sa'id of Wenchi who completed studying *fiqh* (law) and *tawhid* (theology) by his twentieth birthday. In a 1966 interview with Ivor Wilks, al-Hajj Sa'id made reference of having read *al-Shifa* and the *Muwatta'* by his thirty-fifth birthday. However, the majority of *batin* students were older.[4]

Though a comprehensive biography of Muslim scholars in Ghana has yet to be written, what is available from field notes and published records demonstrates patterns of learning worthy of commentary. From 1962 to 1968, Ivor Wilks and his research associate al-Hajj Uthman b. Ishaq Boyo[5] traveled extensively in Ghana researching the history of Muslim communities across the country. Many of the persons interviewed identified themselves as having had grandfathers or great-grandfathers of Dyula Muslim origin.[6] The generation of grandfathers and great-grandfathers was educated either at the Dyula learning centers of Bonduku, Bona, Kong, or at a few locations in Northern Nigeria prior to their dispersion to territories now part of Ghana. Once the older generation of teachers established itself at the various local markets, the rate of sending children to the former centers of learning to pursue studies decreased. It may be deduced from Wilks' field notes that, as the level of the distribution of first and second-generation scholars increased, the need to travel outside local areas became less pressing. Even though none of the local towns could account for a large assemblage of prominent scholars at any given time, there is no doubt that this dispersion of scholars from the late nineteenth century made it possible for future generations of students to be educated closer to home. For example, the aforementioned Liman al-Hajj Sa'id of Wenchi did not go far afield to be educated. He read the Qur'an at Banda under the direction of his maternal uncle al-Hajj Muhammad Banda. Under the same teacher, but now at Wenchi, al-Hajj Sa'id read *tawhid, fiqh, al-Shifa*, the *Muwatta'*, and *Tafsir*. Al-Hajj Muhammad Banda was himself educated by his father (a first generation scholar of the nineteenth century) whose learning was acquired at the old center of Bonduku. Mallam al-Hajj Taminu of Dondoli (of Wa) also identified his father, the twenty-third Imam of the Wa Mosque, as the instructor who taught him *Tafsir, fiqh, nahw* (grammar), and *tawhid*.[7]

The tradition of increasingly teaching students at local mosques continued, and, in 1963, for example, Wilks reported that al-Hajj Taminu of Wa "instructed 12 adult students of his own while, with assistance, he operated a Qura'nic school for children."[8] The evidence presented here is not meant to suggest that travel-study among the Muslim community was eliminated completely. For example, as recently as 1984 Liman Sumaila ibn Mumuni, head of the Asante Nkramo of Kumasi, identified Bonu, Bonduku, and Ojene in the Côte d'Ivoire as places where he had studied. He also spent some time in Senegal to improve his understanding of the Tijani doctrine.[9] This cadre of local Muslim teachers made their knowledge available to children, especially of their extended families, but also to the larger community.

There are no statistical data representing the number of Qur'anic schools that were established in Ghana in the past or are currently in operation. However, Thomas Bowdich and Joseph Dupuis, who led English delegations to Kumasi on two separate occasions in the second decade of the nineteenth century, reported that the operation of Qur'anic schools in the Asante capital dated to that period. Muhammad al-Ghamba, who was a brother of the

Nayiri of Gambaga and also served as head of the Muslim community in the city, was the senior instructor to a small core of Muslim students. From a more recent period, Ivor Wilks noted from the National Census of 1960 that "32 per cent of all male Wala children receiving elementary education of ... [some] sort" were in Qur'anic schools. Of the total adult male population in the region aged "25 years or more" who had received "full-time education, 80 per cent had been at Qur'anic schools" (Wilks 1963, 166). The 1960 information stressed the accessibility of these programs to school-aged persons in their own community. In fact, Qur'anic schools were as widespread as the dispersion of Muslims in the country. The tradition of schooling Muslim children continued and, in 1976 research on *Makaranta* programs in the city of Accra, B.A.R. Briamah (1976) provided a list of Muslim proprietors and their schools at such locales as Cow Lane, Tudu, Accra New Town, Adabraka, and at the Old Zongo Mosque. In visits to some Kumasi-based Qur'anic recitation schools in 1984, David Owusu-Ansah noticed that some of the Imams who were also *Makaranta* proprietors conducted private seminars for more mature and advanced students (Owusu-Ansah, Field notes, 1984, and with Mark Sey, Field notes, 2002). The point, then, is that the *zahir* and *batin* forms of learning that Brenner noted in his work have been preserved as part of the Ghana Muslim learning tradition.

In a yet to be published manuscript, Dr. Mohammed (Mark) Sey of the University of Cape Coast has compiled detailed biographical information on some of Ghana's leading Muslim personalities to illustrate that the tradition of learning under local Mallams has survived. Some of the names on the list include Ustaz Ali Ibn Hassan, who was a former General Secretary of the Ghana Council of Ulama and Imams and is now a leading proprietor of the Kumasi Nuriyya Islamic Institute. Also listed are Ustaz Ibrahim Basha of Tamale, the late Dauda Yusuf Amounyi of Gomoa in the Central Region (a former member of the Council of Muslim Chiefs), Imam Rashid who is the operator of the Rashidiyya Islamic and Herbal Clinic in Tamale, the late Imam Umar Mohmoud of Bolga, and Imam Adubakar b. Hassan b. Yusif of Kotokuraba (Cape Coast). What is interesting from the biographical information provided in this manuscript is that these individuals were trained locally.[10] For example, Imam Rashid had only a small part of his training in

Nigeria and Algeria; and Ustaz Ali Ibn Hassan, born in 1932, started Qur'anic education in Sekondi and, except for a three-month intensive Arabic studies in Cairo in 1986 and a short study tour to Kano in Northern Nigeria, all aspects of Ali Ibn Hassan's learning were done under the instruction of respectable local Mallams. Many such examples abound in Ghana. Most of the Mallams in Northern Ghana — people like Afa Yussuf Ajura, Alhajji Umar of Nyohini, Afa Ibrahim Gushgu, and a host of their own students, were trained locally. This is in no way a suggestion that some of them did not embark on "master seeking," roaming Ghana and other parts of Africa, especially Nigeria for reputed Mallams to complete specific aspects of their studies. But, essentially, the chunk of their studies was carried out locally in Ghana at the time when Christian missionaries were engaged in the spreading of Western schooling to the southern part of the country.

The main focus of the education of most of these prominent Mallams continued to consist of studies in the Qur'an, *Tafsir, hadith, Kitab al-Shifa*, and the *Muwatta'*, but it is on record that the *ulama* had access to other books. For example, Al-Hajj Muhammad Liman Thani of Kete Krakye (died 21 June 1962) showed Wilks and al-Hajj Uthman b. Ishaq Boyo his small library that contained books belonging to illustrious al-Hajj Umar, the famous early twentieth-century scholar. In that collection were such works as the *Tanbih al-Ikhwan* ("Advice to the Brethren," described as poems in seven folios), *Akhbar wa Tanbih al-Kiram* ("History and Advice to the Noble One," also poems in ten folios and about 280 verses), *Ya Khalilu Fa'ajaba* ("Oh, Disordered and Marvelous," poems in seven folios), *Bushra* ("Rejoicings," in eight folios), *Burda* ("Garments," in 18 folios), *Kitab al-Sarhat al-Wariqah fi `ilm al-Wathiqah* ("The Essay Book of Leaves for the Knowledge of Letters"), and *Tarbi' Kitab al-Zahd wa `l-Wasiya* ("Book of Devotions and Injunctions").[11] The titles in the al-Hajj Umar materials are similar to works written by post-*jihad* scholars of the Hausa states of Northern Nigeria. The titles accurately affirmed the scholarly responsibility of ensuring, through advice and instruction, that the Muslim community is sustained in adherence to the teachings and practices of Islam. Al-Hajj Umar's poems appear to take the form of social, religious, and political commentary. Thus, Islamic learning in Ghana continued to have two primary objectives: first, to instruct children in the foundations of Islam; and second, to provide the access for advanced study. Both objectives were consistent with the basic religious philosophy underpinning Islamic education — that Man, as a created being, is obliged to learn about the obligations of Man toward the Creator and in the process accumulate the necessary religious knowledge.

Despite the changes that took place over time in regard to accessing Islamic learning — locally or travel outside — the philosophy has remained the same. While the primary aim of Islamic education is the improvement of a person's religious understanding, *batin*-educated scholars are commonly viewed in the history of West Africa as manufacturers of charms and amulets. As Nehemia Levtzion documented in his *Muslims and Chiefs in West Africa* (1968), clerics associated themselves with several rulers of the Volta Basin, fought in their wars, and ultimately laid the foundation for the conversion of many of their subjects in the eighteenth and nineteenth centuries. During the period of association, some of the *batin*-educated scholars were appointed to important administrative positions. Wilks (1975) points out that Muslims from the northern part of the kingdom and serving at the king's palace became contact persons for the central Kumasi administration. Even more interesting was the fact that the Kumasi Muslims communicated with their co-religionists and received relevant materials for the preparation of amulets and prayers for the protection of Asante's rulers. In other words, *batin* education prepared Muslim scholars for services relevant to the needs of traditional African political systems.[12] Bashir Shehu Galadanci (2000) made similar observations with regard to the benefits and relevance of Islamic education in the history of pre-colonial Nigeria. In that society, Islamic education that was intended to "seek answers first and foremost to the purpose of God's creation and provision [constituted] the content of an academic study that guaranteed a balance between the spiritual and the material obligations of scholars" (Galadanci 2000, 155). This made it possible for Muslims who have had Islamic education to gain employment as judges, clerks of Islamic courts, leaders of Mosques, and, most importantly, teachers of Islamic schools. Galadanci (2000, 155-58) dealt with both Nigeria's pre-colonial Islamic state and its British colonial administration; under indirect rule, the latter preserved Nigeria's traditional Islamic character. Abdulai Iddrisu (1998b, 2004) made a different observation with respect to Ghana, especially northern Ghana which was, together with northern Nigeria, considered at that time to be predominantly Muslim. In Iddrisu's opinion, the British colonial administration did not pretend to prefer Islamic education for obvious reasons. The policy was non-interference with the traditional Qur'anic schools, but an adoption of a progressive policy to restrict free spread of Christian mission programs, especially throughout the Northern Territories of the British Gold Coast (Ghana) was to lead to the stifling of the growth of Qur'anic education. The justification colonial authorities gave for preserving the *status quo* was fear that there would be a clash between Christianity and Islam; or, if allowed to receive a better education, Muslims in their current stage of development would misjudge instructions under the mission system to be equal to the abolishing of class and seniority system by which order has been preserved. But even more important, according to Iddrisu (1998a, 11-21), the *status quo* was maintained so as to convert the place and the people into a labour reserve for the plantations, and then later to war in 1914. As a result, nothing or no policy was designed to guide the transformation of Islamic education; and, even more, those who would have stayed to open more Qur'anic schools were imported to the plantations and mines in the South. It is important to note that not all people in the Gold Coast Northern Territories were Muslim.[13] However, Islam's spread in the region was the longest in the nation's history and the lack of Western-styled schools in the territories to which the Phelps-Stokes reports of 1922 and 1925 pointed was in reference to the obvious absence of secular education to Muslims. Bagulo Bening (1990) suggests that the combined effect of British policy on Islam in the Northern Territories and the supposed dislike of the people for secular education were responsible for the development of an unequal "educational gap" between northern Ghana and the rest of the country. The "educational gap" that has been created led to the impression that Islamic education is incompatible with modernization. From such a perspective, any attempt by Muslims to accept secular educational reforms that affect the structure of the Islamic Qur'anic schools should be viewed as revolutionary.

The Genesis of a Revolution: Observing Change

The literature on the modernization of Islamic education in Ghana is very limited. Braimah (1976), a former lecturer in Religions at the University of Ghana, expressed the need for the modernization of Islamic schools but failed to go beyond listing the existing Qur'anic schools in the Accra area. Skinner (1983) made the first attempt at analyzing efforts to modernize Islamic schools in Ghana. This attempt notwithstanding, Skinner's material centered on few cases in the city of Accra and focused on the educational activities of the Islamic Ahmadiyya movement. Owusu-Ansah (2002) touches on the national movement to modernize Muslims schools in Ghana, but the scope of the discussion on educational reforms only forms a part of his concluding thoughts (see also Owusu-Ansah 1991).

The most instructive contribution is the scholarly essays of Abdulai Iddrisu on colonial policies and practice towards Islamic education in the Northern Territories of the Gold Coast. Iddrisu (2002a) interrogates what he called the conservative and modernizing approaches at forging a meaningful interaction between Islamic and secular education. By concentrating research on the history of Islamic education transformations in the section of the country with the most orthodox Muslim population, Iddrisu's (1998b, 2002ab) research stands to form the basis for any nation-wide application.

Unlike the general Muslim population in Ghana whose acceptance of Western education had been slow, the Ahmadiyya Mission is known for their progressive attitude to secular education. Begun in Lahore (Pakistan) in 1889, the movement initially led by Mirza Ghulam Qadiani challenged the finality of prophecy, which orthodox Muslims accept to reside with Muhammad. Because of doctrinal differences between the Ahmadiyya movement and other Muslim groups, many in the Muslim world describe the teachings of Ghulam Qadiani as heretical and a misrepresentation of Islam. The Nigerian writer Fathuddin Sayyed Muhammad Koya (1995) accused the Ahmadiyyah Mission of supporting colonial rule in West Africa by readily operating Islamic schools modeled on the European style. This characterization notwithstanding, the Ahmadiyya, who arrived in Ghana only in 1923, can now be credited with the establishment and administration of eighty seven pre-school programs, 152 elementary schools, eight secondary institutions, a vocational school, six hospitals, and a teacher training college — all established and operated as modern institutions (Owusu-Ansah, Field notes, 2005). It was for this Ahmadiyya Muslim attitude of modeling their schools and programs along European lines that Skinner (1983) labelled the movement as "progressive." Some authors, such as Abdulai Iddrisu, fault the Ahmadiyya for consistently relegating the Islamic subjects on the school timetable to the background, while imposing upon the curricula a secular schema. For Iddrisu (Iddrisu 2002a, 336-38), the Ahmadis have still not found a progressive means to integrate the two systems of education effectively. But then the Leader of the Ahmadiyya Mission in Ghana, Maulvi Wahhab Adam, sees their record as distinctly different, and argued in an interview that it is rather more forward-looking than their orthodox co-religionists,[14] because secular education, and the rationale for integrating secular with Islamic subjects is to better prepare the child to fit properly into today's world and thus ensure a better practice for Islam.

Conclusion

Even though no comprehensive study of the modernization of the old Qur'anic schools nation-wide is available yet,[15] a number of observations can be drawn from existing research. The first is the fact that Qur'anic schools which are typically associated with orthodox Muslim education are private enterprises operated by Muslim proprietors for the training of children in basic religious knowledge. Given their understanding of the different philosophical orientation of these programs in comparison to secular institutions, Muslim proprietors are less likely to modify the content of instruction and introduce change unless they are convinced that such innovation will not interfere with the purpose of education drastically.[16] The literature also shows that concern expressed by Muslims about the effect of modernization on Islamic schools is not limited to Ghana. Leading Muslim scholars engaged for some time in this discourse about secular education, modernism, and Islam in Egypt, Tunisia, the Sudan, and Nigeria have counselled caution (Cooper, Nettler and Mahmoud 1998). The famous Jamal al-din Al-Afghani (1838-97), the Iranian ideologue who led the nineteenth century Islamic Modernist reform movement, favoured reforms in education that included technical and scientific training

— a position with which Muhammad Abduh (1849-1905), his Egyptian protégée, agreed. However, the latter cautioned that this was the case "[only] if those who adopted these western ways understood it rightly" (see Muhammad Abduh no date). In his discussion on religion and modernism, the Sudanese scholar Mahmud Mohammad Taha favoured an education that provided for the combination of a solid provision of Islamic learning ensuring *taqwa* — the fear of God (Abduh, no date, 110). To borrow Galadanci's phraseology, *ilm* or knowledge must be *Islamized* irrespective of course content so that it is consistent with the teachings of God. In other words, so long as a student's faith remains intact and as long as s/he does not succumb to corrupt Western cultural values, then the modernization of Islamic schools should be acceptable (Galadanci, 2000).

Ghanaian Muslims are beginning to engage with this discourse of whether or not the two systems — Islamic and Western — can be integrated, while ensuring that pupils hold on to their Muslim faith. It is essential to observe that change is taking place in Islamic education, albeit slowly. The first sign of change is that more and more of the old *Makaranta* programs are being moved into bigger mosque structures, some of which are specially built for instructional purposes. Some Muslim communities continue to organize and conduct Qur'anic instruction as private after-school programs for their children. A number of the former *Makaranta* programs are increasingly being consolidated and expanded as restructured Islamic schools where students are grouped by age and placed at levels commensurate with previous Islamic knowledge. The Ghana Education Service duly formed the Islamic Education Unit in 1987 to take control and streamline the activities of the Islamic education system, while introducing the approved national secular curriculum to the schools. A good number of Muslim proprietors have joined the program since then. The Islamic Education Unit (IEU) Northern Regional Office hosts the headquarters of the National Islamic Education Unit. Figures for the academic year 2001-02 remain consistent with that of 2005 and indicate that the Northern Region alone has a registry of 159 pre-school programs, 265 primary (K-6) schools, and 42 three-year junior secondary institutions. The regional capital of Tamale hosted most of the IEU schools in the area, representing seventy-six nursery or pre-school programs, eighty-six primary schools, and twelve junior secondary schools; but every village can also boast of one or two Islamic schools (Iddrisu 2005, 53-67, especially 60-61). While the number of schools within the Northern Region is the largest for the National Islamic Education Unit system, increasing numbers of such schools across the country also reflect acceptance of change. In the Greater Accra Region (in the south), where government, missionary-supported, and municipal council schools were well-represented, the Regional Islamic Education Unit could account for a total of forty-six modernized schools — representing thirteen kindergarten programs, twenty-three primary (K-6) schools, and ten junior secondary schools.[17] There is no doubt, therefore, that the acceptance of the Ghana Education Service secular curriculum by the majority of Ghanaian Muslims proprietors is on the increase. But it is important to ask whether the changes that are taking place in the Islamic schools imply a philosophical reconciliation of the hitherto different worldviews between Islamic learning and secular education. In other words, what caused hitherto *Makaranta* proprietors in the first place to embrace structural modifications in their Islamic schools and thus making them targets for incorporation into the national secular education system?

According to Ustaz Mustafa Kamil al-Din, former Secretary of the Ghana National Council of 'Ulama and Imams, who is also proprietor of the Wataniyya Islamic school system of Kumase, the most important reason for changing the old *Makaranta* system was the pressure felt from the Muslim communities.[18] For the majority of Muslim educators, the age-old philosophical difference between their system and Western education was greatest under colonial rule. When the Wataniyya school was established in 1942 as one of the largest Islamic religious schools in the Asante capital of Kumasi, it was embraced by the community as the appropriate institution to cater for the city's Muslim population. However, with the introduction of Kwame Nkrumah's accelerated education program in 1951, a policy that made basic secular education compulsory and free to children of school age in the Gold Coast at the time when nationalists' agitation for political independence was most intense, many in the Muslim communities who were still distrustful of Western schools but wanted to see improvements in the Qur'anic schools began to pressure their neighbourhood Islamic schools to respond to the changing times by restructuring the Islamic education system. At the same time, there was also pressure from some Muslims who wanted to keep the *Makaranta* system. A compromise emerged whereby the study of the English language was introduced as a subject that Qur'anic school students must learn. This was in 1959, when the Wataniyya School became one of the first English / Arabic schools in the country.

From the perspective of Adam Muhammad Appiadu, who is proprietor of another Islamic school at Suame in Kumasi, the reason for change was not so much due to pressure from the community, but the introduction of change in the Islamic schools should be attributed to the foresight of individual proprietors. Muhammad Appiadu argues that political nationalist developments in the country during the 1950s, in which some leading Muslim personalities such as Ahmadu Banda and Afa Ladan became involved, sensitized the leadership of the Muslim communities to the importance of Western education. Afa Ladan was a Hausa resident scholar in the Gold Coast under whom Appiadu received Qur'anic instruction. Shortly after political independence in 1957, Afa Ladan and others became victim to Prime Minister Kwame Nkrumah's policy of deporting foreigners in the country whose political activities were deemed threatening to the government. Appiadu followed his teacher to Kano where the English / Arabic school system had already found roots under British rule. When Appiadu returned to Ghana in 1959, he established an English / Arabic school at Kumasi Suame, similar to the one he attended in Kano, Nigeria. The goal of this pioneering proprietor was to establish a school equivalent to the public secular schools where Islamic religious knowledge was taught in addition to other secular subjects. Appiadu described his program as a "blackboard school" because students were required to bring their own tables and chairs to school, sit in rows, and listen to a teacher who stood in front of the class to teach. Adam Muhammad Appiadu taught Arabic and Qur'anic knowledge to the students and employed trained non-Muslim staff to teach the other secular subjects.[19] The Muslim communities still had problems with the "blackboard school." In recollecting his thoughts in a 2002 interview, Appiadu observed that some Muslims opposed him because he limited Arabic language instruction to a thirty-minute class per day activity and Islamic religious instruction to two hours in a typical eight-hour instructional school day. In that case, Appiadu's system had become too secular in structure and philosophy while the Wataniyya system was very Islamic with a minor adjustment made for English language instruction.

The criticism levelled at Adam Muhammad Appiadu's Suame Islamic school is important because it underscores the philosophical difference between secular educational and Qur'anic religious programming. Certainly not all Muslim proprietors saw secular education as a threat to Islamic learning, but most of them continue to be concerned that the essential character of the *Makaranta* — the unlimited time for Islamic religious instruction, and the teaching of Arabic language — will be undermined. From the late 1950s onward, Muslim proprietors established various types of schools in the country at which arithmetic and the English language were taught. Some of these schools were more religious than secular but, over time, more and more Muslim proprietors have embraced programs similar to the "blackboard" initiative. Even with the establishment of the Islamic Education Unit to regulate the modernization process, the debate has not disappeared completely. The question is now posed in a more interesting way: does modern education secularize Islamic schools or are Muslims capable of Islamizing secular knowledge? It is important to mention in closing that, these concerns notwithstanding, Qur'anic schools continue to join the Islamic Education Unit and have accepted the national secular curriculum. Many proprietors participating in the secular Islamic Education Unit system have also found ways to instruct basic Qur'anic and Islamic religious knowledge by extending the school day or by running after-school programs in Qur'anic studies; students spend more time studying Islamic subjects after the secular teachers have closed for the day. Some have organized their weekends as an extension of the school week during which time Qur'anic knowledge is instructed in a new way. "The way forward" is for secular and Islamic education philosophies to seek a common ground through compromise, and it is in this regard that the benefits of both systems could be harnessed for the good of the nation. Also, as the newest of the supervisory agencies of the Ghana Education Service, the Islamic Education Units should be expected to face several problems, some of which will be very basic.[20] More research is therefore needed on the performance of the IEU so as to bring to public attention to the challenges faced by those engaged in this quiet revolution.

Notes

[1] The word *Makaranta* is derived from the Arabic *qara'a:* to recite. The *Makaranta* are local schools that originated from the traditional Qur'anic schools. It took the form of secular schools, following the 1951 Accelerated Development Plan for Education initiative, and employed a chalkboard, the use of exercise books, and teacher specialization. For a fuller discussion of the etymology of *Makaranta*, and its evolution in Ghana, see Abdulai Iddrisu (1998a, 42-76).

[2] Efficient instruction had to do with the placing of emphasis exactly on mission work, but the teaching of secular subjects was not neglected at the mission schools.

[3] Mansoor (2005) is a wonderful discussion of European perceptions of Islam and its culture. In this work, the European claim of having an enlightened culture compared to that of Muslims was responded to from the perspective of Muslim scholars.

[4] Ivor Wilks and al-Hajj Uthman b. Ishaq Boyo, Interview with al-Hajj Ibrahim b. al-Hajj Muhammad Sa'id. Wenchi (Ghana), 22 June 1966.

[5] Boyo was a Nigerian with excellent skills in the Arabic language and was thus hired in the 1960s as an assistant to Ivor Wilks at the Institute of African Studies of the University of Ghana.

[6] The hundreds of pages of Wilks' interviews in Ghana (from 1962 through 1968) are now housed at the Herskovits Africana Library at Northwestern University and at the Institute of African Studies at the University of Ghana. The collection includes research notes and field interviews on Asante history as well as on Islam in Ghana.

[7] See Wilks' Ghana field notes deposited at the Africana Library at Northwestern University.

[8] Ivor Wilks and Uthman Boyo, Field Interviews 8 March 1963, Wa, Ghana.

[9] David Owusu-Ansah. Filed notes of 1984. In a more recent conversation with Ghana's National Chief Imam, al-Hajj Sharabutu (July 2006) also indicated his travels to Senegal for further Tijani studies.

[10] We are indebted to the author of this manuscript for allowing us to use it even before it is published.

[11] For a detailed discussion on al-Hajj Umar, see Abdula-Razak (1996). For comparative purposes, see also Balogun (1985).

[12] For a more detailed analysis of Muslim-produced charms and amulets in the history of nineteenth century Asante, see Owusu-Ansah (1991, 2000).

[13] For an excellent description of the peoples of the northwestern sector of the British Gold Coast, colonial labour policy, and the spread of the church, see Hawkins (2002).

[14] David Owusu-Ansah, field interview with Maulvi Wahab bin Adam, Chief of Ahmadiyyah Mission of Ghana, Accra (Ghana), 29 June 2005.

[15] In the past several years, Owusu-Ansah, Abdulai Iddrisu, and Mark Sey of the Department of Religious Studies at the University of Cape Coast have joined together in research on Islamic education. Several interviews have been conducted by the group at several locations in Ghana. A more comprehensive history of Islamic education in Ghana will be forthcoming from this project.

[16] This position seems to cut across most of the interviews, especially with the old *ulama* proprietors.

[17] David Owusu-Ansah, Interviews with Acting Regional Manager of Islamic Education Unit Mr. Shaibo Armiyawo, Accra, 12 March 2002, and 11 July 2005.

[18] David Owusu-Ansah and Mark Sey, Interview with Mustafa Kamil al-Din at Adukrom, Kumase, 10 March 2002.

[19] David Owusu-Ansah and Mark Sey, "Conversation with Adam Muhammad Appiadu, proprietor of Islamic Secondary School at Kumase," 11 March 2002.

[20] A comprehensive discussion of the history, concerns, and successes of the Ghana Islamic Education Unit is being undertaken in the forthcoming manuscript by Owusu-Ansah, Abdulai Iddrisu, and Mark Sey.

A Question of Beginnings

Kenneth W. Harrow

Résumé

*Cet article nous demande de repenser le modèle qui a traditionnellement représenté l'avènement de l'Islam en Afrique: celui d'une entité préétablie, donnée par le monde extérieur d'une unité cohérente, monadique; en quelque sorte, une entité déjà formée. Cet article, évocant les défis jetés par Lacan aux notions conventionnelles d'identité, conteste la version de l'Islam exprimée ci-dessus, la voyant comme une incarnation de l'imago: toujours présente, toujours obéissant à la logique d'un mode de transmission en Afrique, comme apport étranger. La représentation conventionnelle de son irruption en Afrique a toujours impliqué la reconnaissance erronée d'une identité pré-existante, d'un tout qui attendrait de naître, vraisemblablement complètement formé. Ce dont ce modèle ne tient pas compte, c'est que la langue et la forme de ce qu'il a fini par reconnaître et nommer Islam étaient déjà là, et que l'Islam qui a conçu le sentiment nouveau de sa prise de conscience était enraciné dans ce même acte de reconnaissance erronée qui caractérise l'étape du miroir, celle où le sujet en arrive à déclarer "C'est moi." Cet article évoque l'image du père mort pour repenser le modèle identitaire, le "McGuffin" autour duquel le drame **Wangrin** de Hampaté Ba et **Faat Kine** de Sembène Ousmane se déroule. Dans les deux oeuvres, l'exhumation du corps du père prend une dimension fantastique parce qu'elle situe le conflit entre deux tendances rivales qui se font miroir: le narcissisme et l'agressivité, tendances autour desquelles tournent toutes les formes de formation d'identité du sujet.*

Abstract

This article asks us to rethink the models that have conventionally represented the coming of Islam to Africa: that of a pre-established entity, given from the outside, coherent, monadic, unity, like an already formed identity. Using Lacanian challenges to conventional notions of identity, this article contests the above version of Islam, viewing it as an incarnation of the imago: always there, always obeying the logic of a model of transmission into Africa as a reception from abroad. The conventional representation of its irruption into Africa has always involved the *misrecognition of an identity as a pre-existent, already-whole form, waiting to be born, presumably in complete unity. What this model ignores is that the language and form of what it came to recognize and name as Islam were already there, and that the Islam that formed its newly-conscious sense of self was grounded in the same act of misrecognition as characterizes the mirror stage, that is, the stage at which the subject comes to state: "This is who I am." In order to rethink the identitarian model, this article evokes the figure of the dead father, the "McGuffin" on which turns the drama of Hampaté Ba's* **Wangrin** *and Sembène Ousmane's* **Faat Kine.** *In both works, the act of exhuming the father's body takes on a degree of fantastical importance because it situates the struggle between two competing mirror stage tendencies: narcissism and aggression, tendencies around which all forms of subject-identity formation take place.*

> It is of course a beginning that is forever fictional, and the scission, far from being an inaugural act, is dictated by the absence — unless there exists some illusion to discount — of any decisive beginning, any pure event that would not divide and repeat itself and already refer back to some other "beginning," some other "event," the singularity of the event being more mythical than ever in the order of discourse (Derrida 1981, 300).

How did Islam come to West Africa? This is a question Nehemia Levtzion might have set for us, and sought to answer in an examination of the passages of people across time and space, of the conditions of their convergences, and of the accommodations or conflicts that marked their encounters. Ultimately, there was something called Islam that had not previously existed in Mali, Burkina Faso, Niger, Senegal, and Northern Nigeria; we would be tempted to use the language of spreading or diffusing, by means of trade or conquest — the language of contact that depends upon borders, regions of control, power, or influence.

I want to use a slightly different model, though one conceptually parallel to Nehemia's. I do not want to begin with a beginning. What if we were to deny beginnings, deny that there was a time we would label "before Islam" and "after Islam"? To be more precise, we might agree that people began to call themselves Muslim at well-defined moments and in specific places, but claim that their embrace of Islam was not simply a consequence of an originary conversion — except superficially, that is, consciously. What is at stake is the process by which people come to accept a notion of themselves, an idea of an identity. What does it mean for someone to call himself or herself Muslim?

For Lacan, in the mirror stage, the subject's sense of an identity is based on an act of *méconnaissance* — misrecognition. The mirror's reflection — or any commensurate act of the subject's being addressed, any interpellation from an other — presents the subject with an image which it must recognize as an object that is distinct from itself and yet, at the same time, as also being a true reflection of itself. It accepts the image, or "imago," as a gestalt, a whole in which is integrated a unified being it must learn to recognize, to identify, as its own, its self — itself. The infant subject's frustration, anger, and disgruntlement over feeling inadequately coordinated, inadequately empowered to command its movements, to compel others to act and satisfy its needs, finds itself compensated by this sense of becoming a person, a real person, a whole person — of having an identity. For Lacan, this is the process of dissimilation through which a subject forms an ego, an ego position from which to speak itself, to present itself to others.[1] As the act of repression that is the prelude to the entry into the symbolic order has not yet occurred, this stage is marked by the dominance of the imaginary — the image, imaginary relations, accompanied by uncertainty over the boundary between self and other.

The abstraction that might seem to characterize this account of the construction of an identity is concretized in the relations with others on which the process is based. It may well involve an act of negotiating one's relationship with the other as the nurturing mother, whose ties to the subject may threaten the subject's attempt to define a separate space for himself or herself. In that case, the construction of the "devouring mother" or of the rebellious daughter might follow, as Denise Paulme (1986) details. Often, angry and violent reactions mark the mirror stage, as well as their opposite, a narcissism that Lacan describes as the counterpart to the aggression.

The aggression shatters the borders between self and other; the narcissism constructs the identitarian relationship unawares — that is, assumes that self and other were there all along, separated by walls that are protective, upright, inviolable. Islam was yet another incarnation of that imago: always there, always obeying the logic of a model of transmission into Africa as a reception from abroad. The conventional representation of its irruption into Africa has always involved the misrecognition of an identity as a pre-existent, already-whole form, waiting to be born, presumably in complete unity. In Derrida's terms, it is this establishment as a presence that provides the basis for the notions of true identity — what he defines as "the illusion — that is to say, the truth, of that which seems to present itself as the thing itself" (1981, 298).

In this model, Islam is viewed as the gift of the other, and as the foundation for the newly formed Muslim self. It ignores the point of view of the one who had to accept this Islam as marked by an already existent receptiveness (Amselle [1990] 1998); it ignores that whatever was there to recognize Islam, to find in it an identity, had already undergone generations of change, that the language and form of Islam were already there. To be more precise, that the language and form of what it came to recognize and name as Islam were already there, and that the Islam that formed its newly-conscious sense of self was grounded in the same act of misrecognition as characterizes the mirror stage, that is, the stage at which the subject comes to state: "This is who I am."

At the same time, as the subject's claim to identity is made, there are simultaneous claims: this is who I am not, this is the one whom I hate, this is what I could never be; what I want and do not want to acknowledge; what calls me and will not answer me; what I cannot call up, and that still must be there; the place I need in order to be, with Islam, like a mother, like a homeland, like a community, appearing, surging up, just at the right time; an answer that tells me I am here, I exist, I have a name, I see and recognize myself.

Two texts, two key scenes: both scenes are remarkably elusive. One is unstaged, the other barely staged. Both are central to the identities of the key characters as Muslims, Muslims known by virtue of not-being-the-other. In one case the "other" is pagan; in the other case, "other" is Christian. And in both scenes there is a dead body, one that is mostly absent, mostly functioning like a McGuffin that sets the action in motion without itself being present, and therefore, secondly, like the French object "a" whose purpose is not to be actually seized and acquired for itself, but rather to open up the passageway to relationships between others (Žižek 1992).[2] In other words, it is an object that is indispensable to the relationship between others, while remaining, itself, virtually non-existent.

In our two key scenes, that object turns out to be a corpse, or, more precisely, a missing corpse. In *Guelwaar* (1992), it is the missing corpse of the hero himself, Guelwaar. In *The Fortunes of Wangrin* (1973), it is Brildji, the king whose son buried him in a secret location before the heir to the throne, Karibu Sawali, Brildji's brother, could come to the funeral. In both cases, the drama turns on the exhumation of the missing body, and in both cases it is the Muslim injunction against exhumation that presents the narrative with its conflict.

But the narratives are not developed in the same way. In one, the ultimate goal of reconciliation is achieved. Imam and priest see eye to eye; religious differences yield to the originary African cultural identity, and the affirmation of a symbolic order in the name of a rationality, under the sign of the Father, is accomplished. Here the corpse returns from the grave, still embalmed and unrecognizable in its individual features, but present and operant in the minds of the new generation of youth, ready to fight for an autonomous national existence.

The film is built around a classic McGuffin — the missing body. Guelwaar, who has been killed and is lying in the morgue, turns up missing when his son goes to fetch him for the laying out. The police investigation reveals that neighboring villagers have mistaken Guelwaar's body for that of a deceased Muslim villager. Unfortunately, Guelwaar is Christian, and when his family and the police chief go to the village to exhume his body, they are met by resistance from the deceased man's relatives who refuse to dig up the body at the word of a non-Muslim. The conflict then turns on the figure of the buried, enshrouded corpse, and on the full weight of what an exhumation might entail.

If the righteous imam, the police chief, and the Christian adherents overturn the Islamic injunction against exhumation, they can also be said to have restored a wholeness to the community and especially to all the members of a newly recognized African community. This is seen especially in the figure of Barthelémy, Guelwaar's elder son, who had been lost to France, and who finds himself as a Senegalese in the course of his assumption of the struggle over his father's body.

In *Wangrin*, we have the trickster-like Wangrin, the one who can speak not one but all languages, who maneuvers to prevent the "return of the father." If the symbolic order of a dominant colonialism persists, it is in the guise of Wangrin's successfully subverting that order, and turning its power to his own use.

Brildji, a Muslim ruler, dies, and Wangrin is sent to represent the regional French commandant in his funeral. Brildji's son and his brother, heirs according to differing customs to the ruler, are thoroughly manipulated by Wangrin who ends up fleecing them both. Wangrin pretends to convey the Commandant's order to have the body exhumed, and then fabricates the objections of an imam to that order so as not to have the body exhumed. If *Guelwaar* ends with the cementing of Christian righteousness and Muslim righteousness in the concept of African nobility, Wangrin ends with a false harmony between uncle and son, built on the delusions of each fed to them by Wangrin. Further, Wangrin justifies the ascension of the son Loli to the throne by hypocritically evoking the French and Muslim Laws of Paternity that require the son's succession and playing this off the Fulbe Laws of Succession, requiring the brother's succession to his brother. In the end, the governor's ruling, which Wangrin engineers into place, imposes an order and harmony that only superficially covers the competing interests of ruling Christian French, superficially Islamicized African, and fundamentally pagan Fulbe. This is the Hampaté Bâ version of the rule of the trickster, the in-between Wangrin, whose failure to belong entirely to any community is reflected perversely in his facile mastery of all tongues. When the trickster creates the social order, only he is seen to derive benefit, while the others continue on deluded into thinking not only that the benefit but the rule is theirs.

With Sembène, the rule of the Father is reassembled with the succession transference of paternal authority to the son — the same theme he develops in the "feminist" *Faat Kine*. In *Wangrin*, the rule of the Father is subverted; there is no foundational act of self-recognition, the corpse is not exhumed, the religious authority, the colonial authority, the royal authority are all shown to be empty. The Law of the Father is not assumed, not transmitted. There will be no resolution, restitution, or harmonious reintegration of the self, any more than of the society. Wangrin will wind up dead, drunk, drowned, in a ditch, abandoned by his god Gongoloma-Sooke whom he had long since forgotten. And not until the order within which he was able to operate has passed can there come his amanuensis, Hampaté Bâ, who will claim, in a belated afterword, that we had gotten it all wrong, that Wangrin was really a fine fellow, a hero whom we had not recognized.

How much work has to be expended in evoking this figure of the missing dead father to get us to this point. We see Guelwaar's empty suit laid out on his bed as his widow berates him in absentia. We see his sons, literal and symbolic, search for his whereabouts, seek to recover him, and finally, when the body is exhumed, stinking and repulsive, it appears wrapped like a mummy, dark and unshaped, gruesome, abject, repulsive, and, most of all, unrecognizable to our gaze.

Marching back to Thiès in his honor, under his name and bearing his corpse, unintentionally conveys something of the gruesome nature of the religious sacrilege, exactly what Wangrin describes as the greatest sin in Islam. Wangrin invents, or solicits, the opinion of "the great Imam Suleyman" who pronounces the following words, reported by Wangrin:

These are the last three months of my eighty-second year, yet never in my whole life have I had to listen to so execrable a proposal as the one you have just made — to exhume a dead body! Even Satan would take great care to do no such thing. It is written in our holy texts that a somber destiny awaits those inhabitants of earth who dare to order an exhumation. It is also written that the seventh hell will host any man who, during his lifetime, will have made so bold as to enjoy this most macabre of spectacles (Bâ 1999, 121).

What irony, then, that it is the trickster-imposter who can evoke this religious sanction so fervently as to convince even the Imam of the need to intervene to prevent the exhumation; and what irony that for Sembène this greatest blasphemy is to be carried out by the righteous imam, against the objections of the obviously self-interested and corrupt leadership of the Muslim community.

The dead body is the McGuffin and *l'objet "a"* that makes the conflict, and, ultimately, the joining of the two conflicting communities possible. But the exhumation itself is the transgression of the border whose inviolateness, like that of the self, can only be sustained by the abjection, or expulsion, or exclusion of the other.

Islam's presence in Africa, as a site of an African identity, can only be made possible, and can only have been made possible, by the double movement of what Nehemia might have termed accommodation and exclusion — or, in mirror stage terms, narcissism and aggression towards the other. In our metaphor, the act of exhuming the father's body took on its fantastical importance in both texts because it came to situate the struggle between these two competing mirror stage tendencies: tendencies around which all forms of subject-identity formation take place. When the body is exhumed so as to permit the sons to take the father's place, the model of an ultimate accommodation is asserted. When the body is left to rot in an unknown grave, the son's accession is built on an illusion, and the Law of the Father will fail to sustain itself, just as the dominant order will pass into oblivion.

How poignant it is that the parable about the original father to Karibu Sawali's lineage recounted in *Wangrin* rehearses the same fears of the father — warrior evoked at the beginning of Homer's *Iliad*, that is, fear of being turned into an object that will not be remembered, the dead carrion for wild birds and dogs. This is the version Karibu's griot recounts, in a vain effort to sustain those noble qualities once associated with what we have identified as the Law of the Father:

> The Mossi Prince Bila Wobogo swore to procure for his own wives the milk yielded by the white cows reared for the special purpose of quenching the thirst of Boori-Moodi's wives. Bila Wobogo, whose other name was "the angry leopard," pounced on the thirty shepherds in charge of the cattle-pen. Ten were killed, ten wounded, and the remaining ten took to their heels. Outraged, Boori-Moodi jumped on his chestnut thoroughbred. He caught up with Bila Wobogo between Gorongoru and Kumbila, in a spot so lonely that the cry of man could be heard only by birds, and his call answered only by a distant echo. He hailed Bila Wobogo, who responded with a shower of poisoned arrows. Boori-Moodi managed to avoid them by lying flat on his mount, who was leaping about like a wild lion from the Sahel.

Before Bila had time to recharge his bow, Boori's horse collided with his and sent them both — rider and mount — sprawling into the tangle of a thorn bush. Before Bila could rise, Boori's halberd was already poised on his chest. "Boori!" he said. "Kill me if you wish, but don't dishonor my body by leaving it above ground, a prey to vultures." Boori did kill Bila, but he also buried him with his own hands (Bâ 1999, 123).

Bila remains buried, but the sons of Bila fall prey to the tricks of Wangrin, the rule of the French governor, the passage of their honorable past: "'O Wangrin,' replied the imam, 'exhumation is unheard of in Islam and in our own Fulbe tradition'" (Bâ 1999, 122). But Wangrin's rule comes with the passing of tradition, and the imposition of a rule so severe that the only means conceivable to the sons of Wangrin's generation to oppose the new hegemony of the "world community" lies in the exhumation of the father's body, and the evocation of the noble's words calling for an end to the submission of the children to the new world order.

Both *Wangrin* and *Guelwaar* operate on the logic of what has been termed the "metaphysics of presence," a distribution of the economies of self and other into distinct categories of subject and object, that lend themselves to an understanding of the presence of Islam in Africa as entailing accommodation or exclusion. After all, the *dar al Islam* is nothing less that the communal space of the Islamic self, and the *dar al harb* is that of its other.[3] These are the well defined spaces that mark our two texts, *Wangrin*, with its notion of a traditional Africa setting off the Islamic successor, and *Guelwaar*, constructing a similar binary around "traditional" Africa and the interloping Christians and Muslims. Models of "first peoples," "original" or "traditional" faiths or communities, are now viewed as increasingly suspect not just because of poststructural deconstructive moves, psychoanalytical challenges to notions of identity, or postcolonial privileging of hybridity. These challenges to identitarian politics must contend with an African population's sense of itself as being Muslim and as having acquired a Muslim identity through specific historical processes. It is the events that trace those processes that Nehemia Levtzion's work set in motion. Our task is to complicate the model that had seemed so natural for so long, one that presented Islam as a foreign entity that was introduced to a non-Muslim population. Fantastic as it may seem, the challenge to that paradigm has something of the sense of the exhumation of a corpse — an unreal act around a ghostly figure whose effects are felt mostly in the absence of its real body. The gradual challenges to anthropological and historical models of ethnicity and historicity are sometimes best seen in their putatively unrealistic forms, in literature and cinema. Here, the two examples of the exhumation of the corpse function similarly to unsettle the setting in motion of historical truth.

Notes

[1] This is the point at which Derrida's deconstruction of the sovereign subject has its parallel in the notion of *méconnaissance*. Derrida's presentation, in *Dissemination*, of this centering or presence of the subject turns on the location of the self and attribution of the first person pronoun to that location:

> The illusion — that is to say, the truth, of that which seems to present itself as the thing itself, facing me, in the entirely "natural," ceaselessly self-regenerating opening of my face or of the scene on stage — will therefore have been only an effect of what is often called the "apparatus" ("a constantly active, distorting apparatus" 3.43).
> ... *That device was me, it is that device which just wrote this sentence."* Note that the apparatus can be considered my self or my property, but it stands in my place and *I* is only the differentiated structure of this organization, which is absolutely natural and purely artificial, differentiated enough to count within its structure the moment or the place of the autarchic illusion or the sovereign subject (1981, 298-99).

[2] In *Everything You Always Wanted to Know about Lacan (But Were Afraid to Ask Hitchcock)*, Žižek (1992, 6-8) describes the various manifestations of the McGuffin as including one in which it has a material form, and its function is to act as the object of exchange between characters whose relationship takes on a meaningful dimension as a result of that exchange. That object is associated by Žižek with the Lacanian *objet a* since the latter functions as a substitute for the unattainable object of desire, and thus sets in motion the actions of the subject in his or her desire, actions that take their form in relation to the other. For Žižek, this substitutive object is most like a lack, and as such is also essential to the actions of interpretation that construct the symbolic order: *l'objet a* is "a gap in the centre of the symbolic order — the lack, the void in the Real setting in motion the symbolic movement of interpretation" (1992, 8).

The link to our essay here lies in the act of filling the gap or lack in such a way as to make complete or whole sense, in such a way as to construct an identity for oneself or for the other, an identity built in relation to the other, that is marked by wholeness or completeness — in short, to elaborate that understanding of oneself as being a member of a community, be it religious or ethnic or national. This is the psychological state that marks the twin features of our analysis: the sense of oneself as a Muslim, and the sense of one's relations to others.

[3] This is a vision of the world divided into those who belong to the world of believers, *dar al islam*, and those outside that world, *dar al harb*. This is a world with a definite order; similarly, there is the time corresponding to the Islamic period, beginning with Muhammad's revelation, and culminating with the pilgrimage or hegira to Medina, at which point the community of believers comes into existence and time under God's rule begins. The former time, *jahaliyya*, is a time of ignorance; the introduction of God's words through Muhammad introduces faith, or correct knowledge.

"Islamic Music in Africa" as a Tool for African Studies

Michael Frishkopf

Résumé
Convenablement interprété "La Musique islamique en Afrique" offre aux Études africaines un outil analytique utile à l'exploration des relations entre l'expérience affective individuelle et les structures sociales, les valeurs, et les concepts culturels que la musique à la fois reflète et soutient dans les régions musulmanes. La diversité musicale islamique non-discursive a facilité l'expansion islamique en rendant possibles de puissantes adaptations affectives à des conditions socio-culturelles. Les pratiques soniques de l'Islam constituent des sites centraux pour la production sociale chargée d'émotion de l'Islam, modulée au niveau local, et appuyant la défense de l'identité et des normes musulmanes. La diversité de la musique islamique reflète aussi une histoire riche en interactions culturelles, du fait que la musique est un baromètre sensible des conditions sociales et historiques. Pourtant, la diffusion a créé également une certaine uniformité musicale, liant entre elles les utilisations des sons à travers des pays lointains et consolidant des sentiments communs à l'identité culturelle musulmane en Afrique.

Abstract
Suitably interpreted, "Islamic music in Africa" provides African Studies with a useful analytical tool for probing the relation between affective individual experience and the social structures, values, and cultural concepts which music both reflects and supports in Muslim areas. Non-discursive Islamic musical diversity has facilitated Islamic expansion by enabling affectively powerful adaptations to local socio-cultural conditions. The sonic practices of Islam constitute central sites for the affectively charged social production of Islam, as locally inflected, and for the contestation of Muslim identity and norms. The diversity of Islamic music also reflects a rich history of cultural interactions, as music is a sensitive barometer of social and historical conditions. Yet diffusions have bestowed a certain musical consistency as well, linking sound prac-

tices over vast distances, and underpinning common feelings of Muslim cultural identity in Africa.

Introduction

What is "Islamic music in Africa"? What range of social-sonic phenomena does this analytical concept cover? Of what use is it to African Studies? Before addressing these questions, one must begin with a critique, for the phrase is decidedly problematic. The concept of "music" can never be wholly liberated from its long history within the dominant European discursive tradition. In that tradition, "music" centers on a cultivated art of sonic beauty, in which the purity of the aesthetic experience is valued over its socio-cultural embeddedness and individual embodiment. Such "music" is sharply distinguished from linguistic, visual, and body-kinetic arts. Musical performance takes place in particular (mostly secular) social contexts, featuring the "concert" in which "performers" and "audience" are distinctly separated, and where the practice of disembodied "contemplative" listening and its associated ideal of aesthetic pleasure are primary. All this is supported by parallel traditions of writing music, and writing about music, historically and theoretically. As a result of this history, the concept of "music" has accumulated a cluster of associated qualities frequently inducing erroneous distinctions when applied elsewhere.

These errors are particularly salient when "music" is applied to the diverse profusion of largely orally-transmitted social-sonic practices in Africa, in which sonorous, verbal, and body-kinetic performance types are usually inextricably interconnected, while aesthetic and social-ritual functions are often inseparable. Is it really useful to group all this under "music," given this term's weighty European baggage, and the absence of a comparable term in African languages?

The "Islamic" qualifier introduces new problems, not least because it is not always easy to define "Islam" in an area as large as Africa. Exclusive definitions appear arbitrary (even ideological), while inclusive definitions entail a heterogeneity that calls into question the meaningfulness of the term. Beyond such definitional problems, the qualifier "Islamic" is ambiguous, as it can be taken either in a narrower sense ("related to Islamic religion"), or a broader one ("related to Muslims" or "related Muslim-majority societies," that is, "Islamicate" [Hodgson 1974, 57-60]).

Furthermore, the very pairing of "Islamic" and "music" is problematic. Worldwide, Islamic ritual practice centers upon public language performance more than sound (Frishkopf 1999), ranging continuously from heightened speech to elaborate melody; no clear speech-music boundary can be drawn. "Islamic music" is quasi-oxymoronic, insofar as many strict Muslims (relying on particular interpretations of Qur'an and Hadith) regard "music" (or its local lexical proxies, such as Arabic *musiqa*) as *haram* (forbidden); religious performance genres, for which the usual words for music tend to be avoided, carry special names (such as *adhan* for the call to prayer). Finally, the staggering diversity of both "Islam" and "music" in Africa not only renders the phrase "Islamic music" unwieldy, but also misleading. Geographically-defined boundaries further reduce its conceptual coherence, by sundering important cultural connections (such as East Africa and Arabia), while falsely implying the primacy of others (such as West and East Africa).

Nevertheless, "Islamic music" provides a helpful analytical tool for African studies, so long as the aforementioned caveats and limitations are borne in mind. Music (loosely defined) is so ubiquitous, affective, and broadly participatory throughout Africa that its consideration usefully pushes the researcher to consider the relation between individual experience, and the social structures, values, and cultural concepts which music both reflects and supports. Within Muslim-majority areas, much the same is true of Islam, a highly affective and broadly participatory set of discourses and practices strongly linked to personal identity and informing every aspect of life, whose study entails broader socio-cultural considerations as well as more narrowly personal ones. Both "music" and "Islam" are thus highly productive keywords for explorations of Muslim societies in Africa.

At the intersection of these two keywords stands "Islamic music," a form of sonic-social practice critical to the production and maintenance of the affective charges that make social ties and cultural meanings tangible and durable for Muslims, and comprehensible for the researcher. The close connections of "Islamic music" to language, religion, and social life mean that probing the former always reveals much about culture, society, and history generally, as grounded in individual experience. The tension between concepts of "music" and "Islam," far from vitiating "Islamic music" as an analytical tool, actually ensures that this intersection remains a dynamic site of contestation and conflict — a most interesting place for the researcher to be. Among Muslims, the practices of Islamic music broadly construed as "Islamic sound" are primary sites for the production of social identity and cohesion, and for the negotiation of those identities. Islamic music provides a productive window into the affective and discursive nucleus of Muslim societies.

Despite Muslim ideologies of music-rejection, there are, in each locale, real continuities between Islamic sonic practices, and broader musical ones. Muslim modulations of sound are therefore found to be as productive, or reflective, of general social structures and meanings as music in general. While some features of Islamic music are global, representing the worldwide dissemination of Middle Eastern practices at its historical and normative core, these features are everywhere modulated according to local culture and resources. Some African Islamic regions exhibit considerable musical coherence, which is, however, not easily explained as resulting from a simple "Islamic impact." Thus are generated both hypotheses and questions about Muslim history.

For instance, David Ames notes:

... there are far greater similarities in the position of the musician among widely separated Muslim societies located in [the] ... Western Sudan culture area ... than among the much more closely situated Igbo of eastern Nigeria and Hausa of northern Nigeria (1973, 250-51, 272).

Can such similarities be traced to common features of Islamic practice and belief? Or are they better attributed to the ready diffusion of particular practices and values throughout a social network bound by ties of religious confraternity?

But beyond Muslim sound as a feature for understanding the boundaries and history of culture areas in Africa, its centrality and problematic status renders "Islamic music" highly productive of research questions. For instance, research questions such as "Who can play music?" and "What is the musician's status?" typically assume significance far beyond the field of music studies *per se*, precisely because these questions are problematic for members of the society as well. Particularly in regions that cannot be generally characterized as "Islamic" — that is, much of sub-Saharan Africa — the concept of "Islamicate music" becomes ambiguous.[1] This article will therefore treat "Islamic music" as sound-centric, public performance practices freighted — via text, context, associations, or intentions — with Islamic (religious) meanings.

Overview of Islamic Music in Africa

Throughout Islamic history there has been disagreement over the legitimacy of public musical practice — as entertainment, or even (sometimes, especially) as devotion — (Shiloah 1997; Gribetz 1991). Such disputes flared in Muslim Africa, too, particularly during periods of attempted reform (Erlmann 1986; Ames 1973, 273). In West Africa, musicians' social status appears to have declined with the introduction of Islam (Erlmann 1983, 190-201). Given respectable text and context, male vocal forms are most acceptable; accompanying frame drums (Arabic: *tar, duff*), and occasionally flutes (Arabic: *nay*), are often sanctioned, in accord with Hadith and musical traditions.

Other instruments are more suspect in Islamic contexts, especially if they carry un-Islamic associations (for example, with intoxicants, public eroticism, or pre-Islamic rituals). Mixed gender dancing was repressed in some areas, but not in others (Ames 1982). Due to their mystical orientation, Sufi *turuq* (orders [singular *tariqa*]) have frequently (but not always) been more tolerant of "spiritual audition" *(sama')*. Anti-music and -dance polemics have sounded more loudly in some communities (such as *post-jihad* Hausaland) than others (for example, among the Yoruba or Wolof); in Senegal, where most Muslims belong to one of the major orders (Tijaniyya, Qadiriyya, or Mouride), superstar singers (for example, Youssou N'Dour) pay homage to Sufi saints in popular songs featured on radio and television and in nightclubs (McLaughlin 1997).

A genre of Islamic sound is defined by constellations of sonic, textual, and contextual features, all of which may contribute to its meaning. Text typically plays a central role in Islamic music, but context often plays an equally important one in shaping the overall meaning of performance. Each context is associated with a cluster of genres, whose configuration and style of performance may vary, even as the context itself recurs, throughout Muslim communities worldwide.

Across the Muslim world, three categories of recurring performance contexts, each context carrying a uniform meaning, may be discerned, characterized by three degrees of genre variation within each context. Least variable are formal *ritual* contexts, such as *salah* (obligatory prayer). In such contexts, genres of Islamic sound tend to be constrained, at least in part, by Islamic law *(shari`a)*. Such genres are therefore often globalized: the same genres appear everywhere, and they appear everywhere in nearly the same form.

More variable are Islamic festival contexts. Such contexts, which often represent supererogatory rather than core religious practices, are typically celebratory or memorial, and feature informal, looser constraints, because performance in these contexts, though regarded as supererogatory religious worship, is only indicated — not required or closely regulated — by Islamic law. Examples of such contexts include celebrations of *Ashura'* (the tenth of *Muharram*, the first month in the Islamic lunar calendar), *Mawlid al-Nabi* (the Prophet's Birthday), *Ramadan* (month of fasting, and ninth month in the Islamic calendar), `*Id al-Fitr* (fast breaking holiday), `*Id al-Adha* (`*Id al-Kabir*), and the departure or return of Hajj pilgrims. Genres appearing in these contexts tend to be strongly influenced by regional musical or linguistic traditions, or are local genres not recurring elsewhere.

Less constrained still are life-cycle contexts in Muslim societies, such as birth, circumcision, marriage, and funerals. As such contexts are not limited to Muslim communities, they are frequently linked to equivalent ceremonies in non- or pre-Islamic traditions. Such ceremonies naturally vary greatly depending on the cultural context. As a result, the genres performed within these contexts, even while carrying Islamic meanings, are highly localized.

Lying outside these three categories of recurrent contexts are recurring context-types, each subsuming homologous, yet distinctive, contexts characterizing, in part, particular interpretations of Islam. Such context-types include Sufi *hadras* (weekly congregational worship ceremonies), saint festivals, sectarian rites (of various Shi`a groups, for instance), and syncretic spirit possession rituals. Unlike recurring contexts, such as the *Mawlid al-Nabi*, which presents the same essential meanings across Muslim societies, meaning varies dramatically within the homologous contexts grouped within each context-type, such as the Sufi *hadra* (since each *tariqa* features distinctive saintly figures) or the spirit possession ritual (which often exhibits local pre-Islamic cultural features). Finally, one must consider popular music genres carrying Islamic themes, relatively disengaged from specific social contexts, but embedded instead in local or global media-commodity systems.

Formal ritual genres, prescribed by Islamic law, center on vocalized text, often at the expense of musical sound. Musical instruments are infrequent, and insistence upon use of the sacred liturgical language (Arabic) may preclude local understanding. Here variation is primarily in the domain of vocal and social aspects of performance style.

More informal festival genres, associated with supererogatory devotions, exhibit both sonic and textual diversity, often drawing upon local languages, poetic genres, and musical traditions — yet similar genres frequently arise in disparate locales in response to parallel devotional concepts (for example, *madih*, praise, usually for the Prophet Muhammad). Many genres (sometimes textless, such as drumming) develop religious meanings only via contextual association with religious festivals. Life-cycle genres are more diverse still, even more open to local textual and musical sources, carrying Islamic meanings but closely connected to local culture. With the introduction of Islam to a region, formal ritual genres are necessarily injected, whereas festival and life-cycle contexts tend to absorb pre-Islamic practices, subsequently remaining open to extra-Islamic ones, or helping to define a "localized Islam." Subsequent waves of Islamic reformism (especially prevalent in the present day, as a form of Islamic globalization centered on principal centers of Islamic learning and practice, such as Cairo and Saudi Arabia) may clash with these earlier localizations.

Life-cycle contexts tend to draw upon a general category of "musician" who works outside the religious sphere and frequently is not regarded as a religious specialist *per se*. Conversely, religious performers and genres may crossover to the popular music world, transformed (by new instruments, contexts, and meanings) while retaining religious associations via text, sound, intention, and history. In particular, Islamic festival contexts often foster musical specialists who subsequently become artists and entertainers outside the religious domain. Since the early twentieth century, the music media system provides additional incentives; output is commodified via live performance venues, broadcasts, and recorded media. Some of this output is embedded in the local music media system and limited to local distribution; some is absorbed into the global music media system under the guise of "world music," and distributed via international festivals and recordings.

Generally, Islamization of traditional music was an effective means by which the du`ah (literally, those who "call" to Islam) could lead a broad following to the faith. Conversely, this strategy might entail localization of global Islamic expressive forms via absorption of vernacular literary and musical styles (Hiskett 1973, 134-41). The oft-stated opposition of political *(jihadist)* and aesthetic / mystical (Sufi) Islam is inaccurate and misleading, since most Muslim political activists (from Ibn Taymiyya to Osman dan Fodiyo, to Hasan al-Banna) have been influenced by Sufism, and many expressed themselves in poetry carrying their messages within an aesthetic literary matrix. Sung poetry, as a public devotion, serves as an affectively potent vehicle to deliver ideology. A famous example is Asma'u Fodiyo (1793-1863), daughter of Fulani jihadist Osman dan Fodiyo, who taught Islam to Hausa women — many of whom were involved in the non-Islamic Bori spirit-worship cult — via sung poetry (Boyd 2001).

In the remainder of this article, I begin by surveying genres of the principal recurrent Islamic contexts and context-types, progressing from most to least unified, within principal regions of Muslim Africa. This survey is followed by a discussion of recurrent context-types (particular to religious associations and sects), and the emergence of Islamic music into the broader sphere of popular music, both local and global, through flows of musicians, musical styles, or both. Several broad conclusions can then be drawn.

Elements of Islamic Music

Throughout African Islamic performance certain rhetorical elements recur: petitions, praise, and loving devotion (to Allah, the Prophet Muhammad, and the saints), exhortations to the community (Arabic: wa`z), and expressions of religious experience and knowledge (for example, in Egypt [Frishkopf 2000]; in Somalia,

[Orwin 2001, 69]) (in Swahili, [Topan 2001]). Besides Qur'an, these themes are primarily expressed in sung poetry, known in Arabic as *inshad dini* (religious hymns).

One naturally finds a wide distribution of Arabic terminology for Islamic music, though local terms are also used, especially for the instrumentarium, which centers on frame drums and reed flutes due to supportive Prophetic *hadiths*, and long-standing Sufi traditions.[2] Arabic terms tend to acquire a religious hue outside the Arabic-speaking world, where the Arabic language is nearly coextensive with the Islamic domain. Thus, whereas the Arabic word *qasida* simply means "poem," in non-Arabic speaking areas the loan-word *qasida* often refers to a religious devotional song.

Due to centrality of text, vocalists are central and vital to most genres of Islamic music. The most general terms for religious singer in Arabic are *munshid* (hymnodist) or *maddah* (praiser, that is, for the Prophet Muhammad). Other local terms are introduced below. Performers may also be locally known as "singers" as religious shades into popular music. Female performers are common, particularly within domestic life-cycle contexts; thus Hausa women chant poems *(waka)* treating religious topics, such as *shari`a*, veiling, and pilgrimage (Mack 2004, 13, 14, 133-34).

Throughout the Muslim world, the most common themes are petitions (Arabic: *ibtihalat* to God; *tawassul* to Prophet and saints), and praise (Arabic: *madih*). While Allah is broadly glorified and supplicated, detailed panegyric is directed primarily to the Prophet *(madih nabawi)*, centered on appearance and hagiography, expressing loving devotion, calling for God to bless him *(salawat)*, and requesting intercession *(shafa`a)*. Such praise is believed to confer spiritual benefits on singer and listener alike. Though African oral literary traditions of praise exist apart from (and prior to) Islamic ones, the two sets of traditions clearly harmonized.

For instance, traditional Manding griots (praise singers) of West Africa trace their ancestry to Surakata, praise-singer for the Prophet himself (Conrad 1985, 39-40). Likewise, Fulani Muslim reformer `Uthman ibn Fudi (usually transliterated, Osman dan Fodiyo, as per local pronunciation) (1754-1817), who banned much music and dance, nevertheless strove to convert traditional Hausa praise singers into Islamic panegyrists, writing:

Singer, stop, do not waste your time

In singing the praise of men.
Sing the praises of the Prophet and be content (Erlmann 1986, 15, 31, 37).

Henceforth, even non-Islamic praise-singing incorporated Islamic literary conventions (Hiskett 1973, 133-34). Hausa panegyric to the Prophet was composed by Isa dan Shehu (Osman dan Fodiyo's son) and Nana (his daughter) (Hiskett 1973, 141; Boyd 2001, 15), who became a model for Hausa women (Mack 2004, 10).

Certain African *madih* texts exerted global influence, especially the invocation *Dala'il al-Khayrat* by the Moroccan al-Jazuli (died 1465), and poetry of Sharaf al-Din al-Busiri (born 1212), an Egyptian of Berber origin. Two of al-Busiri's Arabic poems praising the Prophet, *al-Burda* and *al-Hamziyya*, are renowned throughout the Muslim world. They have also become models for composers in local idioms throughout Africa, including Nigeria (Hiskett 1973, 133), Sudan (Osman 1990), East Africa (Scheub 1985, 31), North Africa (Sulamiyya 1999), and Egypt (Waugh 1989; Frishkopf 2000).

In Egypt, supplication *(ibtihalat)* and *madih* are the primary themes of sung devotional poetry; both classical *(qasida)* and colloquial *(zajal, mawwal)* forms are used, in a wide variety of contexts, from festivals to Sufi liturgies. Performances may be solo (non-metric), choral, responsorial, or an alternation of the first and second types, a format generally known as *tawashih* (Frishkopf 2006; Barrayn 1994). Other examples of *madih* may be found from West Africa (Schulze 1965), to the North (Fez 2002), from Sudan (Simon 1989, 30-31; Sudan 1980; Osman 1990), to Somalia (Orwin 2001). A distinctive Sudanese *madih nabawi* tradition, featuring local musical style, yet following the broader textual tradition (with strong influence of al-Busiri) is well-established (Osman 1990, 150-52; Sudan 1980). *Madih* is ubiquitous in the Sufi orders, discussed below.

Ritual Contexts

Daily Prayer (Salah)

Ordinary congregational prayer comprises a series of public sonic genres, including the preliminary call to prayer *(adhan)* performed by the *mu'adhdhin* (muezzin), Qur'anic recitation *(tilawa;* also discussed below) performed by the *qari'* ("reader"), *du`a'*, and other short, intoned devotional texts. Such performances are non-metric (there is no regular meter), and strictly vocal. Egyptian *mu'adhdhinin* may precede *adhan* with melodic supplication and *madih*, especially at dawn (Frishkopf 2000). For Friday prayer a *khutba* (sermon), often delivered in local languages, precedes prayer proper. Being obligatory *(fard) salah* is highly-regulated in its textual and contextual aspects. However, its sonic aspect — flexible in vocal timbre, phonetics, stress, tempo, and melodic style — is subjected to local linguistic and musical treatments (for example, among Yoruba, see Adegbite 1989, 35; L. Anderson 1971, 151-52). While *adhan* differences are partly attributable to performer idiosyncrasies, regional and contextual varieties can often be identified; compare North African *(Chants religieux ... au Maghreb; Morocco I: The Music of Islam and Sufism in Morocco)*, Egyptian (La Chadhiliyyah 1999) and West African (Schulze 1965) versions (L. Anderson 1971, 154-56). Yet *adhan* and *tilawa* have also infused Arab sonic style (such as melisma, ornament, modality, solo nasal voice) throughout Muslim Africa, influencing music generally (Charry 2000a, 5; Charry 2000b, 546; Danielson 1991, 114).

Technically, the *adhan's* melodic origins are African, for the first performer was the Prophet's Ethiopian muezzin Bilal ibn Rabah, a fact significant in two other African performance contexts: the Moroccan *Gnawa derdeba* ceremony, and the griot tradition of West Africa. *Gnawas* claim lineal descent from Bilal, while *Manding griots* praise "Bilali Bounama" as ancestor of Sunjata, founder of the Empire of Mali (Schuyler 1981, 3; Langlois 1998, 147; Conrad 1985, 35). In Senegal, the *adhan* is typically performed by *griots* (McLaughlin 1997, 564). Prayer performance differs slightly among the Shi`a (Shiites, mainly in East Africa); for instance, the Shi`i adhan includes an additional phrase, "come to the best of works."

PUBLIC SERMON (KHUTBA)

When detached from Friday prayer, prose sermonizing *(wa`z)* can be considered an independent genre, appearing in a wide variety of contexts (funerals, festivals); such sermons may become an independent spectacle, even valued as entertainment, and distributed on cassette, as in Egypt or in West Africa (Launay 1977, 149-50; Launay 1997, 445-46).

PUBLIC QUR'ANIC RECITATION (TILAWA, TAJWID, TARTIL)
Besides daily prayer, *tarawih* prayers (during *Ramadan*) feature extended passages of Qur'anic recitation. Outside prayer, Muslims memorize and recite the holy Qur'an in public listening sessions for a variety of occasions inside and outside the mosque (Launay 1977, 149; Miner 1942, 623), especially during *Ramadan* (month of its revelation). In theory anyone may chant Qur'an, but professional titled specialists (for example, Arabic *qari'*, Mandinka *fina*) dominate public contexts. The underlying *mushaf* (written text) is fixed, as are rules for its recitation *(ahkam al-tajwid)*, governing phonetics, phrasing, syllable length, and tempo (Nelson 1985). However variant "readings" *(qira'at)* are used in different parts of Africa, for instance the reading of Warsh `an Nafi` in West and North Africa; the reading of Hafs `an `Asim elsewhere. In addition, timbral, melodic, and contextual aspects are highly variable (see Jacobsen 1996, 126; Adegbite 1989, 35). A solo ametric voice is most common in performance, but metered or corporate chanting occurs too, for instance in the distinctive Berber *tolba* of Morocco (hear: Soufis 2003; *Morocco I: The Music of Islam and Sufism in Morocco; Chants religieux ... Au Maghreb*, track #3; *Music in the World of Islam*, 1: track #1; La Chadhiliyyah 1999, track #2).

There are two principal named styles: the melodically elaborate *mujawwad*, and the more recitational *murattal*. Faster and easier to perform, *murattal* is used in *salah*, but is increasingly preferred in other contexts as well, due to reformist perceptions of its greater legality. In Egypt, for instance, performances of *mujawwad* are sometimes criticized as "singing the Qur'an," allowing aesthetic considerations to distract from the Word of God. Traditionally, Egypt's reciters set world-wide standards, but recently a distinctively Saudi style has begun to achieve global recognition as well (Frishkopf 2006).

Ismailis of East Africa may perform additional genres at prayertime; thus among Bohras there is no *khutba*; rather, the prayer leader concludes by praying for forgiveness and asking for the period of *satr* (occultation) to end via manifestation of the Imam (Amiji 1975, 48, 50). Nizaris include recitation of *ginan* poetry (Gillani 2004). Adjacent to the meticulously defined space-time of prayer proper there is more freedom; for example, following Friday prayers, when royal Hausa musicians greet their *sarki* (emir), playing *kakaki* (metal trumpet), *algaita* (shawm), and *kaho* (antelope horn) (Besmer 1972, 197; Ames 1973, 256).

Festival Contexts

Ramadan

The ninth month in the Islamic calendar, *Ramadan* (month of fasting from dawn to sunset) subsumes two principal festival contexts containing musical performances:

(1) Evenings, highlighting religious songs celebrating *Ramadan*, the Qur'an, and the Prophet, and supplicating God. *Ibtihalat* and *tawashih* (featuring classic performers, such as Sayyid al-Naqshabandi and Taha al-Fashni) are often heard on Egyptian radio (Frishkopf 2000), along with *tilawa*. In Kano, royal Hausa musicians perform *Gaisuwar barka da shan ruwa* during the last ten nights of *Ramadan* (Besmer 1972, 195-96), while members of the *Qadiriyya tariqa* roam the streets beating a single membrane drum while chanting praises of the Prophet (Ames 1973, 276 note 8). In the Comoro islands, *mrenge* (boxing matches) are accompanied by drumming after the evening meal (Ottenheimer 1970, 460).

(2) Mornings, when performers rouse the devout for their pre-dawn meal (Arabic: *sahur*; Yoruba: *saari*). This latter function has generated a colourful assortment of sonic traditions. In Marrakech, *ghaita* (oboe) and *nfir* (trumpet) play melodies based on religious chants from mosque minarets (*Morocco I: The Music of Islam and Sufism in Morocco*, track #5; Chottin 1927). In Egypt, the *masahharati* awakens the faithful by calling names and chanting religious formulae, accompanied by a small drum *(baza)*. Among the Dagbamba (Northern Ghana), a *jenjili* (musical bow) player circulates, playing and singing (Chernoff 1979, 131). Yoruba youth may perform *were* or *ajisaari*, whose vocal style is influenced by Islamic cantillations (Adegbite 1989, 39-40; Waterman 1990, 31); formerly *apala* praise singers accompanied by rhythm sticks, and *dundun* drummers, also used to parade from house to house. Drum patterns are taken from the general repertoire of Yoruba traditional music. Later, *apala* combined with drums and *agidigbo (sansa)* to produce evening *Ramadan* entertainment (Euba 1971, 178; Adegbite 1989, 37; Waterman 1990, 85).

Mawlid al-Nabi

The season surrounding the Prophet's birthday (12 Rabi` al-Awwal) is celebrated via musical performances of biographical and panegyric texts (also called *mawlid*), as well as *madih* generally. Sometimes the *mawlid* is performed on other occasions, or even as a weekly devotion. Various *mawlid* texts have been composed based primarily on the classical *sira nabawiyya* attributed to Ibn Ishaq (born c.704), as rendered by the Egyptian, Ibn Hisham (died 828 or 833). In Egypt, the three *mawlids* most frequently performed are Barzanji (by the Medinan Ja`far ibn Hasan al-Barzanji, died 1765), Munawi (by the Cairene `Abd al-Ra'uf al-Munawi, died 1621), and al-Busiri's *Burda*.

Besides Arabic texts, local languages and poetic forms, as well as musical resources, are expressed during *mawlid*. Desert Berbers (Zenatas) of Gourara, Algeria perform *ahallil*, haunting nocturnal vocal-flute-percussion songs of praise (Sahara 2000). The Vai of Liberia sing religious songs during this period, which they call *morodi (Music of the Vai of Liberia)*. In northern Ghana, the week-long Damba festival includes traditional singing, drumming, and dancing honouring the Prophet, and the chief (Corke et al. 2000; Chernoff 1985, 124; Kinney 1970). Festive and entertaining recitations *(kalan)*, centered on sermons, are performed among the Dyula of Ivory Coast for Donba, the Prophet's birthday; spoken text is interspersed with song (Launay 1997, 445-46). Hausa royal musicians — praise singers, drummers, and instrumentalists — perform Sallar Gana for the *mawlid* (Besmer 1972, 288; Hausa 2006), while members of the Qadiriyya chant *madih* to the accompaniment of a drum, as during *Ramadan* (Ames 1973, 276 note 8).

Some of the most elaborate *mawlid* performances are found in East Africa, where enormous sums are expended on a *mawlid* season lasting "more than six months" (Schacht 1965, 96). In Lamu, Kenya, the *maulidi* (= *mawlid*) is highly treasured, observed as a month-long series of "readings" *(kusoma)* culminating in a one-week festival. Each reading comprises solo chanting of texts interspersed with collective *madih (qasida)*. There are five forms, all save one in Arabic; except for the *maulidi Barzanji*, these may be accompanied by drum *(tari, kigoma)*, flute *(nay)*, and stylized male dancing. Self-referential *mawlid* songs defend the performance of *mawlid* music against its fundamentalist detractors, saying, for instance "Do not give up praising Muhammad." The Lamuan *mawlid* thus both reflects and participates in the debate concerning music (Waswahili 1985; Boyd 1981, 88-97). Tanzanian *mawlid* includes *qasidas* and Qur'anic recitation (*Zanzibar: Music of Celebration*, tracks #6 and 7). Somali *madih*, known as *nebi-ammaan*, is composed in the local language and performed for *mawlid* (Orwin 2001, 72-78). In the Comoros, Kandza, featuring a poem about the Prophet's life, is danced (Comores 1994).

Many Sufi shaykhs compose *mawlids* for use in their orders, for example, in the Muhammadiyya Shadhiliyya of Egypt (Al-tariqa 1992; La Chadhiliyyah 1999), or the Khatmiyya of Sudan (Sudan 1980), and nearly all Sufi groups perform enthusiastic *mawlid*. The Senegalese Tivaouane *zawiya* (lodge) of the *Tijaniyya tariqa* performs a yearly *gammu* (or *mawluud*) celebrating the Prophet's birth. The *gammu* is a nocturnal ceremony during which praise poems are sung, especially devotional poetry by the *zawiya's* founder, El Hajj Malik Sy (1855-1922), written for the Prophet (McLaughlin 2000, 194). On the other hand, the more fundamentalist Muslim reformers tend to reject *mawlid* celebrations entirely as *bid`a* (literally "innovation," but implying "heretical").

PILGRIMAGE TO MECCA (HAJJ)

The embarkation and return of pilgrims is a joyous annual celebration. Yoruba women used to welcome returning Muslims with *waka* songs (from Hausa *wak'a*, "song"), evincing Arab influence (melismatic, nasal, embellished), accompanied by metallic idiophones *(seli)* (Euba 1971, 177-78; Waterman 1990, 31); this form derived from Hausa women singers (Mack 2004, 133). *Sakara* praise-singers, accompanied by the *molo* or *goje* lutes, *sakara* clay drum, and other percussion, and synthesizing Arab and local musical styles, have performed at hajj celebrations in Yorubaland (Waterman 1990, 39). Returning pilgrims from the *Khatmiyya tariqa* in Sudan are expected to sponsor a special collective ritual *(karama)* in their honour (Sudan 1980). Nubian women sing call / response songs for pilgrims, accompanied by handclaps (Nubier 1980, 54). Among illiterate Hausa women pilgrims, composition and performance of personal *hajj* songs re-enacting their journey confers cultural capital (Cooper 1999).

'Id Festivals

'Id Festivals, liturgically centred on supererogatory prayers *(salat al-'Id)* marking the end of *Ramadan* fast *('Id al-Fitr)* and the sacrifice of Hajj *('Id al-Adha)*, are sanctioned by Prophetic *Hadith*; these typically incorporate special *takbir* chants, with fixed Arabic texts, whose sonic aspect evinces local linguo-musical influence. However, beyond prayer, the precise form of celebration is not prescribed, so 'Id festivals capaciously absorb a large number of local performance genres, carrying pre-Islamic influence, or exhibiting local developments and adaptations. Many songs reference the 'Id textually, though musical content varies radically: monophonic 'Id songs in Egypt (Frishkopf 2000) contrast with polyphony of the Rasha'ida, an Arab tribe of Eritrea (*Music in the World of Islam* 1: track #7). Some 'Id performances, not religious *per se*, acquire Islamic meanings by association: among the Ivory Coast Dyula, women and children dance (Launay 1977, 149), while Mandinka *jalis (griots)* offer ordinary praise singing (Knight 1973, xiv).

Among Yoruba, *dundun* drum orchestras accompany processions of chiefs to and from prayer ground (Euba 1971, 176-77); *sakara* may also appear — the most famous performer was Abibus Oluwa, "the preacher" (Waterman 1990, 36-39). A famous *hadith* suggests that the Prophet advocated musical celebrations during the 'Id; correspondingly, Othman dan Fodiyo criticized the Hausa's pagan ways but nevertheless allowed the kettle-drum to be beaten at the advent of the 'Id (Ames 1973, 273), and elaborate 'Id festival music continues to be performed there by court musicians *(maroka)*, including praise singers, drums, horns, *shawms*, trumpets, bells, and rattles, for a series of court events and processions (Besmer 1974; Besmer 1972, 256-77; Ames 1973, 256). Spectacular all-night drum history narrations, involving a lead singer-drummer supported by a chorus of up to a hundred others, and climaxing in a dance *(bangumanga)*, are performed for both 'Id festivals among the Dagbamba of Ghana (Chernoff 1985, 110-11; Corke *et al.* 2000).

Ashura'

Shiites in East Africa (primarily of South Asian origin) celebrate Ashura' (commemorating the martyrdom of Husayn and his family at Karbala') with *majalis* (rituals centered on sung elegies and dirges) and *ta`ziyya* (dramatic re-enactment) (Amiji 1975, 50; Qureshi 1981). Sunnis also observe this ancient holiday as commemorating various prophetic events (such as Noah's landfall, Moses' Red Sea passage and receipt of the Ten Commandments, Jonah's deliverance). In North Africa, Ashura' is announced by polyrhythmic drumming *(daqqa)* accompanied by choral chants *(ait)* comprising Divine praises, requests for intercession, prayers for the Prophet, and remembrance of Sufi masters), and trumpets *(neffar)* (La daqqa 1999); children go door to door, singing and collecting for their religious teachers (Marcais, *Encylcopedia of Islam Online*). Some Sunni groups, such as the Sudanese Khatmiyya (see below), display Shiite influence in Ashura' rituals (Karrar 1992, 159).

Life-cycle Contexts

Life-cycle contexts, such as births, circumcisions, weddings, and funerals, celebrated by Muslims and non-Muslims alike, may be viewed as only equivocally Islamic — or even secular — and hence are more likely to accumulate or retain a variety of genres and musical features, resulting in complex convergences, synergies, and syncretisms between Islamic styles (as marked by text and sound) and popular ones. In these familial occasions one generally observes greater liberality in use of musical instruments, musical sounds, dance, and mixing of the sexes. Due to both content and pre-Islamic associations, such performances were often targeted by reformers as un-Islamic (for example, Ames 1982, 136-37). Yet prohibitions typically are less enforceable for domestic contexts peripheral to the sphere of Islamic worship.

Religious songs, especially *madih*, are commonly performed at life-cycle events. In Egypt, *inshad* performed for circumcisions, weddings, or memorials may incorporate popular Arabic songs and instruments (Frishkopf 2002a). *Hausa Bandiri* music transforms Hindi film songs into *madih nabawi* (Larkin 2002). In Kenya, a birth may be celebrated with *mawlid* performance (Boyd 1981, 88); in Zanzibar (Tanzania) a *mawlid qasida* is performed in celebration of a wedding (*Zanzibar: Music of Celebration*, track #6). The *Dyula* traditionally perform sermons *(kalan)* for funerals and memorials (Launay 1997, 445); a new ritual deploys *kalan* for weddings as well (Launay 1977, 148-50). Comorians perform the *deba* — comprising responsorial songs praising the prophets, accompanied by percussion — often closing with a solo *ilahi* (devotion to God), for various family occasions; weddings are celebrated with music and dance called *tari*, filled with praise of the Prophet (Comores 1994). The Comoro *daira* ("circle," or gathering) of the local Shadhiliya *tariqa*, including chant and movement, is performed in memoriam on the seventh and fortieth nights after death, as well as on the final day of wedding festivities (Ottenheimer 1970, 460). Yoruba have performed *waka* and *sakara* for weddings (Euba 1971, 177-78; Waterman 1990, 39). The Songhai (Niger) circumcision ritual (prayers, songs, *tilawa*, dancing, and drumming) fuses Islamic with pre-Islamic performance elements, illustrating how functional homology creates pathways for continuity and syncretism (Miner 1942, 621-31).

Sufi Context-types

Sufi orders (*turuq*, literally "ways") are voluntary religious associations (albeit with strong hereditary tendencies), usually named for a founder-saint, whose "way" they perpetuate. Often erroneously counterpoised to "orthodoxy," Sufi orders have been ubiquitous and socially mainstream throughout much of Islamic history as a means of facilitating spiritual growth beyond what is required by the exoteric ritual and belief of *shari`a*, and as a means of providing a supportive social organization. Sufis emphasize love of God, Prophet, and saints as a means of self-transformation — sometimes even to the point of self-annihilation *(fana')* or Divine Union *(ittihad)*. Each *tariqa* group, providing for the spiritual growth of its members, generates a unique context for public sonic performance, expressing its characteristic world-view shaped by a particular spiritual-social system and doctrines, though these contexts tend to be quasi-homologous in their common emphases upon spiritual development, spiritual hierarchy, and mediation. With a spiritual guide *(shaykh, marabout)*, members gather at a meeting place (mosque, *zawiya, khanqa*) for weekly supererogatory devotional liturgies *(hadra, dhikr, majlis, halaqa, daira, karama, layliyya)*, including remembrance of God *(dhikr)*, love and praise for the Prophet and saints, requests for intercession, and religious guidance, according to the *tariqa's* particular traditions. Language performance (Frishkopf 1999) — often musical — dominates on these occasions.

While mainstream sonic genres *(tilawa, madih, wa`z, mawlid)* are common, the most distinctive Sufi genre is *dhikr (dikr, zikr, dhikiri)*. As a genre, *dhikr* implies collective rhythmic (sometimes melodic) chanting of Divine Names, often accompanied by movement, accelerating to a climax, and possibly leading to ecstatic trance *(wajd, hal)*. Alongside *dhikr*, religious chanters *(munshidun)* may perform poetry (*inshad* Sufi), often composed by *tariqa* founders in local languages, including coded mystical expressions, and standard themes of praise, devotion, and supplication — to God and the Prophet, but also localized to the *tariqa's* saints *(awliya', marabouts)* and regional musical styles. In solo improvisations, or choral responsorial formats, and sometimes with instrumental accompaniment, *inshad* may also appear without *dhikr*, as a catalyst for spiritual connection; such mystical "concerts" are called *sama`*, and draw on local musical traditions (Hear: Fez 2002; Al-Samaa 2004).

Following al-Ghazali (died 1111), Sufism is generally tolerant of music with a spiritual message; though frame drums and reed flutes are often preferred, many local instruments are absorbed into the mix. Sufi emphases upon spiritual love and metaphorical interpretation generate ambiguity between sacred and secular love; any elevated love song supports Sufi interpretations, and may be used in Sufi ritual. As the tolerance and strong social fabric of *turuq* became an important means by which Islam was disseminated through sub-Saharan Africa after the twelfth century, local musical styles were naturally absorbed into Sufi liturgies. Sub-Saharan orders often feature drumming, polyrhythm, and pentatonicism, alongside Arabic elements. Even a reformer such as Othman dan Fodiyo, who initially opposed certain musical traditions, was later softened by mysticism, approving of *madih* and music in his "Najm al-Ikhwan" (1812) (Erlmann 1986, 31). Only in the twentieth century did the twin forces of Saudi-inspired Islamism and secularism lead to the *turuq's* general decline (For general background, see Trimingham 1998; Schimmel 1975; Waugh 1989; Waugh 2005).

Some *tariqas* (Tijaniyya, Qadiriyya, Shadhiliyya) are widespread throughout Africa; others are more localized (Khatmiyya in the Nile Valley, Mourides in Senegal, Aisawa and Sulamiyya in

North Africa). Music varies widely, both from one region to another, and from one *tariqa* to another even within a single region. Tijanis in Hausaland chant religious hymns (Ames 1973, 256); in Senegal, they perform the *gammu* for God, the Prophet, and chief *marabout* (McLaughlin 1997, 566). Qadiris in Hausaland chant *madih* for *mawlid* and *Ramadan* (Ames 1973, 276 note 8); in Sudan their musical rituals exhibit much sub-Saharan African influence, sometimes with instruments (Sudan 1980; Karrar 1992, 155-64); in Senegal they create remarkable percussion pieces on tuned kettledrums *(tabala)* (Tabala 1992; McLaughlin 1997, 565). Throughout East Africa, the *tariqa* spread among non-literate population via colloquial devotional poetry (Reese 2001, 51- 53, 57-62, 66-67; Orwin 2001, 70-72).

Distinctive to far West Africa, the Mourides were founded by Cheikh Amadou Bamba (1850-1927) who composed numerous poems *(khassaids,* from Arabic *qasa'id)* praising the prophet, and inducing trance-like states in listeners (McLaughlin 2000; McLaughlin 1997, 565; Triaud, no date). The *maggal* liturgy is dedicated to Bamba and his family; the Mouride subgroup, Baye Fall, employs Senegalese *sabar*-like drums in devotions (McLaughlin 1997, 565-66). Other Sufi liturgies of Africa have been carefully described (Gilsenan 1973; Frishkopf 1999; Waugh 1989; Waugh 2005; Franken 1986, 95-97). A quantity of recorded African Sufi music is available; for example, liturgies of the Alawiyya and Bouabdaliya of Algeria (Soufis 2003); the Sulamiyya of Tunisia (Ensemble du Cheikh Abdelaziz ben Mahmoud 2000; Sulamiyya 1999); the Shadhiliyya of Egypt (Al-tariqa 1992; La Chadhiliyyah 1999); the Khatmiya of Sudan (Sudan 1980; Simon 1989, 32).

Saint Festival Contexts

With no formal procedure for canonization, the Muslim saint (Arabic: *wali, shaykh, qutb; sayyid, salih* in North Africa; *mallam* (Hausa); *faqir* and *faqih* in Sudan; *pir* among South Asian communities) is ubiquitous in Africa (Radtke, no date). Besides saints recognized throughout the Islamic world (such as Abd al-Qadir al-Jilani [died 1166], Abu al-Hasan al-Shadhili [died 1258]), each region of Muslim Africa contains its local saints (for example, Moulay Idris, patron saint of Fez). As for the Prophet, saints are visited *(ziyara)* and celebrated in an annual festival variously called *mawlid* (birth), *`urs* (wedding), or *mawsim* (season); centered (unlike *mawlid al-nabi*) on the saint's *maqam* (shrine). Sufi orders celebrate their founder-saints (usually eponymous: for example, the Tijaniyya's Ahmad al-Tijani [Algerian, died 1815]); most festivals are public occasions, inviting general community participation.

As opposed to formally closed *tariqa* liturgies, saint festivals are open, socially and sonically; instruments and ecstatic behaviours are more likely to appear. The music of saint festivals includes *tariqa* traditions of *inshad* and *dhikr*, but also draws upon a wider variety of local music, religious or secular; even when not overtly religious, such music acquires spiritual meanings for participants through the dominating presence of the saint. Spectacular processions, including music, often mark celebratory commencements or conclusions. As always, *madih* is central. Enormous *mawlids* in Egypt incorporate musical diversity, from Sufi *inshad*, to secular folk traditions (for example, the *tahtib* stick dance); the renowned Sufi *munshid*, Shaykh Yasin al-Tuhami, performs to upwards of ten thousand listeners for the *mawlid* of the Prophet's grandson, al-Husayn, in Cairo (Frishkopf 2002b; Frishkopf 2001; al-Tuhami 1998). Music praises Moulay Idris at his festival (Chottin 1932; Fez 2002), while Amadou Bamba enjoys musical pride of place during the Grand Maggal, an annual Mouride pilgrimage to his birthplace, Touba (McLaughlin 1997, 565). In Kano, Nigeria, `Abd al-Qadir al-Jilani was celebrated with parades and beating of *bandiri* drums (Radtke).

Spirit Ritual Contexts.

Rituals featuring spirit possession and mixed gender music and dance are widely distributed in "traditional" sub-Saharan African religion. Though many Muslims denounce such rituals as "pagan" *(wathni)* or "pre-Islamic" *(jahili)*, in practice they often evince amalgamation with Islam, typically by associating spirits to elements of Islamic cosmology *(jinn* or saints), recognizing a class of "Muslim spirits," or assimilating social structures and practices to Sufism. Some spirit possession groups may resemble (to a greater or lesser degree) *tariqas* (and may be perceived as such) but the former are more overtly syncretic. Depending on the group, members may regard themselves as Muslims, or merely as interacting with Muslim practices. Such groups often appeal to the publicly marginalized; women, peripheral in most *tariqas*, often play a principal role in musical performances associated with spirit rituals. These rituals, drawing freely on traditional African instruments and music (polyrhythmic, percussive, and pentatonic), center on spiritual therapy (via exorcism or propitiation), frequently feature ecstasy, self-mortification, and possession, and are locally perceived as "African." Commonly, melodic or rhythmic patterns are associated with particular spirits; when performed, such patterns invoke and placate corresponding spirits, thus constituting diagnosis and therapy.

North Africa features a number of different therapeutic spirit-centric musical-ritual types with acknowledged sub-Saharan connections, featuring the *guinbri* lute, such as the Moroccan *derdeba* or *lila* (Schuyler 1981, 3; *Morocco I: The Music of Islam and Sufism in Morocco, Gnawa Music of Marrakesh*) and Algerian *diwan* (Biskra 1996), performed by Gnawas (claiming descent from the Prophet's Ethiopian muezzin, Bilal); the parallel *stambeli* of Tunisia (Jankowsky 2004); the *hadra* of the Moroccan Hamadsha (Crapanzano 1973; Crapanzano, no date; *Morocco I: The Music of Islam and Sufism in Morocco*); and — lying somewhat closer to mainstream Sufi practice — the `Isawiyya hadra* of Morocco, Algeria, and Tunisia (Soufis 2003; Les Aissawa de Fes 1999; Sulamiyya 1999; Standifer 1988, 56; Grame 1970; Michon, no date). In Egypt, Sudan, and Ethiopia, *zar* performances include Muslim spirits (Kenyon 1995, 111; al-Shahi 1984, 28, 35; Natvig 1988). Similar *pepo* spirit possession in Kenya and Tanzania features Muslim spirits (*ki-islamu, ki-arabu*), requesting *dhikiri* or *maulidi* performances (Giles 1989, 94-95, 274-76); spirits are increasingly Islamic in character (Giles 1995, 95, 101). The *ki-pemba* cult of Mombasa reflects Islamic influence in cosmology, songs, and Qur'anic recitation (Topan 1996, 117-22). The Hausa *bori* cult, categorized by some scholars as pre-Islamic (Ames 1973, 256), and condemned by reformers such as Asma'u Fodiyo (Boyd 2001, 12), exhibits Islamic aspects, as spirits *(iskoki)* were assimilated to Islamic *jinn* (Besmer 1972, 66). *Bori* music includes singing, and instrumental performance on calabashes (women), or lutes, rattles, and calabashes (men) (Besmer 1983, 50-52).

Sectarian Contexts

While most African Muslims are Sunni, isolated Ibadi, Ithna`ashari Shi`a (Rizvi and King 1973, 12), Bohra (Amiji 1975), and Nizari Isma`ili groups exist as well (Ranja 2003). These groups feature unique sonic genres and contexts. The Shi`a Ashura' has already been mentioned. Inhabiting the Mzab (six hundred to eight hundred kilometres south of Algiers) are Ibadi Berbers, practicing distinctive patterns of Islamic chant (Alport 1954, 34-42). Nizari Isma`ilis of South Asian descent are concentrated in East Africa; a central liturgical practice is melodic recitation of *ginan*, featuring poetry of founding *pirs*, and a South Asian melodic ethos, often with *tabla* and harmonium accompaniment (Gillani 2004; *Music in the World of Islam*, 1: track #1; Mzab 2006).

Interactions with the Popular Music Sphere

Islamic sonic performance crosses definitively from religious to popular performance when disengaged from specific contexts, and embedded instead in local or global music media-commodity systems. Sometimes popular music genres are inflected with Islamic themes and styles; other times an entire genre may "cross over," freighted with new meanings and often transformed sonically as well. Besides providing sonic resources, connections to traditional Islamic performance may confer artistic legitimacy, ethical propriety, and cultural prestige, tap powerful religious feeling and nostalgia, and serve as a touchstone of cultural authenticity. At least three processes of transformation are at work: restaging, recorded media, and globalization.

The full range of Islamic musical styles and genres, as presented above — including even Qur'anic recitation and the *adhan*, but especially genres of festival, Sufi, and spirit possession contexts — may be restaged and transformed as live entertainment, for example, Gnawa and `Isawiyya performances as spectacle in Marrakesh (Grame 1970, 77-84; Schuyler 1981; *Morocco I: The Music of Islam and Sufism in Morocco*), or the secularization of Nigerian genres *(waka, were, apala, sakara)* via musical, textual, and contextual changes (Euba 1971, 177-79; Adegbite 1989, 40; Collins 1992, 93). Contemporary Sufi singers of Egypt become popular stars, appreciated for *tarab* (musical emotion) as much as spirituality (Frishkopf 2001). Many popular singers of twentieth-century Egypt trained in religious contexts, starting with the traditional schools for mastering Qur'anic recitation *(kuttab)* and continuing with *tawashih diniyya* and Sufi *dhikr*; shifting to the popular domain, they might continue to perform explicitly religious material (Shaykh Naqshabandi), or dwell on ambiguous, elevated Sufi love poetry (Shaykhs `Ali Mahmud and Yusuf al-Manyalawi), or simply enjoy the connotations of authority, authenticity, and propriety bestowed by Islamic training (such as Shaykh Sayyid Darwish and Umm Kulthum) (Danielson 1991, 114-23) even while performing an entirely secular repertoire, provided it maintained a suitable level of decorum.

Such "crossovers" are far less common in Egypt today, not only because the *kuttab* has declined (replaced by governmental schools), but also with the diminished importance of the Sufi sphere and as popular music and religious domains find themselves increasingly at odds: the former increasingly commercialized and eroticized, the latter increasingly puritanical (sometimes to the point of rejecting overly-elaborate Qur'anic recitation). Thus when Nubian pop star Mohamed Mounir produced a post-9/11 album of Islamic music in 2002 entitled *Earth ... Peace* he found himself embroiled in controversy. Emphasizing Islam as a religious of peace and love, he sang "the spilling of any blood is deemed sinful by God." But the music video for this song was banned from Egyptian television, because its petition *(madad*, "help us") to the Prophet was not palatable to the conservative religious establishment (MSN Arabia; Mounir 2002).

Recorded media may play a critical role in the shift to the popular sphere, providing broader markets and disengaging context. In the 1970s, Nigerian *fuji* (including trap set, synthesizers, and traditional Nigerian percussion) emerged from *Ramadan ajisaari*, popularized by early recordings of Muslim musicians Kollington Ayinla and Chief Ayinde Barrister. While *fuji per se* is not Islamic, *fuji* musicians and majority of fans are Muslims (though many are Christian, too), and record companies release special *fuji* LPs on major Muslim holidays (Barber and Waterman 1995, 244; Waterman 1990, 150-51, 231).

In Senegal's bustling music scene, popular singers such as Youssou N'Dour (2004), Cheikh Lo (1996), and Baaba Maal (1998) include on each album one or more songs praising and invoking local Sufi saints, especially Amadou Bamba, his disciple Ibra Fall, and El Hajj Malik Sy; though such music is played in nightclubs and bars, it also expresses a religious message. This phenomenon is testimony to the strength of Sufism there, and reflects also the influence of secular *griot* praise traditions which Senegalese pop stars have inherited (McLaughlin 2000, 191; McLaughlin 1997). The influence of these saints extends beyond Senegal, for example, Mauritanian *griot*-star Malouma who praises Amadou Bamba (Miadeh 1998). Guinean *griot* Mory Kante mixes the call to prayer in one popular song (Kante 1987, track #3). The mixing of sacred and secular is not unproblematic, however; religious conservatives sharply criticized Cheikh Ismael Lo for recording a song ("Wassalia") drawing upon El Hajj Malik's hagiography of Mohammed from the *gammu*, since his cassettes are played in bars and at parties, contexts considered inappropriate for devotional poetry (McLaughlin 2000, 199-200).

The 1970s witnessed the emergence of popular Moroccan groups such as Nass el-Ghiwane and Jil Jilala, which drew eclectically from Moroccan folk and Sufi heritage (including 'Isawiyya and Gnawa), in combination with western popular music (Schuyler 2002). These Moroccan groups also illustrate their transcendence of the local popular scene by touring for Western audiences throughout Europe and North America.

Western consumption generates at least three distinctive categories of African Islamic popular music (all of which tend to be filed as "world music"): what may be termed "global ethnographic," "world beat," and "global pop" musics. "Global ethnographic" includes the numerous recordings and festival performances of what is perceived as "authentic" (that is, rooted in the pre-modern period) Islamic cultural traditions described above, as presented to a Western audience as a kind of auditory travelogue. With the help of program and liner notes, the putative aim of such recordings and concerts is to document the world's cultural diversity and educate Westerners about it. However, despite claims of authenticity, such performances are necessarily transformed, at least by the contextual shift to stage or CD (for example, Tabala 1992; *Morocco I: The Music of Islam and Sufism in Morocco*; Sufi Music Village [London] 1997 [www.culturalco-operation.org]; Al-Tuni 2000).

"World beat" results from eclectic musical hybrids incorporating African-Islamic styles. For instance, Moroccan Gnawa music has generated tremendous interest among Western jazz and rock musicians, resulting in creative fusions; Hasan Hakmoun is an important exponent (such as Hakmoun 1991, with acclaimed jazz trumpeter Don Cherry). Here, creative expression is emphasized over "authenticity"; if an Islamic message appears at all, it is that musical collaborations across cultural divides can facilitate social ones, and demonstrate the spiritual unity of mankind.

Finally, the international music industry and post-colonial connections often enable the uptake of local media scenes into the global market (al-Tuhami 1998; Gharib 2004; Tabala 1992); while *fuji* has remained relatively localized (as compared to other Nigerian genres, such as Afrobeat or juju), Islamically-tinged Senegalese popular music has brilliantly succeeded internationally, especially Youssou N'Dour (2004) who won a Grammy award for "Best Contemporary World Music Album" in 2004. International markets push such music in new directions, sometimes resulting in two versions of releases (local and global) (McLaughlin 1997, 576), or inducing artists to experiment creatively with new fusions (Aichi 2001; Fadhel Jaziri 2000). The striking success of many Muslim West African artists in a global popular music scene strongly conditioned by African-American, Afro-Latin, and Afro-Caribbean forms appears to support speculative arguments made by Gerhard Kubik and others that a large segment of the African diaspora across the Americas was Muslim (Kubik 1999).

Conclusion

From this diverse survey of Islamic music in Africa, several general conclusions can now be drawn. First is the remarkable diversity of Islamic sonic forms, as ritual practices adapt to local socio-cultural conditions, yet generally without any sense of sectarian fissioning, of having "left the faith." The flexibility of Islamic music — and sound generally — plays a critical role in such adaptation as Islamic performance contexts draw on local musical materials, and as musical materials stemming from the Middle East fuse with local musical structures, such as polyphonic drumming, polyrhythm, and pentatonicism. The "unity in diversity" which characterizes Islam in Africa may be attributed to a strong oral tradition coupled with decentralized religious authority, particularly in Sunni Islam, imposing minimal formal ritual and doctrinal requirements.

These requirements centre on discursive performance, allowing freer reign to local adaptation in non-discursive performative dimensions. Sound, operating largely outside Islamic discourse, whose details discourse is unable to precisely reference and therefore unable to precisely regulate, possesses the ability to adapt to local conditions through absorption of local practices. While the concept of "music" *(musiqa)*, usually implying instruments performed for entertainment, may occasionally be subjected to discursive sanctions, the more fundamental concept of "sound" (coupled with "text") remains active and vital, thinly veiled behind a myriad of terminological guises *(adhan, tajwid, inshad,* and *khutba)*. Music's power is all the greater for not being explicitly recognized as such.

The broader picture of Islamic performance is thus one of ramification in its sonic-social aspect, threaded throughout by common filaments of Arabic text, or at least core meanings, most centrally: *tawhid* (affirmation of God's unity), *ibtihalat* (supplication to God), *madih* (praise for His Prophet), and *tawassul* (petitions to Prophet and saints). It is the sense of connectedness, through a genealogical network of performance tradition, rather than uniformity of performance, which supports a common Muslim identity despite outward diversity.

Or, perhaps, because of it. The ability to adapt — which gives rise to the rich variegation of Islamic performative traditions — is also what has enabled Islam to expand by taking root in so many different cultural soils across Africa. In particular, the ability of music to adjust to local socio-cultural conditions, absorbing and transforming local performance materials, while nevertheless bearing core Islamic meanings, combined with the powerful "affecting presence" of socially performed and locally meaningful sound, representing Islam as a whole while remaining deeply enmeshed in local meaning and local sentiment, and thereby connecting, or at least mediating, between the broader world of Islam and other worlds (pre- or extra-Islamic) which impinge upon it, has enabled music to serve as a particularly effective agent of Islamic *da`wa* (missionizing).

Second is the palpable consistency of sound, text, and context across cultural, linguistic, and geographical regions, particularly within ritual and festival contexts, and the recurrence of sounds, textual themes, and performance occasions, albeit with local inflections. Whereas Sufi and (especially) sectarian forms vary more widely in meaning, social and festival contexts often feature the same meanings (expressed in local languages), while ritual contexts (centered on Arabic) vary primarily in sound.

Yet sonic-textual-social forms exhibit considerable consistency across broad geographical areas of Muslim Africa. Recurrent sonic features, throughout both Islamic music and music of Muslims more generally, includes centrality of highly ornamented, melismatic vocalizations; a tense vocal quality and high tessitura; Arabic-inflected tonality (including influence of the seven-toned microtonal modes called *maqamat*); emphasis upon solo, monophonic, or heterophonic textures; salience of poetry over dance; and use of characteristically Islamicate instruments, such as lutes, plucked or bowed. Textual features, especially the ubiquity of praise-song, have already been mentioned. Social-cultural features recur also: a general suspicion of unregulated music; restrictions on mixed-gender dance and female public performance; distinctive male and female repertoires; the appearance of a specialized and professionalized musician-caste and hereditary musician lineages, supported by aristocratic patrons; and centrality of praise-singers, especially as attached to political power. Ames' aforementioned observation of non-correlation between musical similarity and geographical distance (viz. the greater similarity between musicians' social position across Muslim Western Sudan than between Igbo and Hausa in Northern Nigeria) is a case in point (Ames 1973, 250-51, 272).

This consistency, which underpins a measure of Muslim cultural identity, reflects, in turn, the common fund of Islamic norms, meanings, contexts, and practices to which Muslims subscribe, the broad diffusion of Arabo-Islamic culture (crossing to sub-Saharan Africa from Arab North Africa, Egypt, and Arabia) which has infused Muslim-majority areas of East and West Africa (especially the specific practices of Qur'anic recitation and the call to prayer), and the long history of extensive interactions — economic, migrational, cultural, political — across the Muslim world, as supported by the common cultural substrate of Islam.

Third, it is clear that Islamic music reflects these interactions. Music is a sensitive barometer of social and historical conditions in Muslim societies, and for a sound reason: the "sound of Islam" is not merely an epiphenomenonal expression of Islamic faith. Rather, sonic-linguistic practices, what I am liberally calling "music" but might be better known as "language performance," along with the discourse (sometimes heated) surrounding them — including everything from *tajwid*, to *madih*, to prayer itself — are central to the Islamic religion, and to the construction and maintenance of faith of individual Muslims. Such practices, often occurring in intensively social and emotive contexts, inscribe and renew socio-spiritual relationships — to God, to the Prophet, to saints, and to other Muslims — by invoking them within an atmosphere of deeply felt meaning produced by sound and text performed together.

The sonic practices of Islam thus constitute a central site for the affectively charged social production of Islam, as locally inflected, as well as a site for the contestation of what it means to be a Muslim, and the construction of Islamic norms. In musical practice and discourse one observes ongoing debates about what Islam should be, in the broader context of interactions among local, regional, and global social forces. Music's barometric salience becomes most explicit when it emerges into public discourse as yet another instance of the "music polemic" (Nelson 1985), as accusations of heresy are flung against musicians or practices thought by some to deviate too far from Shari`a-sanctioned norms of devotion. But such debates are implicitly present elsewhere as well; for instance, in the striking divergence among ritual practices of Sufi orders in Cairo (Frishkopf 1999), or the silencing effects of contemporary Islamism, rejecting the more musical practices of recitation — especially as carried by the Sufi orders — and thrusting melodically conservative Saudi recitational practices to global prominence, thereby displacing their more traditional Egyptian counterparts (Frishkopf 2006). There is a musical reading of global Islamic politics.

What is striking too is the dearth of historiographic or ethnographic data, across time and space. Though a number of researchers have produced superb scholarship on Islamic musical practices, as indicated by the foregoing survey, coverage is spotty; vast terrains remain uncharted. This fact is linked to another — the undervaluing, within Islamic studies, of research on Muslim performance practices, especially the nuanced cultural modulations to be found even within the most central, and supposedly immutable, of Islamic rituals. While our historical picture of Islamic sound will ever remain incomplete, the contemporary ethnographic scene is far more open to inspection; indeed, a great deal of modern Muslim culture is partially self-documenting, via the local mass media.

A deeper understanding of Islam in Africa depends upon research, both intensive and extensive, of the many local interpretations of Islam. For this purpose, an understanding of the myriad expressive cultural practices carrying Islamic meanings is essential, because of the ability of such practices to represent, and to reproduce or contest, core concepts and social relations characterizing Muslim societies. Among these practices, music is central, due to its collective and affectively charged nature. An enormous amount of feasible research on contemporary Islamic musical practices remains to be carried out. This research promises to illuminate the interactions of local and global forces — ideological, political, or economic — now shaping Muslim societies throughout the region.

Notes

[1] Hodgson himself intended his neologism "Islamicate" to mean "'of or pertaining to' the society and culture of Islamdom," where "Islamdom" is "the society in which the Muslim and their faith are recognized as prevalent and socially dominant" (1974, 58).

[2] *Sahih Muslim* supports beating the *duff* (frame drum) for `Id celebrations. With its symbolism of the human body, and plaintive sound, the reed flute has been a fixture of many Sufi liturgies at least since the thirteenth century, when it was documented by Jalal al-Din Rumi's poetry and established in the ritual practice of the Sufi order founded in his name, the Mevleviyya.

Hidden in the Household: Gender and Class in the Study of Islam in Africa

E. Ann McDougall

Résumé

Le ménage, si on le conçoit comme un organisme dynamique doté de statuts multiples, d'une culture multiple, composé de plusieurs générations et des deux sexes, peut offrir un cadre conceptuel permettant de réinterpréter pratiques, processus et modèles d'islamisation de l'Afrique. Ce cadre contraste avec celui privilégié en littérature qui se concentre sur l'activité des commerçants, des religieux et des directeurs d'institutions publiques. Il nous rappelle qu'ils ont "vécu l'Islam" près de leurs mères, épouses, soeurs et esclaves dans le ménage. Cette première exploration préliminaire des femmes et esclaves considérées d'ordinaire comme marginales à l'islamisation se propose de défier les perceptions existantes: les femmes et esclaves ne sont pas que "réceptrices" de l'Islam, elles en sont aussi les agents. Dans leurs ménages, elles ont modelé la manière dont l'Islam a été vécu autour d'elles. Aussi, au lieu de ne considérer que l'histoire des personnalités et des lieux publics, l'intérêt porté au ménage et aux changements encourus au fil du temps peut nous permettre de voir une facette différente de l'Islam et des différents processus d'islamisation.

Abstract

The household, if understood in a dynamic multi-status, multi-generational, multi-cultural, "gendered" way, can provide a conceptual framework for reinterpreting practices, processes, and patterns of Islamization in Africa. This framework contrasts with the one privileged in literature that focuses on the agency of traders, clerics and chiefs in public institutions. It reminds us that they "lived Islam" next to their mothers, wives, sisters, and slaves in households. This preliminary exploration of women and slaves usually seen as marginal to Islamization is intended to challenge extant perceptions: women and slaves were not only "recipients" of Islam but its agents. In their households, they shaped how Islam was lived by all around them. So instead of looking only at the history of more public Islamic people and places, addressing attention to the household and its changing nature over time may allow us to see a different face of Islam and different process of Islamization.

Introduction

The History of Islam in Africa (Levtzion and Pouwels 2000a) is a remarkable collection, many years in the making, which assembles voices of key scholars working in the area of Islam and history in Africa. And thanks to the vision of its editors, it is even more. The introduction (Levtzion and Pouwels 2000b)[1] echoes the understanding Nehemia Levtzion developed over a long career of how and why Islam became rooted throughout the continent over many millennia.[2] This lifetime of exploring different facets of Islam's history in Africa clearly fashions the lens through which readers are asked to read *Islam in Africa*'s subsequent twenty-four chapters. It is a lens that, in turn, focuses attention on a combination of patterns of Islamic expansion and varieties of Islamic experience: it has a strong geographical character (patterns as they emerge in different regions of Africa) and an equally strong emphasis on process (experience as measured through conversion). Across time and space, readers encounter stories of how and why African merchants, politicians, diplomats, scholars, and "holy men" — Africa's royal, upper and middle classes — became Muslim and in turn shaped African history.[3] These are, without exception, stories of "progress" in which the processes of Islamization move Braudelian-style — in simultaneous historical "moments" moving at different speeds and different societal levels — towards fully Muslim societies. What this means in any given moment or place varies greatly; as the introduction states: "the *advance* of Islam has profoundly influenced religious beliefs and practices of African societies, while local traditions have `Africanized' Islam" (Levtzion and Pouwels 2000a, ix [my emphasis]). Nevertheless, Levtzion and Pouwels (2000b, 2-4) make it clear that, ultimately, "progress" is achieved when the traditional or the pre-Islamic can be overcome. "Africanized Islam" — in spite of the attention given to the dynamics of conversion — remains a less-clearly articulated concept than "Islam in Africa." And "Islam in Africa," Africanized or not, remains firmly within the domain of trade, politics, and war (Levtzion and Pouwels 2000a, ix).

To elaborate, the model of "Islamization" presented derives from Levtzion and Pouwels' understanding of conversion. They argue that while merchants opened "routes" (through the "gateways" of north and east Africa, the title of the first section), they merely exposed Africans to Islam; "conversion to Islam was the work of men of religion, communicating primarily with local rulers. The latter were often the first recipients of Islamic influence," underscoring the importance of "states" in the process. In turn, rulers and associated aristocracies took a middle position between the Muslims who "helped them" and "the rest" who remained attached to traditional beliefs (Levtzion and Pouwels 2000b, 2). Out of this situation developed a "negotiated Islam" where people either publicly proclaimed Islam and privately continued to "fear fetishes" or sought a symbiotic relation between the traditional and the Muslim (Levtzion and Pouwels 2000b, 3). A sort of structural parallelism prevailed: "Muslim clerics who rendered religious services to Islamized chiefs became integrated into the sociopolitical system of the state by playing roles similar to those of traditional priests"; clerics were neutral like priests, and mosques resembled shrines in function (Levtzion and Pouwels 2000b, 3). Over time, these clerics and saints *(wali)* taught rulers, but even so, many remained "unable to relieve the monarchy of pre-Islamic heritage"; in many instances, those who became "too Muslim" were deposed or killed (Levtzion and Pouwels 2000b, 4). The historical watershed occurred in the seventeenth and eighteenth centuries, when Islamic learning moved from the town (where rulers and learned teachers lived) to the countryside. It was "rural" Islamic scholarship that gave rise to a new class of Muslims — those who took up *jihad* against those urban literates who had incompletely embraced Islam (Levtzion and Pouwels 2000b, 10, 11).[4]

> The challenge to the marginal role of Islam in African societies did not come from "ulama" [learned men] who were spokesmen for the traders, nor from clerics who rendered religious services in the chiefly courts; it came mostly from the autonomous rural and pastoral enclaves (Levtzion and Pouwels 2000b, 11).

The editors emphasize the role of emergent vernacular Islamic literature — in particular, poetry and oral renderings of Islamic thought — in popularizing Islam among the illiterate peasants and pastoralists of those enclaves (Levtzion and Pouwels 2000b, 12). In these ways, changing realities of conversion shaped both the patterns and the progress of Islamization.

Historians of Africa will recognize in this approach a well-entrenched framework that gives organizational priority to region — the traditional North, West, East and South Africa, and places thematic emphasis on power-related activities like state building, commerce, politics, religious hierarchies, and war. Most will also note that this traditional approach is one that is both elitist and male oriented: because it concerns itself with activities that were largely (though not exclusively) the domain of men — and men primarily of middle and/or upper classes; it privileges an elitist, male world-view. Put another way, if it is assumed that the essentials of Islamization were processes and patterns of conversion that were in the hands of "learned religious men," "successful merchants," and "powerful chiefs," then Islamization by definition becomes an understanding of what these men did and why and how they did it. In this case, the tendency to adopt this perspective is strengthened by the fact that Islam itself is usually understood as a patriarchal, patrilineal ideology.[5] It seems legitimate to ask, then: to what extent can this model incorporate practices and experiences of conversion that are not about traditionally recognized power, whether gender or class defined? One might equally pose the question: how might such alternative practices and experiences reshape or challenge the existing model?

Gender, Class and "Islamization"

The editors give few indications as to how they might respond to the first question. In the introduction, apart from an indirect reference to "spouses and their relatives" converting in the context of East Central African trade (Levtzion and Pouwels 2000b, 7), women literally enter the picture only during the last section addressing colonial rule. And even in this context, women are merely observed taking an active part in popular movements and preaching to other women, among a range of voluntary services. The most significant impact they are credited with having on the practice of Islam is creating what came to be known as "the women's pilgrimage" — the off-season journey to Mecca that was largely populated by women (Levtzion and Pouwels 2000b, 15). As for non-elites, other than taking up the anonymous role of those who occupied the above-mentioned "rural and pastoral enclaves" (presumably the non-literate peasants and herders responding to the process of "popularization"),[6] we see them referenced, on occasion, as slaves. In this model, slaves are either the cause of Islam's lack of progress (only non-Muslims can be legitimately enslaved; therefore, territories regularly raided for slaves marked the frontiers of *Dar al-Islam*) (Levtzion and Pouwels 2000b, 5), or its embracers as an expression of resistance to Christian masters (this in what is presented as an unusual situation, addressed only in the chapter on South Africa) (Levtzion and Pouwels 2000b, 7).

The geographically and chronologically organized core of the book (some fourteen chapters) does not provide that much more material with which to engage the question, but that which is offered up is very suggestive. For example, in the context of West Africa and the rise of eighteenth- and nineteenth-century *jihads*, David Robinson highlights the role of the use of vernacular languages in expanding the audience receptive to a revitalized Islam.[7] He notes that in the Futa Jalon such literature was primarily in Pulaar (not Arabic): "much of it was designed for recitation and the edification of the women, slaves and other less literate members of the population" (Robinson 2000b, 134). Similarly, in Northern Nigeria (Sokoto), such literature was written in Fulbe and Hausa, again, intended for recitation to the "less literate — women, slaves, farmers, pastoralists." Key texts were copied and circulated to other parts of the savanna, becoming the "Sokoto model" of *jihad*. In both regions, and in spite of being "contained in a patriarchical framework," free women could be teachers and pedagogues (Robinson 2000b, 134, 138-39). Probably the most famous of these who made "vital contributions" to vernacular literature was Nana Asma'u, daughter of *jihadist* Uthman dan Fodio:

> ... encouraged by father, brother, and husband [she] developed organization and pedagogy to reach the women of the region.... By her poetry in Fulfulde, Hausa and Arabic, and by her training of teachers, she probably accomplished more thorough going Islamization in the northwestern part of Hausaland than anyone else in the caliphate (Robinson 2000b, 138-39).

According to Robinson, Nana Asma'u was promoting a particular form or "version" of Islam over what was at the time regarded as "traditional" *(bori)* belief.[8] What is also striking here is that there was a collaborative effort to incorporate "women, slaves, pastoralists, farmers" between Nana Asma'u and her male family; it was recognized that this audience needed to understand Islam not only in a local language because of their illiteracy but through a different genre, the oral recitation of poetry. Both practice and process were reshaped to respect different worldviews and to respond to different local belief systems, central of which in both the Futa Jalon and the broader savanna were those of women and slaves.[9]

A second set of material can be drawn from the East and East /

Central African region. The "conversion model" is presented as evolving in a different pattern in this region, as well as at a later date, effectively the nineteenth century. The "slow process of Islamization" moved beyond coastal regions only as Africans who had converted in the coastal urban environments returned home to the interior with the growth of the ivory and slave trade. This commerce, in turn, was buttressed by the arrival of new merchants and landowners who invested in Islam (mosques, schools), the rise of sufi brotherhoods and the development of the Omani "empire" based on the prosperous island of Zanzibar. Levtzion and Pouwels note that even in this environment,

> ... not many Africans accepted Islam.... Those who converted were mostly members of the immediate entourage of the Arab and Swahili merchants: spouses and their relatives, porters and other employees of the merchants (Levtzion and Pouwels 2000b, 7)

Yet the emphasis here remains firmly on the traders as agents and trade as practice.

The reference given for this "slow process" is David Sperlings' fascinating chapter on the hinterland. A few examples will suffice to argue that his material is far more revealing of both process and practice than the introduction suggests, and with some probing, far more provocative in terms of our understanding of "the model." The above statement about the immediate entourage of merchants is made in the context of discussing the major trading centres of the interior (Tabora and Ujiji) and commenting upon the "surprising lack of Islamization" in the area; while difficult to define, Sperling points to "an apparent lack of interest among most Muslim traders in spreading their religion."[10] He then goes on to note that Africans who adopted Islam were generally "wives [of Arabs and Swahili] and sometimes relations of their wives, retainers or porters, and slaves" (Sperling 2000, 289).[11] Wives and slaves — each category of converts plays a significant role in Sperlings' account. In fact, numerous examples of Islamization being driven by Muslim merchants marrying local African (non-Muslim) women are provided, ranging from the coastal region of Mombassa to the deep interior. The process of "rural Islamization" he dates largely to the latter nineteenth century and to the "remigration" of urban converts, just as Levtzion and Pouwels outline. But the actual Islamization in each instance can be located in the heart of newly-formed households. In the case of the Segeju and Vumba Swahili, the latter settled near Segeju villages, took Segeju wives, and the children of these marriages were brought up as Muslims; other Segeju (friends? relatives?) "must have been attracted" as well.

Thus the Seguju came to be among the first indigenous African people of the coastal hinterland to adopt Islam on a large scale, and this was not so much because of trading contacts but as a result of close relations arising out of interspersed settlement and intermarriage (Sperling 2000, 282).[12]

A similar situation is described between the Swahili and Sigua of the Mrima Coast hinterland and between the Digo and the Tangana Swahili (south of Mombasa) (Sperling 2000, 282).[13]

A few interesting observations are relevant here. First, in the case of the Digo and Tangana, an early twentieth-century observer noted:

Side by side with Mohammedan practices, they continue their tribal religious observances. Most of their wives and women folk are pagans and their husbands do not seem to consider it necessary for them to be anything else (Sperling 2000, 282).

This led Sperling to conclude: "They [Digo Muslims] seem to have had no difficulty leading their traditional way of life and responding to the demands of their new faith"; from the 1870s, the number of Digo Muslims increased gradually but steadily; while continuing to live in their villages, "[they] would go to pray in neighbouring Tanzania mosques." While the outside observer saw Islam literally in the persons of the men who would have been praying in the mosques and, by default, "paganism" in the "women folk" who remained in the villages, Sperling eschews such simplification in acknowledging that there was a dynamic created in the early marriages that "gradually but steadily" created Muslims of the Digo. Children were clearly being brought up Muslim (creating the generation of Digo Muslims, undoubtedly men, who went to pray in neighbouring mosques), as well as the next generation of Digo Muslim women. The observer, in attributing "paganism" to the women, overlooks his own comment that "they" continue their tribal religious observances, "side by side with Mohamedan practices." Men and women were experiencing Islam within an environment that women ensured continued to protect their cultural "tradition" (Sperling 2000, 282).[14]

There is another point of relevance here, raised by Edward Alpers in his related chapter: everywhere in East and East Central Africa this "culture" was matrilineal.[15] Alpers notes the same strategies as

Sperling in terms of the role of intermarriage between Muslim merchants and "local" women in the "initial expansion of Islam in Macuana" but concludes that "since Makua culture was strongly matrilineal, it is not at all clear that such marriages ought to be considered as part of a pattern of Islamic conversion" (Alpers 2000, 306). In effect, he (like Sperling, above) then goes on to show very clearly why indeed they were central to this region's "pattern of conversion." He notes how Islamic and indigenous forms of belief were gradually being "mediated," giving examples of law,[16] initiation ceremonies, and mourning (Alpers 2000, 313). He also comments on Swahili scribes and traders as being important "not least for their knowledge of Islamic charms" (Alpers 2000, 308), again suggesting a resonance with "traditional" beliefs that facilitated the mediation he identifies. As Sperling's evidence suggests, the arena in which such mediation occurred was the household and the "traditional" village — the reproductive sites of matrilineal society.[17]

This raises yet a third point — where, exactly, Islamic teaching, learning, and praying took place. As Sperling notes, outsiders looked for signifiers of Islam such as mosques and Qur'anic schools, and tended to conclude that people were not Muslims in the absence of these institutions (Sperling 2000, 275-76, 289). While to some extent accepting this association in the early parts of the chapter,[18] he cautions against the weakness of such sources by referencing the fact that such practices were undoubtedly going on unobserved in the privacy of homes (providing the example of Zanzibaris) (Sperling 2000, 289).[19] Alpers is even more explicit. He accepts that "Islam was spreading peacefully by Muslim traders" but specifies that the local holy men *(walimu)* and *shurfa*, "with their religio-magical knowledge," as well as "innumerable *mafundi* (masters)" were teaching village children "in any hut, on a veranda or under the shade of a tree as school" (Alpers 2000, 309), largely out of sight or recognition of European visitors. "Huts" and "verandas" again situate the locus of process and practice back in the household. Sperling concludes that "because of the limitation of our sources and consequent lack of knowledge, the history of Islam necessarily lies hidden behind the secular and commercial activities whose details are so much better known" (2000, 289). That said, looking more closely at how matrilineal societies and the women who were powerful in them actually "mediated" between Islam and traditional culture just might reveal more of what "lies hidden" than we have recognized to date.[20]

Sperling's observations about Muslim converts also included attention to "non-elites" — specifically to slaves. Indeed, his chapter deals more extensively with them than any other, but just as sources for "hidden teaching and learning" pose a problem for historians, Sperling notes that "the practice of Islam by slaves is not well documented" either.

> Illiteracy was high, opportunities for learning few, and knowledge of the faith rudimentary. Slave villages had no Qur'an schools, and slaves and the children of slaves had little chance to learn about their faith. Slaves who lived in town had better access to education and sometimes studied to quite high standards.... But even slaves without a solid grounding in Islamic doctrine acquired a veneer of Muslim attitudes and practice.... [According to a European observer, they] "sometimes learn by rote sufficient of the Koran, though in an unknown tongue to them, to take part with their betters in the religious exercises of the mosque" (2000, 280).

One cannot help but be struck by the fact that these measures of "being Muslim" echo some of the issues Sperling addresses elsewhere as being perhaps over-emphasized (for example, the presence of mosques and schools). They also resonate with Robinson's evidence discussed above regarding those who learned without Arabic literacy and the role such people played in the process of Islamization in West Africa. And finally, one might be tempted to comment that the description of slaves learning the Qur'an "by rote, in an unknown tongue [Arabic]" correlates well with the description of any non-Arabic speaking *talibe* (student) — slave or free — learning to be Muslims in a Qur'anic school or mosque.

In spite of the doubts his initial discussion of slaves and conversion might raise about this sector of society being significant to the "model," Sperling's actual evidence argues strongly to the contrary. For example, when he recounts that slaves were among the "entourage of Swahili and Arabs" who converted in the Tabora-Ujiji region, he notes these "Islamized Manyema slaves" were sufficiently large in number that "the town [was] as much like a plantation as [a] trading settlement" (Sperling 2000, 288).[21] Alpers adds to this impression. He notes that in the mid-eighteenth century the Portuguese restricted Muslims in Mozambique from acquiring new slaves because "Muslim owners indoctrinated the slaves with `their damned Mohammedan faith'" (2000, 305). A century later, no attempts had been made to convert free Makonde at Cape Delgado, but Makonde slaves on the coast had become Muslims (Alpers 2000, 307). He also notes two significant institutional developments deriving from conversion practices that built on the region's tradition of slavery. First, while noting the "challenges" that Islam posed for matrilineal kinship and inheritance practices in East Central Africa, he also recounted one "mediation" that permitted the Yao to benefit from both the new and the old: chiefs quickly discovered how to exploit Islamic "patrilateral means" of inheritance to attach slave women and children to their own matrilineages (Alpers 2000, 313). Second, north of Quelimane, schools were established that recruited students from the coast:

> When a child enters that school, the first condition that is imposed on him is to embrace the religion of Mohammed, then the father of the child accepts the obligation to furnish a domestic servant to the Arabs as a slave when the child has completed his studies — normally three years.... On completion of his studies the disciple takes the name of *Malimu* and is a *doctor*. Upon fulfillment of payment by his father, he then returns to his kin and his people and exercises his art among them (Alpers 2000, 308 [emphasis in the original]).

Alpers comments that this is "solid evidence" of a missionary strategy for Islam; he might also have noted that it was one firmly rooted in East African slavery and ultimately would have had the impact of linking coastal and hinterland Islam through the expansion of that institution, as well as through the concomitant expansion of Muslim education (2000, 308-09).[22]

A final point, significant in its comparison with the West African situation described by Robinson: both women and slaves could be teachers and *walimu*. Sperling (2000, 280) identifies one of the last *liwali* of Mombasa as having been a slave,[23] and Alpers describes the Shaykh who introduced the Qadiriyya brotherhood to Malawi in 1929 as "the most important woman in Malawi Islamic history."[24] Having studied and received her credentials in Zanzibar, "her leadership and teaching brought many women into an active role in the revitalized *umma* [Muslim religious community] through the use of *tariqa* [brotherhood] banners, *dhiker* [trance-inducing singing] and occasions for collective religious celebration" (Alpers 2000, 312-13). While we, unfortunately, are told nothing about how being of slave background might have shaped the Shaykh's experience or his influence in the "Islamization" of Mombasa, clearly the Malawian Shaykh had, like Nana Asma'u, responded as a woman to the needs of potential female converts. Where the latter had attempted, with the "Sokoto model," to use vernacular language and local forms of poetry to compete with traditional belief practices like *bori*, the former incorporated such practices as *dhikr* (religious recitations of the names of "God" that lead to a trance-like condition; tied to mysticism, not orthodox practices) into an Islam women would be attracted to (one with collective ceremonies, dancing not unlike *bori* custom, and symbols like banners). What is significant about these two cases is the fact that each Shaykh — one a slave, one a woman — was an integral part of the larger process of Islamization taking place in their respective regions. They, their practices, the experiences of those who followed them, have to be incorporated into the "model" we use. Either that — or the model has to be reshaped such that they can be fully embraced.

Such a path is more easily identified than followed, it would appear, given the strength of current gender and class readings of the evidence. In the final section of the book (disappointingly entitled "General Themes"),[25] there is no chapter exploring the "theme" of class — or more specifically slaves — and Islam.[26] There is, however, a brief but highly impressive contribution dealing with "Muslim women" by Roberta Ann Dunbar (2000, 373-96). In light of the discussion above, I would argue that it constitutes one of the most important points of departure in *Islam in Africa*. In terms of content, it fleshes out much of the material I have teased from Robinson, Sperling, and Alpers above; essentially it adds many more women and their activities to the Levtzion-Pouwels "model." But it stands out precisely because it argues that simply adding more women to the equation is not enough. Dunbar concludes:

> The relationship between religion and other aspects of their life [Muslim women in sub-Saharan Africa] is complex. It is shaped by contextual elements of ideology, social structure and political economy, on the one hand and by women's strategies on the other.... Differences of demography, underlying social structures, the age of Islam and colonial history account for regional differences in women's experience of Islam to a greater degree than particular features of Muslim ideology. That does not mean, however, that ideology lacks importance.... This is particularly

visible in the domain of law and the state.... Family law often lies at the frontier of ... debates [between Islamic and secular law / authority] because it touches people close to home. The status of women more than that of men is linked to family law because of their centrality to the biological and cultural reproduction of the system....

... While the processes of these developments require further study, these features characterize Islam *and* Muslim women. If the exercise of condensing such rich and varied experience into so few pages has any merit, it is to broaden our conceptualization of Islam as well as to embrace our understanding of the condition of Muslim women (Dunbar 2000, 412-13 [emphasis in original])

We must "use Muslim women's lived experiences of Islam to influence our conceptualization of Islam": this is essentially the challenge Dunbar issues to readers and to the "model" the editors currently offer up. In the remainder of this article, I would like to engage with that challenge, expanding it to embrace both women and slaves along the lines suggested to us by the chapters by Robinson, Sperling, and Alpers. I have chosen to draw on the experiences of three Muslim women living, respectively, in North, West, and East Africa during the twentieth century; they represent, between them, lives of both freedom and slavery. The stories are not new — indeed Baba, Bi Kaje, and Fatma are probably familiar to most readers interested in Muslim African women and/or slaves.[27] However, their lived experiences as recounted in the published versions of their lives have yet to be interrogated in terms of what it meant to be Muslim from their gender and class perspectives and, in turn, how these perspectives might help us reshape our own with respect to understanding "lived Islam."[28] The material teased out of *Islam in Africa* (above) drew primarily on the late eighteenth and nineteenth centuries; the lives of Baba, Bi Kaje, and Fatma move us into the colonial era and beyond — an evolution of the processes and practices discussed above. These explorations are preliminary and tentative but hopefully they will succeed in "engaging with the legacy" of Nehemia Levtzion in a way that will stimulate further discussion and further debate.

Lives of Women, Lives of Slaves: "Lived Experiences of Islam"

"Baba of Karo" (1877-1951, "Woman of the Muslim Hausa,"

NORTHERN NIGERIA)
To understand Islam as Baba appears to have lived it is to understand her experience as wife, co-wife, mother, and slave owner on a daily basis. Islam seems to have impinged upon her reality primarily in terms of prayer — not because she prayed (she actually never mentions herself or other women praying),[29] but because prayers ordered daily routine and work.[30] Her account of her own life, ceremonies and rituals, her husband and/or the household slaves, is repeatedly ordered with reference to prayers: what is done before them, between them, after them; how women's and slaves' labour was organized in terms of different prayers; how children's studying of the Qur'an was similarly scheduled (Smith 1954, 120, 131-34). When she was married to an Islamic teacher (*alim* or *malam* in Hausaland), Islam also marked the seasons. After the harvest was in, she traveled with her husband and a group of young students *(talibe)* for several months, staying in different towns while he both taught and learned. She did little or no work during this time, visiting with the women in the families with whom they stayed, living largely on the alms given to her husband (Smith 1954, 131-34). Other than this, she was secluded during her adult life and her concerns were largely those of food (and organizing the labour to make sure it was prepared) and rituals like marriage, divorce, and childbirth. In her world, the most important aspect governed by Islam seems to have been *iddah*, the period of time a woman had to remain celibate and secluded after divorcing and before remarrying. This Islamic requirement (that was meant to ensure the divorcée was not pregnant)[31] played a huge role in Baba's life because she spent so much time involved in facilitating marriages and divorces; in a society where multiple marriages in one's lifetime was the norm, it clearly was an important part of all women's lives, determining where and how they would live for much of them (Smith 1954, 25, 48, 111, 130, 152-53, 167, 171, 179, 259 note 3, 270 note 21). Islamic judges *(qadis)* also intruded upon her reality primarily in terms of the decisions they made regarding the divorces of Baba's friends and relations — if these respected legal voices had another role in society, one would never know it from Baba's account (Smith 1954, 107-08, 165, 170-82). It is interesting, however, that while Baba mentioned covering her face and head while traveling (so that she could peek out but no one could see her), it was only because it was so rare that she spoke of it — when secluded, this was not an issue (Smith 1954, 132).[32] Nor did she seem to link being

veiled or secluded to her religion. In fact, she noted that some men secluded their wives and others did not, even within the same neighbourhood. She seemed to associate seclusion more with being urban than anything else, noting that "in Kano" men secluded their wives with nice food and lovely clothes but did not permit visits outside even with their kinfolk (a particularly "bad" thing in her view and not true of seclusion in her area) (Smith 1954, 80). And in recounting that one of her husbands had paid boys to fetch firewood and water for her and her co-wife until, when he fell ill, they were no longer confined to the compound and went out to fetch wood and water themselves, she suggested indirectly that seclusion was also an issue of status and labour availability (Smith 1954, 210-11).[33]

Consciousness of "being Muslim" was most prevalent when she spoke about slaves. On one occasion she commented to her interviewer, Mary Smith, that if a slave had four wives, he was probably Muslim; she mentioned that masters freed slaves in order to be rewarded: "It is like giving alms," she said. "But if masters of slaves do not attend to religion, they did not do it [manumit] at all" (Smith 1954, 40). Slaves were inherited like all other property; her story is peppered with mentions of how a man would inherit two slaves, a woman one. She pointed out to Smith that the important process of dividing up slaves was according to Islamic law but slaves could not, themselves, inherit (Smith 1954, 39-40, 75, 119). This aspect of "being Muslim" was central to her reality and to women in general, because of the important role that slaves played in their lives. Baba emphasized in particular how children born to family slaves were "freed" after their Islamic naming ceremony and considered "kin." By this she did not mean "free" but rather "special" with rights that purchased slaves did not enjoy.

> We took part in one another's ceremonies, there was "Kinship" ...
> If we had a ceremony, they all brought things to give us; if they had one we all took things to them ... (Smith 1954, 40, 42).[34]

She did speak of slaves who were fully freed: for example, the one she had been given. The process of "adoption" was an Islamic one with *malams* and sacrifices and prayers involved. The slave was given a new name (a "free Muslim" name — in this case "Allah the Remedy" became "Usuman") and became his former master's son. He, in turn, gave his new "son" to Baba to be her child (she was infertile), "just as if I had born him" (Smith 1954, 122).[35] Issues of birth and children were intricately linked to Allah and his name was invoked on many occasions to assure conception and successful deliverance of children (Smith 1954, 124, 142, 145). Again, Baba's personal situation as an infertile woman underscores even more strongly in what ways Islam was central to life: it brought children or created them from slaves. Children of slaves married to each other were considered Muslim, regardless of the faith of their parents, and were given a name at the seventh-day naming ceremony (Smith 1954, 40, 257 note 6). Frequently, slaves had what Baba called "double names" — most seem to have in some fashion invoked "Allah" or Islam: "Gift of Allah," "Wealth belongs to Allah," "May Allah prolong our father's life" or, as in Usuman's case "Allah the Remedy" (Smith 1954, 50).[36] It was their master's religious duty to see that they were brought up Muslim (Smith 1954, 257 note 6).[37]

There are three particularly interesting elements in Baba's life history that reflect upon more orthodox views of "women and Islam." First, there is the degree to which the presence of the British seems to have had no impact on how Baba lived or experienced Islam. Even in connection with slavery, she argues that most slaves (and certainly most of their slaves) "continued to live as before" (Smith 1954, 67, 128);[38] they, in turn, continued to treat their slaves as before. Nothing in her account suggests that the rituals involved in the childbirth, marriage, or freeing of slaves changed, even when slaves were in principle "freed" in law. She gave no indication of being aware that the British in any way interfered with Islamic law or its practice by *qadis*. Other than providing peace so that she and her husband could travel on their annual teaching circuit, and putting an end to kidnappings in which anyone could be taken for purposes of being ransomed back, from her perspective, the British had no impact whatsoever on life in Northern Nigeria.[39]

Second is the degree to which Islam did not provide a sense of common identity with the other Muslim group in the area, the Fulani, even in the context of British (Christian) colonial Nigeria. She very strongly and clearly differentiated herself, her family, and her "people" from the "cattle Fulani." Indeed, from her account it would be difficult to know that they were Muslim, let alone the "orthodox" group who had carried out the *jihad* of Shaykh Uthman dan Fodio in the early nineteenth century. She portrayed them as "having no humanity" because they did not pass children around the kin-group in forms of pseudo-adoption as did the Hausa. Fulani "have no compassion"; they have "no human feelings," they "are not good people. They care only for themselves and their own children. According to Baba, only when they married Hausa women did they begin to adopt and "become better people" (Smith 1954, 127-28). The only "interaction" she recognized was the selling of grain to them as they passed during the season in which they pastured cattle in the region (Smith 1954, 119). Intermarriage, while it did occur, was rare and frowned upon (Smith 1954, 146).

And lastly, there was the integration of *bori* (spirit possession) and "charms" into her experience of Islam. While she noted that the men did not like to have *bori* practiced in their hamlet (Smith 1954, 43) and that chiefs publicly objected to it, she just as often talked about the presence of prostitutes known to be involved in *bori* coming to the compounds (Smith 1954, 43, 63). A relative of hers was even welcomed back as a wife after spending years in the city in a "*bori* brothel" (Smith 1954, 135). She also recounted how *bori* spirits (one, somewhat surprisingly, a Muslim named Malam al-Haji) were involved in the creation of their new village and how expert *bori* dancers had been called upon by the Chief to help generate an active market (Smith 1954, 219-21).

> [The Chief] likes *bori* but only in private, because he is afraid.... All of the rulers like the *bori* — if they didn't, would their work be any good? Of course they all agree with them ... (Smith 1954, 222).

She went on to explain at some length how *bori* and *malams* co-existed, in one instance tying the concept to seclusion:

> Of course they [chiefs] all agree with them [*bori* spirits]. So do the *malams*, secretly. The *malams* call on the *bori* in private, in the darkness at night. Everyone wants spirits, kings and noblemen want them, *malams* and wives shut away in compounds — it is with them that we work in this world, without them would our labour be of any use? The work of the *malams* is one thing, the work of *bori* experts is another, each has his own kind of work and they must not be mixed up ... (Smith 1954, 222).[40]

To some extent this could be viewed as consistent with the orthodox view of "*bori*" existing as a "remnant" of earlier beliefs, as contrasted with the reformed Islam Nana Asma'u attempted to teach for example, or as referenced by European observers talking of "pagan" women folk in East Central Africa. But there is a sense here that this is really a shared Islamic reality in which everyone accepted the broad framework and participated at different times in life and in different ways, in its articulation — more along the lines of my interpretation of Sperling's evidence (above), of living Islam within a "traditional" cultural environment in which women were key "mediators." And in this case, ironically, the ostensibly Islamic practice of seclusion, according to Baba, promoted the clearly non-Islamic invoking of *bori*. This interpretation tends to be reinforced by Baba's casual mentioning of "charms" that were used to bring run-away women home (including the above-mentioned relative who had lived in a *bori* brothel). These were drawn up by *malam* (in this case, her father and, on another occasion, one of her husbands who was also a *malam*) (Smith 1954, 135-37). There is no question that this particular magic united the sexes and was the base of a particular power men exercised over women, a power greater than any given in law. And it would seem that, at least in Baba's world, it was resorted to frequently. Baba attributed to this power the fact that her relative stayed in seclusion for fifteen years with her father, even after she had been on her own for so long "in town."

Another version of this kind of "sharing" of so-called magic concerned the important issue of conception. Baba talked about various ways to prevent pregnancy (including wearing a kola nut around one's waist [Smith 1954, 148]); most interesting was "writing medicine" — when a *malam* wrote out a text from the Qur'an on a slate, washed off the ink, and gave it to the woman to drink. Baba implied that only greedy *malams* did this but she also gave the impression that like the use of "charms," this was not uncommon. It was also used to encourage conception. Baba knew this first hand because, in her childless condition, she had tried it. She had also tried drinking *bori* medicine; neither delivered the desired result. She subsumed both failures, equally, to the will of Allah: "you can only have that which Allah gives you — isn't that so? That's your destiny" (Smith 1954, 179). For Baba, this may have been the most important of all internalizations of Islam, given the absolute centrality of reproduction to the identity of a Hausa woman and, as Dunbar reminded us (above), of the centrality, in turn, of that biological reproduction to the cultural continuity of society. It also exemplified that sense of a shared set of beliefs between men and women, between *bori* and *malam* medicine, that marked "lived" Islam.[41]

One last observation concerns what seems to be an unusual (if not unique) custom: the marriage of alms. Baba mentions this peculiar marriage in which a woman was given as alms to a *malam* without the usual bride-price payment by the groom's kin (Smith 1954, 99, 100). On one occasion, her family participated in a marriage ceremony in the morning (wherein the woman was "married" to a representative of the Prophet) only to find out in the evening that the "bride" was being given to them (and that was the way she expressed it — to "them," the family, not just to her husband) (Smith 1954, 129). On another occasion, a relative of Baba's had run away from a marriage of alms and this was seen as a very serious breach of community that reflected badly on the family (Smith 1954, 151-52). In terms of what it meant to Baba to be Muslim, we see it articulated on every page as she emphasized the centrality of "family" to life and her role in that family. But in her last thoughts recorded with Smith, she spoke of marrying off her adopted daughter. "I should prefer to give her as alms" she said,

> I haven't many children so I should like to give her to a good *malam*, a student but a young man, because maidens don't like old men; then we should give her as alms. I should be happy ... [and] if it is a marriage of alms, our kinsfolk will all help me.

In this wish, we see what being a good Muslim woman meant to Baba, in the context of being Hausa, in the 1940s: Islam as it was being lived and experienced aided women like Baba (as well as those in families poorer than hers) and put issues of family and reproduction at the forefront.

"Bi Kaje" (1890-1981/82, Swahili Woman of Mombasa, Kenya)

The account of Bi Kaje's life in Mombasa is considerably shorter and less revealing than that of Baba's (Mirza and Strobel 1989, 1-65); however, there are some interesting parallels. She too was Muslim, freeborn, and conscious of her "superior" identity, culturally speaking. Whereas Baba expressed that identity in the context of neighbouring Fulani Muslims, Bi Kaje did so in terms of the origins of Arab settlement on the coast. She claimed descent from the original "twelve tribes" who were responsible for integrating strangers to the land; interestingly she said they had not initially intermarried with "foreign Arabs":

> This is not their place. When the Arab came in the past and wanted a wife, he couldn't marry someone's daughter from here. If he came, he would be told "Who is this person?" We didn't want

intermarriage with those Arabs. Perhaps he was a slave back home" (Mirza and Strobel 1989, 28).
However, they did marry *shurfa*, those who claimed direct descent from the prophet:

... those *masharifu* mix with people from here. We accept them. We can't refuse the *masharifu* (Mirza and Strobel 1989, 28).

With this statement, she was both establishing the key role of women as the agents of coastal integration and linking this process with a "pure" Islam. This was also meant as a repudiation of the recently-arrived Omani Arabs who she considered to be as much outsiders as the earlier strangers of whom she spoke. She insists they did not automatically receive respect (Mirza and Strobel 1989, 18, 19).[42] Her account of origin also placed marriage at the centre of "being a good Muslim." This association was made explicit in Bi Kaje's explanation of the intricate kinship relations that defined her life.[43] Moreover, just as Baba's account illustrated how central maternal relations remained in the practice of marriage, childbirth, and divorce, Bi Kaje's led Mirza and Strobel to comment on the same phenomenon "despite [the] strong patrilineal bias[es] of Islam" (1989, 18). The cultural matrilineality we observed in earlier accounts of this region (and discussed above), seem to have continued in the twentieth century to negotiate successfully the patrilineal world of Islam.

It is also notable that much of Bi Kaje's identity, both as a Muslim and as a woman, was tied to slaves and slavery (Mirza and Strobel 1989, 30-40). She spoke extensively of the slaves in her family, of how they were divided between sons and daughters (although her divisions did not so neatly reflect Islamic inheritance practices as had Baba's), and of the distinctive status of "slaves of the household" — those born to the family or of "mixed" slave-free marriages rather than those purchased in the market. And she used similar terminology: where Baba spoke of children born of household slaves as being "freed" to the family and as being "kin," Bi Kaje declared directly that they were not slaves. They were *mzalia*.

Among us, if a person is an *mzalia* once or twice [that is, in terms of generations] you treat them like your own child, if you like.... they say: two times an *mzalia* and their father is a freeborn man. But they keep the slave name because the grandmother was purchased [she is speaking of a particular slave history here]. We say you let them free. You write, "This person is free. He is neither my slave nor anyone else's. I will not make him serve." Now you have set him or her free; he or she is a freed slave, an *mzalia* of the lineage, and is not a person to be ordered about.... You seclude her [if a female] like your own child (Mirza and Strobel 1989, 33).[44]

While she is not as explicit as Baba in linking this lineage extension to religious conversion, it is understood here in the reference to seclusion. Indeed, she gives the impression that conversion was the definition of "freedom" and that with respect to female slaves, seclusion was the mark of their "freed" status (Mirza and Strobel 1989, 33).[45] In another section of her account, she addresses "becoming Muslim" more directly:

A person says, "I want to become a Muslim," along with his wife. He will convert, he will become a Muslim, he will be taken to the mosque, he prays, he fasts during *Ramadan*. Now, if he has a child, that child isn't anyone's slave. The father isn't a slave, he has converted.... A person who leaves his religion and follows ours has surpassed us. In praying, in fasting, he has surpassed those of us who were born into the hand of Islam (Mirza and Strobel 1989, 29).

In this account, conversion accomplishes the equivalent of being "born into the household"; it is a direct way to alter both one's own status and that of one's children. And again, while less explicit than Baba's statements about masters' duties regarding the Islamic education of their slaves and slaves' children, Bi Kaje's reference to "his being taken to the mosque" implied that this would be undertaken by the master or someone appropriate in the family.

Bi Kaje spoke of a very special intersection between being female and being slave in a Muslim household: the concubine.[46] Concubines were not unique to Muslim societies but Islamic law regulated the institution. Only slaves could be taken as concubines; sexual relations with a free woman required marriage. And children born to a master by a concubine had to be recognized as free.[47] Generally speaking, the concubine too was freed;[48] in any case, she could not be sold. Concubinage provided social mobility for female slaves and even potential freedom if masters respected the law. In Bi Kaje's experience, "cultural custom" also played a role. She recounted how the woman who had raised her father gave him a farm and two slaves, one of which, Faida, he took as a concubine:

He secluded her; she did not have to go out.... She had a child, but it died. So, she lived with my father and when the child died, Faida had no work. My father didn't live with her anymore. By our custom, if you make a person a concubine and then want to let her go, you should marry her off. You look for another husband and marry her off. If she is not married because you, her master, didn't find a husband for her, if she stays unmarried and then gets another man, if she gets pregnant and delivers a child, it must be yours. My father said, "I made her a concubine, she had a child. When she delivered, the child died." My father didn't want her again. She built a house for herself and lived there.... Then my father found a person named Msengesi, a slave of people from Zanzibar. He returned and married Faida. They stayed here in town. He didn't build a house; they rented other people's houses and lived in them. She had no children (Mirza and Strobel 1989, 32).

Because Faida's child died, her contribution to Bi Kaje's family was largely that of any other female slave. Had the child lived, she would have both biologically and culturally contributed to the family lineage. But that did not negate her status of *umm al-walid*, mother of the child; she could not be sold. Being Muslim and being a concubine bought her a life she would otherwise have been unable to access;[49] her reality also became a part of Bi Kaje's experience and family life.

Bi Kaje, like Baba, emphasized the ongoing relations one expected between former female slaves and the household. For example, Faida, although living in her own house, was expected to assist at family ceremonies:

If there was something happening at the main house, naturally she would come. If there was a wedding, she would come. When it was over she would return home. If there was a funeral, she would come and sit through the funeral with everyone else. When it was over, everyone would go home (Mirza and Strobel 1989, 32).

Then there was her aunt's cook who, although freed, continued to live in the same house as her former mistress and attend to her needs until she died. After this, the freed slave lived out her days in a house with Faida, reflecting the way in which the concept of an "extended family" in this case had been internalized not just by means of master-slave relations but laterally, through the "slave-slave" kinship that "family" provided (Mirza and Strobel 1989, 32-35).

Echoing Baba, she linked freeing slaves inextricably to Islam. She recounted the story of a woman who had been freed by the British rather than her mistress — a secular, rather than a religious manumission. The woman then went to market and sold palm wine; when told that this was contrary to Islam, she stopped. In the end, she sold all she had accumulated to build a mosque. Unfortunately, she did not have enough to complete the building but later it was finished by others and named after her. The inference here is that in spite of the slave's considerable personal commitment to Islam, being "on her own," away from her Muslim family, she simply did not know enough. And, most importantly, because she had not been properly emancipated, she could not succeed "properly" as a Muslim woman (Mirza and Strobel 1989, 37-38).

Even Bi Kaje's account of seclusion involved slaves: she recounted that the contemporary buibui (outer gown worn by women) is a recent phenomena and that when she was a child and young woman, women went out together with a tarpaulin-like cover that slaves carried. They walked, literally, in a sort of moving room that took their secluded part of the house into the street. Then a version of it that covered a single person, the buibui was developed; this required neither company nor slaves (Mirza and Strobel 1989, 46) — presumably, a reference to the ending of slavery under British colonial rule and a subsequent shortage of personal servants.[50] She also noted the issue of labour, as had Baba, when recounting differences between urban and rural practices. She noted that for those living on farms where water was some distance away, married women who did not have anyone to fetch it for them would go out themselves — covered, of course (Mirza and Strobel 1989, 47).

On the other hand, she seems to have articulated a stronger association between seclusion and Islam than did Baba and, ultimately, between seclusion and prestige. For her, having been very strictly secluded was clearly a status symbol and her only regret seemed to be that women in contemporary Mombassa are at a disadvantage when they suddenly find they have to use the shops and they are uneducated in that respect. But she did not seem to regret her own situation (Mirza and Strobel 1989, 46-49).

One other point of interest with respect to the issue of "lived Islam" was Bi Kaje's extensive account of New Year's Day rituals. They involved sacrifices on the ocean shore in order to assure prosperity to the community. The ritual involved walking a cow around town while reciting prayers from the Qur'an, then sacrificing the cow on the beach where meat would be distributed and eaten. It was important that the meat did not come back into the city. Bi Kaje feared that "now" that people take meat back home, this was going to bring an epidemic on the town: what was not eaten was supposed to be disposed of into the water to eliminate ritual pollution and sickness (Mirza and Strobel 1989, 45-46). This is a striking example of a shared "un-orthodox" Muslim ceremony that united both men and women, cultural tradition and Islam, but that was also distinctly urban.

Bi Kaje and Baba clearly experienced similar satisfaction in their role as marriage facilitators and the former's stories of marriages and the role of the local *shaykh* in overseeing divorce are comparable to Baba's (Mirza and Strobel 1989, 50-55). So too are accounts of the rituals involved in childbirth and in "adoption" — the sharing of children among kin-folk (Mirza and Strobel 1989, 57-58). However, formal Qur'anic education appears to have been more important to Bi Kaje than to Baba. While Baba noted that sometimes girls were educated at Qur'anic schools, she also said that sometimes even boys were not; it was not a central issue for her, perhaps because in the end, she came to live for many years with a *malam* and associated Islamic learning with the "informal" (largely hidden) seasonal and household instruction her husband provided. Bi Kaje clearly valued education but in a different way. She noted that girls were taught at home by other women (another example of "private Islam") but saw the denial of "school" as an attempt to keep her from writing to men (Mirza and Strobel 1989, 43), an interesting link between gender relations and Islamic education.

"Fatma Barka" (1900/10-1994, Malian Slave, Goulimine, Southern Morocco)

Finally, I turn to the story of Fatma, drawing upon an analysis that has been extensively developed elsewhere (McDougall 1998) in order to explore the class aspect of this topic of women's lived experiences of Islam. Fatma was a slave for a large part of her life. Then, she was a "freed slave" until her death. Both Baba and Bi Kaje spoke extensively of slaves and of how they were governed by the same Islamic rules as free people; nevertheless, they noted a range of "exceptions" that continued to affirm slave status. Fatma allows us to see these similarities and differences from the slave's point of view. Explicit references to religion in Fatma's story are rare. Other than making a reference to "her" Shaykh on one occasion in her account and her decision not to look at a picture of herself she had given me permission to take because "it was against her religion," Fatma's faith was not evident in her interviews.[51] And yet the fact that she was a female Muslim slave in a Muslim society shaped so much of her life. Probably the most significant way was also the least visible in her story, namely the fact that she was at some time a concubine to her master. This I learned only after her death but it helped put several pieces of her story into context. First, she told of having arrived from Mali with her master's family in Goulimine — in fact she repeated this story of crossing the Sahara in a camel caravan from Timbuktu on two occasions, almost as a kind of performance. On each occasion, at one point or another, she repeated that she was not Mohamed Barka's daughter, that he had bought her in Mali and that she was his "servant" (McDougall 1998, 296). Initially I missed the significance of this; only when put together with the information about her relationship with her master did this make sense. It was important that her slave status was publicly recognized because only as a slave could she have been a legitimate concubine within Islamic law. And this was important to her, as she considered herself a good Muslim (McDougall 1998, 300).

Looking closely at Fatma's account, in which so much of her total identity was developed in terms of her relationship to her "family," that is, the extended family of her master Mohamed Barka, we can see several instances where her presentation of her master as a "good Muslim" was also about herself. In recounting their arrival in Goulimine, she reiterated that Barka's wealth came as a reward for his faith, not as a consequence of a materialistic marriage (McDougall 1998, 296-97). She also noted that he had freed a household slave, Messoud, in recognition for an act of bravery; this was an especially highly-regarded pious act for a Muslim to undertake (McDougall 1998, 300-01). Perhaps the instance that resonates most with Baba's and Bi Kaje's accounts has to do with inheritance. Upon his deathbed, Barka had instructed his children not to treat "Faytma" (his name for her) as inheritable property. As a slave, she was legally exactly that (property), but as it happens she had not had a child with him. He had gone on to articulate this unusual request, in effect, a request to free her, in Islamic terms: he had said "she is your Mother." Again, this phrase makes no sense on its own but taken in the context of religion, it acquires significance (McDougall 1998, 288, 301). In the metaphors Fatma used to present her former master to us, she was adopting important symbols of who she was as well. She was revealing to us, albeit obliquely, something of the Muslim slave culture, which had been a part of her reality over time and by which she defined her own religiosity.

In closing this discussion of Fatma, it is worth noting that in her descriptions of her relations with the Barka family — her continuing participation as cook for family celebrations, her assistance when family members were ill, and the family's involvement (including assistance by Messoud) in the marriage of her son (McDougall 1998, 289, 301-02) — she echoes almost eerily both Baba's and Bi Kaje's descriptions of the slave women in their families. In addition to the repeated emphasis on "kin" underlying her discourse, the centrality of food and food preparation to defining these relations is striking. Where Baba frequently referenced "gifts" of food moving between the free and slave communities to characterize relations between what were essentially fictive kin, both Bi Kaje and Fatma tied female slaves to masters and mistresses through the process of cooking. For the former, family pride was expressed in the *mzalia* extensions to the lineage; for the latter, similar pride was derived from being incorporated in such an extended family. Fatma articulated both the pride and the status in her testimony that: "I am the mother of a very large tribe."[52] While one might argue that this was simply a function of slave society, I am inclined to interpret this more in terms of the specific set of relationships Muslims incorporate into the concept of "family."[53] The year before she died, she applied for and received her first ever *carte d'identité*. It stated that she was born in Goulimine. Clearly, this was not a biological birth but a familial one: in Goulilmine she became "Faytma," concubine of Barka. And over the years, as members of Barka's "biological" family died, she became the embodiment of Barka's memory and it, in turn, enshrined her own identity. So, this was the name she chose for her *carte*, "Faytma Barka" (McDougall 1998, 305). In contrast to the unfortunate freed slave in Bi Kaje's story, Fatma was "properly" emancipated (freed some years after Barka's death, by his son), and lived a "proper" life as a good Muslim; in so doing, she took her place in the Barka lineage and flourished in the reflection of her "good Muslim master" of so many years ago.

Conclusion

In *Islam in Africa*, Levtzion and Pouwels (2000a) set out to establish a "continent-wide" approach, a model to understanding the process and progress of Islamization in Africa. As developed in the Introduction, it was an approach that by and large attributed agency to free, middle- and-upper-class men and measured progress by their activities. Yet, there were hints of the voices of others — women, for example, and slaves. And when we pursued these voices in some of subsequent chapters, they became sufficiently loud as to suggest there might be some dynamics at play not yet "accounted for" in the model. Robinson expanded upon the editors' attention to the role of vernacular language in the process of conversion and the emergence of "rural Islam" by drawing our attention to the fact that many (if not most) of these converts were women and slaves, and that women were often the teachers and mediators between literate written (Arabic) Islam and illiterate oral vernacular Islam. Sperling and Alpers located women and slaves among the main converts in hinterland and interior East Central Africa; they clearly identified marriage as a key "process" in conversion, and located Islamic teaching and learning among women, children and slaves in the household and village. They also spoke directly to the issue of the co-existence of so-called "traditional" and "Islamic" beliefs within those households and villages, implying that "mediation" and "negotiation" underlay this co-existence but stopping short of suggesting that women within the household were the primary agents undertaking it. Finally, from the only thematic chapter to focus on women, we drew on Dunbar's conclusion (buttressed by reference to Wright's trailblazing 1970s work) that we need to understand women's experiences of "being Muslim" not only to learn more about women *per se* — but to learn more about Islam.

The stories of Baba, Bi Kaje, and Fatma took us into their households and allowed us to see how lived experiences of being female or being slave (or being both) may have shaped being Muslim. These stories are of the twentieth century, but in their detail and their voices they resonate with the glimpses our historical sources left from earlier times. For them, being Muslim was experienced in many ways but almost all of these were located within the household. Many were very personal, if not intimate in nature: prayer shaped life and work on a daily basis; Allah was invoked in names, in songs, in ceremonies concerned with the essentials of life and death; Islam and Islamic practices were central to the identity of slaves born to the household and especially to female slaves taken as concubines; *malams* and *qadis* were called upon to shape marital relations, either by the power of law or "charms." Seclusion emerged as a more complex factor, being, on the one hand (somewhat ironically), a "public" marker of being Muslim, but on the other, a combined reflection of class and location (rural-urban). The reason for secluding was clearly rooted in religious beliefs, the ability to do so limited by other factors. Bi Kaje's account suggested one more nuance — seclusion as distinguishing between slave and *mzalia*.[54] Even veiling ("seclusion in public" as the story of the *buibui* illustrates so well) was imbued with Muslim modesty, cultural custom and, frequently, class sensitivity. Finally, these stories echoed each other in emphasizing the shared sense of "kinship" that Islam facilitated between free, freed, and slave household members — Baba and Bi Kaje used Islamic ritual and ceremony to "extend" their families; Fatma used her position in such a family to acquire an identity as a proper Muslim woman.

In what ways, however, do these "lived experiences" speak to Levtzion and Pouwel's approach to "Islamization" and to Dunbar's plea that we allow women's experiences to help us re-conceptualize Islam in Africa? First, I would argue, they help us move beyond the dichotomy of "traditional / pre-Islamic versus modern/Islamic" that underpins notions of "rural and urban" and "public and private" Islam, and more towards the "complementarity" and "permeability" emphasized in work on identity (Askew 1999, 73). And contrary to what arguing for a "women's perspective" might suggest, these stories also challenge in subtle ways the assumption that in Muslim African societies women's and men's worlds were completely separate. Certainly age and class cross-cut such divisions, but Baba in particular gave the impression that those worlds intersected more often than one might expect. Looking at life from within the household, we can see both custom and culture providing an architecture for "being Muslim" that is quite distinct from that which governs life at the mosque or the Qur'anic school. Unlike the latter, which tended to be the domain of men, the household embraced both men and women, albeit in clearly defined roles. Studies that have attempted to explain this complexity in terms of men's and women's Islam, or as in the East African context as "African women, Islamic men" have not moved much beyond the early twentieth century observer we met above who saw Muslim men going to prayer and so-called pagan women staying home[55]. Moreover, they miss three dynamics that are central to the practice and experience of Islam that are only evident within the household: marriage, childrearing, and "family" slavery. As we saw in more general terms in Sperling and Alpers' chapters, marriage was a key factor to converting women of non-Muslim backgrounds but, simultaneously, those marriages were also uniting different cultural traditions[56] and in East Central Africa (as well as early on in much of Sahelian and Saharan West Africa [McDougall 2004]), uniting matrilineal with patrilineal custom. Within these marriages — Muslim by law and religion, culturally tied to women's locality and ethnic identity — children, boys and girls, were raised Muslim. Women usually taught young children, then boys turned to clerics and schools (where they existed) while girls continued to be educated in the household. Bi Kaje's story as a Swahili woman is a wonderful illustration of all of these issues.

Finally, there were the household slaves who, through Islamic practices like concubinage and naming practices, became "kin" to the lineage. Bi Kaje's story emphasizes a fairly well-defined family that had been formed by incorporating concubines, adoptees, and *mzalia* — surprisingly similar to the one Fatma lived in so very far away in Morocco. Baba seemed to extend the concept of "household" even further to include whole slave villages descended from the Hausa equivalent of *mzalia*;[57] nevertheless, they were "personalized" through her immediate family's ongoing involvement in arranging marriages and adopting children. This kind of slavery, often called "Islamic slavery" in the literature, is usually studied in isolation from Islam — that is, these stories, these slave narratives, are well known in discussions of the history of slavery. But, as is evidenced in the Levtzion and Pouwels volume, they are not seen as part of the history of Islam. Alpers asked if marriage in matrilineal societies "ought to be considered as part of a pattern of Islamic conversion." I argued in the affirmative above; here, I would suggest in addition that perhaps the process was so successful over the long term because of the way in which Muslim slaves (converts, adoptees, concubines, and *mzalia*) became incorporated into the larger lineages. Not only were they and their progeny extending the family, including its labour and reproductive resources,[58] but also they were extending and shaping the practice of Islam in ways special to their slave and gender status.

The household, if understood in this dynamic multi-status, multi-generational, multi-cultural, "gendered" way, can provide a conceptual framework for understanding the practices, processes, and patterns of "Islamization" as they were experienced by others than the traders, clerics, and chiefs. Or, one might also argue that these leading figures of society also "lived Islam" next to their mothers, wives, sisters, and slaves and were themselves, at least at times, part of this household "world of Islam." Without denying the importance of recognizing the agents and activities privileged in most studies of the history of Islam in Africa, including the Levtzion and Pouwels volume now certainly considered the "seminal" work on the subject, this preliminary exploration of "others" usually seen as marginal to the process of Islamization, notably women and slaves, is intended to expand the parameters of that process. It argues that women and slaves were not only "recipients" of Islam but agents of conversion as the religion rooted itself in Africa. In their households, they shaped how Islam was lived by all around them. And instead of only looking at the history of more public activities, if we address attention to the household and its changing nature over time, perhaps we will see a different face of Islam and Islamization emerging.[59]

Notes

[1] Entitled "Introduction: Patterns of Islamization and Varieties of Religious Experience Among Muslims of Africa."

[2] It reflects Levtzion's earliest publications on Islam in West Africa's Volta Region (1968), through his penning of the seminal *Ancient Ghana and Mali* ([1973] 1980) in which he explored state growth, through his co-editorship of the invaluable *Corpus* ([1981] 2000) that made selected, excerpted Arabic texts available to non-Arabophones, to his numerous conference-based edited works on a range of specific issues including "rural and urban Islam" (1986) and "Renewal and Reform" (1987). [For full references to these works, see Levtzion's CV republished in this volume].

[3] Topics of "Progress" and "conversion" in the context of "North and West Africa" and "Horn and Sub-Saharan Africa" are central to the Introduction (especially Levtzion and Pouwels 2000b, 2-8); chapters following are organized according to geographical region (with the exception of "Themes," grouped together at the end).

[4] Or, put another way, had continued to embrace an "accommodation of Islam with traditional religions." The Fulani *jihad* of Uthman dan Fodio in Northern Nigeria was justified in these terms (Levtzion and Pouwels 2000b, 10); the continued persistence of "pre-Islamic elements" in Bornu also legitimized extending the *jihad* against this ostensibly Muslim neighbour (Levtzion and Pouwels 2000b, 5).

[5] See chapters on East and Central Africa (David Sperling, Edward Alpers) in

which matrilineal societies are addressed. For Alpers, Islam's patrilineality is so central that he questions whether marriages to women of matrilineal societies "ought [even] to be considered as part of a pattern of Islamic conversion" (2000, 306), a point to which I will return, below. Kelly Askew (1999, 67-70) notes that the association of Islam with patriarchy and "male domination of women" has distorted the writing of Swahili Coast history.

[6] This characterization underscores the dichotomy between the "rural, Arabic illiterate countryside" and the "urban, commercial, educated" communities (Levtzion and Pouwels 2000b, 7).

[7] Corroborating the point made in the introduction; see Voll's discussion of Levtzion's contribution to this issue in this volume.

[8] Roberta Ann Dunbar contributed "Sufism and Muslim Women in Africa: An Opportunity to Shape the Public Sphere?" to the original ASA memorial panels, in which Nana Asma'u's contributions were highlighted; regrettably, family circumstances prevented Dunbar from preparing that paper for publication in this volume.

[9] Robinson (2000b, 145 note 21) cites additional information on Futa Jalon literature. This realization is not in itself so revolutionary (for example, Jean Boyd's *The Caliph's Sister*, 1989); what is noteworthy is that this analysis has not in any significant way influenced the vision presented to readers.

[10] This observation is repeated later in the article (Sperling 2000, 290-91).

[11] A significant change in Levtzion and Pouwels' rendering of this statement substituted "other employees of the merchants" for "slaves" (compare 7 and 289).

[12] Segeju are linguistically Mijikenda but considered culturally distinct (Eastman 1988, 7); on the Mijikenda in general, see Willis (1993).

[13] The Digo were also Mijikenda, one of the original "nine groups" (Askew 1999, 71).

[14] These observations invoke a larger discussion about women, gender, culture, and religion given definition by Carol Eastman (1988). She addressed Strobel's (1983) earlier argument that women (mostly of slave origin) tended to assimilate into coastal Swahili culture, including Islam, and that, thereafter, their children were similarly acculturated. Eastman argued that the opposite was equally as likely, that what developed were gender-specific cultural and religious "worlds." With reference to the Diogo, the female slaves, noted as being particularly numerous among Digo (Mijikenda) in the nineteenth century, maintained their culture and religion. She goes on to hypothesize that this "gender defined world" was a dichotomous one in which Muslim men raised Muslim boy children in an Islamized Swahili culture, while "African" (non-Muslim) women raised African girl children in a non-Muslim African culture. Sperling's comments (above) raise questions about this interpretation. Patricia Romero's (1988, 154-60) life history of Mama Khadija also supports an "accommodation" model showing that,

among Lamu household slaves, the practice was to follow the example of the master's family. Yet Khadija did maintain "traditional African" culture as a healer and mid-wife, and attempted (in a rare situation) to bring the Swahili "aristocracy" into that African world. The direct challenge is Kelly Askew's (1999) work on music and dance. She questions this historically-gendered analysis and attributes the widespread acceptance of gender dualism to the equally widespread assumption that Muslim-rooted patriarchy and patrilineality had shaped culture. "Because a vaguely conceived Islam is the perceived cause for gender segregation, and because the coast has been predominantly Islamic for more than seven centuries," Askew states, "the conclusion that pervades Swahili studies is that gender segregation has been around a very long time" (1999, 91). She argues that the "duality" of contemporary Swahili society is recent.

Both she and Eastman take "Islam" as a given, Askew's nod to a "vaguely conceived" ideology notwithstanding. It is worth noting that Strobel's argument is not as clear-cut as Eastman suggested. Strobel allowed that household domestics might have adopted freeborn culture in order to signify a "class" difference between themselves and slaves more removed from the house who retained a more traditional, "Africanized" lifestyle. This was not an "either-or" situation. Most recently, linguist Katrin Bromber's (2007, 115-16) preliminary work with terminology used for female slaves underscores a lack of dichotomy between expected categories like "noble / slave," "master / slave," "mistress / female slave" that she attributes to the transitional situation in which household slaves found themselves as they sought to disassociate with "uncivilized" traditions and adopt "civilized" Swahili culture. The "dichotomy" was expressed in cultural, not gender or class terms.

[15] The question of how patrilineal or matrilineal the "Swahili" were remains debated and debatable (Askew 1999, 86-88).

[16] To judge one's innocence in the Mozambique hinterland, one was to eat an uncooked ball of rice in which was written a phrase from the Qur'an without vomiting (Alpers 2000, 307).

[17] Sperling (2000, 290) recounts the story of slave-trader Tippu Tib: he was able to pass himself off as the son of a "long lost" daughter of an important chief; drawing on the matrilineal inheritance practices of that society, he laid claim to all the ivory that would normally have been brought to the chief. Elsewhere, I have drawn attention to the role of matrilineality in shaping how Islam came to be both embraced and practiced during an even earlier era (McDougall 2004).

[18] In particular in his discussion of the Islamic conversion of slaves (Sperling 2000, 279-81).

[19] Another reference to this "hidden" education is Romero's (1988, 144) Khadija. As a freed-slave child, she learned the Qur'an from visitors to the

house and most particularly from her sister.

[20] I include here the Swahili who appear, at least in earlier centuries, to have been largely matrilineal (McDougall 2004; Askew 1999).

[21] In the context of Tippu Tib: "some Manyema made their way to Tabora and Ujiji — more often than not as slaves, and became Muslim" (Sperling 2000, 290).

[22] Children learned to read and write in Arabic, as well as "a little medicine" (Alpers 2000, 309).

[23] Shaykh Mbarak bin Ali al-Hinawi.

[24] Shaykh Mtemwe bint ali bin Yusuf.

[25] There are eight contributions covering art, literature, music, education, and law (curiously, Sufism is also relegated to this section). Constituting one-third of the book, they are under-reflected in the Introduction.

[26] This is surprising given the "growth" in studies of this particular intersection by the mid 1980s and into the 1990s. Fred Cooper's *Plantation Slavery on the East African Coast* delineated a framework for studying "slaves and Islam" in 1977, followed by his "Islam and Cultural Hegemony: The Ideology of Islamic Slave Owners on the East African Coast" (Paul E Lovejoy's influential *The Ideology of Slavery*, 1981). Lovejoy's (1988, 1990) work on slavery in the Sokoto Caliphate (especially attention to Islamic concubinage and slavery) focused attention on this area of study. Joseph Miller's "world bibliography" of slavery carved a niche for "Muslim slavery" in 1985, updated in 1993; (see especially "Muslim Slavery and Slaving" in Elizabeth Savage [1992]). John R. Willis' two-volume collection *Slaves and Slavery in Muslim Africa* also appeared in 1985. By the mid-1990s, studies of Islam, slaves, and slavery were central to the field of Islam in Africa.

[27] The first story: "Baba" of Karo (Hausaland, Northern Nigeria, 1877-1951) as recorded by anthropologist Mary Smith in 1949-50 and published in 1954. The second: *Three Swahili Women*, specifically that of Kaje wa Mwene Katano (Bi Kaje of Mombassa, Kenya, c.1890-1981), collected by Sarah Mirza and Margaret Strobel in the 1970s and published in 1989. The third: Fatma Barka (southern Morocco, c.1900/10-1994), collected in 1993-94 and published in 1998. Most recently, Baba's story is referenced several times in Coquery-Vidrovitch's (2007) overview of "women, marriage, and slavery" and Bi Kaje's life experience is drawn upon by Bromber (2007) to flesh out literary terminology.

[28] This approach echoes Marcia Wright's innovative work in the 1970s, in which she sought to understand slavery through the experiences of the most vulnerable — the women. In the 1993 collection that brought together much of that work, *Strategies of Slaves and Women*, a 1975 essay is reprinted that argues for an erasure of the "boundaries" historians usually impose between slave and free. It draws attention to the importance of gender in determining the strategies open to slaves in making their own world. Manipulation of,

and insertion into, kinship networks and idioms feature centrally in her analysis (for an excellent review of this work and its significance, see Glassman 1995b).

[29] The exception to this was when she discussed a widow mourning for her late husband: during the 130 days of morning, "you say your prayers and pray for your husband" (Smith 1954, 211-12).

[30] Romero (1988, 146) comments on the significance of daily prayers in Mama Khadija's life in relation to the work involved in fetching water for ablutions.

[31] This mirrors the practice of female slaves remaining with their seller before being turned over to a new owner to be certain no pregnancy was in play. Islamic practice shaped by gender in this instance cross-cuts class.

[32] The only other time she mentioned covering the head was in speaking of coming into a household as a new wife. In her second marriage, she remained with her head covered for six days; after that, she became a "daughter of the house" and uncovered. A first wife remained covered for seven months because she must become "accustomed to the house." Head covering was a cultural rather than religious practice, embedded in customs of family more than Islam or gender *per se* (she did not, for example "uncover" in the presence of other women in the household until she had become its "daughter").

[33] She also mentioned that she and other women had fetched water when the whole village had been moved and water was scarce (Smith 1954, 188). Her mother had been a "secluded wife" and, as a child, she had gone to market to trade on her mother's behalf; that she personalized this information suggests that being secluded (*aurem kulle* in Hausa) was by no means the norm (Smith 1954, 55, 259 note 8).

[34] See also Bi Kaje's and Fatma's stories (below) on this point; Romero's (1988, 154) Khadija participated regularly in the ceremonies of her former master's family as well.

[35] Islamic law governed who would be free in slave marriages: children "followed the milk line," that is, the mother. No matter what the status of the father, if the mother was still legally slave, the children were slave and belonged to her master. Baba said her family had "no problem" with males marrying outside the family; they would give the children to the woman's master once they were grown (Smith 1954, 41, 119-20).

[36] One would call the first part of the name (such as "Gift" or "Wealth belongs ...") and the slave answered accordingly "of Allah ..." or "to Allah...."

[37] In her family, when slave boys were seven years old they were taught prayers and sent to Qur'anic school; sometimes girls went too (Smith 1954, 43).

[38] Her interpretation of the ending of slavery is revealing. After the British said no master was allowed to call a slave "slave," "those who were younger than you became younger brothers, those older became older brothers."

From her perspective, this was an extension of existing custom with respect to the children of house slaves. And, according to her, only "some slaves" who had been bought in the market fled; the rest remained in the family (Smith 1954, 67). Her perspective on the British seems to have been shaped by local *malams* (learned men) who had said that the Europeans would "stop wars, they would repair the world, they would stop oppression and lawlessness, we should live at peace with them."

[39] "Before the world was settled, there was no traveling about" — Baba's reference to the arrival of the British (Smith 1954, 132). Smith notes that she talked of a time when "everyone became free"; as no such law had been passed at the time (c. 1910-11), Smith queries Baba's meaning. It is likely that the reference to "free" here was the same as above — that is, that slaves were no longer purchased in the market, therefore all slaves became the equals of "family-born" slaves.

[40] One is reminded of Khadija, a mid-wife who also "dealt with problems of the spirit world" for both her own former slave community and her former master's family (Romero 1988, 152). On *bori* among the Hausa, see the work of Susan O'Brien (for example, 1999, 2001).

[41] It is clear from Baba that most *bori* adepts were women but yet there were two male dancers in her own family, one of whom was her father's younger brother (and her father was a *malam*) (Smith 1954, 63). With respect to *malams*, she also noted that women went to them to get "medicine" to drive co-wives mad (Smith 1954, 156). It may be that "*malams* and *bori* had their own work" but in terms of women's domain, it would seem their "efforts" were often aimed towards the same or very similar goals. For an inside view of how Islam and "sorcery" (including spirit possession) can co-exist and feed each other, see Lambeck (1993).

[42] "[Bi Kaje's attitude] corrects a view commonly held in the literature of the coast which was written during the colonial period and inherited the colonialists' view of the Omani aristocrats as superior to Africans. This Arab ascendance in the historiography reflected the rise of the Omani sultanate in Zanzibar in the nineteenth century, but has been inappropriately projected backwards into earlier periods" (Mirza and Strobel 1989, 19). Elsewhere, I have observed in similar fashion how the process of Islamization itself coloured the evidence that we are reading to understand Islamization, both in West and East Africa (McDougall 2004). Louise Rolingher (2009) adds that we may also be seeing the view from Mombasa as opposed to that of Zanzibar. Lamuan (Waamu) and Mombasan (Watu wa Mvita) Swahili Muslims think / thought of themselves as having a more direct and "purer" link to Islam than the Omani upstarts.

[43] Mirza and Strobel (1989, 18) comment upon the "language" of kinship that fails to easily differentiate between relationships and makes explanations confusing when translated; Smith also commented upon this issue with

respect to Baba and noted that Baba would only use names when it was clear that Smith was confused.

[44] Curiously, Bromber (2007, 132) does not mention the term *mzalia* either in her discussion of *suria* (concubine) or *hadimu*, freed slave. Deutsch (2007), on the other hand, devotes a paragraph to their status.

[45] Or, as we will see below in the case of Faida, of a special status that incorporated elements of both freedom and slavery. While Faida was "free" to live independently when no longer wanted by her master and was given the means to build her own house, had she subsequently had a child, it would have belonged to Bi Kaje's father who was still legally her master. That she remained his property was underscored by the fact that he eventually "married her off" (as was his customary obligation); at that point it would seem she lost the right to the house she had built (property of a slave is the property of his/her master) and spent the rest of her life living in rented accommodation. However, at least from what we know, even though not formally manumitted, she was not included as inheritable property on the death of Bi Kaje's father (33).

[46] *Suria* (plural *Masuria*). See Bromber (2007, 116-17, 120-21). She raises questions about the Islamic practice around *suria*, suggesting it may have been different among the Swahili but has no evidence to that effect. (She links the Ibadite legal system with Zanzibar, implying *masuria* may have been treated differently there; the Ibadi influence was introduced in the nineteenth century with the establishment of Sultan Said Sayid's rule. It was therefore chronological and class specific, not geographical — and Ibadis spread well into the interior during the course of the century.) Also see Deutsch (2007, 134).

[47] The following quotation from Mtoro bin Mwinyi Bakari does raise a question with respect to Swahili society: "If a freeman marries a slave woman, their child is a slave; but if a free woman marries a slave man, their child is not a slave, because free birth is matrilineal" (1981, 175). According to Islamic law, a freeman can take a slave woman as concubine but not as "wife" — if married, she must be freed, so it is difficult to understand exactly what is meant here. Elsewhere, it was rare for a free woman to marry a slave man but the same distinction pertained; marriage could only take place with a slave partner if the other was also slave or ex-slave. "Ex slave" is officially "free" but not necessarily regarded as such socially; perhaps this was the "freeman" Bakari referred to, in which case it is true that the child would be "slave" because the mother still belonged to her master. As for the "ex-slave women" marrying with a slave man and the reference to matrilineality, it may indeed have been a reflection of a matrilineal society (as Askew infers [1999, 88]). Or, it may possibly reflect the "norm" of a child of a slave relationship tracing "possession" back through the female to the master as articulated in the transitional societal moment Bakari was observing. The

differences between slave, freed slave, and "free" appear to have been negotiable to some extent. See Strobel's discussion (1983, 119-21); she notes that while a slave woman may not marry her master without being freed, she can marry another man while still a slave. There is still some ambiguity as to whether this was true of any free man or only "freed men." Bromber's (2007, 120-21) discussion of this issue confuses several of these points. She notes the Islamic injunction against marriage between partners of unequal social status, then suggests it is ignored in cases where a free person was not yet married *(and was thus eligible to have extramarital relations)*: free males married female slaves *"whom they had to free before marriage"* [my emphasis]. Married men were entitled to sexual relations with as many concubines (who, in turn must be slaves) as they wished; the point of freeing them before marriage was just that — no law was ignored; marriage took place between a free man and a "freed" woman. The real question here is the one raised above: the ambiguity between free and freed.

48 If not immediately, then on the death of her master.

49 Bromber (2007, 120) notes that she initially doubted the claims that *masuria* enjoyed a special "higher" status "as respected figures within the household who upon the birth of a child advanced to highly regarded members of the community." However, she is now convinced as "the respected status of many of these women has ... been confirmed by numerous interviews" [17 interviews in Bagamoyo 2000] (Bromber 2007, 114).

50 Strobel confirms this memory: the tent-like covering carried by slaves was called the *ramba* or *shira* (in Swahili). In 1910 it gave way the wearing of the *buibui*; Strobel (1983, 122) also surmises that this was related to the abolition of slavery.

51 The details of how, when, and where the interviews took place can be found in McDougall (1998, 305-06, notes 2 and 3). Fatima once mentioned Allah in the context of: "If you lower your head to God [Allah], he will give you everything you wish" (McDougall 1998, 298).

52 Fatma's experiences resonate with Strobel's observations and analyses of female slaves involved in reproductive labour (broadly defined to include more than biological reproduction) in a Mombassan urban household (1983 — interviews conducted 1972-73, 1975).

53 This in turn derives from the role kinship played in the initial articulation of Islam, as first argued by Fred Cooper (1977, 25-26) in the context of East African Muslim society. He argued that laws and customs were less about Islam *per se* than about the concept of kinship rooted in Islam. In this respect, so-called "Islamic Slavery" was no different from lineage-based slavery. Herein lies the intersection with Wright's (1993, 21-45) analysis, which also derives from East African narratives. Her accounts deal with slaves who interacted with the newly-established Christian mission communities rather than the coastal Muslim Swahili ones, for the most part. All retained

roots of some depth in "non-Christian, African" society as well. Wright emphasized how these enslaved women drew on kinship idioms to be wives, mothers, sisters, and daughters, as well as "slaves." Kinship was not "fictive" in the anthropological sense, but it had specific meanings within each of these different societies. I suspect Wright would privilege class and gender over religious ideology with respect to the operating of kinship as an integrative and protective mechanism. However, similarities seen across three very different cultural and geographical regions (including colonial identity — Fatma's Morocco being French, Baba's northern Nigeria and Bi Kaje's Kenya British) that shared belief in Islam, suggest that some "dialogue" between the perspectives would yield useful results and that Cooper's observations about Islam and kinship must remain central to any such discussion.

[54] Fatma had not been secluded but, like many Saharan women in southern Morocco, she wore *melhafa*, the sari-type veil that totally covers the hair and can be drawn over the face to leave only the eyes visible.

[55] This "discussion" deserves more attention. I.M. Lewis takes on the issue critiquing, among others, Ernest Gellner, J Spencer Trimingham, and H J Fisher; he reiterates the role played by the dichotomy historians set up between the literate, well-informed *ulamma* of the towns and their illiterate (or semi-literate) country cousins. Lewis (1996, 140-42, 152-54) argues that "what in a particular cultural context is regularly categorized as `pre-Islamic survival' is in many cases nothing of the sort." While I remain uncomfortable with his notion of a "spectrum" with orthodox, fundamentalist Islam at one end and "magical *maraboutism*" at the other, I agree with his point that these cannot be unambiguously be identified with the dichotomies between town and tribe, male and female. Askew's (1999, 1-4) work engaged with frequently (above) argues similarly, as we have seen, particularly with respect to the "dominance" of gendered worlds and patriarchy. However, Eastman's challenge remains. While arguing for a "process" almost identical to the one I will return to below, Eastman concludes:

> Islam leaves girls and women at home, together, and in seclusion. African practices remain in a position to be maintained, transmitted, transformed and reaffirmed (as dynamic cultural processes) from generation to generation. Boys, in contrast, are socialized by their fathers into an Islamic lifestyle and remain relatively isolated from the African cultural influences at play in women's groups. *Even in marriage, where the dual sub-cultures meet and where it has been thought that Swahili women act in accord with a code of behaviour that is expressive of Islam,* Muslim / Arab influences may be more illusory than factual (1988, 3 [my emphasis]).

In effect, this chapter revisits precisely this point.

[56] Eastman contrasts "Arab men" with "African women." But in East / East

Central Africa, most Muslim men taking non-Muslim wives were either Swahili (of coastal, not Arab culture *per se*) or other African converts to Islam (often businessmen). The notion of pure "Arab" as distinct from pure "African" is neither consistent with the evidence we have from Sperling and Alpers, nor resonant with recent studies on Swahili identity (such as Askew 1999).

[57] This recollects Sperling's description of "Islamization" among the slaves of the Tabori-Ujiji region.

[58] For a detailed discussion of "productive and reproductive slave labour" in a Swahili household, see Strobel (1983, 116-23).

[59] As Sperling said, the "secular and commercial"; I would add the political. It is striking that once women appeared in the political arena, as occurred frequently during the colonial era, they became part of the discussion of "Islamization" (Levtzion and Pouwels 2000b, 15). Even Dunbar's chapter focuses principally on contemporary political activities and speaks of women "using" Islam to gain rights and protect against social / governmental oppression. However, our view of these activities might change if we were able to situate "Islamization" in a context that placed the household at the base (if not the centre) of the analysis. Perhaps women were / are simultaneously engaging with Islam and shaping its practices in different domains of their lives, in the context of different familial and social relations (such as food — obtaining it, preparing it, exchanging it, eating it). The rules and rituals surrounding "food" are rooted both in religion and in the household, as each of the "stories" above reveal; yet I am unaware of studies to date that have attempted to explore Muslim identity or experience through food. Rolingher's (2009) thesis, "Edible Identites," goes some significant way towards responding to this oversight.

Resurgent Islamic Fundamentalism as an Integrative Factor in the Politics of Africa and the Middle East

Nehemia Levtzion

Introduction

Studies of the resurgence of Islamic fundamentalism, otherwise called the Islamist movements, brought the debate about Orientalism back to public attention. Those who postulate a cultural essence that underlies and unifies Islamic history are considered to beneo-Orientalists. It is significant, however, that there is a convergence between the view of the so-called neo-Orientalists and that of the Islamists, who insist on the monolithic universality of Islam (Zubayda 1997, 103; `Ali 1999, 2).

The politicization of Islam in the 1980s and 1990s must be explained in terms of social, political and economic context (Carapico 1997, 31). Algeria's armed Islamist insurgency arose from political exclusion, economic misery and social injustice. Likewise, the violent clashes in the poor quarter of Imbaba in Cairo should be explained by the living conditions there, which might have caused even more violence (Beinin and Stork 1997, 17). In other words, we should pay careful attention to political and economic conjunctures, national particularities and local histories (Vitalis 1997, 102).

For Muslims, history is of great significance, particularly the period of the Prophet and his Companions, known as the days of the

---

This chapter was first presented to the Conference on "Islam and the West: the African Perspective," Evangelische Akademie Loccum, 21–23 October 2002.

Reproduced with minor editorial modifications from *Islam in Africa and the Middle East: Studies on Conversion and Renewal*, edited by Michael Abitbol and Amos Nadan, XIV 1-14. Farnham, UK: Ashgate Variorum, 2007.

salaf, and the following three centuries, when Muslims ruled the world and Islamic civilization was more advanced than other civilizations. I have researched the simultaneous emergence of renewal and reform movements throughout the Muslim world in the eighteenth century, which has some parallels with the recent resurgence of Islam as a worldwide phenomenon. In other words, the universality of Islamic militancy cannot be accidental, and should also be viewed as derived from an historical process, based on legal, ideological and cultural foundations (Khurshid 1983, 222–25, 203).

The Public Sphere

The relationship between state and society is a favorite topic in the study of Islam. Our contribution to this discourse consists of analysing the concept of public sphere, which in Islamic societies may be taken as replacing the Eurocentric term, civil society. The public sphere is defined as the autonomous space between the official and private spheres. The most important institutions of the public sphere in pre-modern societies were the *sharî`a* courts, the *muhtasib* and the marketplace, the *waqf*, the *madrasa*, Sufi brotherhoods and craft associations.

Papers collected in *The Public Sphere in Muslim Societies*, edited by Hoexter, Eisenstadt and myself, demonstrate the existence of a vibrant public sphere that was of crucial importance in shaping the dynamics of pre-modern Muslim societies. The papers dispute the concept of "Oriental despotism" and the notion of a total separation and estrangement of the society from its rulers. In reality, the autonomous institutions of the public sphere placed limits on the absolute power of the ruler.

Institutions of the public sphere in pre-modern Muslim societies remained vital until the end of the eighteenth century. But from the beginning of the nineteenth century these institutions faced the challenge of Western influence, modernity and the nation state. The power of the *sharî`a* courts was eroded. *Waqf* endowments were appropriated by the modern state, and the religious institutions lost financial autonomy. The craft guilds were destroyed by capitalist penetration. The `ulamâ' lost their monopoly in the field of education to Western-style schools. Modernist movements attacked Sufi brotherhoods as one of the principal reasons for the decadence of Islam. The modern state further undermined the autonomy of those institutions, and the vacuum created in the public sphere has been filled by the Islamist movements. Religion is a good source for political ideas: its symbols are indigenous and easily recognized. The Islamist movements win public support because they articulate the authentic values of Islam that are close to the heart of every Muslim (Crystal 1995, ii: 259-86, 275; Tripp 1996, 51-69). From an historical perspective, religion emerged as a banner under which the oppressed and dispossessed rallied in periods of economic and social hardship. Where it was, or is, the official state religion (the Ottoman Empire, Saudi Arabia, Pakistan and Iran), Islam is a legitimating ideology for the ruling class and constitutes part of the state mechanism. Unofficial Islam, on the other hand, has throughout history frequently expressed popular protest, and often assumed unorthodox, sectarian, or mystical (Sufi) forms in order to challenge the centre's religious and political legitimacy (Margulies and Yildizoglu 1997, 144-45).

The declared political target of all Islamist movements is to rebuild Islamic societies and states on the foundations of the *sharî'a*. However, the *sharî'a* as interpreted and articulated by modern Islamists is not the same as that elaborated by the *'ulamâ'* over the centuries. Most radical Islamists did not originate from the circles of the *'ulamâ'*. They oriented themselves to a broad public, rather than to a restricted circle of scholars. To many *'ulamâ'*, the language and modes of thought of the Islamists appear un-Islamic, as they mix passages from the Koran with discussions of current affairs. The resurgence of Islam involves a broader awareness of the social and political dimensions of the faith, and calls on believers to be more active participants in public life (Heffner 2001, 491-514).

The Islamists developed networks of voluntary organizations that dispensed charity, looked after the needs of the poor, built mosques and ran schools and clinics. They provided services that the state was unwilling or unable to undertake. They created a new autonomous public sphere that challenged state power. Funding for these social services came partly from public contributions, but also from businessmen who favoured the Islamists' economic programmes of tax cuts, deregulation and economic incentives for business development. In Syria, the Islamic opposition to the Ba'th Party in the early 1980s developed out of the *sûq*, where religious institutions and the trading economy came together. The Islamic movement expressed the worldview of the *sûq* against the radical policies of the Ba'th. In Algeria, the "commercial bourgeois" were important financial contributors to the Islamic Salvation Front (FIS) party, because of its programme of tax cuts, deregulation, and economic incentives for business development. It is significant that the propaganda of the pro-Islamic Refah Party in Turkey was not concerned with Allah, but with social and economic issues like privatization, unemployment, prices, salaries and wages (Margulies and Yildizoglu 1997, 150).

Al-Ikhwân al-Muslimûn (the Muslim Brotherhood) in Egypt was the first organized movement of Islamists. Having emerged between the two world wars, in the age of liberalism, it continued the discourse of the modernists by demonstrating the viability of Islam in the modern world. It used a somewhat apologetic tone, unlike the affirmation of Islam's authenticity by contemporary Islamists. Even today, the mainstream of the *Ikhwân* is committed to broad-based social reforms, and not to seizing political power.

By the end of the 1980s, a broader range of intellectuals and professionals had become involved in the reaffirmation of the Islamic tradition and the Islamization of daily life. With its greater political activism, the non-violent mainstream of Islamic fundamentalism attracted a broader group of people (Voll 1991, 386–87). From the universities, student activists moved on to join the professional associations. The victory of the Islamic trend in the professional associations indicates the growing alienation of the educated middle class both from the ruling elites and their secular opposition, and the emergence of the Islamic trend as the only credible political alternative to the Egyptian regime. The Muslim Brothers are the only independent political force with broad-based mass support. Since the mid-1970s, when its leaders renounced the use of violence, the Brothers have been working towards Islamic reform through institution building, persuasion, and increased participation in legal, mainstream channels of public life.

Support for the Brothers crosses class and generational lines, but their recruitment efforts have been particularly successful among recent secondary school and university graduates — doctors, engineers, pharmacists, lawyers and other professionals — in large cities and provincial towns. Islamic schools, health clinics and community centres created by the Muslim Brothers have provided employment for young doctors, teachers and other professionals. Islamist leaders are close in age to new graduates and are familiar with the same deprivations. Muslim Brothers and more militant groups have indoctrinated the youth with the idea that the reform of society is a religious duty incumbent on every Muslim. They are imbuing the educated youth with a new sense of civic obligation, and a new perspective on their own capacity to effect social change. The Mubarak regime may be able to contain the activity of armed Islamic groups through increased intimidation and repression, yet it is far less equipped to stem the Islamic trend's social and ideological incorporation of new groups at the grassroots level (Wickham 1997, 133).

In Jordan, the tolerance of the Hashemite regime encouraged moderation in the Muslim Brotherhood, which supported the king in moments of crisis (Boulby 1999). Even the Hizballah decided to participate in the parliamentary elections of August and September 1992, and scored a brilliant victory (Langohr 2001, 591–610).

In Morocco, the pragmatic and moderate Islamic Party for Justice and Development opted for dialogue and a degree of consensus. In September 2002 the party participated for the second time in the general elections, seeking to increase its representation, but was concerned that a landslide that might generate reaction among the pro-Western elite, similar to the events in Algeria more than ten years earlier. Leftist and liberal observers acknowledge the Islamists' superior election campaign organization, financing and tactics, which together with public sympathy, strengthened by communal involvement, gave them an advantage in free elections (Wickham 1997, 129). Government policy is therefore an important factor in determining the nature of the political discourse, and the resorting to violence by Islamist movements depends to a large extent on the way that a government deals with Islamist activists. It was under the oppressive regime of Nasser that Sayyid al-Qutb developed an ideology that became the banner of the extreme Islamist movements that branched off from the *Ikhwân*. They advocated withdrawal from society and the formation of a new, alternative, believing society that would eventually supplant the unbelieving one (Voll 1991, 381–82). Heated debates took place among the extreme Islamists as to whether, and under what conditions, it was permissible to declare Muslims to be infidels and therefore legitimate targets for *jihâd*. Differences among Islamists also revolve around whether an Islamist society should precede, or succeed, an Islamist state. Answers to such questions chart different political strategies, and determine the role of Islamists in the public sphere.

The Challenge of Islam to the West

Of all world religions, Islam has had the greatest political success, with the creation of a worldwide empire shortly after the rise of the new faith. The success of Muslims contrasts with the historical experience of the Jews, who had no state of their own for long periods, and with the early history of the Christians, who were persecuted during their first three centuries. Jews await messianic redemption, whereas for Christians the Kingdom of God is in heaven. Muslims, on the other hand, seek to establish the Kingdom of God on earth, here and now, through the implementation of the law of God, the *sharî`a*. This is the task of the Muslim state, which therefore has a sacred religious mission.

The basic political concepts of Islam were formulated during the period of political success, and they bear the mark of a triumphant religion. Thus, the political ascendancy of Islam is so deeply inherent in the mind of Muslims that periods of decline are viewed as deviations from the natural course of history, and as temporary aberrations that must be reversed. Indeed, there was a point at which contemporary Muslims believed that history had returned to its natural course. The 1973 oil boycott by OPEC, a predominantly Muslim organization, shocked the industrialized West. The 1960s was the period of the "Cold War" between Egypt and Saudi Arabia over hegemony in the Arab world; between Nasser's Egypt with its adherence to Arab nationals and socialism, and Saudi Arabia with its Islamic orientation. The defeat of Nasser in 1967 and the flow of petrodollars to Saudi Arabia after 1973 helped to shift the emphasis in the Arab world to Islam (Sidahmed and Ehteshami 1996, 1-15). Although oil politics lost their momentum, the moral boost reasserted Muslim identity and authenticity.

The Islamic concept of international relations, also formulated during periods of military expansion, is embedded in the *sharî`a*, and divides the world into two: *dâr al-Islâm*, where the law of Islam is supreme under Muslim rule, and *dâr al-Harb*, lands still under the rule of infidels. Muslims are obliged to exert every effort to extend *dâr al-Islâm* at the expense of *dar al-Harb*. The Arabic word for exertion is *jihâd*, a term that became a synonym for holy war. *Jihâd* is central to the theory of international relations as the instrument for implementing the expansion of Islam throughout the rest of the world.

Whatever political entities exist in *dâr al-Harb* are necessarily temporary and lack any legitimacy. In theory, the Muslim state cannot even make valid treaties with these political entities. Hence, the conduct of the Muslim state in the international arena is unilateral, not bilateral. The Ottoman Empire, the last great Muslim power, put this theory into practice. The Ottoman sultan accepted European ambassadors at his court, but did not send ambassadors to Europe until the nineteenth century. The change came about when the Ottoman Empire was forced to sign the Treaty of Karlovic with the Habsburg Empire and the Republic of Venice in 1699, and to recognize the existence of legitimate political entities in *dâr al-Harb*. Thus the perpetual *jihâd* gave way to permanent co-existence. In modern times, Muslim states operate within a world order based on Western diplomatic code and agreements, the same world order that sanctioned imperialism and colonialism, and which continues to favour the rich industrialized nations.

The challenge to the West began with Nasser, from a secular position of non-alignment. But Mu`ammar al-Qadhafî of Libya, who considered himself Nasser's successor, challenged the West from a militant Islamic position. Radical Islamist movements claim that full restoration of Islam is not possible within the existing world order (George 1996). For Khumeinî, the United States was the symbol of evil, the leader of a distorted illegitimate world order that must be destroyed. Saddâm Husayn came to power as the leader of the secularist Ba`th Party. But when he challenged the West in 1991, he resorted to Islamic rhetoric.

The attack on the United States of 11 September 2001 turned the spotlight onto the non-state Islamic terrorist challenge to the West. The worldwide terrorist network was made up of *mujâhidûn* from many Muslim nations who had originally volunteered for the cause of Islam in Afghanistan. They had been supported and armed by the United States to resist the Soviet Union. Many of them later went on to fight for the cause of Islam in Bosnia and Chechnya. They were joined by members of extremist Islamist groups, mainly from Egypt, who had earlier been supported by Saudi Arabia, and were recruited by Sadat in the battle against the Nasserites and leftists. The Islamist movement broke with the Egyptian regime after Sadat's autocratic tendencies were clearly manifested, and when the promises of economic prosperity failed to materialize and the peace treaty with Israel was signed (Beinin and Stork 1997, 9, 11).

Saudi Arabia's pro-Western policy supports the existing world order because it serves the economic and political interests of the royal house. This policy, however, is in conflict with the doctrines of the Wahhâbiyya movement that gave birth to the kingdom The eighteenth-century Wahhâbiyya, the most radical Islamic movement in pre-modern times, followed the teachings of the fourteenth–century Ibn Taymiyya, whom contemporary radicals Islamists adopted as their spiritual mentor.

The Islamic discourse is the only legitimate one in Saudi Arabia, but the threat to the regime is from radicals who point to the contradictions between realities and the doctrinal principles of the Wahhâbiyya. Hence, whenever a clash between Islamic and Western values is apparent, the royal house tips the scales towards Islam in order to perpetuate the alliance between the religious establishment and the political elite. This alliance goes back to the eighteenth-century concordat between the Shaykh Muhammad Ibn `Abd al-Wahhâb, who gave his name to the Wahhâbiyya movement, and the Emir Sa`ûd, who gave his name to the kingdom of Saudi Arabia. Because the authority of the established `ulamâ' is still acknowledged in charting rules of social behaviour, any criticism of the royal family is presented as being against Islam itself (Nehme 1998, 291, 292, 294, 298).

Pragmatism and Accommodation in Islam

The Wahhâbi-Saudi case illustrates the accommodation of a radical Islamic movement to practical realities. Pragmatism and accommodation in Islam find expression in the political concept that any authority is better than anarchy, and that any effective government is legitimate. This concept had evolved as early as the first century of Islam, in the wake of the traumatic civil war that brought about the great schism between the Sunna and the Shî`a.

Pragmatism and accommodation helped Sunni Islam to attain two of its greatest historical achievements: the end to schisms in Sunni Islam after the split with the Shî`a, and the spread of Islam across continents and over cultural barriers. All Muslims in the outer lands of Islam are Sunnis, and they accepted Islam not as a result of a military conquest, but through a long and peaceful process of accommodation.

Ijmâ`*, or the general consensus, is one of the four principles of jurisprudence in Sunni Islam. *Ijmâ` is reached through a process by which an innovation *(bid`a)* becomes a *sunna*, or orthodoxy, after it has been practised for generations, with the tacit consensus of the `*ulamâ'*. This process might be conceived as a legal mechanism guided by pragmatism. Yet almost everything that was endorsed through *ijmâ`*, such as the visitation of saints' tombs, is controversial. For centuries, these rulings were challenged by the radicals of every generation. Indeed, Muslim radicals may be defined as those who strictly adhere to the ideals of Islam, and reject pragmatism and accommodation.

Perhaps the most important concept that evolved out of the general consensus is that a Muslim does not become *kâfir*, an infidel, even if he commits a grave sin. But extreme radicals claim that Muslims can be declared infidels, and that *jihâd* against them is therefore permitted. Sayyid al-Qutb developed the view that contemporary Muslim societies, particularly which of Egypt, live in the *jâhiliyya* because they follow man-made laws and not the divine law. According to al-Qutb, there is no contemporary state that is ruled by the law of Islam, and therefore the whole world is *dâr al-Harb*, and *jihâd* is the only recourse (Choueiri 1996, 19–33). The *jihâd*, which had originally been an instrument for expanding the land of Islam at the expense of the land of the infidels, was transformed, in the ideology of the modern radicals, into an Islamic revolution against the infidels within.

The process by which pragmatism mitigates radical movements has been repeated also in Iran. The approved arena of Islamic politics has featured a continual struggle between different factions of political clerics and their supporters, who represent a spectrum from radicals to pragmatists. Radicals wish to carry on the revolutionary momentum, and advocate exporting the revolution to other countries. They call for uncompromising opposition to the United States and to Western influence. The conservatives who comprise the mainstream of Iranian clerics, seek to reinforce Islamic values and religious morality, including censorship of art, culture and the media. The third group, the pragmatists who won the presidential and parliamentary elections, support reform and foreign investment, which also implies a conciliatory attitude towards the West (Zubaida 1997, 112).

Africa

In Africa, one may also observe radicalism contained by pragmatism. The drive for reform in West Africa was initiated in the 1950s by those known as Wahhâbis, graduates of al-Azhar, who criticised the worship of saints. They provoked a violent and bloody confrontation with the Sufi brotherhoods.

The Wahhâbî movement in Mali, like Islamist groups elsewhere, established a range of institutions, such as mosques, modernized Muslim schools, clinics, pharmacies and cultural centres. Funding has come from contributions of local communities or individuals, migrant workers, and foreign Arab and Muslim sources. Yet the most important source of funding, in Africa as in the Middle East, is wealthy merchants. Acts of piety enhance the prestige of merchants and raise their commercial credability. They perform the pilgrimage to Mecca, and dispense charity by building mosques and financing other religious activities. Thus they benefit the reform movement (Brenner 1993, 59–78, 67, 74, 70).

In Nigeria in the 1950s there were violent clashes between adherents of the Qâdiriyya, which was associated with conservative "establishment" Islam, and the Tijâniyya, which had developed in reaction to the perceived elitist bent of the Qâdiriyya. The reformists in Nigeria, represented by the Izala movement, provoked friction and physical confrontation with the Sufis that often resulted in loss of life and damage to property. In 1980, the violence of Maitatsine, the fundamentalist prophet, and his followers in Kano shocked Muslims of all persuasions. The widespread destruction that resulted from these disturbances forced a reconsideration of questions of religious differences. The state security apparatus became more meticulous in monitoring religious organizations and banned open-air preaching, which affected the Izala more than other religious organizations (Umar 1993, 154-78).

Since the early 1980s there have been periodic clashes between Muslims and Christians in Nigeria, which may be related to the growing militancy among Muslims, particularly the call for the implementation of the *sharî`a*, which would change the status of non-Muslims. The Christians became alarmed, and also more violent.

In the Ivory Coast, riots represented the revival of rivalries between the mainly Muslim north and the predominantly Christian south. Muslims in the Ivory Coast, who comprise about half of the population, are mainly migrants from neighbouring countries, particularly Burkina Faso. The succession dispute after Felix Houphouet's death in 1993 was between the Catholic Henri Konan Bedie and the Muslim Alassane Ouattara. The former became interim president, and harassed Outtara's supporters. Muslim officers were purged from the army and the civil service. In 1994, Bedie legislated a citizenship bill that created a dual system favourable to the Christians of the south. People of the north complain of being treated as second-class citizens, and have been determined to defend their rights (Kaba 2000, 189-208).

Facing the common enemies of secularism and Christianity, there has been, since the late 1980s a tendency towards reconciliation between the rival Islamist and Sufi shaykhs. In the process, radicalism has lost much of its violent and sectarian connotations in West Africa, and a consensus has grown among the different groups about the orthodox tradition of Islam. This culture of tolerance caused praying styles to lose a good deal of their significance. Old adversaries joined together in organizations sponsored by governments. Reformist schools co-exist and co-operate with the religious or *zâwiya*-operated schools, to compete with secular education. Koranic schools improved their appearance with tables, blackboards and modern equipment and the curriculum was expanded to cover non-religious subjects (Kaba 2000, 202-04).

With independence, Islam became politically marginalized, as the new political elite opted for a secular order. Only in Senegal did Muslims play a significant role, because Léopold Senghor's political interests converged with those of the Sufi brotherhoods. These brotherhoods, particularly the Mourides, successfully adapted to modern conditions. The urban Mourides have developed a viable associative organization, which reflects the understanding that the brotherhood's commercial community thrives best within its own networks. Mouride ritual in this case serves as the bond of a commercial association. The successful Mouride entrepreneur appears to have taken on something of the social function of the rural shaykh, who provides for the material existence of his clientele (Cruise O'Brien 1988, 135-36, 141).

Yet the Mourides' traditional leadership is challenged from two sides in the town: from the brotherhood's more successful traders, who can be very much richer than the shaykhs, and from the new generation of Western-educated urban disciples. As the state opened schools in Mouride areas and Mouride parents were encouraged to enrol their children. The outcome was an assertive Mouride presence in the university, in the form of militant Mouride students with an active association (a *dâi'ra*), a programme of proselytism among the young, and an ideological restatement of the Mouride faith. Ahmadou Bamba is represented as the pioneer of the struggle against Western decadence. The young Mourides are against pop music, the use of drugs and Western dress. Mouride defence of African cultural pride is a powerful attraction to the young. A Mouride reform movement defends the Brotherhood from the attacks of the reformists. Bamba, who had created an independent African Sufi movement, also represents the refusal to subordinate to the Arab world, which Mourides claim distinguishes them from the Senegalese Tijâniyya and Qâdiriyya, who defer to Fez or Baghdad (Cruise O'Brien 1988, 136, 144, 146, 153).

Sudan

Sudan, an Arab-African state, is the only Sunni country that has experienced a genuine Islamic revolution. Hasan al-Turâbî, who emerged as the leader of the country's Islamist movement, advocated the reformation of the Muslim Brotherhood in the Sudan as a popular, potentially mass, political association. He opted to cooperate with President Ja`far al-Numayrî when the latter called for national reconciliation in 1978. With the new openings that this provided, the Brotherhood laid the foundations for the National Islamic Front (NIF) and for the emergence of the Islamists as an effective, if still relatively small, political force.

The September Laws of 1983, enacted by Numayrî, were

considered by al-Turâbî to be only the first step, however imperfect, in the actual Islamization of society. Following the military coup of 1989 led by General `Omar Bashîr, the revolutionary government soon became identified with the NIF, and al-Turâbî emerged as the major articulator of the ideology and programme of the new regime.

The Bashîr government actively suppressed all opposition, and the human rights record of the regime has been widely condemned (Voll 2000, 153-67). It has tried to control all social, political and cultural activities through "popular committees" that are entitled to forbid "non-Islamic" behaviour in the streets, in living quarters and in places of work. The explanation was that the function of such organizations is based on the traditional Islamic duty "to enjoin justice and forbid evil" (`Ali 1999, 14).

Conclusion

The modern state completed the destruction of pre-modern institutions in the public sphere of Islamic societies that had already been eroded under the impact of modernization and Western influence. The Islamists filled up the public sphere, and through their communal welfare projects also took over many functions of state institutions. The debate among Islamists was whether they should first work to create an Islamic society, or should seize state power in order to impose change from above, as the Sudanese regime has done. The reaction of governments may to a large extent determine both the nature of the political discourse and the level of violence.

Sunni Islam has always inclined towards pragmatism, which contemporary Islamists strongly reject, because they dismiss all compromises. These Islamists continue a long radical tradition in Islam, epitomized in the figure of the fourteenth-century Ibn Taymiyya, whom contemporary Islamists consider their spiritual mentor. The radicals reject legal constructions that developed out of the *ijmâ`*, which represents a process of compromise and accommodation. The most extreme radicals also reject the basic concept that there is no *takfîr* of Muslims. By addressing Muslim governments as infidels, extreme radicals legitimize a *jihâd* against Muslim societies and a total attack against the world order by every means, including international terrorism.

Is there any comfort in our analysis that Muslim radicals might accommodate to other systems and values, or at least be partially pragmatic? Does this depend also on the reaction of the international community? Is there a way to fight international terrorism other than by force? Scholars can hardly propose answers to these questions, which are political in nature. We can only suggest that politicians be more attentive to the nuances of scholarly analyses of society, history, religion and culture.

Epilogue: Islam and the New Public Sphere

John O. Voll

"If you want to liberate a society, just give them the Internet."
Wael Ghonim (2011)

Wael Ghonim, a Google marketing manager, became one of the heroes of the revolution that forced Hosni Mubarak of Egypt from power in 2011. His Facebook page, "We are all Khaled Said," which evoked the name and image of the young Egyptian who was beaten to death by the secret police, was an important tool for mobilizing the mass demonstrations in Tahrir Square. Ghonim's arrest and detention made him a symbol of the opposition to the Mubarak regime. In broader terms, Ghonim's actions illustrate the importance of the electronic social media – Facebook, YouTube, Twitter, cell phones, and others – in the events of what has come to be called the "Arab Spring." Regardless of the long term outcomes for specific movements, people using the resources of these media have dramatically changed the dynamics of popular political participation in the public sphere.

The evolution of the public sphere in Muslim societies has distinctive features but is also part of the broader global changes in the nature of popular participation in the modern era. The concept of the "public sphere" in modern society was influentially defined by Jürgen Habermas as "a social space – distinct from the state, the economy, and the family – in which individuals could engage each other as private citizens deliberating about the common good" (Mendieta and Vanantwerpen 2011b, 2). The reality of the "public sphere" has changed over the past two centuries, but the arena for popular action in society between the state and the domestic sphere continues to be of great importance in modern society and politics.

Nehemia Levtzion's interest in understanding the nature of the public sphere in the Muslim world is reflected in some of his final writings (Levtzion 2002, and Levtzion 2008). Issues that he raised in the first years of the twenty-first century provide a useful foundation for examining the nature of the public sphere as reflected by the new style of public participation involved in the Arab Spring of 2011 and movements elsewhere. Specifically, he and other scholars emphasized the changing institutional base of the public sphere as modern state systems developed in the Muslim world. This broad foundation is being transformed again by new communications technologies, creating a new public sphere that still involves the institutional public sphere, but also is significantly different in the ways that people are mobilized.

The New Public Sphere

The nature of the public sphere itself is changing significantly throughout the world. Among the major elements in these processes are the media, which played important roles in the Arab Spring. Already by the late 1990s, it was possible to say that there is "wide agreement that the Internet is dramatically changing the dynamics of political participation" (Ayres 1999, 140). A discussion in *Wired*, a major magazine covering the new media, describes the changes in 1996:

> The public square of the past – with pamphleteering, soapboxes, and vigorous debate – is being replaced by the Internet, which enables average citizens to participate in national discourse, publish a newspaper, distribute an electronic pamphlet to the world, and generally communicate to and with a broader audience than ever before possible. It also enables average citizens to gain access to a vast and literally world-wide range of information.
> (Wired 1996, 84, quoted in Warf and Grimes 1997, 261)

Looking at this description of the "new" public sphere fifteen years later, it becomes apparent that the public sphere continues to change in many important ways. Viewed from the perspective of the dynamics of participation in the Arab Spring, the 1996 portrayal of electronic participation in the public sphere seems almost archaic. In 2010, Chris Anderson, the editor-in-chief of *Wired*, could declare, "The Web is Dead. Long Live the Internet." In terms of participation in the public sphere, Anderson noted the dramatic changes: "The Internet is the real revolution, as important as electricity; what we do with it is still evolving. As it moved from your desktop to your pocket, the nature of the Net changed" (Anderson 2010). In this perspective, the global Internet-based activism of the 1990s, as seen in the global support for the Zapatista movement in Mexico, can be viewed as an emerging "desktop public sphere," while the dynamics of Arab Spring participation combined utilizing in-your-pocket technology, not available in 1996, with direct political engagement "in the streets" (Ghonim 2012, 153–158).

Just as "We Are All Khaled Said" helped to mobilize popular support for opposition in Egypt, the new social media were crucial in mobilizing opposition in Tunisia, the first successful movement of the Arab Spring. There had been a number of local protests against the repressive Tunisian regime that the police quickly suppressed. However, when Tarak Bouazizi set himself on fire in protest against the local police in Sidi Bouzid, social media mobilized.

As an early activist recounted, the government "had total control of media, so almost no one wrote about Bouazizi... We had to take advantage of our only weapon, the biggest open and free media in the world: the Internet" (El Mekki 2012, 58). Internet activists, bloggers, and cyberactivists transformed the Tunisian public sphere.

At the beginning of the twenty-first century, scholars like Nehemia Levtzion were examining changes in the public sphere in the Muslim world. In the tradition of examination of the public sphere in Western societies from the seventeenth and eighteenth centuries to the present, much of this analysis concentrated on institutional developments. Levtzion and a group of colleagues published a volume of essays (Hoexter 2002) which "demonstrate the existence of a vibrant public sphere that was of crucial importance in shaping the dynamics of pre-modern Muslim societies" (Levztion 2008, 547). This analysis involved a major challenge to the secular-oriented analyses of "civil society" that viewed historic Muslim societies as not having a functional "public sphere."

While the studies in the Hoexter-Levtzion volume concentrated on institutions in pre-modern society, Levtzion extended this analysis to modern and contemporary developments. He argued that the "modern state" weakened the old Muslim institutions in the public sphere and "the vacuum created in the public sphere has been filled by the Islamist movements" (Levtzion 2008, 547–548). An important element in this process was that "Islamists developed networks of voluntary organizations... . They created a new autonomous public sphere that challenged state power" (Levtzion 2008, 548).

Levtzion suggested that one of the major institutions of the pre-modern Muslim public sphere, the Sufi brotherhoods (*tariqahs*), made a successful transition to modern forms. In their reformist mode, pre-modern tariqahs "could have led Muslim societies into the modern period with a sense of revival," although their efforts to resist European imperial expansion in the nineteenth century were unsuccessful (Levtzion 2002, 117). However, Sufi organizations may be viewed as precursors to the twentieth-century Islamists and were influential in shaping the thought and organization of the modern Islamists. In addition, the organizations of many of the tariqahs themselves were successful in adapting to conditions of modernity and have millions of followers throughout the world. Levtzion noted the modern success of the Murid brotherhood in Senegal as an example (Levtzion 2008, 547–548).

The public sphere for politics in the Muslim world during the 1990s and the first years of the twenty-first century was still institutional in format but changing. In specific terms of politics in the Arab world, already by 1997 Asad Abukhalil observed that the "shape of Arab politics is rapidly evolving" and that "the tide has been turning in favour of democratisation for some time" (Abukhalil 1997, 150, 160). Similar changes were taking place in other parts of the Muslim world. One of the first major successful anti-authoritarian movements overthrew the long-term dictator in Indonesia, Suharto, in 1998. In Turkey, the political arena was significantly changed when a reformist, Islamically-identified political party, the Adalet ve Kalkinma Partisi (AKP) won elections in 2002, signaling the decline of the old-style secularist politics of the twentieth century. However, in most analyses at that time, little attention was given to the potential impact of electronic social media.

During the first decade of the twenty-first century, the nature of the available electronic social media was being transformed. Facebook was launched in 2004, YouTube began in 2005, and Twitter in 2006. The expansion of the capacities of cell phones and other handheld informational and transmission devices substantially changed the way that many people in the world communicated with others, creating the capacity for new types of societal networks. Scholars began to note the impact of these new resources on the nature of collective activity and the changing nature of institutional organization. "For most of modern life, our strong talents and desires for group effort have been filtered through relatively rigid institutional structures because of the complexity of managing groups... . The current change, in one sentence, is this: most of the barriers to group action have collapsed, and without those barriers, we are free to explore new ways of gathering together and getting things done" (Shirky 2008, 21,22).

This new mode of group action was important in the movements in the Arab Spring. "The new media played an important role in mobilizing the Arab uprisings," and the "symbiotic interaction of new media and mobile phones with more familiar communications channels such as television and newspapers has fundamentally transformed political communication" (El Difraoui 2012, 18). However, as El Difraoui argues, the media were the means for mobilizing people, but "it was the people rather than the media that were the decisive factor for change" (El Difraoui 2012, 18).

Old and New Activism in the Evolving Public Sphere

A striking aspect of the experience of Egypt and elsewhere in the Arab Spring is the absence of institutional organizations in the shaping of the initial movements. The Tahrir movement did not end up creating a formal political organization in the model of the older institutional action in the public sphere. This mode was summed up by Wael Ghonim:

> Revolutions of the past have usually had charismatic leaders who were politically savvy and sometimes even military geniuses. Such revolutions followed what we can call the Revolution 1.0 model. But the revolution in Egypt was different: it was truly a spontaneous movement led by nothing other than the wisdom of the crowd.
>
> (Ghonim 2012, 293)

The "wisdom of the crowd" was frequently expressed in what might be thought of as the new vernacular language of those mobilized by the new media. Rather than creating grand statements of ideology, like the famous tracts involved in the Revolution 1.0 model (Thomas Paine's *Common Sense* or Marx's *Communist Manifesto*, for example), the most visible and audible voices in the Arab Spring were frequently the pop-singers and rappers. Popular singers like El Général in Tunisia, Ramy Essam in Egypt and Haked in Morocco were said to provide "the soundtrack" for the movements (Hebblethwaite 2011; Lynskey 2012; Schemm 2012).

The new vernaculars of hip hop and other pop-music forms were important vehicles for strengthening the enthusiasm of the participants. This aspect reflects an important dimension of pre-modern movements of revival and reform that Levtzion noted. Those movements in the pre-modern public sphere often utilized vernacular languages in the presentation of their message to the general public. "The efficiency of preaching and exhortation in the vernacular to mobilize popular support" was important, for example, in movements like the jihad of Uthman dan Fodio in early nineteenth-century Nigeria (Levtzion 2002, 115). Although the actual vernacular may be new, the principle of addressing people in the language of their daily life in order to encourage their participation in the movement is a significant shared characteristic of the earlier and later modes of activism.

The new populist activism brought a new element into the public sphere but it did not replace or eliminate existing institutions. The new autonomous public sphere of the late twentieth century, observed by Levtzion, involved "the emergence of the Islamic trend as the only credible political alternative to the Egyptian regime" (Levtzion 2008, 549). The Muslim Brotherhood had well-established networks of social and charitable groups. These structures were an important part of the older institutional style of public sphere in Egypt and in other parts of the Muslim world. However, while the Brotherhood is the most visible political alternative, the Sufi tariqahs, with millions of followers, provide popular religious foundations for identity in the public sphere. Having successfully adapted to modernity, their importance means that the public sphere cannot be viewed, as it is by many analysts, as a basically "secular" domain.

In the year following the overthrow of Mubarak in Egypt, tensions sometimes developed between those involved in the various styles of activity in the newly powerful public sphere. Although all involved supported replacement of the existing regime and called for elections, the older institutional-style groups, like the Muslim Brotherhood, were better prepared for the actualities of participating in elections. The result in the first Egyptian parliamentary elections was a very substantial victory for the Islamist parties organized by the Muslim Brotherhood and the Salafis. There were similar results in other Arab countries where Arab Spring incentives led to holding major elections. Al-Nahdah, the longtime Islamist opposition to the Ben Ali regime in Tunisia, won the first elections in the new era, and a moderate Islamically-identified party in Morocco that had been in the opposition won the 2011 elections there. After fourteen months of continuing conflict in Syria, the Syrian

Muslim Brotherhood emerged as the best organized group within the opposition movement, despite having been rigorously suppressed for decades.

It is possible to see two quite different competitions in these developments. The old authoritarian institutions of post-colonial politics faced anti-authoritarian populism representing the new forms of political opposition. However, the organizations of the older institutional movements of opposition emerged as both competitors and allies of the new populists. In this way, the new public sphere is the arena for a three-way competition between the old dictatorial establishment, the new populist democrats, and the older organizations that have had long experience in the politics of opposition.

The post-Arab Spring public sphere is lively and powerful and is a public and political space within which powerful populist political forces operate. Whether the long-term results of the Arab Spring involve the establishment of new and more democratic political regimes or a reversion to authoritarianism in some new mode, the political realities of the public sphere have been transformed. The victory of those Arab Spring movements that were successful in bringing an end to the existing autocratic regimes represents a challenge not only to the old political regimes but also a challenge to the conceptual paradigms that were used to analyze the old-style politics.

Secularism, Islamism, and the Changing Place of Ideology

Many of the longstanding activities and conflicts within the public sphere have been changing in their nature in recent years. Many analyses of the public sphere have emphasized its political aspects and it is the arena within which the major social movements of contention operate. In the Muslim world, as elsewhere, competitions have often been among actors *within* the public arena, rather than *between* civil society actors and the state.

One significant rivalry in the Muslim public sphere has been between "secularists" and "Islamists," each with distinctive and competing ideological positions. An important assumption made by many analysts since the middle of the twentieth century was that the "secularists" were progressive and more "modern" than the religious advocates. A pillar of the old modernization theory was that modernity meant the inevitable secularization of societies. However, in the early twenty-first century, "religion is on the rise" globally and the "major world religions are all taking advantage of the opportunities provided by globalization to transform their messages and reach a new global audience" (Thomas 2010, 93, 101). This new importance for religion is generally not a part of state policy but is an important element in the changing public sphere.

The radical secularist ideologies of the twentieth century have failed. In the Arab Spring, the first two rulers to be overthrown were identifiable as secular autocrats. Similarly, Saddam Hussein in Iraq and Bashar Asad in Syria are identified with the old secularist radicalism of different branches of the Ba'th

Party. While it would not be accurate to say that the advocates of democratic opposition to authoritarian regimes were specifically opposing secularist ideologies, it would be equally inaccurate to say that pro-democracy people were advocating secularism. The legacy of secularist modernization in the Middle East, from the Shah in Iran to Mubarak in Egypt, was authoritarian rule, not modern democracy.

Similarly, the extremist Islamist ideologies of the twentieth century, which were the rivals of the secularist visions, had little part in the activism of the Arab Spring. Old-style jihadism may have lost "one of its major selling points: that only armed struggle can bring down the regimes in the region" (Brynjar Lia, quoted in Lahoud 2011, 4). The 2011 movements have been interpreted in many ways, but in broad terms, "the revolutions transcend the Islamist politics that reigned in the region just a few years ago" (Bayat 2011).

The nature of the Tahrir Square movement suggests that the old dichotomy between "religious" and "secular" in the public sphere needs to be redefined. At the end of the twentieth century, the most visible religious elements in the public sphere, as noted by scholars like Levtzion, were the Islamist movements, who filled the vacuum created by the weakening of the old basic institutions of the pre-modern public sphere (Levtzion 2008, 547–548). However, the new movements of the Arab Spring were neither Islamist (in the old definition of that term) nor secularist. Asef Bayat suggests that these movements are "post-Islamist," in which "Post-Islamism is not anti-Islamic or secular; a post-Islamist movement dearly upholds religion but also highlights citizens' rights. It aspires to a pious society within a democratic state" (Bayat 2011). For example, Wael Ghonim's beginning as a social media figure was the creation of a Web site that would "serve as a kind of public library featuring a complete range of moderate Islamic opinions" and after two years it had tens of thousands of daily users (Ghonim 2012, 15). In the time when Tahrir Square was occupied, the Muslim Friday prayer services were major events, but they were a part of the group life more than an ideological declaration.

This new blending of "religious" and "secular" elements in the new public sphere is well illustrated by the evolving public roles of Sufi associations. In important ways, the tariqahs utilized modern types of activities to continue their important role in pre-modern society in which they "maintained lines of communications between the common people and the authorities" (Levtzion 2002, 117). In this way, although the brotherhoods were an important political force, they were outside of the state and active in the public sphere.

An important modern and contemporary example of this role is the case of the Murids in Senegal, who, as Levtzion noted, had "successfully adapted to modern conditions" (Levtzion 2008, 556). In Senegal, allegiance to one of the major Sufi orders "has never seriously been called into question as the public and dominant mode of religious devotion for the great majority – some 90 per cent – of the Senegalese population" (Villalón 2007, 173). The Murids are central to what has been and continues to be a "vibrant and religiously based 'civil society' that has facilitated a popular engagement with the state... The Senegalese democratic polity has been built on religious foundations" (Villalón 2007, 173).

Since independence, Senegal has had a series of strong, long term leaders. In each transition from one dominant figure to another – in 1981 from the "founding father," Leopold Senghor to Abdou Diouf, from Diouf to Abdulaye Wade in 2000, and in 2012 from Wade to Macky Sall – the brotherhoods played important roles in the processes that avoided military coups or the establishment of a one-man, one-party state. Each transition reflected the nature of the public sphere of the time. The transition in 2011–2012 involved a rejection of an attempt by Wade to amend the constitution to enable him to stay in power. Wade attempted to utilize the old-style, more institutional ethnic-Murid alliance with the presidency. His loss may show the changing nature of Sufi involvement in the public sphere. Part of the opposition to Wade was expressed by a globally-known popular singer, Youssou N'Dour, who was associated with the Murid tradition but not a leader in the order. Although he was disqualified as a presidential candidate, he became culture and tourism minister in the first cabinet of Macky Sall.

In the new public sphere, "religion" blended with pragmatic issues of protest against authoritarian rule. Neither ideological secularism nor old-style jihadism was a significant element in the emerging new modes of protest. Emad Shahin of the Kroc Institute at University of Notre Dame noted, "It's not an age of ideology anymore... . There are more pressing issues that all the players, including the Islamists, are interested in now and have to deal with" (Slackman 2011). The old competitions for ideological leadership in the Middle East between people like Saddam Hussein in Iraq and the Ayatollah Khomeini in Iran have been replaced by more pragmatic calls for improvement of the conditions of daily life and an end to police state repression. The demands of the demonstrators were basic, with the simple slogan, "The People Want to Overthrow the Regime." being heard from North Africa to the Gulf (Lynch, 2011).

The shift from ideological Islamism to more pragmatic approaches of participation in the public sphere was visible in many areas in the first decade of the twenty-first century. In Turkey, for much of the second half of the twentieth century, a series of Islamist parties led by Necmettin Erbakan presented the old-style institutional Islamist positions. When the Virtue Party (*Fazilet Partisi*) was closed by the government in 2001, the Islamist movement split. "The older generation of politicians around Erbakan... were traditionalists... . They saw their mission as establishing a 'new civilization' based on traditional Islamic values and were reluctant to make practical compromises with the secular establishment" (Rabasa and Larrabee 2008, 46). In contrast, the new trend, articulated by Recep Tayyip Erdoğan and Abdullah Gül in forming the Justice and Development Party (AKP; *Adalet ve Kalkınma Partisi*) was "a sharp departure from the political Islam represented by Erbakan... Erdoğan explicitly stated that the party was not going to be an Islamist party and that the party members were simply 'Muslim democrats'" (Rabasa and Larrabee 2008, 54).

A similar transition to more pragmatic political positions is visible in the long-term evolution of PAS (*Parti Islam Se-Malaysia*) in Malaysia. PAS began in the 1950s as a party advocating the establishment of an Islamic state and maintained that older mode of Islamist political platform until late in the twentieth century. In these later PAS platforms, as analyzed by Syed Ahmad Hussein, "Islamic governance was increasingly presented not in the dogmatic legalistic-institutional form of the mid-1980s but one highlighting the centrality in Islam of social justice, rights of the citizen, honest elections and clean government" (Quoted in Liow 2004, 368).

In Egypt, one aspect of the blending of longstanding religious identities and pragmatic approaches can be seen in some interesting initiatives by some Sufi leaders. Historically, the leadership of the orders has avoided overt political involvement except to continue the traditional function of expressing concerns of the common people to the rulers. However, in the transition period following the overthrow of Mubarak, important Sufi leaders became concerned by the prospect of the growing political power of the Brotherhood (which opposes many of the popular Sufi religious customs and festivals). They "quickly aligned with liberals and revolutionary youth groups" and participated in the establishment of "the first Sufi political party, the Egyptian Liberation Party" (Brown 2011, 12). One of the founders of the party, Mohamed Alaa Eddin Abu Azayem, the head of the Azmiyya Tariqah expressed the fears clearly: for the Salafis, "Sufis, Shia, and unveiled women are nonbelievers... . Hence the need for a moral party that would make people feel safe" (El Hennawy 2011). However, despite the large following that the orders have in Egypt, the tariqah-based party did not do well, possibly because it is "too much a part of Egyptian life to stand out as an identifying political motivator" (Brown 2011, 13).

This move away from dogmatic institutional-ideological modes has taken different forms in many parts of the Muslim world. It is a significant element in the Arab Spring. However, this shift also reflects a more general and longstanding tendency in Muslim history, as noted by Levtzion in his analysis. He notes the importance of "pragmatism and accommodation" in Sunni Islam and the tendency of radical movements to be "contained by pragmatism," citing examples like the Wahhabi-Saudi movement in eighteenth-century Arabia, and modern "fundamentalist" movements in Mali and Nigeria.

The non-ideological nature of the new public sphere visible in the events of the Arab Spring is thus a part of developments visible in many parts of the contemporary Muslim world. One analyst speaks of this time as the "seemingly new era of political and leaderless actors who are weary of the burdens of ideologies" (Lahoud 2011, 4). This is a move away from the ideological dogmatisms of the earlier "new" institutional public sphere in which ideological Islamism was a significant force. However, the shift from radicalism to pragmatism in the public sphere, as noted by Levtzion, has clear precedents in Islamic history.

Conclusion

Populist activism is an important part of participation in the public sphere in all societies. By the second decade of the twenty-first century, radically new ways of expressing this activism interacted with established institutional modes of participation. In Muslim societies, this new-style public sphere became visible in the Arab Spring movements of 2011, although this new populism had roots in twentieth-century developments. These antecedents were noted and analyzed by scholars like Levtzion at the beginning of the new century.

In this "new public sphere," electronic social media provided important new mechanisms for mobilization of participants without utilizing the older forms of institutional organization. However, the older organizational forms continued to be effective means for managing popular participation in more formally structured activities like forming political parties and participating in elections. In this way, while both the new populists and the older organizations of opposition joined forces in opposing autocratic regimes, there was always a potential for conflict between the older and newer modes of participation in the public sphere.

In the new public sphere, more formally-articulated ideologies play a less important role than they did in the politics of the later twentieth century. The ideologies of both Islamism and secularism, which had been major forces in the earlier public sphere, play a less crucial role. Most participants in the public sphere seem tired and mistrustful of more dogmatic ideologies and even formerly ideological Islamist groups articulate their visions in more pragmatic terms. Populism is increasingly expressed in the vernacular of the rapper rather than the sermons and lectures of imams and secular intellectuals.

Strong continuities with the past remain an important part of the Muslim public sphere. However, by the second decade of the twenty-first century, populist activism in the social arena between the state and the private domestic realms has taken many novel forms, giving shape to a new Muslim public sphere.

References

Abukhalil, As'ad. 1997. "Change and Democratisation in the Arab World: The Role of Political Parties," *Third World Quarterly* 18, No. 1 (March): 149-163.

Anderson, Chris. 2010. "The Web is Dead. Long Live the Internet," *Wired* 18.02 (February). Available at: www.wired.com/magazine/2010/08/ff_webrip/all/1.

Ayres, Jeffrey M. 1999. "From the Streets to the Internet: The Cyber-Diffusion of Contention," *Annals of the American Academy of Political and Social Science* 566 (November): 132-143.

Bayat, Asef. 2011. "The Post-Islamist Revolutions," *Foreign Affairs*, 26 April 2011. Web 23 April 2012. Available at: www.foreignaffairs.com/articles/67812/asef-bayat/the-post-islamist-revolutions?page=show.

Brown, Jonathan. 2011. *Salafis and Sufis in Egypt*. Washington: Carnegie Endowment for International Peace.

El Difraoui, Asiem. 2012. "No 'Facebook' Revolution' – But an Egyptian Youth We Know Little About," in *Protest, Revolt and Regime Change in the Arab World*, ed. by Muriel Asseberg. SWP Research Paper No. 6. Berlin: Stiftung Wissenschaft un Politik.

El-Hennawy, Noha. 2011. "Egypt's Sufi-dominated party aims to counterbalance Salafism in politics," *Egypt Independent*, 9 May 2011. Available at: www.egyptindependent.com.

Ghonim, Wael. 2011. "Egypt's Facebook Revolution: Wael Ghonim Thanks The Social Network," *The Huffington Post* 25 May 2011. Updated Report by Catharine Smith. Available at: www.huffingtonpost.com/2011/02/11/egypt-facebook-revolution-wael-ghonim_n_822078.html.

Ghonim, Wael. 2012. *Revolution 2.0: The Power of the People is Greater than the People in Power, A Memoir*. Boston: Houghton Mifflin Harcourt.

Hebblethwaite, Cordelia. 2011. "Is hip hop driving the Arab Spring?", *BBC News Middle East*, 24 July. Available at: www.bbc.co.uk/news/world-middle-east-14146243.

Hoexter, Miriam, Shmuel N. Eisenstadt, and Nehemia Levtzion. 2002. *The Public Sphere in Muslim Societies*. Albany: State University of New York Press.

Lahoud, Nelly. 2011. "Revolution in Tunisia and Egypt: A Blow to the Jihadist Narrative?", *CTC Sentinel* 4, No. 2 (February): 4-5.

Levtzion, Nehemia, 2002. "The Dynamics of Sufi Botherhoods," in Hoexter, 2002, pp. 109-118.

Levtzion, Nehemia. 2008. "Resurgent Islamic Fundamentalism as an Integrative Factor in the Politics of Africa and the Middle East," *Canadian Journal of African Studies/ Revue Canadienne des Études Africaines* 42, Nos. 2-3, 546-559.

Liow, Joseph Chin Yong. 2004. "Exigency or Expediency? Contextualizing Political Islam and the PAS Challenge in Malaysian Politics," *Third World Quarterly* 25, No. 2, 359-372.

Lynch, Mark. 2011. "The Big Think Behind the Arab Spring," *Foreign Policy* (December). Available at: www.foreignpolicy.com.

Lynskey, Dorian. 2011. "Ramy Essam – the voice of the Egyptian Uprising," *The Guardian*. 19 July. Available at: www.guardian.co.uk/music/2011/jul19/ramy-essam-egypt-uprising-interview.

Mendieta, Eduardo, and Jonathan Vanantwerpen. 2011a. *The Power of Religion in the Public Sphere*. New York: Columbia Univesity Press.

Mendieta, Eduardo, and Jonathan Vanantwerpen. 2011b. "Introduction: The Power of Religion in the Public Sphere," in Mendieta and Vanantwerpen, 2011a, pp. 1-14.

Rabasa, Angel and F. Stephen Larrabee. 2008. *The Rise of Political Islam in Turkey*. Santa Monica: RAND.

Schemm, Paul. 2012. "A year on, Morocco's democracy movement founders," *Washington Post* 19 February. P. A17.

Shirky, Clay. 2008. *Here Comes Everybody: The Power of Organizing Without Organizations*. New York: Penguin Books.

Slackman, Michael. 2011. "In Mideast Activism, a New Tilt Away From Ideology," *New York Times*, 23 January. Available at: www.nytimes.org.

Thomas, Scott M. 2010. "A Globalized God: Religion's Growing Influence in International Politics," *Foreign Affairs* 89, No. 6 (November/ December): 93-101.

Van Bruinessen, Martin, and Julia Day Howell, eds. 2007. *Sufism and the 'Modern' in Islam*. London: I. B. Tauris.

Villalón, Leonardo A. 2007. "Sufi Modernities in Contemporary Senegal: Religious Dynamics between the Local and the Global," in van Bruinessen 2007, pp. 172-191.

Warf, Barney and John Grimes, 1997. "Counterhegemonic Discourses and the Internet," *Geographical Review* 87, No. 2 (April): 259-274.

Wired, 1996. "Internet v. United States Department of Justice, Janet Reno et al," *Wired* 4.05 (May): 84-91.

Works Cited

Abduh, Muhammad. No date. *al-Islam wa-'l-muslimun*, edited by Mahmud Abu Rayyah. Cairo: Dar al-Ma'arif.

Abdula-Razak, Idris. 1996. "Alhaji Umar of Kete Krachi: A Muslim Teacher, a Poet, and a Social Commentator of His Time." MPhil thesis, Department of Religion, University of Ghana.

Ackroyd, Peter. 2000. *The History of Britain*. London: The Biography. New York: Doubleday.

Adegbite, Ademola. 1989. "The Influence of Islam on Yoruba Music." *Orita* 21, no.1: 32-43.

Adeleye, Remi. 1971. *Power and Diplomacy in Northern Nigeria 1804-1906*. London.

Aichi, Houria. 2001. "Khalwa: chants sacrés d'Algérie." Virgin Classics.

Ajayi, J.F. Ade and Michael Crowder, eds. 1971. *History of West Africa*. London: Longman Press.

al-Khafaji, Rasoul. 2006. "The Case of Shifts in Lexical Repetition in Arabic-English Translations." *Babel* 52, no.1: 39-65.

al-Samaa. 2004. "Al-Samaa: Ecstatic Spiritual Audition." Ihsan Rmiki. Paris: Institut du Monde Arabe.

al-Shahi, Ahmed. 1984. "Spirit Possession and Healing: The ZAR among the Shaygiyya of the Northern Sudan." *Bulletin (British Society for Middle Eastern Studies)* 11, no.1: 28-44.

al-Tariqa. 1992. "Al-Tariqa Al-Hamidiyya Al-Chaziliyya." France: Arion.

al-Tuhami, Yasin. 1998. "The Magic of the Sufi Inshad." Montreuil, France: Long Distance.

al-Tuni, Ahmad. 2000. "The Sultan of All Munshidin." Montreuil, France: Long Distance.

al-Yassini, Ayman. 1995. "Wahhâbîya." In *The Oxford Encyclopedia of the Modern Islamic World*, edited by John L. Esposito, 4: 307-08.

Alexander, Archibald. 1969. *A History of Colonization of the Western Coast of Africa*. New York: Negro Universities Press.

'Ali, Haydar Ibrahim. 1999. "Civil Society and Democratization in Arab Countries with Special Reference to the Sudan." In Islamic Area Studies Project — Islamic Area Studies working paper series no. 12. Tokyo, Japan.

Alpers, Edward A. 2000. "East Central Africa." In *The History of Islam in Africa*, edited by N. Levtzion and R.L. Pouwels, 303-26. Athens: Ohio University Press.

Alpha Ba, M. 1991. "The Status of Muslims in Sierra Leone and Liberia." *Journal Institute of Muslim Minority Affairs* 12, no.2: 464-81.

Alport, E.A. 1954. "The Mzab." *Journal of the Anthropological Institute of Great Britain and Ireland* 84, nos.1-2: 34-44.

Ames, David W. 1973. "Igbo and Hausa Musicians: A Comparative Examination." *Ethnomusicology* 17, no.2: 250-78.

——. 1982. "Contexts of Dance in Zazzau and the Impact of Islamic Reform." In *African Religious Groups and Beliefs: Papers in Honor of William R. Bascom*, edited by Simon Ottenberg, 110-47. Meerut, India: Published for the Folklore Institute by Archana Publications.

Amiji, Hatim. 1975. "The Bohras of East Africa." *Journal of Religion in Africa* 7, no.1: 27-61.

Amselle, Jean-Loup. [1990] 1998. *Mestizo Logics: Anthropology of Identity in Africa and Elsewhere*. Translated by Claudia Royal Stanford, California: Stanford University Press.

Anderson, Benjamin. 1971. *Journeys to Musadu*. London: Frank Cass and Company Limited.

Anderson, Lois Ann. 1971. "The Interrelation of African and Arab Musics: Some Preliminary Considerations." In *Essays on Music and History in Africa*, edited by Klaus Wachsmann, 143-69. Evanston: Northwestern University Press.

Ansari, Muhammad Abdul Haq. 1986. *Sufism and Shari'ah: A Study of Shaykh Ahmad Sirhindi's Effort to Reform Sufism*. Leicester: The Islamic Foundation.

Arnaud, Robert. 1912. "La singulière légende des Soninkés: Traditions orales sur le royaume de Koumbi." In *L'Islam et la politique musulmane française en Afrique occidentale français*, 156-84. Paris, Comité de l'Afrique Française.

Ashmun, J. 1827. "Latest from Liberia." *African Repository* 3, no.6: 10-15.

Askew, Kelly M. 1999. "Female Circles and Male Lines: Gender Dynamics along the Swahili Coast." *Africa Today* 46, nos.3-4, Summer / Autumn): 67-102.

Assombang, R. 1999. "Sacred Centers and Urbanization in West Central Africa." In *Beyond Chiefdoms: Pathways to Complexity in Africa*, edited by S. McIntosh, 80-87. Cambridge: Cambridge University Press.

Bâ, Amadou Hampaté. [1973] 1999. *L'Etrange destin de Wangrin*. Paris: Editions 10/18. Translated as *The Fortunes of Wangrin*. Translated by Aina Pavolini Taylor. Bloomington: Indiana University Press.

Bâ, Amadou Hampâte et Jean Daget. 1955. *L'Empire peul du Macina, Volume 1*. Bamako: IFAN.

Bahilu, James Ayarna Bahir. 1988. "A Survey of the History and Impact of the Ahmadiyyah Muslim Mission in Wa." MPhil thesis, Department of Religion, University of Ghana.

Bakari, Mtoro bin Mwinyi. 1981. *The Customs of the Swahili People:*

The Desturi Za Waswahili of Mtoro Bin Mwinyi Bakari and Other Swahili Persons. Edited and translated by J.W.T. Allen. Berkeley: University of California Press.

Balogun, S.U. 1985. "Arabic Intellectualism in West Africa: The Role of the Sokoto Caliphate." *Journal: Institute of Muslim Minority Affairs* 6, no.2: 394-411.

Barber, Karin, and Christopher Waterman. 1995. "Traversing the Global and the Local: Fuji Music and Praise Poetry in the Production of Contemporary Yoruba Popular Culture." In *Worlds Apart: Modernity Through the Prism of the Local*, edited by Daniel Miller, 240-62. London: Routledge.

Barrayn, Sheikh Ahmad. 1994. "Sufi Songs." Paris: Long Distance.

Barth, Heinrich. 1857 [1965]. *Travels and Discoveries in North and Central Africa, Being a Journal of an Expedition Undertaken under the Auspices of HBM's Government in the Years 1849-1855. Volume 3*. New York: Harper & Brothers.

Basso, Keith H. 1984. "'Stalking with Stories': Names, Places, and Moral Narratives among the Western Apache." In *Text Play and Story: The Construction and Reconstruction of Self and Society*, edited by Stuart Plattner and Edward M. Bruner, 19-55. 1983 Proceedings of the American Ethnological Society.

———. 1988. "'Speaking with Names': Language and Landscape among the Western Apache." *Cultural Anthropology* 3, no.2: 99-130.

———. 1996. *Wisdom Sits in Places: Landscape and Language among the Western Apache*. Albuquerque: University of New Mexico Press.

Baynes, N. 1913. "The Successors of Justinian." In *The Cambridge Medieval History, Volume II: The Rise of the Saracens and the Foundation of the Western Empire*, 263-300. Cambridge: Cambridge University Press.

Beach, David N. 1980. *The Shona and Zimbabwe 900-1850*. Gwelo: Mambo Press.

Bedaux, R., J. Polet, K. Sanogo, and A. Schmidt, eds. 2003. *Recherches archéologiques à Dia dans le Delta Intérieure du Niger (Mali)*. Leiden: CNWS Publications.

Beidelman, Thomas O. 1965. "Myth, Tradition and Oral History." *Anthropos* 65, no.6: 74-97.

Beinin, Joel and Joe Stork. 1997. "Introduction." In *Political Islam: Essays from Middle East Report*, 3-27. Berkeley: University of California Press.

Belcher, Stephen, ed. 2005. *African Myths of Origin*. London: Penguin Books.

Bello, Shaykh Muhammad. 1820-21. *Tanbih ahl al-Fuhum ala wujub ijtinab ahl al-sha dhaba wa I-nujum.* Cairo.

Ben-Ari, Nitsa. 1998. "The Ambivalent Case of Repetitions in Literary Translation. Avoiding Repetitions: A `Universal' of Translation." *Meta* 63, no.1: 1-11.

Bening, Bagula. 1990. *History of Education in Northern Ghana, 1907-1976.* Accra: Ghana Universities Press.

Benson, S.A. 1863. "Message of the President of Liberia, December 5, 1862." *African Repository* XXXIX, no.3: 76-85.

Berthier, S. 1997. *Recherches archéologiques sur la capitale de l'empire de Ghana: Etude d'un secteur d'habitat à Koumbi Saleh, Mauritanie. Campagnes II-III-IV-V (1975-1976)-(1980-1981).* Oxford: Archaeopress.

Besmer, Fremont E. 1972. "Hausa Court Music in Kano, Nigeria." PhD thesis, Columbia University.

———. 1974. "Kídan dárán sállOL 203 \f `WP MultinationalA Roman' \s 12: Music for the Eve of the Muslim Festivals of Id al-fitr and Id al-kabir in Kano, Nigeria." Bloomington: African Studies Program, Indiana University.

———. 1977. "Initiation into the Bori Cult: A Case Study in Ningi Town." *Africa* 47, no.1: 1-13.

———. 1983. *Horses, Musicians, and Gods: The Hausa Cult of Possession-Trance.* South Hadley, Massachusetts: Bergin & Garvey.

Bidmos, M.A. 2003. *Islamic Education in Nigeria: Its Philosophy and Research Methods.* Lagos: Panaf.

Biskra. 1996. "Algerie Le Diwân De Biskra." Paris: Ocora.

Blanchard, I. 2001. *Mining, Metallurgy and Minting in the Middle Ages, Volume 1.* Stuttgart: Franz Steiner Verlag.

Blyden, Edward Wilmot. 1887a [1967]. *Christianity, Islam and the Negro Race.* Edinburgh: Edinburgh UP.

———. 1887b [1971]. *Christianity, Islam and the Negro Race,* edited by Hollis R. Lynch. London: Franck Cass & Co.

———. 1971. *Black Spokesman,* edited by Hollis R. Lynch. London: Franck Cass & Co.

———. 1978. *Selected Letters of Edward Wilmot Blyden,* edited and with an Introduction by Hollis R. Lynch. Millwood, New York: KTO Press.

Boulby, M. 1999. *The Muslim Brotherhood and the Kings of Jordan, 1945-1953.* Atlanta: Scholars Press.

Boutros-Ghali, Boutros. 1994. "The OAU and Afro-Arab Cooperation." In *The Organization of African Unity after Thirty Years,* edited by Yassin el-Hyouti, 147-68. Westport: Preager Publishers.

Bovill, E.W. 1933. *Caravans of the Old Sahara.* Oxford: Oxford

University Press.
———. 1968. *Golden Trade of the Moors*. Second edition. London: Oxford University Press.
Bowen, T.J. 1857 [1968]. *Adventures and Missionary Labours in Several Countries in the Interior of Africa from 1849 to 1856.* Charleston [reprinted London].
Boyd, Alan. 1981. "Music in Islam: Lamu, Kenya, a Case Study." In *Discourse in Ethnomusicology II: A Tribute to Alan P. Merriam*, edited by Caroline Card, Jane Cowan, Sally Carr Helton, Carl Rhkonen, and Laurie Kay Sommers. Bloomington, Indiana: Ethnomusicology Publications Group, Indiana University.
Boyd, Jean. 1989. *The Caliph's Sister: Nana Asma'u 1793-1865*. London: Frank Cass & Co.
———. 2001. "Distance Learning from Purdah in Nineteenth-Century Northern Nigeria: The Work of Asma'u Fodiyo." *Journal of African Cultural Studies* 14, no.1: 7-22.
Bragdon, Kathleen J. 1993. "Vernacular Literacy and Massachusett World View, 1650-1750." In *Algonkians of New England: Past and Present*, edited by Peter Benes, 26-35. Boston: Boston University Press.
———. 1996. *Native People of Southern New England, 1500-1650*. Norman and London: University of Oklahoma Press.
Braimah, B.A.R. 1976. "Islamic Education in Ghana." In *Religion in a Pluralistic Society*, edited by J.S. Pobee, 201-16. Leiden: E. J. Brill.
Braimah, J.A. 1997. *History and Traditions of Gonja*. Calgary: University of Calgary Press.
Bravmann, Rene. 1983. *African Islam*. Washington, DC: Smithsonian Institution Press and Ethnograhica.
———. 2000. "Islamic Art and Material Culture in Africa." In *The History of Islam in Africa*, edited by Nehemia Levtzion and Randall Pouwels, 489-517. Athens: Ohio University Press.
Brenner, Louis. 1971. "Review of Muslims and Chiefs in West Africa." *American Historical Review* 76: 533-34.
———. 1993. "Constructing Muslim identities in Mali." In *Muslim Identity and Social Change in Sub-Saharan Africa*, edited by Louis Brenner, 59-78. Bloomington: Indiana University Press.
———. 1995. "Sufism in Africa." African Studies Association Annual Conference, Orlando, Florida.
Brett-Smith, Sarah C. 1994. *The Making of Bamana Sculpture: Creativity and Gender*. Cambridge, UK: Cambridge University Press.
———. 1996. *The Artfulness of M'Fa Jigi: An Interview with Nyamaton Diarra*. Madison: University of Wisconsin African Studies Program.
Bromber, Katrin. 2007. "Mjakazi, Mpambe, Mjoli, Suria: Female Slaves in

Swahili Sources." In *Women and Slavery, Volume 1: Africa and the Western Indian Ocean Islands*, edited by Gwyn Campbell, Suzanne Miers, and Joseph C. Miller, 111-28. Athens: Ohio University Press.

Brooks, George. 1993. *Landlords and Strangers: Ecology, Society, and Trade in Western Africa, 1000-1630.* Boulder, Colorado: Westview Press.

Brown, William. 1969. "The Caliphate of Hamdullahi c.1818-1864." PhD thesis, University of Wisconsin.

Buehler, Arthur F. 1997. "Currents of Sufism in Nineteenth and Twentieth Century Indo-Pakistan: An Overview." *The Muslim World* 87, no.3-4: 299-314.

Bühnen, Stephan. 1994. "In Quest of Susu." *History in Africa* 21: 1-47.

Bulliet, Richard W. 1990. *The Camel and the Wheel.* New York: Columbia University Press.

Butler, Judith. 1990. *Gender Trouble: Feminism and the Subversion of Identity.* New York: Routledge.

Camara, Laye. 1980. *The Guardian of the Word: Kouma Lafôlô Kouma.* London: William Collins & Co.

Camara, Seydou. 2005. "Le Manden et l'occupation coloniale française: histoire d'une vie, histoire d'une frontière." 6th International Conference on Mande Studies, Kankan, Guinea, 25-26 June.

Camps, G. 1987. *Les Berbères: Mémoire et identitée.* Paris: Editions Errance.

Carapico, S. 1997. "Introduction to Part One." In *Political Islam: Essays from Middle East Report*, edited by Joel Beinin and Joe Stork, 29-32. Berkeley: University of California Press.

Carbonell Cortes, Ovidi. 2003. "Semiotic Alteration in Translation. Othering, Stereotyping, and Hybridation in Contemporary Translations From Arabic Into Spanish and Catalan." *Linguistica Antverpiensia* (New Series) 2: 145-59.

———. 2004. "Exoticism, Identity, and Representation in Western Translation from Arabic." In *Cultural Encounters in Translation From Arabic*, edited by Said Faiq, 26-39. Cleavedon, UK: Multilingual Matters.

———. 2006. "Misquoted Others: Locating Newness and Authority in Cultural Translation." In *Translating Others: Volume 1*, edited by Theo Hermans, 43-63. Manchester: St. Jerome Press.

Cardinall, A.W. 1927. *In Ashanti and Beyond.* London.

Cashion, Gerald. 1982. "Hunters of the Mande: A Behavioral Code and Worldview Derived from a Study of Their Folklore." PhD thesis, Indiana University

Chang, Kwang-Chih. 1962. "China." In *Courses Towards Urban Life:*

Archaeological Considerations of Some Cultural Alternatives, edited by Robert J. Braidwood and Gordon R. Willey, 177-92. Chicago: Aldine.

Chants religieux. "Volume 2: Au maghreb." Paris: Club du disque Arabe, 1996.

Charry, Eric S. 2000a. *Mande Music: Traditional and Modern Music of the Maninka and Mandinka of Western Africa*. Chicago: Chicago Studies in Ethnomusicology, University of Chicago Press.

——. 2000b. "Music and Islam in Sub-Saharan Africa." In *The History of Islam in Africa*, edited by Nehemia Levtzion and Randall Lee Pouwels: 545-73. Athens: Ohio University Press.

Chernoff, John Miller. 1979. *African Rhythm and African Sensibility: Aesthetics and Social Action in African Musical Idioms*. Chicago: University of Chicago Press.

——. 1985. "The Drums of Dagbon." In *Repercussions: A Celebration of African-American Music*, edited by Geoffrey Haydon and Dennis Marks, 101-27. London: Century Pub.

Chottin, A. 1927. "Note sur le "Nfir" (trompette du Ramadan)." *Hesperis* v, no.vii: 376-80.

——. 1932. "Airs populaires marocains." *Le Menestrel* XCIV: 351-53.

Choueiri, Y. 1996. "The Political Discourse of Contemporary Islamist Movements." In *Islamic Fundamentalism*, edited by A. Sidahmed and A. Ehteshami, 19-33. Boulder, Colorado: Westview Press.

Cissé, Youssouf Tata and Wâ Kamissoko. 1975. *L'empire du Mali*. Paris: Fondation SCOA Pour la Recherche Scientifique en Afrique Noire.

——. 1988. *La grande geste du Mali des origins à la fondation de l'empire*. Paris: Éditions Karthala Association ARSAN.

——. 1991. *Soundjata la gloire du Mali*. Paris: Éditions Karthala Association ARSAN.

Cleaveland, Timothy. 2002. *Becoming Walata: A History of Saharan Social Formation and Transformation*. Portsmouth, New Hampshire: Heinemann.

Cohen, R. 1971. "Cultural Strategies in the Organization of Trading Diasporas." In *The Development of Indigenous Trade and Markets in West Africa*, edited by C. Meillassoux, 266-81. Oxford: Oxford University Press.

Collins, John. 1992. *West African Pop Roots*. Philadelphia: Temple University Press.

Colvin, Lucie. 1974. "Islam and the State of Kajoor: A Case of Successful Resistance to Jihad." *Journal of African History* 15, no.4: 587-606.

Comores. 1994. "Comores: Musiques traditionnelles de l'Île D'Anjouan." Paris: Maison des Cultures du Monde.

Conrad, David C. 1981. "The Role of Oral Artists in the History of Mali." Volume 2. PhD thesis, SOAS, University of London.
———. 1985. "Islam in the Oral Traditions of Mali — Bilali and Surakata." *Journal of African History* 26, no.1: 33-49.
———, ed. 1990. *A State of Intrigue: The Epic of Bamana Segou According to Tayiru Banbera*. Oxford: Oxford University Press for the British Academy.
———. 1992. "Searching for History in the Sunjata Epic: The Case of Fakoli." *History in Africa* 19: 147-200.
———. 1994. "A Town Called Dakajalan: The Sunjata Tradition and the Question of Ancient Mali's Capital" *Journal of African History* 35: 355-77.
———. 1997. "Jousting with Jinn and 'Doing the Sifili': Mande Ritual Ordeals on Paths to Power." International Symposium on West Africa and the Global Challenge, Dakar, Senegal, 24-26 June.
———, ed. 1999. *Epic Ancestors of the Sunjata Era: Oral Tradition from the Maninka of Guinea*. Madison: University of Wisconsin African Studies Program.
———, ed. 2002. *Somono Bala of the Upper Niger: River People, Charismatic Bards, and Mischievous Music in a West African Culture*. Leiden: Brill.
———, ed. 2004. *Sunjata: A West African Epic of the Mande Peoples*. Indianapolis, Indiana and Cambridge, Massachusetts: Hackett Publishing Company, Inc.
Conrad, David C. and Humphrey J. Fisher. 1982. "The Conquest That Never Was: Ghana and the Almoravids, 1076. I. The External Arabic Sources." *History in Africa* 9: 21-59.
———. 1983. "The Conquest That Never Was: Ghana and the Almoravids, 1076. II. The Local Oral Sources." *History in Africa* 10: 53-78.
Cooper, Barbara M. 1999. "The Strength in the Song: Muslim Personhood, Audible Capital, and Hausa Women's Performance of the Hajj." *Social Text* 60: 87-109.
Cooper, Fredrick. 1977. *Plantation Slavery on the East African Coast*. New Haven & London: Yale University Press.
———. 1981. "Islam and Cultural Hegemony: The Ideology of Slaveowners on the East African Coast." In *The Ideology of Slavery in Africa*, edited by Paul E. Lovejoy, 271-307. Beverly Hills & London: Sage Publications.
Cooper John, Ronald L. Nettler, and Mohamed Mahmoud, eds. 1998. *Islam and Modernity: Muslim Intellectuals Respond*. London and New York: I.B. Tauris Publishers.
Coquery-Vidrovitch, Catherine. 2007. "Women, Marriage, and Slavery in

Sub-Saharan Africa in the Nineteenth Century." In *Women and Slavery, Volume 1: Africa and the Western Indian Ocean Islands*, edited by Gwyn Campbell, Suzanne Miers, and Joseph C. Miller, 43-62. Athens: Ohio University Press.

Corke, Penny, Geoffrey Haydon, Louis Mahoney, Alhaji Ibrahim Abdulai, John Miller Chernoff, Third Eye Productions, RM Arts (Firm), Channel Four (Great Britain), and Films for the Humanities (Firm). 2000. "The Drums of Dagbon." 1 videocassette (58 min.) Videorecording. Repercussions: a Celebration of African Influenced Music. Princeton, New Jersey: Films for the Humanities & Sciences.

Coulon, Christian. 1979. "Les Marabouts sénégalais et l'état." *Revue française d'études politiques africaines* 158: 15-24.

Crapanzano, Vincent. 1973. *The Hamadsha: A Study in Moroccan Ethnopsychiatry*. Berkeley: University of California Press.

———. "Hamadisha (Hmadsha)." In *Encyclopaedia of Islam*, edited by P. Bearman, T. Bianquis, C.E. Bosworth, E. van Donzel and W.P. Heinrichs. *The Encyclopaedia of Islam Online* <http://www.brillonline.nl.login.ezproxy.library.ualberta.ca/subscriber/entry?entry=islam_SIM-8593>. Leiden: Brill. Accessed 19 May 2008.

Creevey, Lucy. 1968. "The Political Influence of Muslim Brotherhoods in Senegal." PhD thesis, Boston University.

Cronon, William. 1983. *Changes in the Land: Indians, Colonists, and the Ecology of New England*. New York: Hill and Wang.

Crosby, Constance A. 1993. "The Algonkian Spiritual Landscape." In *Algonkians of New England: Past and Present*, edited by Peter Benes, 35-41. Boston: Boston University Press.

Cruikshank, Julie M. 1981. "Legend and Landscape: Convergence of Oral and Scientific Traditions in the Southern Yukon Territory." *Arctic Anthropology* 18, no.2: 67-93.

———. 1990. "Getting the Words Right: Perspectives on Naming and Places in Athapaskan Oral History." *Arctic Anthropology* 27, no.1: 52-65.

———. 2002. "Oral History, Narrative Strategies, and Native American Historiography: Perspectives from the Yukon Territory, Canada" in *Clearing a Path: Theorizing the Past in Native American Studies*, edited by Nancy Shoemaker, 3-27. New York: Routledge.

Cruise O'Brien, Donal. 1971. *The Mourides of Senegal: The Political and Economic Organization of an Islamic Brotherhood*. Oxford: Clarendon Press.

———. 1998. "Charisma Comes to Town: Mouride Urbanization, 1945-1986." In *Charisma and Brotherhood in African Islam*, edited by

D.B. Cruise O'Brien and C. Coulon, 135-57. Oxford: Oxford University Press.

Crystal, Jill. 1995. "Civil Society in the Arabian Gulf" in *Civil Society in the Middle East*, edited by Augustus Richard Norton, 259-86. Leiden: Brill.

Cuoq, J. 1975. *Recueil des sources arabes concernant l'Afrique occidentale du VIIIe au XVIe siècle: (Bilad al-Sudan)*. Paris: Editions de Centre national de la recherche scientifique.

Curtin, Philip. 1975. *Economic Change in Precolonial Africa: Senegambia in the Era of the Slave Trade*. Madison: University of Wisconsin Press.

Curtis IV, Edward E. 2002. *Islam in Black America*. Albany: State University of New York Press.

Danielson, Virginia. 1991. "'Min al-Mashayikh': A View of Egyptian Musical Tradition." *Asian Music* 22, no.1: 113-27.

Davies, Kenneth Gordon. 1957. *The Royal African Company*. London: Longman's, Green and Co.

Davis, Moshe. 1995. *Teaching Jewish Civilization: A Global Approach to Higher Education* New York: New York University Press.

D'Azevedo, Warren Leonard. 1962. "Continuity and Integration in Gola Society." PhD thesis, Northwestern University.

DeCorse, C.R. and G.L. Chouin. 2003. "Trouble with Siblings: Archaeological and Historical Interpretation of the West African Past." In *Sources and Methods in African History: Spoken, Written, Unearthed*, edited by T. Falola and C. Jennings, 11-13. Rochester: University of Rochester Press.

Delafosse, Maurice. 1912. *Haut-Sénégal-Niger (Soudan Française)* 3 vols. Paris: Emile Larose. Reprinted, Paris: G.-P. Maisonneuve et Larose, 1972.

Deme, A. and S.K. McIntosh. 2006. "Excavations at Walaldé: New Light on the Settlement of the Middle Senegal Valley by Iron-Using Peoples." *Journal of African Archaeology* 4, no.2: 317-47.

Depont, Octave and Xavier Coppolani. 1897. *Les confreres religieuses musulmanes*. Alger: Adolphe Jourdan.

Derrida, Jacques. 1981 *Dissemination*. Translated by Barbara Johnson: Chicago: University of Chicago Press.

——. [1999] 2001. "What is a 'Relevant' Translation?" Translated by Lawrence Venuti. *Critical Inquiry* 27: 174-200.

Deutsch, Jan-Georg. 2007. "Prices for Female Slaves and Changes in Their Life Cycle." In *Women and Slavery*, edited by Gwyn Campbell, Suzanne Miers and Joseph Miller, 129-44. Athens: Ohio University Press.

Devisse, J. 1983. *Tegdaoust III: Recherches sur Audaghost*. Paris: Editions recherche sur les civilisations.

Diabaté, Massa Makan. 1970. *Janjon et autres chants populaires du Mali*. Paris: Présence Africaine.

———. 1975. *L'aigle et l'épervier ou La geste de Sunjata*. Paris: Editions Pierre Jean Oswald.

Diamond, Jared M. 1997. *Guns, Germs and Steel: The Fates of Human Societies*. New York: Norton.

Dieterlen, Germaine. 1951. *Essai sur la Religion Bambara*. Paris: Presses Universitaires de France.

Diop, Samba. 2000. *The Epic of El Hadj Umar Taal of Fouta*. Madison: University of Wisconsin African Studies Program.

Doumbia, Paul-Emile-Namoussa. 1936. "Etude du clan des forgerons." *Bulletin du comité d'études historiques et scientifiques de l'Afrique occidentale française* 19: 334-53.

Dubois, Felix. 1896. *Tombouctou la mysterieuse*. Paris.

Du Bois, W.E.B. 1962. "A Statement Concerning the Encyclopaedia Africana Project." 1 April 1962. *Encyclopedia Africana Project History Archive* <http://www.endarkenment.com/eap/legacy/620401duboisweb.htm>. Accessed 21 May 2008.

Dumestre, Gérard, éditeur et traducteur. 1979. *La geste de Segou*. Paris: Armand Colin.

Dumestre, Gérard et Lilyan Kesteloot, eds. 1975. *La Prise de Dionkoloni*. Paris: Armand Colin.

Dunbar, Roberta A. 2000. "Muslim Women in African History." In *The History of Islam in Africa*, edited by N. Levtzion and R. Pouwels, 397-418. Cape Town: David Philip.

Eastman, Carol M. 1988. "Women, Slaves and Foreigners: African Cultural Influences and Group Processes in the Formation of Northern Coastal Swahili Society." *The International Journal of African Historical Studies* 21, no.1: 1-20.

Eisenstadt, S.N., Michel Abitbol and Naomi Chazan, eds. 1988. *The Early State in Africa*. The Hague: E.J. Brill.

Eisenstadt, S.N. and W. Schluchter. 1998 "Introductory Paths to Early Modernities: A Comparative View." *Daedalus* 127: 1-18.

El-Wakkad, Mahmoud (with I. Wilks). 1961-62. "Qissatu Salga Tarikhu Gonja." *Ghana Notes and Queries* 3: 8-31 and 4: 6-25.

Ensemble du Cheikh Abdelaziz ben Mahmoud. 2000. "Soulamia de Tunisie." Chérif Khaznadar, and Maison de la Culture de Rennes. France: Arion.

Erlmann, Veit. 1983. "Marginal Men, Strangers and Wayfarers:

Professional Musicians and Change among the Fulani of Diamare (North Cameroon)." *Ethnomusicology* 27, no.2: 187-225.
———. 1986. *Music and the Islamic Reform in the Early Sokoto Empire: Sources, Ideology, Effects.* Abhandlungen Für Die Kunde Des Morgenlandes, Stuttgart: Deutsche Morgenländische Gesellschaft. Kommissionsverlag F. Steiner Wiesbaden.
Euba, Akin. 1971. "Islamic Musical Culture among the Yoruba: A Preliminary Survey " In *Essays on Music and History in Africa,* edited by Klaus Wachsmann, 171-81. Evanston: Northwestern University Press.
Evans, C. 1998. "Historicism, Chronology and Straw Men: Situating Hawkes' 'Ladder of Inference.'" *Antiquity* 72, no.276: 398-405.
Fadhel Jaziri. 2000. "Hadhra." France: Universal Records (France).
Fairclough, Norman. 1989. *Language and Power.* London: Longman.
Fairhead, James and Melissa Leach. 1996. *Misreading the African Landscape: Society and Ecology in a Forest-Savanna Mosaic.* Cambridge, UK: Cambridge University Press.
Feierman, Steven. 1974. *The Shambaai Kingdom.* Madison: University of Wisconsin Press.
Fenn, Thomas. 2008. "Technology and Trans-Saharan Commerce: Early Medieval Metals Trade in the Middle Sahel Zone, Sub-Saharan West Africa." Biennial Meeting of the Society of Africanist Archaeologists. 8-11 September. Frankfurt, Germany.
Ferguson, Phyllis. 1970. "Review of Muslims and Chiefs in West Africa." *Africa* 40: 181-82.
———. 1972. "Islamization in Dagbon: A Study of the Alfanema of Yendi." PhD thesis, University of Cambridge.
Fetter, Bruce. 1979. *Colonial Rule in Africa: Readings from Primary Sources.* Wisconsin: At the University Press.
Fez. 2002. "Morocco: the Art of Sama` in Fez." VDE.
Filopowiak, W. 1979. *Etudes archéologiques sur la capitale médiévale du Mali.* Szczecine: Muzeum Narodowe w Szczecinie.
Fisher, Humphrey. 1971. "Introduction" to *Journeys to Musadu,* by Benjamin Anderson, ix-xxiii. London: Frank Cass and Company Limited.
———. 1975. "The Modernization of Islamic Education in Sierra Leone, Gambia, and Liberia: Religion and Language." In *Conflict and Harmony in Education in Tropical Africa,* edited by Godfrey N. Brown and Mervyn Hiskett, 187-99. London: George Allan & Unwum Ltd.
———. 1987. "Liminality, Hijra, and the City." In *Rural and Urban Islam in West Africa,* edited by Nehemia Levtzion and Humphrey Fisher,

147-71. Boulder, Colorado: Lynne Rienner.

Fletcher, R. 1992. "Time Perspectivism, Annales, and the Potential of Archaeology." In *Archaeology, Annales, and Ethnohistory*, edited by A.B. Knapp, 35-49. Cambridge: Cambridge University Press.

Franken, Marjorie Ann. 1986. "Anyone Can Dance: A Survey and Analysis of Swahili Ngoma, Past and Present." PhD thesis, University of California, Riverside.

Frishkopf, Michael. 1999. "Sufism, Ritual, and Modernity in Egypt: Language Performance as an Adaptive Strategy." PhD thesis, UCLA.

——. 2000. "Inshad Dini and Aghani Diniyya in Twentieth Century Egypt: A Review of Styles, Genres, and Available Recordings." Middle East Studies Association.

——. 2001. "Tarab in the Mystic Sufi Chant of Egypt." In *Colors of Enchantment: Visual and Performing Arts of the Middle East*, edited by Sherifa Zuhur, 233-69. Cairo: American University in Cairo Press.

——. 2002a. "Inshad Dini: Islamic Hymnody in Egypt." In *The Garland Encyclopedia of World Music (Volume 6)*, edited by Virginia Danielson, Scott Marcus, and Dwight Reynolds, 165-75. New York: Garland Pub.

——. 2002b. "Shaykh Yasin al-Tuhami: A Typical Layla Performance." In *The Garland Encyclopedia of World Music (Volume 6)*, edited by Virginia Danielson, Scott Marcus, and Dwight Reynolds, 147-51. New York: Garland Pub.

——. 2009. "Mediated Qur'anic Recitation and the Contestation of Islam in Contemporary Egypt." In *Music and the Play of Power: Music, Politics and Ideology in the Middle East, North Africa and Central Asia*, edited by Laudan Nooshin. London: Ashgate Press.

Froelich, J.C. 1962. *Les musulmans d'Afrique noire*. Paris: Editions de l'Orante.

Galadanci, A. Bashir Shehu. 1993. "Islam and Education in Africa: Past Influence and Future Challenges." In *Islam in Africa*, edited by Nura Alkali et al., 97-106. Ibadan: Spectrum Books.

——. 2000. *Islamization of Knowledge: A Research Guide*. Kano: The International Institute of Islamic Thought, Nigeria Office.

De Ganay, Solange. 1949. "Aspectes de mythologie et de symbolique bambara." *Journal de Psychologie Normale et Pathologique* 42: 181-201.

Garrard, Timothy. 1982. "Myth and Metrology: The Early Trans-Saharan Gold Trade." *Journal of African History* 23, no.4: 443-61.

Geertz, Clifford. 1968. *Islam Observed: Religious Development in Morocco and Indonesia*. New Haven: Yale University Press,

Gellner, Ernest. 1983. *Muslim Society*. Cambridge: Cambridge

University Press.

George, D. 1996. "Pax Islamica: An Alternative New World Order." In *Islamic Fundamentalism*, edited by A. Sidahmed and A. Ehteshami, 71-91. Boulder, Colorado: Westview Press.

Gharib, Sabah. 2004. "Sufi Spirit." Hollywood Music Center.

Ghazala, Hasan. 2004. "Stylistic-Semantic and Grammatical Functions of Punctuation in English-Arabic Translation." *Babel* 50, no.3: 230-45.

Gibb, Hamilton A. R. 1953. *Mohammedanism: An Historical Survey*. Second edition. New York: New American Library.

Giles, Linda L. 1989. "Spirit Possession on the Swahili Coast: Peripheral Cults or Primary Text?" PhD thesis, University of Texas, Austin.

———. 1995. "Sociocultural Change and Spirit Possession on the Swahili Coast of East Africa." *Anthropological Quarterly* 68, no.2: 89-106.

Gillani, Karim. 2004. "The Ismaili Ginan Tradition from the Indian Subcontinent." *Bulletin of the Middle East Studies Association* 38, no.2: 175-86.

Gilsenan, Michael. 1973. *Saint and Sufi in Modern Egypt: An Essay in the Sociology of Religion*. Oxford: Oxford Monographs on Social Anthropology, Clarendon Press.

Glassman, Jonathon. 1995a. *Feasts and Riot: Revelry, Rebellion, & Popular Consciousness on the Swahili Coast, 1856-1888*. Portsmouth, New Hampshire: Heinemann, Social History of Africa Series.

———. 1995b. "Marcia Wright's *Strategies of Slaves and Women: Life-Stories from East / Central Africa*." *Journal of African History* 36, no.1: 149-52.

Gnawa Music of Marrakesh: Night Spirit Masters. New York, New York: Axiom, 1990.

Gold Coast. 1951. *Report on the Educational Development for the Year 1949-50*. Accra: Government Printing Department.

———. 1952. *Accelerated Development Plan for Education, 1951*. Accra: Government Printing Department.

Gondonneau, A. and M. F. Guerra. 2002. "The Circulation of Precious Metals in the Arab Empire: The Case of the Near and the Middle East." *Archaeometry* 44, no.4: 573-99.

Goody, Jack, ed. 1968. *Literacy in Traditional Societies*. Cambridge: Cambridge University Press.

Gouilly, Alphone. 1952. *L'Islam dans l'Afrique occidentale française*. Paris: Larose.

Graham, C.K. 1971. *The History of Education in Ghana*. London: Frank Cass & Co. Ltd.

Grame, Theodore C. 1970. "Music in the Jma al-Fna of Marrakesh." *The Musical Quarterly* LVI, no.1: 74-87.

Grébenart, D. 1985. "Le Néolithique final et l'age des métaux. La région d'In Gall-Teguidda n Tesemt (Niger): Programme archeeologique d'urgence II." *Etudes Nigériennes* 49: 1-418.

Green, Kathy. 1984. "The Foundation of Kong: A Study in Dyula and Sonangui Ethnic Identification." PhD thesis, Indiana University.

Gribetz, Arthur. 1991. "The Sama` Controversy: Sufi vs Legalist." *Studia Islamica* 74: 43-62.

Guannu, Joseph Sey. 1972. "Liberia and League of Nations: The Crisis of 1929-1934." PhD thesis, Fordham University.

Guerra, M. F., C.-O. Sarthre, A. Gondonneau, and J-N Barrandon. 1999. "Precious Metals and Provenance Inquiries Using LA-ICP-MS." *Journal of Archaeological Science* 26: 1101-10.

Gumi, Abu Bakr. 1972. *Al-'Aqida al-sahiha bi-muwafaqat al-shari'a.* Beirut: Dar al-'Arabiyya.

Hakmoun, Hassan. 1991. "Gift of the Gnawa." Chicago: Flying Fish.

Harbeson, John, Donald Rothchild and Naomi Chazan, eds. 1994. *Civil Society and the State in Africa.* Boulder, Colorado: Lynne Rienner Publishers.

Hardymen, J.T. and R.K. Orchard. 1977. *Two Minutes from Sloane Square: A Brief History of the Conference of Missionary Societies in Great Britain and Ireland, 1912-1977.* London: CBMS.

Harley, Brian J. and David Woodward, eds. 1987. *The History of Cartography, Vol 1. Cartography in Prehistoric, Ancient, and Medieval Europe and the Mediterranean.* Chicago: University of Chicago Press.

Harrison, Christopher. 1988. *France and Islam in West Africa (1860-1890).* Cambridge: Cambridge University Press.

Harwood, Frances. 1976. "Myth, Memory and Oral Tradition: Cicero in the Trobriands." *American Anthropologist* 78, no.4: 783-96.

Haskell, H., R. McIntosh and S. McIntosh. 1986. "Archaeological Reconnaissance in the Region of Dia, Mali." Unpublished Report to the National Geographic Society <http://www.ruf.rice.edu/~anth/arch/research.html>.

Hausa. "Nigeria: Hausa Music: Traditions of the Emirate of Kano." Inedit: Maison des Cultures du Monde, 2006.

Hawkes, Christopher. 1947. "Archaeology and the History of Europe." Inaugural Lecture to the Oxford Chair.

Hawkins, Sean. 2002. *Writing and Colonialism in Northern Ghana: The Encounter between the LoDagaa and "The World on Paper."* Toronto: University of Toronto Press.

Heffner, Robert W. 2001. "Public Islam and the Problem of Democratization." *Sociology of Religion* 62, no.4: 491-514.
Hegel, G.W.F. [1822-30] 1956. *The Philosophy of History*. Translated by J. Sibree. Amherst, New York: Dove Books.
Henige, David. 2007. "'This is the Place:' Putting the Past on the Map." *Journal of Historical Geography* 33, no.2: 237-53.
Herbert, Eugenia. 1995. "Metals and Power at Great Zimbabwe." 10th Congress of the Pan-African Association for Prehistory and Related Studies, Harare.
Hiskett, Mervyn. 1973. "The Origin, Sources, and Form of Hausa Islamic Verse." In *Essays on African literature*, edited by W.L. Ballard, 127-53. Atlanta: School of Arts and Sciences, Georgia State University.
———. 1975. "Islamic Education in the Traditional and State Systems in Northern Nigeria." In *Conflict and Harmony in Education in Tropical Africa*, edited by Godfrey Brown and Mervyn Hiskett, 134-51. London: George Allan & Unwum Ltd.
———. 1984. *The Development of Islam in West Africa*. New York: Longman.
———. 1994. *The Sword of Truth: The Life and Times of Shehu Uthman Dan Fodio*. Evanston, Illinois: Northwestern University Press.
Hodgkin, Thomas. 1966. "The Learning Traditions in Ghana." In *Islam in Tropical Africa*, edited by I.M. Lewis, 442-43. Cambridge: Cambridge University Press.
Hodgson, Marshall GS. 1974. *The Venture of Islam. Volume 1: The Classical Age of Islam*. Chicago: University of Chicago Press.
M. Hoexter, S. N. Eisenstadt and N. Levtzion. 2002. *The Public Sphere in Muslim Societies*. Albany, New York: SUNY Press.
Hoffman, Valerie J. 1999. "Annihilation in the Messenger of God: The Development of a Sufi Practice." *International Journal of Middle East Studies* 31: 351-69.
Hofheinz, Albrecht. 1999. "Internalizing Islam: Shaykh Muhammad Majdhub, Scriptural Islam and Local Context in the Early Nineteenth-century Sudan." PhD thesis, University of Bergen.
Holsoe, Svend Einar. 1967. "The Casava Leaf People: An Ethnohistorical Study of the Vai People with a Particular Emphasis on the Tewo Chiefdom." PhD thesis, Boston University.
Houdas, O. editor and translator. 1913. [1964] *Ta'rikh es-Soudan*. Paris: UNESCO.
Houdas, O. and M. Delafosse. editors and translators. 1913. [1964] *Ta'rikh el-Fettach*. Paris: UNESCO.
Hourani, Albert. 1961. *A Vision of History: Near Eastern and Other Essays*. Beirut: Khayats.

Huffman, Thomas. 1996. *Snakes and Crocodiles: Power and Symbolism in Ancient Zimbabwe.* Johannesburg: Witwatersrand University Press.

———. 2000. "Mapungubwe and the Origins of the Zimbabwe Culture." *The South African Archaeological Society Goodwin Series* 8: 14-29.

Humblot, P. 1951. "Episodes de la légende de Soundiata." *Notes Africaines* 52: 111-13.

Hunwick, John. 1969. "Review of *Muslims and Chiefs in West Africa*." *African Affairs* 68: 363-64.

———. 1997. "Sub-Saharan Africa and the Wider World of Islam: Historical and Contemporary Perspectives." In *African Islam and Islam in Africa: Encounters between Sufis and Islamists*, edited by Eva E. Rosander and David Westerlund, 28-53. London: Hurst.

———. 1999. *Timbuktu and the Songhay Empire: Al-Sa`di's Ta'rikh al-Sudan down to 1613 and Other Contemporary Documents.* Leiden: Brill.

———. 2003. *Arabic Literature of Africa. Volume 4: The Writings of Western Sudanic Africa,* compiled by John O. Hunswick. Leiden: Brill.

Hunwick, John and Eve Troutt Powell, eds. 2002. *The African Diaspora in the Mediterranean Lands of Islam.* Princeton, New Jersey: Markus Wiener.

Iddrisu, Abdulai. 1998a. "A History of the Development of Islamic Education in Northern Ghana in the Nineteenth and Twentieth Centuries." MPhil thesis, History Department, University of Cape Coast, Ghana.

———. 1998b. "British Colonial Responses to Islamic Education: The Case of the Northern Territories of the Gold Coast, 1890-1940." *Journal of the Institute of Education* 4, no.2: 1-20.

———. 2002a. "Between Islamic and Western Secular Education in Ghana: A Progressive Integration Approach." *Journal of Muslim Minority Affairs* 22, no.2: 335-50.

———. 2002b. "The Growth of Islamic Learning in Northern Ghana and Its interaction with Western Secular Education." 10th Codesria General Assembly Meeting, Nile International Conference Centre, Kampala, Uganda 8-12 December.

———. 2004. "In Northern Ghana, 1900-1925: Colonial Control and Muslim Education." *Islam et Sociétés Au Sud Sahara* 17-18: 11-21.

———. 2005. "The Growth of Islamic Learning in Northern Ghana and Its Interaction with Western Secular Education." *Africa Development* 30, nos.1-2: 53-67.

Ilesanmi, Simeon O. 2001. "Constitutional Treatment of Religion and the Politics of Human Rights in Nigeria." *African Affairs* 100: 529-44.

Izard, Michel. 1970. *Introduction à l'histoire des royaumes Mossi*. Paris: College de France.

———. 1992. *L'odyssée du pouvoir. Un Royaume africain. Etat, société, destin individual*. Paris: Ecoles des Hautes Etudes en Sciences Sociales.

Jabr, Abdul-Fattah M. 2001. "Arab Translators' Problems at the Discourse Level." *Babel* 47, no.4: 304-22.

Jacobsen, K.O. 1996. "Ramadan in Morocco + Fundamental Divisions and Differences in Islamic Ritual Celebrations: An Analysis of the Interaction of Formal and Local Traditions." *Temenos* 32: 113-35.

Jakobson, Roman. 1959. "On Linguistic Aspects of Translation." In *On Translation*, edited by R.A. Bower, 232-39. Cambridge: Harvard University Press.

Jankowsky, Richard C. 2004. "'The Other People': Music, Race, and Rituals of Possession in Tunisian Stambeli." PhD thesis, The University of Chicago.

Jansen, Jan, Esger Duintjer and Boubacar Tamboura, translators and editors. 1995. *L'Epopée de Sunjara, d'après Lansine Diabate de Kela (Mali)*. Leiden: Research School CNWS.

Johnson, John William. 1986. *The Epic of Son-Jara: A West African Tradition*. Text by Fa-Digi Sisókó. Bloomington: Indiana University Press.

———. 1979. *The Epic of Sun-Jata According to Magan Sisòkò*. 2 volumes. Bloomington: Indiana University Folklore Publications Group.

Johnson, Marion. 1976. "The Economic Foundations of an Islamic Theocracy: The Case of Masina." *Journal of African History* 17, no.4: 481-95.

Kaba, Lansiné. 1974. *The Wahhabiyya: Islamic Reform and Politics in French West Africa*. Evanston, Illinois: Northwestern University Press.

———. 2000. "Islam in West Africa: Radicalism and the New Ethic of Disagreement, 1960-1990." In *The History of Islam in Africa*, edited by N. Levtzion and R.L. Pouwels, 189-208. Athens: Ohio University Press.

Kamal, Youssouf. 1926-51. *Monumenta Cartographica Africae et Aegypti*. 5 volumes. Cairo.

Kante, Mory. 1987. "Akwaba Beach." New York: Polydor.

Kanté, Souleymane. 1994. *Manden dòfò. Kafa 3nan Kurukanfuwa gbara kurundu lu, ani kaja 4nan, mèn kèda Sonjada taminnèn kò*, edited by Baba Diané. Translated as "Les fameux 150 articles de la

Constitution Mandingue lors du sommet de Kroukan-Fouwa a Kaaba en 1236 et les evenements qui ont lieu pendant 4 siecles et demi apres Soundiata Ketta." Cairo.

Kaplan, Robert D. 2000. *The Coming Anarchy: Shattering the Dreams of the Post Cold War.* New York: Random House.

Karrar, Ali Salih. 1992. *The Sufi Brotherhoods in the Sudan.* Series in Islam and Society in Africa. Evanston, Illinois: Northwestern University Press; London: C. Hurst.

Kenyon, Susan M. 1995. "Zar as Modernization in Contemporary Sudan." *Anthropological Quarterly* 68, no.2: 107-20.

Kesteloot, Lilyan, ed. 1972. *Da Monzon de Segou: Epopée Bambara.* 4 volumes. Paris: Fernand Nathan.

———. 1994. "La filiation mythique et historique entre la royauté du Tekruur et celle des Wolof." In *Senegal-Forum: Litterature et Histoire,* sous la direction de P.S. Diop. Dakar: IFAN.

Khurshid, Ahmad. 1983. "The Nature of the Islamic Resurgence." In *Voices of Resurgent Islam,* edited by J.I. Esposito, 218-29. Oxford: Oxford University Press.

Kinney, S. 1970. "Drummers in Dagbon: Role of Drummer in Damba Festival." *Ethnomusicology* 14, no.2: 258-65.

Knight, Roderic. 1973. "Mandinka Jaliya: Professional Music of the Gambia." PhD thesis, UCLA.

Konneh, Augustine. 1993. "Mandingo Integration in the Liberian Political Economy." *Liberian Studies Journal* 18, no.1: 44-62.

———. 1996a. *Religion, Commerce and the Integration of the Mandingo in Liberia.* Langham: University Press of America.

———. 1996b. "Citizenship at the Margins: Status Ambiguity, and the Mandingo of Liberia." *African Studies Review* 39, no.2: 141-54.

Koya, Fathuddin Sayyed Muhammad. 1995. *Islam and the Ahmadiyyah Movement.* Bauchi, Nigeria: College of Islamic Studies.

Kramer, Robert. 1996. "Islam and Identity in the Kumase Zongo." In *The Cloth of Many Colored Silks: Papers on History and Society Ghanaian and Islamic in Honor of Ivor Wilks,* edited by John O. Hunwick and Nancy Lawler, 287-318. Evanston: Northwestern University Press.

Kubik, Gerhard. 1999. *Africa and the Blues.* Jackson: University Press of Mississippi.

La Chadhiliyyah. 1999. "Sufi Chants From Cairo, Egypt." Mohammed El Helbawy. France: Institut Du Monde Arabe.

La Daqqa. 1999. "La Daqqa: Sacred Drums From Marrakesh." Paris: Institut du Monde Arabe.

Lambek, Michael. 1993. *Knowledge and Practice in Mayotte: Local*

Discourses of Islam, Sorcery and Spirit Possession. Toronto: University of Toronto Press.

Langlois, T. 1998. "The Gnawa of Oujda: Music at the Margins in Morocco." *World of Music* 40, no.1: 135-56.

Langohr, V. 2001. "Of Islamists and Ballot Boxes." *International Journal of Middle East Studies* 33: 591-610.

Larkin, Brian. 2002. "Bandiri Music, Globalization and Urban Experience in Nigeria." *Cahiers d'études africaines* 168: 739-62.

Last, D. Murray. 1967. *The Sokoto Caliphate.* London: Longman.

Launay, Robert. 1977. "The Birth of a Ritual: The Politics of Innovation in Dyula Islam." *Savanna* 6, no.2: 145-54.

———. 1997. "Spirit Media: The Electronic Media and Islam among the Dyula of Northern Côte d'Ivoire." *Africa* 67, no.3: 441-53.

Law, R. 1980. *The Horse in West African History.* Oxford: Oxford University Press.

Lawler, Nancy. 1996. "Ivor Wilks: A Biographical Note." In *The Cloth of Many Colored Silks,* edited by Nancy Lawler and John Hunwick, 5-13. Evanston: Northwestern University Press.

Le Chatelier, A. 1887. *Les Confrères Musulmanes du Hedjaz.* Paris: Ernest Laroux.

Le Gall, Dina. 2005. *A Culture of Sufism: Naqshbandis in the Ottoman World, 1450-1700.* Albany: State University of New York Press.

Les Aissawa de Fes. 1999. "Trance Ritual." Paris: Institut du Monde Arabe.

van Leuwen, Richard. 2004. "The Cultural Context of Translating Arabic Literature." In *Cultural Encounters in Translation From Arabic,* edited by Said Faiq, 14-25. Cleavedon, UK: Multilingual Matters.

Levtzion, Nehemia. 1967. "The Long March of Islam in the Western Sudan." In *The Middle Age of African History,* edited by R. Oliver, 13-18. London: Oxford University Press.

———. 1968. *Muslims and Chiefs in West Africa: A Study of Islam in the Middle Volta Basin in the Pre-Colonial Period.* Oxford: Clarendon Press.

———. 1971a. "Patterns of Islamization in West Africa." In *Aspects of West African Islam,* edited by D.F. McCall and N.R. Bennett, 31-39. Boston: Boston University Press. Reprinted in *Conversion to Islam,* edited by N. Levtzion, 207-16. New York: Holmes & Meier, 1979.

———. 1971b. "The Early States of the Western Sudan to 1500." In *History of West Africa,* edited by J.F.A. Ajayi and M. Crowder, 1: 120-57. London: Longman.

——— 1971c. "A Seventeenth-Century Chronicle by Ibn al-Mukhtar: A Critical Study of Ta'rikh al-Fattash." *Bulletin of the School of*

Oriental and African Studies 34: 571-93.

———. 1973. *Ancient Ghana and Mali*. London: Methuen. 2nd edition, New York: Holmes & Meier, 1980.

———. 1975. "Northwest Africa: From the Maghrib to the Fringes of the Forest in the Seventeenth and Eighteenth Centuries." In *Cambridge History of Africa*, edited by J.R. Gray, 4: 142-222. Cambridge: Cambridge University Press.

———. 1977. "North Africa and the Western Sudan from 1050 to 1590." In *Cambridge History of Africa*, edited by R. Oliver, 3: 331-462. Cambridge: Cambridge University Press.

———. 1978. "The Sahara and Sudan from the Arab Conquest of the Maghrib to the Rise of the Almoravids." In *Cambridge History of Africa*, edited by J.D. Fage, 2: 637-84. Cambridge: Cambridge University Press.

———. 1979. *Conversion to Islam*. New York: Holmes & Meier.

———. 1980. *An Introduction to African History*. Tel Aviv: The Open University of Israel (Hebrew).

———. 1986. "Eighteenth-Century Renewal and Reform Movements in Islam." In *Renewal (tajdid) and Reform (islah) in Islam*. Special issue of *Hamizrah Hehadash* 31: 48-70 (Hebrew).

———. 1987a. "Rural and Urban Islam in West Africa." In *Rural and Urban Islam in West Africa*, edited by N. Levtzion and H.J. Fisher, 1-20. Boulder, Colorado: Lynne Rienner.

———. 1987b. "Merchants vs Scholars and Clerics: Differential and Complementary Roles." In *Rural and Urban Islam in West Africa*, edited by N. Levtzion and H.J. Fisher, 21-37. Boulder, Colorado: Lynne Rienner.

———. 1987c. "The Eighteenth Century: Background to the Islamic Revolutions in West Africa." In *Eighteenth Century Renewal and Reform in Islam*, edited by N. Levtzion and J. Voll, 21-38. Syracuse, New York: Syracuse University Press.

———. 1990a. "Conversion to Islam in Syria and Palestine, and the Survival of Christian Communities." In *Conversion and Continuity: Indigenous Christian Communities in Medieval Islamic Lands*, edited by M. Gervers and R.J. Bikhazi, 289-312. Toronto: Pontifical Institute of Medieval Studies.

———. 1990b. "Conversion and Islamization in the Middle Ages: How did Jews and Christians Differ?" *Pe'amim* 42: 8-15 (Hebrew).

———. 2000. "Islam in the Bilad al-Sudan to 1800." In *The History of Islam in Africa*, edited by N. Levtzion and R.L. Pouwels, 63-91. Athens, Ohio: Ohio University Press.

———. 2002. "The Dynamics of Sufi Brotherhoods." In *The Public Sphere in Muslim Societies*, edited by M. Hoexter, S.N. Eisenstadt and N. Levtzion, 109-18. Albany: SUNY series in Near Eastern Studies.

———. 2007. *Islam in Africa and the Middle East: Studies of Conversion and Renewal*. Edited by Michel Abitbol and Amos Nadan. Burlington, Vermont: Variorum-Ashgate.

Levtzion, Nehemia and J.F.P. Hopkins, eds. 1981. *Corpus of Early Arabic Sources for West African History*. Cambridge, UK: Cambridge University Press (Fontes Historiae Africanae: Series Arabica IV). Reprinted in 2000 by Markus Wiener Publishing Inc.

Levtzion, Nehemia, Ivor G. Wilks and Bruce M. Haight. 1986. *Chronicles from Gonja: A Tradition of West African Muslim Historiography*. Cambridge, UK: Cambridge University Press (Fontes Historiae Africanae: Series Arabica IX).

Levtzion, Nehemia and Humphrey J. Fisher, eds. 1987. *Rural and Urban Islam in West Africa*. Boulder, Colorado: Lynne Rienner. Originally published as a special issue of *Asian and African Studies* 20, no 1 (1986).

Levtzion, Nehemia and John O. Voll, eds. 1987a. *Eighteenth Century Renewal and Reform in Islam*. Syracuse, New York: Syracuse University Press.

———. 1987b. "Eighteenth-Century Renewal and Reform Movements in Islam: An Introductory Essay." In *Eighteenth Century Renewal and Reform in Islam*, edited by N. Levtzion and J. Voll, 13-20. Syracuse, New York: Syracuse University Press.

Levtzion, Nehemia, Daphna Ephrat and Daniela Talmon-Heller. 1998. *Islam: A History of the Religion. Volumes 1 and 2*. Ra`anana: The Open University of Israel.

———. 2000. *Islam: A History of the Religion. Volume 3*. Ra`anana: The Open University of Israel.

Levtzion, Nehemia and Randall L. Pouwels, eds. 2000a. *The History of Islam in Africa*. Athens: Ohio University Press.

———. 2000b. "Introduction: Patterns of Islamization and Varieties of Religious Experience among Muslims of Africa." In *The History of Islam in Africa*, edited by N. Levtzion and R.L. Pouwels, 1-18. Athens: Ohio University Press.

Lewicki, T. 1960a. "Quelques extraits inédits relatifs aux voyages des commerçants et des missionnaires ibadites nord-africains au pays du Soudan occidental et central au moyen âge." *Folia Orientalia* II: 1-27.

———. 1960b. "al-Ibadiyya." In *The Encyclopedia of Islam*. Second edition. Volume 3: 648-60. Leiden: Brill.

———. 1961. "L'Etat nord-africain de Tahert et ses relations avec le Soudan occidentale à la fin du 8e et au 9e siècle." *Cahiers d'Etudes Africaines* 2: 513-35.

———. 1971. "The Ibadites in Arabia and Africa." *Journal of World History* 13: 51-130.

Lewis, I.M. 1996. *Religion in Context: Cults and Charisma.* Cambridge, New York: Cambridge University Press.

Leynaud, E. et Y. Cissé. 1978. *Paysans Malinké du Haut Niger.* Bamako: Imprimerie Populaire.

Liebenow, J. Gus. 1987. *Liberia: The Quest for Democracy.* Bloomington: Indiana University Press.

Liverani, M. 2000. "The Libyan Caravan Road in Herodotus IV.181-185." *Journal of the Economic and Social History of the Orient* 43, no.4: 496-520.

Lo, Cheikh. 1996. "Ne La Thiass (Gone in a Flash)." World Circuit Nonesuch.

Loimeier, Roman. 1994. "Chiekh Touré: Du reformisme à l'islamisme, un musulman sénégalais dans le siècle." *Islam et Sociétés au Sud du Sahara* 8: 55-66.

———. 1997. "Islamic Reform and Political Change: The Example of Abubakar Gumi and the Yan Izala Movement in Northern Nigeria." In *African Islam and Islam in Africa: Encounters between Sufis and Islamists,* edited by Eva E. Rosander and David Westerlund, 286-307. London: Hurst.

———. 1999. "Political Dimensions of the Relationship between Sufi Brotherhoods and the Islamic Reform Movement in Senegal." In *Islamic Mysticism Contested: Thirteen Centuries of Controversies and Polemics,* edited by Frederick de Jong & Bernd Radtke, 341-56. Leiden: Brill.

———. 2000. "L'Islam ne se vend plus: The Islamic Reform Movement and the State in Senegal." *Journal of Religion in Africa* 30, no.2: 168-90.

Lovejoy, Paul E., ed. 1981. *The Ideology of Slavery.* Beverly Hills and London: Sage Publications.

———. 1988. "Concubinage and the Status of Women Slaves in Early Colonial Northern Nigeria." *The Journal of African History* 29, no.2: 245-66.

———. 1990. "Concubinage in the Sokoto Caliphate (1804-1903)." *Slavery and Abolition* 11: 158-89.

Lugard, Fredric. 1923. *The Dual Mandate in British Tropical Africa.* Edinburgh: W. Blackwood.

Ly-Tall, Madina, Seydou Camara and Bouna Diouara, editors and translators. 1987. *L'Histoire du Mande d'après Jeli Kanku Madi Jabaté de Kéla.* Paris: Association SCOA.

Lynch, Hollis R. 1970. *Edward Wilmot Blyden: Pan-Negro Patriot, 1832-1912*. Oxford University Press.
Maal, Baaba. 1998. "Baaba Maal Nomad Soul." New York: Island Records / Palm Pictures.
MacDonald, K.C. and R.H. MacDonald. 2000. "The Origins and Development of Domesticated Animals in Arid West Africa." In The Origins and Development of African Livestock, edited by R. Blench and K. MacDonald, 127-162. London: UCL Press.
——. Forthcoming. "Mammalian, Avian, and Reptilian Remains." In *Archaeological Investigations in the Middle Senegal Valley, 1990-1993*, edited by R. McIntosh, S. McIntosh, and H. Bocoum. Oxford: Archaeopress.
MacDonald, K., R. Hutton MacDonald and T. Togola. 1998. "Excavations at Tonga Maare Diabel: A 1st Millennium AD Malian Town." *Nyame Akuma* 50: 51 (abstract).
Mack, Beverly B. 2004. *Muslim Women Sing Hausa Popular Song*. Bloomington: African Expressive Cultures, Indiana University Press.
Mahmud, Saka S. 2004. "Islamism in West Africa: Nigeria." *African Studies Review* 47, no.2: 83-95.
Malgras, Denis. 1992. *Arbres et arbustes guérisseurs des savanes maliennes*. Paris: ACCT-Karthala.
Mansoor, Moaddel. 2005. *Islamic Modernism, Nationalism, and Fundamentalism: Episode and Discourse*. Chicago: University of Chicago Press.
Marcais, P. "Ashura' II." *Encyclopaedia of Islam Online*. Leiden: Brill.
Margulies R. and E. Yildizoglu. 1997. "The Resurgence of Islam and the Welfare Party in Turkey." In *Political Islam: Essays from Middle East Report*, edited by Joel Beinin and Joe Stork, 144-53. Berkeley: University of California Press.
Martin, B.G. 1976. *Muslim Brotherhoods in 19th Century Africa*. Cambridge: Cambridge University Press.
Mattingley, D. 2003. *The Archaeology of Fazzan, Volume 1*. Tripoli: Society for Libyan Sudies.
Mauny, R. 1961. *Tableau géographique de l'Ouest African au Moyen Age*. Dakar: IFAN.
Mbembe, Achille. 2001. *On the Postcolony*. Berkeley: University of California Press.
Mbillah, Johnson. 1987. "A Comparative Study on the Kusasi Responses to Christian Mission and Muslim Dawah." In Partial Fulfillment of Certificate in Mission, Selly Oak College, Birmingham, UK.
Mbow, M.-A. 1997. "Les Amas Coquilliers du Delta du Sénégal: Etude Ethno-archéologique." Thèse de Doctorat, Universitée de Paris,

Pantheon-Sorbonne.

McCann, J.C. 1999. "Causation and Climate in African History." *International Journal of African Historical Studies* 32, nos.2-3: 261-79.

McDougall, E. Ann. 1983. "The Sahara Reconsidered: Pastoralism, Politics, and Salt from the Ninth through the Twelfth Centuries." *African Economic History* 12: 263-86.

———. 1985. "The View from Awdghust: War, Trade and Social Change in the Southwestern Sahara, from the Eighth to the Fifteenth Century." *Journal of African History* 26, no.1: 1-31.

———. 1998. "A Sense of Self: The Life of Fatma Barka (North / West Africa)." *Canadian Journal of African Studies* 32, no.2: 398-412.

———. 2004. "Women in African Islamic Cultures, 1400-1700." *Encyclopedia of Women and Islamic Cultures.* Leiden: Brill.

McIntosh, Roderick J. 1998. *The Peoples of the Middle Niger.* Island of Gold. Oxford: Blackwell.

———. 2005. *Ancient Middle Niger: Urbanism and the Self-Organizing Landscape.* Cambridge: Cambridge University Press.

McIntosh, Roderick J., Joseph A. Tainter, and Susan Keech McIntosh, eds. 2000. *The Way the Wind Blows.* New York: Columbia University Press.

McIntosh, R., S. McIntosh, and H. Bocoum, eds. Forthcoming. *Archaeological Investigations in the Middle Senegal Valley, 1990-1993.* Oxford: Archaeopress.

McIntosh, Susan Keech, ed. 1995. *Excavations at Jenné-jeno, Hambarketolo, and Kaniana: The 1981 Season.* University of California Monographs in Anthropology. Berkeley: University of California Press.

———, ed. 1999a. *Beyond Chiefdoms: Pathways to Complexity in Africa.* Cambridge: Cambridge University Press.

———. 1999b. "Floodplains and the Development of Complex Society: Comparative Perspectives from the West African Semi-Arid Tropics." In *Complex Polities of the Ancient Tropical World,* edited by Elizabeth A. Bacus and Lisa J. Lucero, 151-65. Archaeological Papers of the American Anthropological Association, No. 9.

———. 1999c. "A Tale of Two Floodplains: Comparative Perspectives on the Emergence of Complex Societies and Urbanism in the Middle Niger and Senegal Valleys." *East African Urban Origins in World Perspective: Proceedings* <http://www.arkeologi.uu.se/afr/projects/BOOK/Mcintosh/mcintosh.pdf>. Accessed 7 July 2008.

———. 2001. "Analyses of Cubalel and Sincu Bara Pottery Assemblages."

In *Fouilles à Sincu Bara, un site de l'âge de fer dans la moyenne vallée du Sénégal,* edited by S. McIntosh and H. Bocoum. Dakar: IFAN/Ch. A. Diop, Nouakchott: CRIAA.

McIntosh, S., and H. Bocoum. 2001. *Fouilles à Sincu Bara, un site de l'âge de fer dans la moyenne vallée du Sénégal.* Dakar: IFAN/Ch. A. Diop/ Nouakchott CRIAA.

McIntosh, S. and R. McIntosh. 1984. "Archaeological Reconnaissance in the Region of Timbuktu, Mali." *National Geographic Research* 2, no.3: 302-19.

McLaughlin, Fiona. 1997. "Islam and Popular Music in Senegal: The Emergence of a 'New Tradition.'" *Africa* 67, no.4: 560-81.

——. 2000. "'In the Name of God I Will Sing Again, Mawdo Malik the Good': Popular Music and the Senegalese Sufi Tariqas." *Journal of Religion in Africa* 30, no.2: 191-207.

Maier, Hendrick M.J. 1995. "Malay and Indonesian Literature." In *The Oxford Encyclopedia of the Modern Islamic World,* edited by John L. Esposito, 28-34. New York: Oxford University Press.

Margoliouth, D.S. 2008. "Kadiriyya." *Encyclopaedia of Islam, Second Edition.* Edited by P. Bearman, T. Bianquis, C.E. Bosworth, E. van Donzel and W.P. Heinrichs. Brill Online. Tel Aviv University Sourasky <http://www.brillonline.nl/subscriber/entry?entry=islam_COM-0411>. Accessed 15 December 2008.

Miadeh, Malouma Mint. 1998. "Desert of Eden." Newton, New Jersey: Shanachie.

Michon, JL. "'Isawa." *The Encyclopaedia of Islam Online.* Leiden: Brill.

Miles, William F.S. 1994. *Hausaland Divided: Colonialism and Independence in Nigeria and Niger.* Ithaca: Cornell University Press.

——. 2001. "Report on an International Symposium: 'Third World Views of the Holocaust,' Northeastern University, Boston, April 18-20, 2001." *Journal of Genocide Research* 3: 511-13.

——. 2004. "Third World Views of the Holocaust." *Journal of Genocide Research* 6, no.3: 371-93.

Miller, Joseph C. 1985. *Slavery: A Worldwide Bibliography, 1900-1982.* White Plains, New York: Kraus International Publications.

——. 1993. *Slavery and Slaving in World History: A Bibliography.* 2 volumes. Millwood, New York: Kraus International Publications.

Miner, Horace. 1942. "Songhoi Circumcision." *American Anthropologist* 44, no.4, Part 1: 621-37.

Miran, Marie. 2006. *Islam, histoire et modernité en Cote d'Ivoire* Paris: Editions Karthala.

Mirza, Sarah and Margaret Strobel, editors and translators. 1989. *Three*

Swahili Women: Life Histories from Mombasa, Kenya. Bloomington and Indianapolis: Indiana University Press.

Mitchell, P. 2005. *African Connections.* Walnut Creek: Altamira Press.

Moaddel, Mansoor. 2005. *Islamic Modernism, Nationalism, and Fundamentalism: Episode and Discourse.* Chicago: University of Chicago Press.

Monteil, Charles. 1924. *Les Bambara du Segou et du Kaarta.* Paris: G.-P. Maisonneuve & Larose.

Monteillet, J., H. Faure, P.A. Pirazolli, and A. Ravisé. 1981. "L'invasion saline du Ferlo (Sénégal) à l'Holocene Supérieure (1900 bp)." *Palaeoecology of Africa and the Surrounding Islands* 13: 205-15.

Montrat, M. 1958. "Notice sur l'emplacement de la capitale du Mali." *Notes Africaines* 79: 90-93.

de Moraes Farias, Paulo. 1974, "Great States Revisited," *Journal of African History* 15, no.1974: 479-88.

———. 2003. *Arabic Medieval Inscriptions from the Republic of Mali: Epigraphy, Chronicles and Songhay-Tuareg History.* Oxford: Oxford University Press.

"Morocco I: The Music of Islam and Sufism in Morocco." Philip Daniel Schuyler. Cambridge: Rounder, 1999.

MSN Arabia. 2006. "Mohamed Mounir" <http://www.arabia.msn.com/entertainment/spotlight86/>. Accessed 12 September 2006.

Mounir, M. 2002. "Earth ... Peace." Mondo Melodia

Munson, P.J. 1980. "Archaeology and the Prehistoric Origins of the Ghana Empire." *Journal of African History* 21, no.4: 457-66.

Music in the World of Islam. Jean Jenkins Loewer, and Poul Rovsing Olsen. London: Topic, 1994.

Mzab. "Mzab photos" <http://www.taha.online.fr/welcome.htm>. Accessed 2006

Natvig, Richard. 1988. "Liminal Rites and Female Symbolism in the Egyptian Zar Possession Cult." *Numen* 35, no.1: 57-68.

N'Dour, Youssou. 2004. "Egypt." Fathy Salama. New York: Nonesuch.

Nehme, M.G. 1998. "The Islamic-Capitalist State of Saudi Arabia: The Surfacing of Fundamentalism." In *Islamic Fundamentalism: Myths and Realities,* edited by A.S. Moussalli, 275-302. London: Ithaca Press.

Nelson, Kristina. 1985. *The Art of Reciting the Qur'an.* Austin: Modern Middle East Series no. 11, University of Texas Press.

Neumann, K. 2003. "The Late Emergence of Agriculture in Sub-Saharan Africa: Archaeobotanical Evidence and Ecological Considerations." In *Food, Fuel and Fields: Progress in African Archaeobotany,* edited by K. Neumann, A. Butler and S. Kahlheber, 71-92. Koln: Heinrich Barth Institute.

Niane, D.T. 1960. *Soundjata: où l'épopée mandique*. Paris: Présence Africaine.

———. 1965. *Sundiata: An Epic of Old Mali*. Translated by G.D. Pickett. London: Longmans.

Nicholson, Sharon. 1980. "Saharan Climates in Historic Times." In *The Sahara and the Nile*, edited by M.A.J. Williams and H. Faure, 173-200. Rotterdam: A.A. Balkema.

———. 1986. "The Spatial Coherence of African Rainfall Anomalies: Interhemispheric Teleconnections." *Journal of Applied Meteorology* 25, 1365-81.

———. 1994. "Recent Rainfall Fluctuations in Africa and Their Relationship to Past Conditions Over the Continent." *The Holocene* 4, no.2: 121-31.

———. 1996. "Enviromental Change within the Historical Period." In *The Physical Geography of Africa*, edited by W.M. Adams, A.S. Goudie, and A.R. Orme, 60-87. Oxford: Oxford University Press.

Nubier. 1980. "Musik Der Nubier / Nordsudan." Artur Simon, Museum für Völkerkunde (Berlin, Germany), and Musikethnologische Abteilung. Berlin: Musikethnologische Abteilung Museum für Völkerkunde Berlin, Staatliche Museen Preussischer Kulturbesitz.

O'Brien, Susan. 1999. "Pilgrimage, Power and Identity: The Role of the Hajj in the Lives of Northern Nigerian Hausa Bori Adepts." *Africa Today* 46, nos.3-4: 11-41.

———. 2001. "Spirit Discipline: Gender, Islam and Hierarchies of Treatment in Post-Colonial Northern Nigeria." *Interventions: The International Journal of Postcolonial Studies* 3, no.32: 222-41.

O'Fahey, R.S. 1990. *Enigmatic Saint: Ahmad Ibn Idris and the Idrisi Tradition*. Evanston, Illinois: Northwestern University Press.

O'Fahey, R.S. and Bernd Radtke. 1993. "Neo-Sufism Reconsidered." *Der Islam* 70, no.1: 52-87.

O'Sullivan, John. 1976. "Developments in the Social Stratification of Northwest Ivory Coast during the Eighteenth and Nineteenth Centuries: From Malinke Frontier Society to the Liberation of Slaves by the French, 1907." PhD thesis, UCLA.

Ofosu-Asante, Alfred. 1997. "Christian Missions to Muslims in Ghana: A Case Study of the Converted Muslim's Christian Ministries and Markaz al-Bishara." MPhil Thesis, Department of Religion, University of Ghana.

Oliver, Roland, ed. 1967. *The Middle Age of African History*. Oxford: Oxford University Press.

———. 1997. *Realms of Gold: Pioneering in African History.* Madison: University of Wisconsin Press.

Olivier, Laurent and Anick Coudart. 1995. "French Tradition and the Central Place of History in the Human Sciences: Preamble to a Dialogue between Robinson Crusoe and his Man Friday." In *Theory in Archaeology: A World Perspective,* edited by Peter J. Ucko, 363-81. New York: Routledge.

Omole, Bamitale. 1987. "Bilateral Relations between Senegal and Nigeria, 1960-1980: Cooperation and Conflicts." *Genève Afrique* 25, no.2: 80-102.

Orwin, Martin. 2001. "Language Use in Three Somali Religious Poems." *Journal of African Cultural Studies* 14, no.1: 69-87.

Osborn, Emily. 2000. "Gender, Power and Authority in Kankan-Baté." PhD thesis, Stanford University.

———. Forthcoming. *Making States: Power, Gender, and Colonial Rule in Kankan Baté.* Columbus: The Ohio University Press.

Osman, Ahmed Ibrahim. 1990. "In Praise of the Prophet: The Performance and Thematic Composition of the Sudanese Religious Oral Poetry." PhD thesis, Indiana University.

Ottenheimer, H.J. 1970. "Culture Contact and Musical Style: Ethnomusicology in the Comoro Islands." *Ethnomusicology* 14, no.3: 458-62.

Owusu-Ansah, David. 1991. *Islamic Talismanic Traditions in Nineteenth Century Asante.* Lewiston, New York: Edwin Mellen Press.

———. 2000. "Prayers and Healing." In *The History of Islam in Africa,* edited by Nehemia Levtzion and Randall Pouwels, 477-88. Athens and Oxford: Ohio University Press.

———. 2002. "History of Islamic education in Ghana: An Overview." *Ghana Studies* 5: 61-82.

Paulme, Denise. 1986. *La Mère dévorante.* Paris: Gallimard.

Pearce, Margaret Wickens. 1998. "Native Mapping in Southern New England Indian Deeds." In *Cartographic Encounters: Perspectives on Native American Mapmaking and Map Use,* edited G. Malcolm Lewis, 157-86. Chicago and London: University of Chicago Press.

Perinbam, B.M. 1988. "The Political Organization of Traditional Gold Mining: The Western Loby c.1850 to c.1910." *Journal of African History* 29, no.3: 437-62.

Quiquandon, F. 1892. "Histoire de la puissance Mandingue." *Bulletin de la Société de Géographie Commerciale de Bordeaux, Second Series* 15: 305-18, 369-87, 401-29.

Qureshi, Regula Burckhardt. 1981. "Islamic Music in an Indian

Environment: The Shi'a Majlis." *Ethnomusicology* 25, no.1: 41-71.
Radtke, B. et al. "Wali." *The Encyclopaedia of Islam Online*. Leiden: Brill.
Rahman, Fazlur. 1968. *Islam*. New York: Anchor Books.
Ranger, Terence. 1979. "The Mobilization of Labour and the Production of Knowledge: The Antiquarian Tradition in Rhodesia." *Journal of African History* 20: 507-24.
Ranja, T. 2003. *Success Under Duress: A Comparison of Indigenous African and East African Asian Entrepreneurs*. Working Paper No. 7. Tanzania: Economic and Social Research Foundation.
Reese, Scott S. 2001. "The Best of Guides: Sufi Poetry and Alternate Discourses of Reform in Early Twentieth-Century Somalia." *Journal of African Cultural Studies* 14, no.1: 49-68.
Reynolds, Jonathan. 2001. "Good and Bad Muslims: Islam and Indirect Rule in Northern Nigeria." *The International Journal of African Historical Studies* 34, no.3: 601-18.
Riddell, Peter. 2001. *Islam and the Malay-Indonesian World: Transmission and Responses*. London: Hurst.
Riechmuth, Stefan. 1993. "Islamic Learning and its Interaction with 'Western' Education in Ilorin, Nigeria." In *Muslim Identity and Social Change in Sub-Saharan Africa*, edited by Louis Brenner, 179-99. London: Hurst.
———. 2000. "Islamic Education in Sub-Saharan Africa." In *The History of Islam in Africa*, edited by Nehemia Levtzion and Randall Pouwels, 419-40. Athens and Oxford: Ohio University Press.
Rinn, Louis. 1884. *Marabouts et Khouan*. Alger: Adolphe Jourdan.
Rizvi, Seyyid Saeed Akhtar and Noel Q. King. 1973. "Some East African Ithna-Asheri Jamaats (1840-1967)." *Journal of Religion in Africa* 5, no.1: 12-22.
Robertshaw, Peter. 2000. "Sibling Rivalry? The Intersection of Archaeology and History." *History in Africa* 27: 261-86.
Robinson, David. 1985a. *The Holy War of Umar Tal: The Western Sudan in the Mid-Nineteenth Century*. Oxford: Clarendon Press.
———. 1985b. "L'espace, les métaphores et l'intensité de l'Islam ouest-africain." *Annales ESC* 40, no.6: 1395-1405.
———. 1992. "Ethnography and Customary law in Senegal." *Cahiers d'Etudes Africaines* 32, no.2: 221-37.
———. 2000a. *Paths of Accommodation: Muslim Societies and French Colonial Authorities in Senegal and Mauritania, 1880-1920*. Athens: Ohio University Press.
———. 2000b. "Islamic Revolutions in the Western Sudan." In *The History of Islam in Africa*, edited by Nehemia Levtzion and Randall

Pouwels, 131-52. Athens and Oxford: Ohio University Press.

———. 2004. *Muslim Societies in African History.* Cambridge: Cambridge University Press.

Rolingher, Louise. 2009. "Edible Identities: Food, Cultural Mixing and the Making of East African Identities in the Nineteenth and Twentieth Centuries." PhD Thesis, University of Alberta.

Romero, Patricia W. 1988. "Mama Khadija: A Life History as Example of Family History." In *Life Histories of African Women,* edited by Patrica W. Romero, 140-58. London: Ashfield Press.

Rosaldo, Renato. 1980a. *Ilongot Headhunting, 1883-1974.* Stanford: Stanford University Press.

———. 1980b. "Doing Oral History." *Social Analysis* 4: 89-99.

Rosander, Eva E. 1997. "Introduction: The "Islamization of 'Tradition' and 'Modernity.'" In *African Islam and Islam in Africa: Encounters between Sufis and Islamists,* edited by Eva E. Rosander and David Westerlund, 1-27. London: Hurst.

Ross, Eric. 1995. "Touba: A Spiritual Metropolis in the Modern World." *Canadian Journal of African Studies* 29, no.2: 222-59.

Rothchild, Donald and Naomi Chazan, eds. 1988. *The Precarious Balance: State and Society in Africa.* Boulder, Colorado: Westview Press.

Sadir, Karim. 2003. "The Neolithic of Southern Africa." *Journal of African History* 44: 195-209.

Sahara. 2000. "Sacred Songs From the Sahara." Barka Foulani, and Ahallîl de Gourara. Paris: Institut du Monde Arabe.

Said, Edward. 1978. *Orientalism.* New York: Vintage.

———. 1993. *Culture and Imperialism.* New York: Vintage.

Sanankoua, Bintou. 1990. *Un empire peul au XIXe siècle: la Diina du Maasina.* Paris: Karthala.

Sanneh, Lamin. 1976. "Origins of Clericalism in West Africa." *Journal of African History* 17, no.1: 49-72.

———. 1979. *The Jakhanke: The History of an Islamic Clerical People of Senegambia.* London: Oxford University Press.

———. 1987. "Rural Factors in the Futa Jallon 1867-1912." In *Rural and Urban Islam in West Africa,* edited by Nehemia Levtzion and Humphrey J. Fisher, 73-102. Boulder, Colorado: Lyne Reinner.

———. 1989. *The Jakhanke Muslim Clerics: A Religious and Historical Study of Islam in Senegambia.* Lanham: University Press of America.

Savage, Elizabeth, ed. 1992. *The Human Commodity: Perspectives on the Trans-Saharan Slave Trade.* London, Frank Cass.

Schacht, Joseph. 1957. "Islam in Northern Nigeria." *Studia Islamica* 15:

123-46.

———. 1965. "Notes on Islam in East Africa." *Studia Islamica* 23: 91-136.

Schele, Linda and David Freidel. 1990. *A Forest of Kings: The Untold Story of the Ancient Maya*. New York: William Morrow

Scheub, Harold. 1985. "A Review of African Oral Traditions and Literature." *African Studies Review* 28, nos.2-3: 1-72.

Schildkrout, Enid. 1996. "Politics and Poetry: Mohammed Rashid Shaaban's *History of Kumasi*." In *The Cloth of Many Colored Silks: Papers on History and Society Ghanaian and Islamic in Honor of Ivor Wilks*, edited by John O. Hunwick and Nancy Lawler, 367-91. Evanston: Northwestern University Press.

Schimmel, Annemarie. 1975. *Mystical Dimensions of Islam*. Chapel Hill: University of North Carolina Press.

Schulze, Gary. 1965. "Music of the Mende of Sierra Leone Sound Recording." Ethnic Folkways Library. Old Catalog. np: Folkways Records FE 4322.

Schuyler, Philip D. 1981. "Music and Meaning among the Gnawa Religious Brotherhood of Morocco." *World of Music* 23 no.1: 3-13.

———. 2002. "A Folk Revival in Morocco." In *Everyday Life in the Muslim Middle East*, edited by Donna Lee Bowen and Evelyn A. Early, 287-93. Bloomington: Indiana University Press.

Sedgwick, Mark J. R. 1998. "The Heirs of Ahmad Ibn Idris: The Spread and Normalization of a Sufi Order, 1799-1996." PhD thesis, University of Bergen.

Sela, Avraham. 2002. "Islamic Radicalism and Movements." In *The Continuum Political Encyclopedia of the Middle East*, edited by Avraham Sela, 425-41. New York: The Continuum International Publishing Group.

Sembène Ousmane. 1992. *Guelwaar*. 35 mm. 115 min. Channel IV, Doomireew, France 3 Cinéma, Galatée Films, New Yorker Films, Westdeutscher Rundfunk (WDR). Senegal.

Sesay, S.I. 1966. "Koranic Schools in the Provinces." *Sierra Leone Journal of Education* 1: 24-26.

Shaibu Armiyawo. 1994. "Conflict over Imamship in Ghana: The Case of Sekondi / Takoradi Municipal Area." BA thesis. Legon: Department of Religion, University of Ghana.

Shiloah, Amnon. 1997. "Music and Religion in Islam." *Acta Musicologica* 69, no.2: 143-55.

Sidahmed, A. and A. Ehteshami. 1996. "Introduction." In *Islamic Fundamentalism*, edited by A. Sidahmed and A. Ehteshami, 1-15. Boulder, Colorado: Westview Press.

Simon, Artur. 1989. "Musical Traditions, Islam, and Cultural Identity in the Sudan." In *Perspectives on African Music*, edited by Wolfgang Bender Bayreuth, 25-42. West Germany: Bayreuth University.

Sirriyeh, Elizabeth. 1999. *Sufis and Anti-Sufis: The Defence, Rethinking and Rejection of Sufism in the Modern World*. Richmond, Surrey: Curzon.

———. 2000. "Sufis, Colonialists and Islamists: Old and New Encounters in Africa." *Journal of Religion in Africa* 30, no.2: 249-55.

Skinner, David. 1973. "Islam and Education in the Colony and Hinterland of Sierra Leona (1750-1914)." *Canadian Journal of African Studies* 10, no.3: 499-510.

———. 1983. "Islamic Education and Mission Work: Ghana, Gambia in the Post-Colonial Era." Stanford University African Social History Workshop.

Smith, A.B, K. Sadr, J. Gribble, and R. Yates. 1991. "Excavations in the South-Western Cape, South Africa, and the Archaeological Identity of Prehistoric Hunter-Gatherers within the Last 2000 Years." *South African Archaeological Bulletin* 46: 71-91.

Smith, Mary F. *Baba of Karo: A Woman of the Muslim Hausa*. New Haven: Yale University Press, 1954.

Soufis. 2003. "Soufis d'Algérie." Universal.

Sperling, David C. 2000. "The Coastal Hinterland and Interior of East Africa." In *The History of Islam in Africa*, edited by N. Levtzion and R.L. Pouwels, 273-302. Athens: Ohio University Press.

Stahl, Ann. 1993. "Concepts of Time and Approaches to Analogical Reasoning in Historical Perspective." *American Antiquity* 58, no.2: 235-60.

Standifer, James A. 1988. "The Tuareg: Their Music and Dances." *The Black Perspective in Music* 16, no.1: 45-62.

Stein, Gil. 2002. "From Passive Periphery to Active Agents: Emerging Perspectives in the Archaeology of Interregional Interaction." *American Anthropologist* 104, no.3: 903-16.

Steiner, George. 1975. After Babel: Aspects of Language and Translation. Oxford: Oxford University Press.

Stewart, Charles C. 1976a. "Southern Saharan Scholarship and the Bilad al-Sudan." *Journal of African History* 17, no.1: 73-93.

———. 1976b. "Frontier Disputes and Problems of Legitimation: Sokoto-Masina Relations, 1817-1837." *Journal of African History* 19, no.4: 497-514.

———. 1990a. "Islam." In *The Colonial Moment: Essays on the Movement of Minds and Materials 1900-1940*, edited by Andrew Roberts, 191-222. Cambridge: Cambridge University Press.

———. 1990b. "Review of *Rural and Urban Islam in West Africa* by

Nehemia Levtzion and Humphrey Fisher." *International Journal of African Historical Studies* 23, no.1: 126-27.

———. 1997. "Colonial Justice and the Spread of Islam in the Early Twentieth Century." In *Le temps des Marabouts*, edited by Robinson, David and Jean-Louis Triaud. Paris: Karthala: 53-66.

Stoddard, Lothrop. 1921. *The New World of Islam*. New York: Charles Scribner's Sons.

Straight, H. Stephen. 1981. "Knowledge, Purpose, and Intuition: Three Dimensions in the Evaluation of Translation." In *Translation Spectrum*, edited by Marilyn Gaddis Rose, 8-22. Albany: SUNY Press.

Strobel, Margaret 1983 "Slavery and Reproductive Labor in Mombasa." In *Women and Slavery in Africa*, edited by Claire C. Robertson and Martin A. Klein, 111-29. Madison: University of Wisconsin Press.

Sudan. 1980. "Dikr Und Madih." Artur Simon, Museum für Völkerkunde (Berlin, Germany), and Musikethnologische Abteilung. Berlin: Musikethnologische Abteilung, Museum für Völkerkunde Berlin, St atliche Museen Preussischer Kulturbesitz.

Sulamiyya. 1999. "Sufi Songs From Tunis." Paris: Institut du Monde Arabe.

Summer, D.L. 1963. *Education in Sierra Leone*. Freetown: Government of Sierra Leone.

Sutton, J. 1983. "West African Metals and the Ancient Mediterranean." *Oxford Journal of Archaeology* 2, no.2: 181-88.

Tabala. 1992. "Tabala Wolof: Sufi Drumming of Senegal." Boubacar Diagne. Village Pulse.

Takezawa, S and M. Cissé. no date. "Le Méma et les grands empires de l'Afrique de l'Ouest." Unpublished document provided by M. Cissé.

Tal, Tamari. 1997. *Les castes de l'Afrique occidentale. Artisans et musiciens endogames*. Nanterre: Societe d'Ethnologie.

Thiaw, I. 1999. "Archaeological Investigations of Long-Term Culture Change in the Lower Falemme (Upper Senegal Region) AD 500-1900." PhD thesis, Rice University.

Tibenderana, P.K. 1983. "The Emirs and the Spread of Western Education in Northern Nigeria (1910-1946)." *Journal of African History* 24: 517-34.

Togola, T. 2008. *Archaeological Investigations of Iron Age Sites in the Mema Regions, Mali*. Oxford: Archaeopress.

Togola, T., M. Cissé and Y. Fané. 2004. "Reconnaissance archéologique à Gao (Mali) et environs." *Nyame Akuma* 62: 50-60.

Topan, Farouk. 1996. "Muslim Perceptions in a Swahili Oral Genre " In *The Marabout and the Muse: New Approaches to Islam in African*

Literature, edited by Kenneth W. Harrow, 116-23. London: Heinemann.
———. 2001. "Projecting Islam: Narrative in Swahili Poetry." *Journal of African Cultural Studies* 14, no.1: 107-19.
Traoré, Dominique. 1947. "Makanta Djigui, fondateur de la magie soudanaise." *Notes Africaines* 35: 23-25.
Triaud, J.L. 1997. "Introduction." In *Le temps des Marabouts*, edited by David Robinson and Jean-Louis Triaud. Paris: Karthala: 11-30.
———. "Muridiyya." *The Encyclopaedia of Islam Online*. Leiden: Brill.
Trimingham, J. Spencer. 1959. *Islam in West Africa*. Oxford: Clarendon Press.
———. 1962. *A History of Islam in West Africa*. Oxford: Clarendon Press.
———. 1971 [1998]. *The Sufi Orders in Islam*. New York: Oxford University Press.
Tripp, Charles. 1996. "Islam and the Secular Logic of the State in the Middle East." In *Islamic Fundamentalism*, edited by A. Sidahmed and A. Ehteshami, 51-69. Boulder, Colorado: Westview Press.
Tsiga, A. Ismaila and Abubakar Gumi, 1992. *Where I Stand*. Ibadan: African Books Collective.
Umar, Muhammad Sani, 1993. "Changing Islamic Identities in Nigeria from the 1960s to the 1980s: From Sufism to Anti-Sufism." In *Muslim Identity and Social Change in Sub-Saharan Africa*, edited by Louis Brenner, 154-78. London: Hurst.
———. 1999. "Sufism and its Opponents in Nigeria: The Doctrinal and Theological Aspects." In *Islamic Mysticism Contested: Thirteen Centuries of Controversies and Polemics*, edited by Frederick de Jong and Bernd Radtke, 359-85. Leiden: Brill.
"Music of the Vai of Liberia." Produced and Recorded by Jeanne Monts and Lester Parker Monts. New York: Ethnic Folkways Records, 1982.
Vansina, Jan. 1965. *Oral Tradition: A Study in Historical Methodology*. London: Routledge & Kegan Paul.
———. 1995, "Historians, Are Archaeologists Your Siblings?" *History in Africa* 22: 369-408.
Venuti, Lawrence. 1995. *The Translator's Invisibility*. New York: Routledge.
———. 1998. *The Scandals of Translation*. New York: Routledge.
———. 2004a. "Foundational Statements." In *The Translation Studies Reader*, 13-20. New York: Routledge.
———, ed. [2000] 2004b. *The Translation Studies Reader*. Second edition. New York: Routledge.
Vernet, R. 1993. *Préhistoire de la Mauritanie*. Sepia: Paris.
Vidal, J. 1924. "La légende officielle de Soundiata." *Bulletin du comité*

d'études historiques et scientifiques de l'Afrique occidentale française 7: 317-28.

Vikør, Knut S. 1995. *Sufi and Scholar on the Desert Edge: Muhammad b. Ali al-Sanusi and His Brotherhood*. Evanston, Illinois: Northwestern University Press.

———. 2000. "Sufi Brotherhoods in Africa." In *The History of Islam in Africa*, edited by Nehemia Levtzion and Randall L. Pouwels, 441-75. Athens: Ohio University Press.

Villalon, Leonardo A. 1995. *Islamic Society and State Power in Senegal: Disciples and Citizens in Fatick*. Cambridge: Cambridge University Press.

———. 1999. "Generational Change, Political Stagnation and the Evolving Dynamics of Religion and Politics in Senegal." *Africa Today* 46, nos.3-4: 129-34.

———. 2004. "Islamism in West Africa: Senegal." *African Studies Review* 47, no.2: 61-71.

Vitalis, Robert. 1997. "Islam and the Struggle for the State in the Middle East." In *Political Islam: Essays from Middle East Report*, edited by Joel Beinin and Joe Stork, 97-102. Berkeley: University of California Press.

Voll, John O. 1991. "Fundamentalism in the Sunni Arab World: Egypt and the Sudan." In *Fundamentalisms Observed*, edited by Martin E. Marty and R. Scott Appleby, 345-402. Chicago: University Of Chicago Press.

———. [1982] 1994. *Islam: Continuity and Change in the Modern World*. Second edition. Syracuse, New York: Syracuse University Press.

———. 1999. "Foundations for Renewal and Reform: Islamic Movements in the Eighteenth and Nineteenth Centuries." In *The Oxford History of Islam*, edited by John L. Esposito, 509-47. New York: Oxford University Press.

———. 2000. "The Eastern Sudan, 1822 to the Present." In *The History of Islam in Africa*, edited by N. Levtzion and R. Powels, 153-67. Athens: Ohio University Press.

Waswahili. 1985. "Music of the Waswahili of Lamu, Kenya." Alan W Boyd. New York City: Folkways Records.

Waterman, Christopher Alan. 1990. *Juju: A Social History and Ethnography of an African Popular Music*. Chicago: Chicago Studies in Ethnomusicology, University of Chicago Press.

Waugh, Earle H. 1989. *The Munshidin of Egypt: Their World and Their Song*. Columbia, South Carolina: Studies in Comparative Religion, University of South Carolina Press.

———. 2005. *Memory, Music, and Religion: Morocco's Mystical Chanters*.

Columbia, South Carolina: Studies in Comparative Religion, University of South Carolina Press.

Webb, J. 1995. *Desert Frontier: Ecological and Economic Change along the Western Sahel 1600-1850*. Madison: University of Wisconsin Press.

Whitely, Peter M. 2002. "Archaeology and Oral Tradition: The Scientific Importance of Dialogue." *American Antiquity* 67, no.3: 405-15.

Wickham, C.R. 1997. "Islamic Mobilization and Political Change: the Islamist Trend in Egypt's Professional Associations." In *Political Islam: Essays from Middle East Report*, edited by Joel Beinin and Joe Stork, 120-35. Berkeley: University of California Press.

Wilks, Ivor. 1961. "The Northern Factor in Ashanti History: Begho and the Mande." *Journal of African History* 2, no.1: 25-34.

———. 1963. "The Growth of Islamic Learning in Ghana." *Historical Society of Nigeria* 2: 409-17.

———. 1968. "The Transmission of Islamic Learning in the Western Sudan." In *Literacy in Traditional Societies*, edited by Jack Goody, 161-97. Cambridge: Cambridge University Press.

———. 1975. *Asante in the Nineteenth Century: The Structure and Evolution of a Political Order*. London: Cambridge University Press.

———. 1989. *Wa and the Wala: Islam and Polity in Northwestern Ghana*. Cambridge: Cambridge University Press.

———. 2000. "The Juula and the Expansion of Islam into the Forest." In *The History of Islam in Africa*, edited by N. Levtzion and R.L. Pouwels, 93-115. Athens: Ohio University Press.

———. 2002. "'Mallams Do Not Fight with the Heathen': A Note on Suwarian Attitudes to Jihad." *Ghana Studies* 5: 215-30.

———. 2003. "Off to Northern Ghana in the Morning." In *Ghana in Africa and the World: Essays in Honor of Adu Boahen*, edited by Toyin Falola, 25-35. Trenton, New Jersey: Africa World Press.

Willis, C. Armine. 1921. "Religious Confraternities of the Sudan." *Sudan Notes and Records* 4, no.4: 175-94.

———. 1922. "Memorandum, 11 January 1922." In *Sudan Monthly Intelligence Report*, No. 328 (November 1921).

Willis, John Ralph. 1975. "Ancient Ghana and Mali." *International Journal of African Historical Studies* 8, no.1: 175-81.

———, ed. 1985. *Slaves and Slavery in Muslim Africa*. 2 volumes. London: Frank Cass.

Willis, Justin. 1993. *Mombasa, the Swahili, and the Making of the Mijikenda*. Oxford: Oxford University Press; New York: Clarendon Press.

Wilson John. 1963. *Education and Changing West African Culture*. New

York: Teachers College.
Wolfers, M. 2007. *Thomas Hodgkin: Wandering Scholar*. London: Merlin Press.
Wooten, Stephen R. 2000. "Antelope Headdresses and Champion Farmers: Negotiating Meaning and Identity Through the Bamana Ciwara Complex." *African Arts* 33, no.2: 19-33 and 89-90.
Wright, F. 1905. "The System of Education in the Gold Coast." *Special Report on Educational Subjects* XII, no.II: 3.
Wright, Marcia. 1993. *Strategies of Slaves and Women: Life-Stories from East / Central Africa*. New York: L. Barber Press; London: J. Currey.
Zahan, Dominique. 1963. *La dialectique du verbe chez les Bambara*. Paris and La Haye: Mouton & Co.
"Zanzibar: Music of Celebration." London: Topic, 2001.
Zelkina, Anna. 2004. "The `Wahhabis' of the Northern Caucasus vis-à-vis State and Society: The Case of Daghestan." In *The Caspian Region II: The Caucasus*, edited by Moshe Gammer, 146-78. London: Routledge.
Zeltner, Franz De. 1913. *Contes du Sénégal et du Niger*. Paris: Ernest Leroux.
Žižek, Slavoj, ed. 1992. *Everything You Always Wanted to Know about Lacan (But Were Afraid to Ask Hitchcock)*. London and New York: Verso.
Zubayda, Sami. 1997. "Is Iran an Islamic State." In *Political Islam: Essays from Middle East Report*, edited by Joel Beinin and Joe Stork, 103-19. Berkeley: University of California Press.

Index

Page numbers in **Bold** represent figures.

Abduh, M. 249
Abitbol, M. 21, 82
Abukhalil, A. 350
Accra: Makaranta 243
activism: popular 352, 357
Adalet ve Kalkinma Partisi 351
adhan 276
adoption: children 310–11
Afghani, J. al-din al- 248
Afghanistan 340
Africa: rainfall variations **139**; Sahel 59, 145, *see also* West Africa
Africa Research Unit: Harry S Truman Research Institute for Advancement of Peace 79
African Affairs 57
African Studies: Hebrew University 21, 76, 83
African Studies Association (ASA) 66; (2003) meeting 2; (2004) meeting 2, 72
African Unity Organization (OUA) 225
Africanization: Islam 59, 297
Ahmadiyya movement 247, 248
akhbar wa Tanbih al-Kiram 244
alcohol 221
algaita: shawm 278
Algar, H. 114
Algeria 279, 287; insurgency 334; Islamic Salvation Front (FIS) 337
Almagor, U. 80
Alowi, Sherif 219
Alpers, E. 302, 303, 304, 305
Amadu, S. 95, 96, 97, 98, 99
American Colonization Society (ACS) 198, 202–5
American Historical Review 57
Americano-Liberians 202
Ames, D. 269

Ancient Ghana and Mali: archaeology 163–71; bio-physical and social evolution of landscape 169; climate change 168; climate change, subsistence and mobility 138–42; equestrian terracotta figurine **147**; fauna 146; horses 146–7; nomads and sedentaries 142–8; political organization 154–9; project 8–11; radical propositions 163–4; sources 163; trans-Saharan trade 148–54; updating 135–6
Ancient Ghana and Mali (Levtzion) 22, 58, 135–6
Anderson, B. 205, 207
Anderson, C. 349
Anglicization 130–1
Appiadu, A.M. 251–2
Arab League 225
Arab Spring 348, 349, 353, 354; group action 351
Arab Stimulation 163
Arabic 70, 236
archaeology 145; Ancient Ghana and Mali 163–71
Asad, B. 353
Asante 91
Ashura' 271, 281–2
Asma'u, N. 300, 306, 311
Ayinla, K. 289
Azarya, V. 21

Baba, A. 90
Baba of Karo 307–13
Back, I. 12, 14
Bakemi 201
Bakhtin, M. 123
Bakri, M. al- 112, 146–7, 154, 156, 157
Bamana creation myth 180, 181, 191

INDEX

Bamba, A. 217, 285, 286, 290, 345
Banda, A. 251
Banda, M. al-hajj 242
Bantamba 186, 187, 188
Barrister, Chief A. 289
Basel mission 237, 238
Bashîr, O. 346
Basso, K. 179, 183
Ba'th Party: Syria 336
batin 240, 241
Battuta, Ibn 71
Bayat, A. 354
Bedie, H.K. 344
Be'er-Tuvia 18
beginnings 256
Bello, M. 96
Ben-Zvi Institute 23; Study of Jewish Communities of the East 54
Bening, B. 246
Berber camel-drivers 71, 148
Berlin: General Act of the Conference 238
Bi Kaje 313–18
Bidmos, M.A. 240
birth 282, 309
Bissandougou (Guinea) 180
black Islam 63
blackboard school 251, 252
Blyden, E. 206–9, 236, 237; *Christianity, Islam and the Negro Race* 235
Boahen, A. 47
Bohras 277
Bois, W.E.B. du 45
Book of Gonja, Kitab Ghanja 51
Boporo 201, 203, 205
bori 311, 312; Hausa cult 287
Bornu 89
Bouaziz, T. 349
Bounama, B. 276
Bowdich, T. 242
Boyo, al-Hajj O. 46, 47, 50
Bravmann, R. 92
Brenner, L. 57, 240
Briamah, B.A.R. 243
British Gold Coast 246; Education Ordinance 238
British Royal Company 237
Brooks, G. 139
Bühnen, S 186–7
Bulletin of the School of Oriental and African Studies 94
Burda, al- (al-Busiri) 275
Buré 191
Burgess, Rev E. 203

Burkina Faso 344
Busiri, S. al-Din al- 275

Cairo: Imbaba 334
Cambridge History of Africa 22, 60
camels: drivers (Berber) 71, 148; herders 144
Cape Coast Castle 237
Carbonell, O. 123
Cardinall, A.W.: *In Ashanti and Beyond* 41
Castle schools 237
charity 202
charms 311
Charry, E. 12
Chazan, N. 4, 5, 9, 65, 66; memories of Nehemia 76–83
children 310; adoption 310–11. Wala 243
Christian missionaries 203, 235, 237–9
Christianity 198, 239
Christianity, Islam and the Negro Race (Blyden) 235
Chronicles from Gonja: A Tradition of West African Muslim Historiography (Levtzion) 23
circumcision 282, 283
Cissé, D. 156
Cissé, Y. 156, 189
class: Islamization 299–307
Cleaveland, T. 93
climate change 138–42, 168
Cohen, R. 156
Collins, D. 7
colonialism 79, 122
Colvin, L. 93
Comoros Islands 278, 280
conception 312
concubines 315
Condé, J.B. 189
Condo confederation 200, 203, 205
Conrad, D. 2, 9, 24, 58, 83
conversion 297; model 301
Conversion to Islam (Levtzion) 22, 59, 60
copper 153
Coppolani, X. 104
Corpus of Early Arabic Sources for West African History (Levtzion and Hopkins) 7, 8, 22, 120–33; cultural studies of translation strategies 121–6; translation 126–32
Coulon, C. 227
creation myth: Bamana 180, 181, 191

INDEX

Cruickshank, J. 194
cultural integration: Islam 201
cultural values: European 239
culture: matrilineal 302–3
Cuoq, J. 127
Curtin, P. 61

Dagbamba 278
Dagomba 41, 51, 91
Dahiratoul Moustarchidina wal Moustarchidaty 228
Dakajalan 186, 193
Dala'il al-Khayrat 275
Damba festival 279
dancing: mixed gender 270
dar al-Harb 340
Dar al-Islam 89, 97, 339
Davies, K.G. 237
deaths 282
Delafosse, M. 58, 93
democratization 350
Depont, O. 104
Derrida, J. 256, 258
Dia, M. 223, 224
Digo 302
Diouf, A. 228, 355
divorce 308
Dò 182
drought 141
drugs 345
drums 278, 281
du'ah 273
Dunbar, R.A. 12, 306–7
Dupuis, J. 242
Dutch Charter (1621) 237
Dyula 236, 241

ecological zones: location (1600) **142**; location (1850) **143**
education 318; Portuguese 237, *see also* schools
Education Conference of Missionary Societies of Great Britain 239
Education Ordinance: British Gold Coast 238
Egypt 248, 278, 281, 286; Imbaba (Cairo) 334; Liberation Party 356; *madih* 275; Muslim Brotherhood 337–8; Sufi singers 288
Eighteenth Century Renewal and Reform in Islam (Levtzion and Voll) 24, 62, 107, 116
Eisenstadt, S.N. 80; Levtzion, N.; and Hoexeter, M. 62, 108, 335

El Difraoui 351
El General 352
Elmina castle 237
empire problem 165
Encyclopaedia Africana Project (EAP) 45, 46
English/Arabic schools 251
epic tradition 194
equestrianism 146–7, **147**
Erbakan, N. 355
Eritrea 281
Essam, R. 352
Europe: cultural values 239
evolutionary principles 169
exoticism 8, 124

Facebook 348, 351
Fadama 191, 192
Fage, J. 55, 60
Fairhead, J. 183
Fajigi 193
Fall, I. 290
Fansuri, H. 114
Farakoro 191
Fatma Bakra 318–20
fauna: Ancient Ghana and Mali 146
Ferguson, P. 51, 57
films: *Guelwaar* 259–63; Hindi 282
Fisher, H. 49, 61
Fletcher, R. 170
Fodio, U. dan 96, 215, 223, 274, 281, 310
Fodiyo, A. 273, 287
foreigners' expulsion: Ghana 42
foreignizing translation 122, 127
Fortes, M. 41
Fortunes of Wangrin, The (Hampaté Bâ) 259–63
freedom: seclusion 315
Frishkopf, M. 12, 14–15, 16
fuji: Nigeria 289, 291
Fulani 310
Fulbe scholars 89, 99
fundamentalism *see* Islamic fundamentalism

Galadanci, B.S. 245, 249
Galajo, A. 96–7
Garamantian trade network 148–9
Gasikiya ta fi kwabo (Hausa newspaper) 223
Geertz, C. 214
Gellner, E. 214, 231
gender: Islamization 299–307

INDEX

Gershoni, Y. 12, 15
Ghamba, M. al- 242
Ghana 89; Academy of Learning (Accra) 45; Empire **158**; expulsion of foreigners 42; leading Muslim personalities 243; Muslim Council 49; Tamale 20, *see also* Ancient Ghana
Ghana Education Service: Islamic Education Unit 235, 249, 250, 252
Ghana University 43; Institute of African Studies 39–40, 45, 49
Ghana's Islamic schools 235–48; modernization 247–8; narrative 235–46
Ghazali, Abu H. al- 115
Ghiwane, N. el- 290
Ghonim, W. 348, 351, 354
Ghulam Qadiani, M. 247
Gibb, H.A.R. 105
globalization 225
Gnawa derdeba (Morocco) 276
Gnawa music: Morocco 291
Golan, D. 81
gold: Ghana 200; production 150, 151, 152, 156, 192
Gold Coast 41, 42; British 238, 246; schools 237; University College 40, 42
Goody, J. 57
Gould, S.J. 169
Graham, C.K. 237
Grand Cape Mount Region 205–6
Great Britain Education Conference of Missionary Societies 230
Great States Revisited (de Moraes Farias) 11
Green, K. 92
griots 290; Manding 274, 276
Guelwaar (film) 259–63
Guggisberg, Sir G. 238
Guinea: Bissandougou 180
Gumi, A. 222–3, 225, 226
Guttmann, E. 76

Habermas, J. 348
Hadith 201
Haight, B. 23, 52
Hajj 220, 271, 280
Haked 352
Hamdullahi 94, 95, 96, 97, 99
Hampaté Bâ, A.: *The Fortunes of Wagrin* 259–63
Hamziyya (al-Busiri) 275
Harrow, K. 12, 13
Harwood, F. 177

Hashemites 338
Hausa 280; *bori* cult 287; *Gasikiya ta fi kwabo* (newspaper) 223; royal musicians 279; women 307–13
Hausa Baniri 282
Hausaland 89, 95, 285; purification 209
Hausaland Divided (Miles) 74
Hawkes, C. 167
Hawqal, Ibn 155
Hebrew University 19, 55, 64; African Studies Department 21, 76, 83
Henige, D. 193
Herodotus 149
Heyd, Professor U. 20
Hindi film 282
History of Islam in Africa, The (Levtzion and Pouwels) 12–17, 60, 73, 297
Hizballah 338
Hodgkin, T. 40, 45, 46
Hoexeter, M.: Eisenstadt, S.N. and Levtzion, N.; *The Public Sphere in Islamic Societies* 62, 108, 335
Hoffman, V. 111
Hofheinz, A. 111
Holocaust parallelism 75
holy wars 209
Hopkins, J.F.P. 59; and Levtzion, N.; *Corpus of Early Arabic Sources for West African History* 7, 8, 22, 120–33
horses: Ancient Ghana and Mali 146, **147**
Houdas, O. 93
Hourani, A. 115
Hunwick, J. 57, 224
Hussein, S. 340, 353
Hussein, S.A. 356

Ibn al-Arabi 111; Neo-Sufism 112–16
Ibrahim, H. 20, **25**, **37**, 56
Ibtihalat 278
'Id al-Adha 271, 281
Id al-Fitr 271, 281
'Id festivals 281
iddah 308
Iddrisu, A. 12, 13, 246–8
identity 257, 258
ideology: changing place 353–6
Idris, Ibn 111
Idrisi tradition 113
illiteracy 304
Imbaba (Cairo) 334
In Ashanti and Beyond (Cardinall) 41
Indonesia 350

INDEX

inshad 282
inshad dini 274
Institute of African Studies: Ghana University 39–40, 45, 49; Islam in Ghana 43–8
insurgency: Algeria 334
International Center for University Teaching of Jewish Civilization 24
International Islamic Solidarity and its Limitations (Levtzion) 23
internet: political participation 349
iron production 185
Islam: Africanization 59, 297; beginnings in Africa (new model) 256; cultural integration 201; as a gift 258; missionary strategy 305; modernisation 212; peaceful spread 201; rural 321; Sunni 346, *see also* Muslim
Islam in Ghana: Institute of African Studies 43–8; introduction 39–40; Levtzion - to come or not to come? 48–9; Levtzion - what's to be done? By Whom? 49–52; to come or not to come? 48–9; where had all the Muslims gone? 40–3
Islam in West Africa: Religion, Society and Politics to 1800 (Levtzion) 25
Islamic Education Unit: Ghana Education Service 235, 249, 250, 252
Islamic fundamentalism: Africa 343–5; challenge to West 339–41; conclusion 346–7; introduction 334–5; pragmatism and accommodation 341–3; public sphere 335–9; Sudan 345–6
Islamic Modernist reform movement 248
Islamic music in Africa: conclusion 291–5; elements 273–5; festival contexts - Ramadan 278; interactions with the popular music sphere 288–91; introduction 267–70; life-cycle contexts 282–3; overview 270–3; ritual contexts - Ashura' 281–2; ritual contexts - daily prayer 275–6; ritual contexts - 'Id Festivals 281; ritual contexts - Mawild Al-Nabi 279–80; ritual contexts - pilgrimage to Mecca 280; ritual contexts - public Qur'anic recitation 277–8; ritual contexts - public sermon 276; saint festival contexts 285–6; sectarian contexts 288; spirit ritual contexts 286–7; Sufi Context-types 283–5

Islamic Party for Justice and Development: Morocco 338
Islamic Salvation Front (FIS): Algeria 337
Islamism 353–6
Islamization 6, 55, 91, 297; class 299–307; gender 299–307; marriage 301; media 225; rural 289, 299, 301; and West Africa 89–90; wives 301
Ismailis 277
Israel Oriental Society 25
Israeli Council for Higher Education 23, 25
Israeli Information Center 19
Ittihâd Thaqâfi al-Islâmi (ITI) 220–1, 223, 231
ivory 301
Ivory Coast 279, 281, 344
Izala movement 343

Jakhanke 61
Jalayan, T. al- 240
jamâ'as 226
Jama'at Nasril al-Islam (JNI) 226, 227
Jazuli al- 275
jazz 291
jeli memory 187
jeliw 173
Jenne 184
Jenne-jeno 150–1, 155
Jewish Studies 73
jihad 59, 62, 93, 215, 340, 342; of the sword 89
Jilala, J. 290
Jones, D.H. 49
Jordan 338
Journal of African History 22, 166
Juula 199

Kaduna television 223
kaho 278
kakaki 277
Kalassa 185, 193
Kamanjan 184, 192
Kamara, F. 193
Kambasiga 186, 187, 188
Kamissoko, W. 189
Kangousa 184, 192
Kano 219, 278; Law School 222; Maitatsine 343; music 286
Kanté 187
Kante, M. 290
Karlovic Treaty (1699) 340
Karrar, A.S. 109

INDEX

Kati, M. 97
Kenya 282, 287; Mawlid performances 279
Khaldûn, Ibn 22
Khatmiyyah 109
Khomeini, A. 225
Khubta 276
ki-pemba cult 287
kibbutzim 54
kinship 322; ceremonies 309
Kirina 185
Kissidougou 183
Kitab al-Shifa 241
Kitab Ghanja: Book of Gonja 51, 52
Klein, M. 3, 4, 8
Kokoro river 190
Konfara 190, 191, 192
Kong 92
Konkomba 42
Konneh, A. 200
Koranic schools 235–48, 344
Koulikoro 185, 189
Kourossa 180
Koya, F.S.M. 247
Kubik, G. 291
Kukuba 186, 187, 188
Kumase 250
Kumasi 242, 245
Kumasi Nuriyya Islamic Institute 243
Kumbi Saleh 147-8
Kunta 96

Lacan, J. 257
Ladan, A. 251
landscape: bio-physical and social evolution (Ancient Ghana and Mali) 169; spiritually significant 173
Le Chatelier, A. 104
Le Gall, D. 114
Leach, M. 183
Leonard Davis Institute 23
Levinas, E. 122
Levtzion, A. 22, 25
Levtzion, M. 21, 23
Levtzion, N. 22, 24, **25**; *Ancient Ghana and Mali* 22, 58, 135–6; BA studies 19–20; Ben Zvi Institute 23; bibliography 26–35; birth 18, 54; *Chronicles from Gonja: A Tradition of West African Muslim Historiography* 23; *Conversion to Islam* 22, 59, 60; CV 35–7; Dean of Faculty of Humanities 23; death 25, 83; early years 19, 54; the educator 64–7; family 25; head of research committee 22; *The History of Islam in Africa* 12–17, 60, 73, 297; Hoexeter, M. and Eisenstadt, S.N., *The Public Sphere in Islamic Societies* 62, 108, 335; and Hopkins, J.F.P., *Corpus of Early Arabic Sources for West African History* 7, 8, 22, 120–33; *International Islamic Solidarity and its Limitations* 23; *Islam in West Africa: Religion, Society and Politics* 25; Jewish Studies 24; MA studies 20; marriage 20; meeting villagers **37**; memoirs and memories 3–5; *Muslim Chiefs* 4, 6, 50–1, 55–7, 90–3, 245; name 72; Open University 24; pastoralists 62; PhD 20–1; PhD supervisor 77; *Rural and Urban Islam in West Africa* 23; sabbaticals UK 22, 23; sabbaticals US 22, 23; scholarly agendas 57–64; *A Seventeenth-Century Chronicle by Ibn al-Mukhtar: A Critical Study of Ta'rikh al-Fattash* 94; Sufi brotherhood 24; Van Leer Institute 24
Levtzion, O. 21, 24
Levtzion, T. (nee Gindel) 3, 20–1, 39, 85–7, **87**
Liberia: conclusion 208–10; from ideological to practical approach 204–8; introduction 198–9; Islam essence 202; Muslims in the forest and Christians on the coast 199–204
Liberians: Americano 202
Lo, C. 289, 290
London University: School of Oriental and African Studies (SOAS) 20, 55
Lugard, Lord 216

Maal, B. 289
McDougall, E.A. 15, 16; memories of Nehemia 83–5
McIntosh, R. 9, 24, 58, 158, 183
McIntosh, S.K. 9, 24, 58, 192
maddah 274
madih 282; Egypt 275
Maghan Konfara 190, 191
Mahadists: Sudan 220
Maigari, D. 226
Maitatsine 343; violence 343
Majdhub, M. al- 111
Makaranta 236, 240, 249, 250, 251, 252
malams 311, 312
Malawi 305
Malaysia 356

INDEX

Mali 89, 98, 186, 276; pre-imperial 175–6, *see also* Ancient Ghana and Mali
Maliki law 236
Malinke 199
Mallams 243–4
Malouma 290
Mamprussi 91
Mande history 168; heartland 187; heartland map **176**; heartland and related *Jamanaw* **174**; oral narrative 173; pilgrimage tales 176–8, 192–3; sacred geography 177; spiritual landscape 173; wealth 191
Mande Studies Association (MANSA) 64, 66
Manding griots 274, 276
Mandingo 200
maraboutic power 227–8
marriage 308; alms 313; Islamization 301; Swahili 314
Masina 95
Masu Sarauta 216
maternalism 314
matrilineal culture 302–3
Mawlid al-Nabi 271, 279–80
Mbeme, A. 232
Mecca 220; Mande pilgrimage 178
media: Islamization 225; revolution 224–5; social 348
metallurgy 168
Middle Volta Basin 41
Miles, W. 4; *Hausaland Divided* 74; memories of Nehemia 72–6; *Third World Views of the Holocaust* 74
militancy 335
Mills, Rev S.J. 203
Miran, M. 93
mirror stage 257
Mirza, S. 313–18
missionaries: Christian 203, 235, 237–9
mobility 138–42
Monrovia 202
Moraes Farias, P. de 58; *Great States Revisited* 11
Morocco 277, 278, 352; *Gnawa derdeba* 276; Gnawa music 291; Islamic Party for Justice and Development 338; popular music 290; spirit-centric music 287
Mounir, M. 289
Mourides 285, 344, 345
Moustarchidine 228
Mozambique 304
Mrima Coast 302

Mubarak, H.: fall from power 348
muezzin 275–6
Muhammad, A. 97
Mujaddidi 113
mujâhidûn 340–1
munshid 274
Murîdiyya (Murid Brotherhood) 217, 218, 224, 350
Murids: Senegal 350, 354–5
music: Gnawa 276, 291; Kano 286; Morocco 276, 290, 291; pop (popular) 288–91, 345; rejection 269; world 290; Yoruba traditional 278, *see also* Islamic music in Africa
musicians 272; status 270; Sufi singers 288
Muslim: being 309, *see also* Islam
Muslim Brotherhood 337–8, 338, 352; Egypt 337
Muslim Chiefs (Levtzion) 4, 6, 50–1, 57, 90–3, 245
Muslim clerics 201
Muslim Council: Accra 47
Muslim schools 201
Muslim women 306
Muslim World League 222
Muwatta 241
mzalia 314

Naamu 191
Nallino, C.A. 110
Naqshbandis, M. 114
Naqshbaniyyah 113
Narena 189
Nasser, G.A. 338
National Census (1960) 243
National Islamic Front: Sudan 345
Native American Hopi tradition 175, 179
native mapping 175, 179, 193
N'Dour, Y. 270, 289, 291, 355
Neo-Sufism: concept 104–8; conclusion 117–18; Ibn al-Arabi 112–16; introduction 103; objections: not new 108–9; *Union with the Spirit of the Prophet* 110–12; vernacular 116–17
Neuberger, B. 21, 81
Niamanko 189
Niamina 189
Niani 188, 189
Niass, I. 219, 224
Niasse, A. 218
Niasse, S.L. 231
Nicholson, S. 139, 168

INDEX

Nigeria 207; *fuji* 289, 291; Kano 286; Muslim-Christian clashes 344; Sufis and Wahhâbîsts 211–32
Nketia, K. 43, 45
Nkrumah, K. 44, **44**, 46, 47, 250, 251
nomads 142–8; Sanhaja 142, 148
Norasoba 185
Northern Factor in Ashanti History, The (Institute of African Studies, University of Ghana) 43
Northern People's Congress 219
Noukouma: battle (1818) 96
Nuh, A. 97
Nyèmi-Nyèmi 186, 187, 188

Obasanjo, O. 230
O'Brien, C.C. 49
Odienne 93
O'Fahey, R.S. 103, 105, 107, 110, 113, 117
oil: Nigeria 226; OPEC boycott 339
Oliver, R. 4, 55, 60; memories of Nehemia 70–2
Open University 64; Emerging States of Africa 81
oral tradition 57, 179; weakness 192
oriental despotism 335
Osborn, E. 93
Oslo agreement 66
O'Sullivan, J. 93
othering 8, 122
Ottoman Empire 340
Ou'aranic schools 235–48, 344
Ouattara, A. 344
Owusu-Ansah, D. 12, 13, 92, 243

paganism: women 302
Pan-Islamism 104
pastoralism 143
paternity laws 260
patriarchal ideology 299
Paulme, D. 257
Pearce, M.W 175, 178
Phelps-Stokes Commission 238, 239, 246
place names 186
Pliny 149
poetry 274; sung 273
pop (popular) music 288–91, 345
populist activism 352, 357
Portuguese education 237
post-colony 232
Pouwels, R. 25; *The History of Islam in Africa* 12–17, 60, 73, 297

pregnancy: avoiding 312
Presbyterians 237
Price, J. 40
prostitutes 311
protest: popular 336
public space 232
public sphere 63, 335–9; new 348–51; old and new activism 351–3
Public Sphere in Islamic Societies, The (Levtzion, Hoexeter and Eisenstadt) 62, 108, 335
purification: Hausaland 209

Qadhafi, M. 340
Qadiriyya 202, 214, 216, 343
qasida 274
Qur'anic schools 235–48, 344; revolutionary 246–8
Qutb, S. al- 338

Radtke, B. 103, 105, 107, 110, 113, 117
Rahman, F. 105, 106
rainfall variations: Africa **139**
Ramadan 271, 277, 278
Ranger, T. 166
Rashid, Imam 243
Refah party (Turkey) 337
religious hymns 274
Revolution 1.0 model 351, 352
Rinn, L. 104
risala 241
Roberts, President J.J. 207
Robinson, D. 6, 217, 305, 321
Ronen, D. 74
Rosaldo, R. 193–4
Royal African Company 237
rural Islam 321
rural Islamization 289, 299, 301
Rural and Urban Islam in West Africa (Conference and paper) 23, 60–1

Sabar, G. 81
Sadat, A. 341
Sahara 59; climate 140; trade **141**, 148–54
Sahel: African 59; ecologically-mediated change 145
Said, E. 7, 122
Said, K. 348
Sa'id, L. al-Hajj 242
saints 285
Sakara 280
salaf 335
Salafia 212

INDEX

Salah 275–6
Sall, M. 355
Salla Gana 279
salt 155; trade 149
Sammaniyyah 109
Samori Turé, A. 208
Sanhaja nomads 142, 148
Sankaran 182, 183, 187
Sanneh, L. 61, 236
Sanusi, M. al- 109
Saradauna 223
Sa'ûd, Emir 341
Saudi Arabia 225, 339
Schleiermacher, F. 122, 123
scholars: Fulbe 89, 99
School of Oriental and African Studies (SOAS), London University 20, 55
schools: blackboard 251, 252; Castle 237; English/Arabic 251; Ghana Islamic 235–48; Kano Law 222; maraboutic 221; modernisation 248; Muslim 201; Muslim-Christian 207; Qur'anic 235–48, 344; Western 207
seclusion 309, 315, 317, 322
secularism 353–6; modernisation 354; radicalism 354
sedentary agriculturalists 142–8
Segou 180
Seguju 301–2
Senegal 276, 285, 344; *gammu* 280; Murid brotherhood 350; Murids 354–5; music scene 289–90; Sufis and Wahhâbîsts 211–32
Senghor, President L. 224, 344, 355
September 11th terrorist attack 340
Seventeenth-Century Chronicle by Ibn al-Mukhtar: A Critical Study of Ta'rikh al-Fattash (Levtzion) 94
Sey, Dr M. (Mark) 243
Shahin, E. 355
shari'a 62, 199, 201, 230, 336, 339; sound 271
shawm: *algaita* 278
Shaykh 305–6
Shehu, I. dan 275
Shershevsky, R. 21
Shi'a adhan 276
Shinnie, P.L. 43
Shoah 75
Sierra Leone 198, 207, 236
Sigua 301
Sirhindi, A. 113
Skinner, D. 236, 247
slavery 145, 203, 205, 206, 301, 305

slaves 299; household 314; Islam 304, 310; kinship 316; life of Fatman Barka 318–20; teachers 305; wives 309
Smith, M. 309, 313
social media 348
Sokoto 95, 99, 216; model 306
Somalia 280
Songhay 89
Soso 186, 187
Sperling, D. 301, 302, 303, 304
spirit possession 286
spiritual audition 270
spiritual landscape 173
spiritual services 201
Stoddard, L. 104
Strabo 49
Straight, S. 133
Strobel, M. 313–18
Suame 251
subsistence 138–42
Sudan 248, 275; Islamic fundamentalism 345–6; Mahadists 220
Sufi brotherhood 24, 63, 202, *see also* tarîqas
Sufi and Islamist relations: colonial period 214–20; comparative analysis 229–31; conclusion 231–2; decolonization and independence 220–4; introduction 212–14; radicalism and responses to post-colonialism 224–9
Sufi singers 288
Sufism 61, 89; hadras 271, 272; liturgies 275; *mawlid* 280; orders 283–5
Sumanguru 185
Sumaworo 189
Sunjata 173, 179, 181, 185, 189, 190
Sunni Islam 346
sûq 336–7
Surakata 274
Suwari, al-hajj S. 51, 92
Suwarian tradition 92
Suyuti, al- 204
Swahili 302; Tangana 302; women 313–18
Sy, El H.M. 218, 280, 290
Sy, M. 228
symbolic reservoir 169
Syria 352; Ba'th Party 336

Taha, M.M. 249
Tahrir Square 348
Tait, D. 41

406

INDEX

Tal, T. 98
Tallensi 42
Tamale: Ghana 20, 87; IEU schools 249
Tanbih al-Ikhawan 244
Tangana Swahili 302
Tanzania 280, 282, 287
taqwa 249
tarawih 277
Ta'rikh al-Fattash 93, 97, 98
Ta'rikh as-Sudan 93
tarîqas 216–19, 224, 227, 231, *see also* Sufi brotherhood
Tassey Condé, D. 192
tawashih 278
Taymiyya, Ibn 115, 212, 341, 346
teachers: slaves 305
Teaching Jewish Civilization: A Global Approach to Higher Education 73
Tel-Aviv: Africanist 81
television: Kaduna 223
Third World Views of the Holocaust (Miles) 74
Thomas Hodgkin: Wandering Scholar (Wolfers) 47
Tijani, A. al- 286
Tijâniyya 216, 219, 224, 226, 286, 343
Timbuktu 97; histories 93
Tokolor Empire 215
tolerance 344
Touba: Great Mosque 224
Touré, C. 220, 223
trade 301; confederation 200; diaspora 156; Garamantian network 148–9; Islam spread 199, 200; Sahara route map **141**; salt 149; trans-Saharan 148–54
translation 119–33; foreignizing 122, 127
Trimmingham, J.S. 89, 94, 105
Truman Research Institute for the Advancement of Peace (Africa Research Unit) 79, 80, 83
Tunisia 248, 287, 349, 352
Turâbî, H. al- 345
Turkey 350–1, 355; Refah party 337
Twitter 348, 351

Umar, al-H. 244
Umar Tal 215, 218, 231
Union with the Spirit of the Prophet: Neo-Sufism 110–12
United States of America (USA) 340
Usmanniya 223

Vai (Liberia) 279

Van Leer Institute 24, 64
Vansina, J. 4, 10, 21, 57, 166–7, 169
veil 308, 309
Venuti, L. 122
vernacular language 300
Vikor, K. 12
Villalon, L. 218
Virtue Party 355
Voll, J. 6–7, 62
Vumba Swahili 301

Wa 51, 91, 242
Wa Fadjiri 231
Wade, A. 355
Wade, M. 80
Wahhabism 62, 115, 212–32; Mali 343
waka 274
Wakkad, M. el- 48
Wala children 243
walâya 226
Wangara 193, 199
War of Independence (1947/8) 19
Wataniyya Islamic schools 250, 251
wa'z 273
Webb, J. 144
weddings 282
Weslyans 237
West: education 237, 239; schools 207
West Africa: Christianity 198, explorations in *Muslim* 93–9; explorations in *pagan* 90–3; and Islamization background 89–90; political and economic change *145*
Whiteley, P. 179
Wilks, I. 3, 23, 40, **44**, 51, 55; Dyula 236, 241, 242; Kumasi Muslims 245; National Census (1960) 243; transmission of learning 92
Willis, C.A. 104
Wired (magazine) 349
wives: Islamization 301; slaves 309
Wolfers, M., *Thomas Hodgkin: Wandering Scholar* 47
Wolof 221, 222
women: Hausa 307–13; lives 307–24; Muslim 306; paganism 302; pilgrimage 299; Swahili 313–18; teachers 305
world beat 290–1
world music 290
Wujudiyyah 114

Yoruba 280, 281; traditional music 278
YouTube 348, 351

INDEX

Yuviler Center 86

Zabidi, M. al- 115
Zahir 240
Zamfara 230
Zanzibar 301, 305
Zapatista movement 349
Zongos 40, 41

For Product Safety Concerns and Information please contact our EU representative GPSR@taylorandfrancis.com
Taylor & Francis Verlag GmbH, Kaufingerstraße 24, 80331 München, Germany

www.ingramcontent.com/pod-product-compliance
Lightning Source LLC
Chambersburg PA
CBHW060549230426
43670CB00011B/1743